UNCANNY X-MEN

THE NEW AGE

ON ICE

writer
CHRIS CLAREMONT

ALAN DAVIS & TOM RANEY pencilers
MARK FARMER & SCOTT HANNA inkers
**DEAN WHITE, MATT MILLA &
GINA GOING** colors
**CHRIS ELIOPOULOS & VIRTUAL CALLIGRAPHY'S
RUS WOOTON** letterers
**STEPHANIE MOORE &
SEAN RYAN** assistant editors
MIKE MARTS editor

JENNIFER GRÜNWALD collections editor
JEFF YOUNGQUIST senior editor, special projects
DAVID GABRIEL director of sales
LORETTA KROL production
MEGHAN KERNS book designer
TOM MARVELLI creative director

JOE QUESADA editor in chief
DAN BUCKLEY publisher

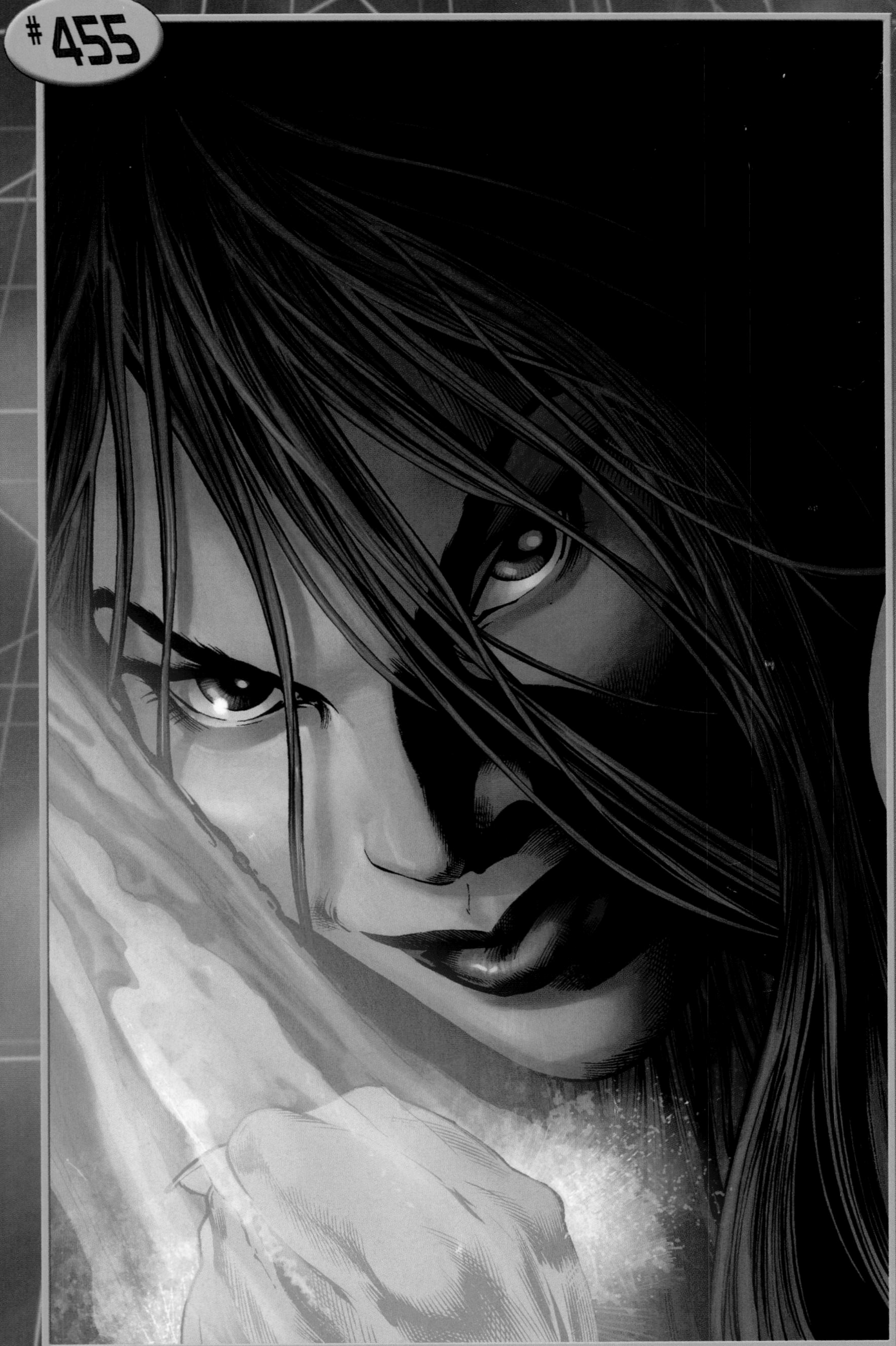
#455

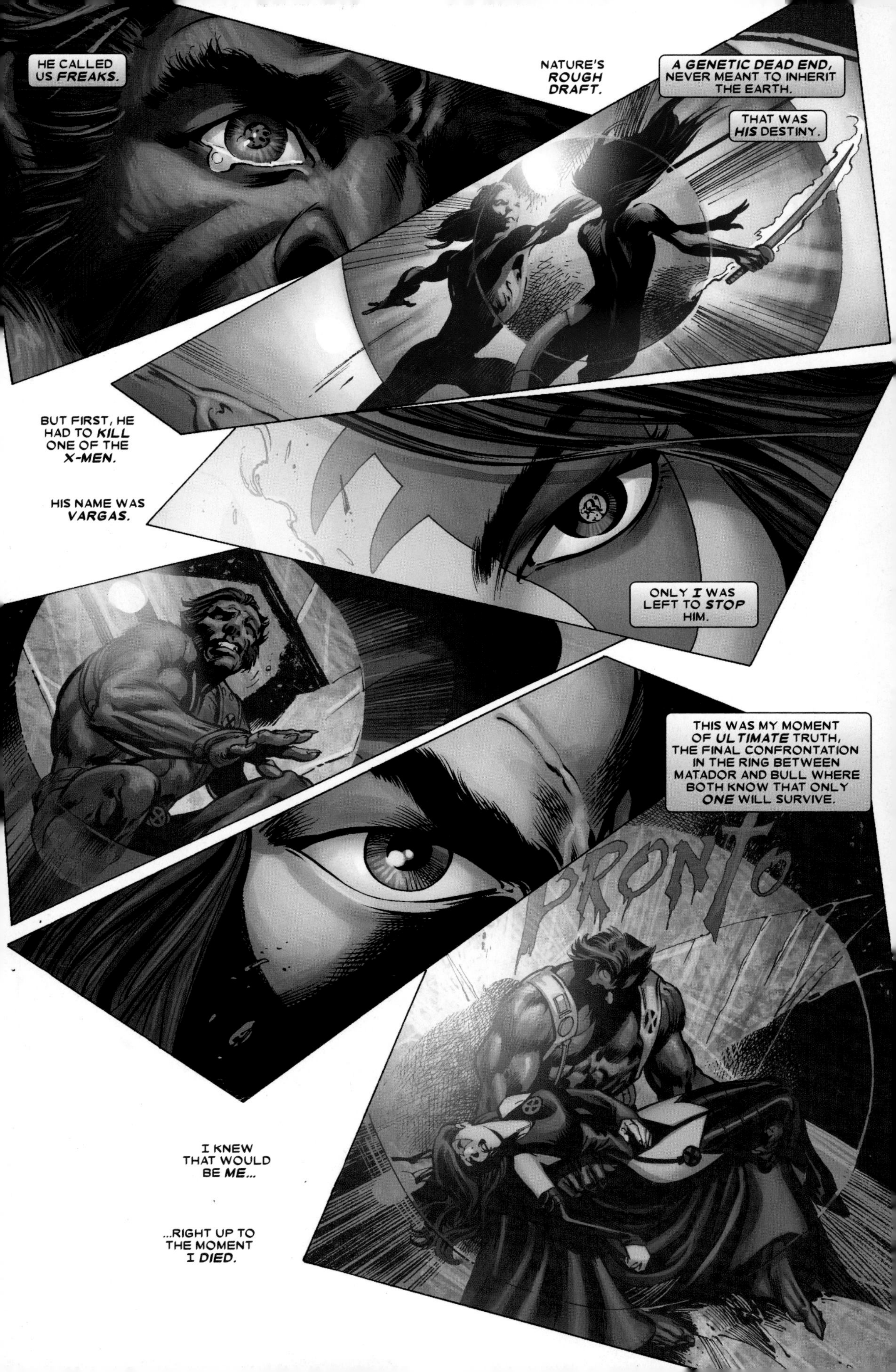
HE CALLED US FREAKS.
NATURE'S ROUGH DRAFT.
A GENETIC DEAD END, NEVER MEANT TO INHERIT THE EARTH.
THAT WAS HIS DESTINY.
BUT FIRST, HE HAD TO KILL ONE OF THE X-MEN.
HIS NAME WAS VARGAS.
ONLY I WAS LEFT TO STOP HIM.
THIS WAS MY MOMENT OF ULTIMATE TRUTH, THE FINAL CONFRONTATION IN THE RING BETWEEN MATADOR AND BULL WHERE BOTH KNOW THAT ONLY ONE WILL SURVIVE.
I KNEW THAT WOULD BE ME...
...RIGHT UP TO THE MOMENT I DIED.

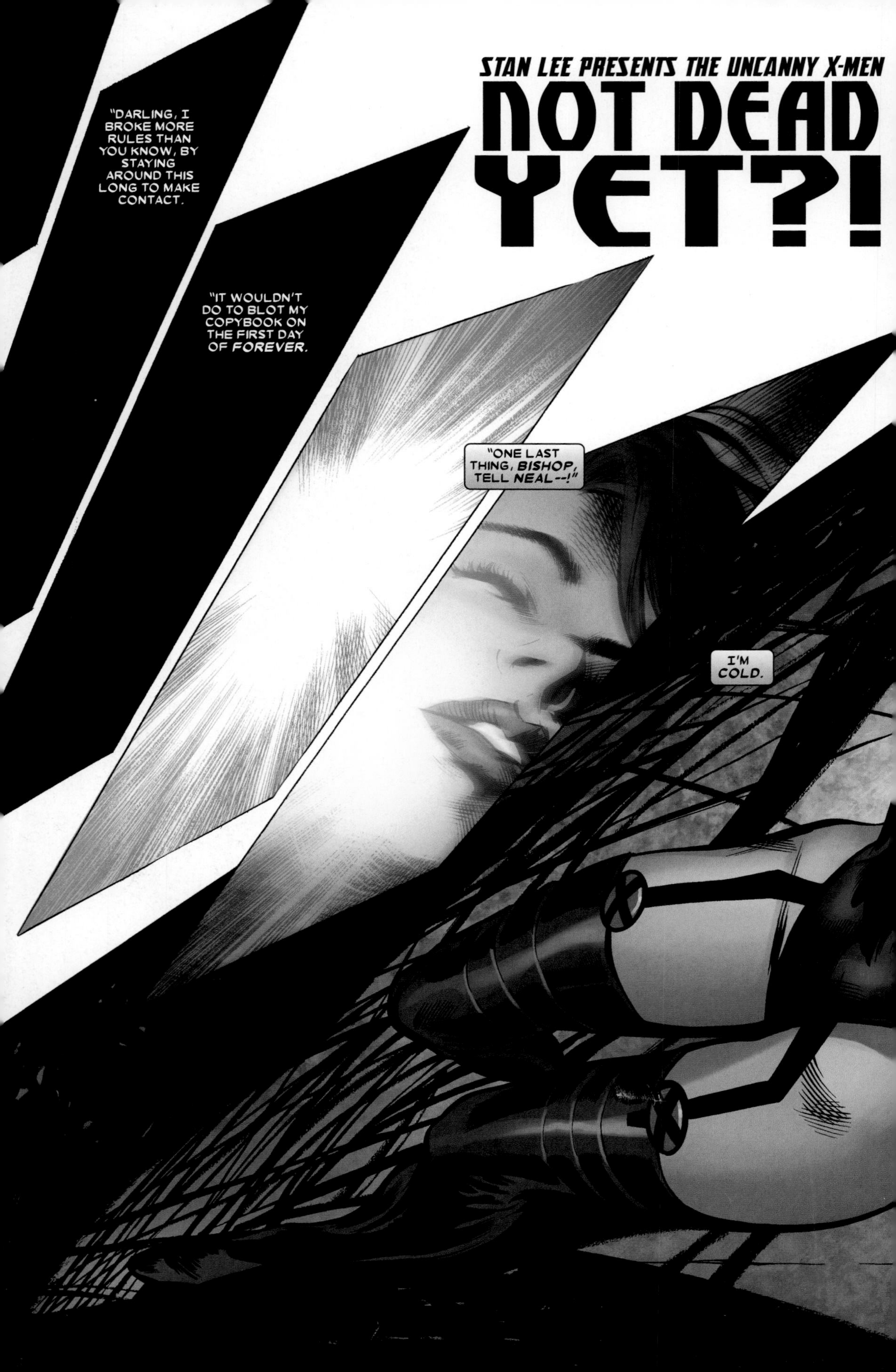
STAN LEE PRESENTS THE UNCANNY X-MEN
NOT DEAD YET?!
"DARLING, I BROKE MORE RULES THAN YOU KNOW, BY STAYING AROUND THIS LONG TO MAKE CONTACT.
"IT WOULDN'T DO TO BLOT MY COPYBOOK ON THE FIRST DAY OF FOREVER.
"ONE LAST THING, BISHOP, TELL NEAL--!"
I'M COLD.

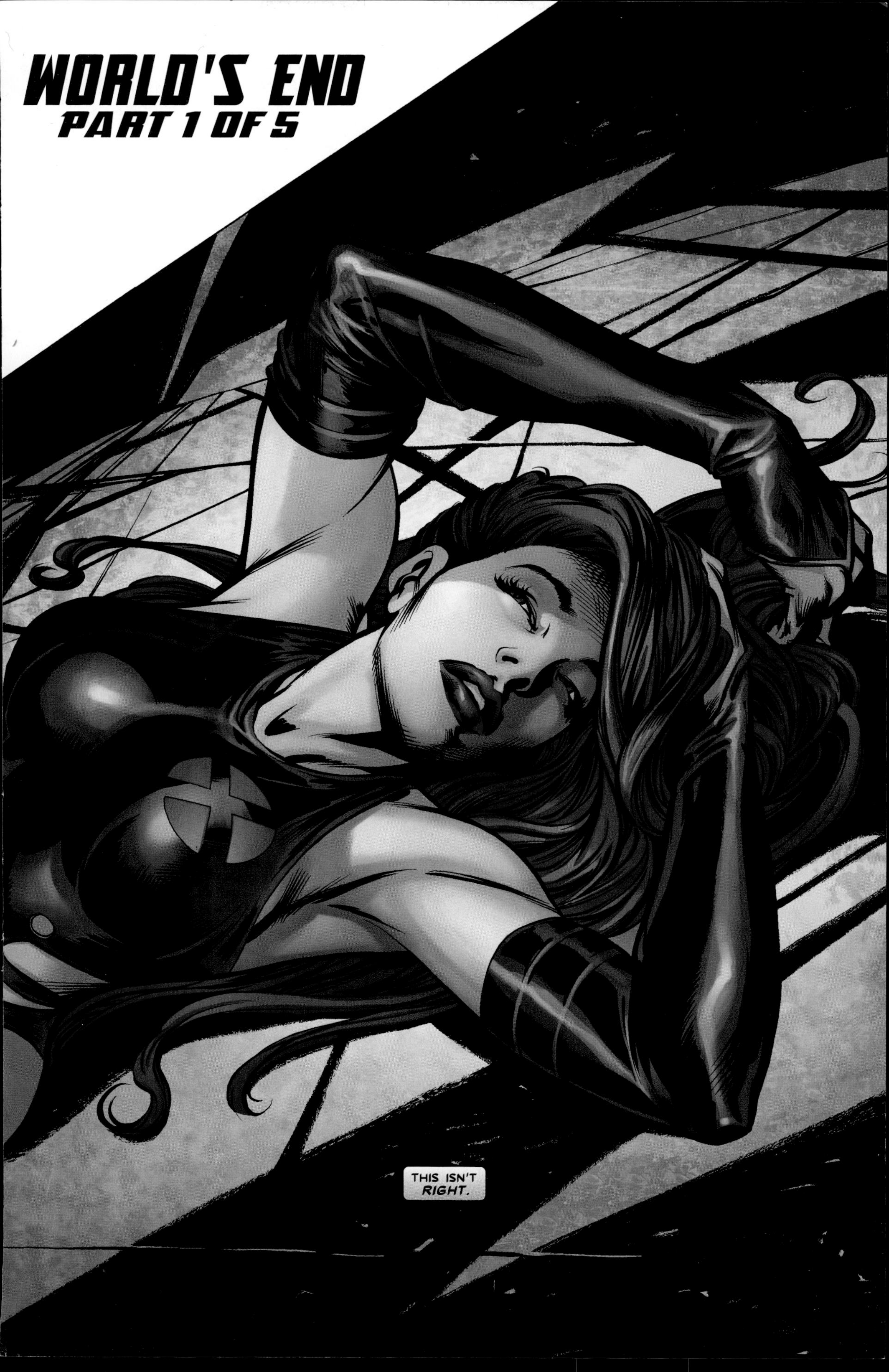
WORLD'S END
PART 1 OF 5
THIS ISN'T RIGHT.

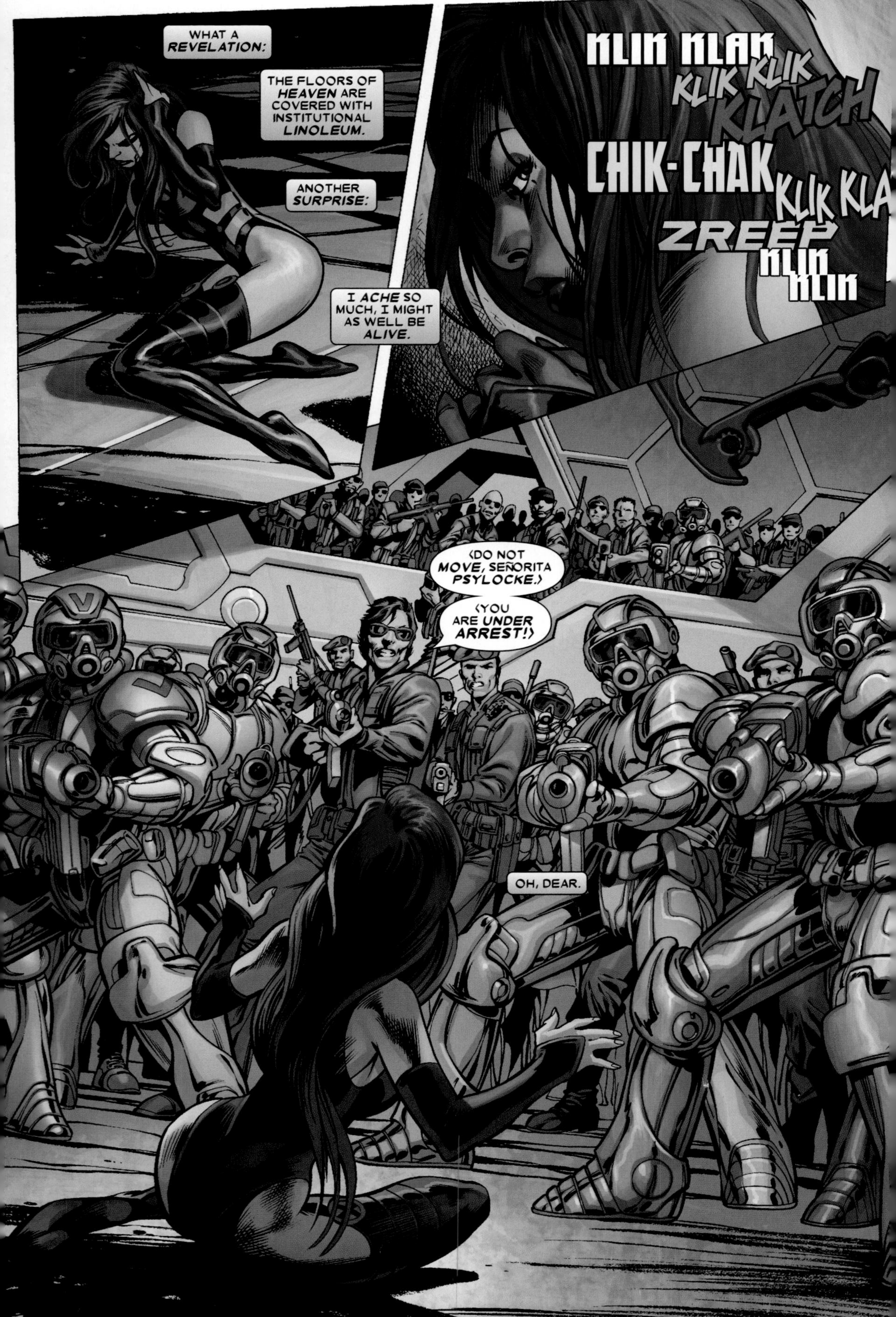

WHAT A REVELATION:
THE FLOORS OF HEAVEN ARE COVERED WITH INSTITUTIONAL LINOLEUM.
ANOTHER SURPRISE:
I ACHE SO MUCH, I MIGHT AS WELL BE ALIVE.
KLIK KLAK
KLIK KLIK
KLATCH
CHIK-CHAK
KLIK KLA
ZREEP
KLIK
KLIK
‹DO NOT MOVE, SEÑORITA PSYLOCKE.›
‹YOU ARE UNDER ARREST!›
OH, DEAR.

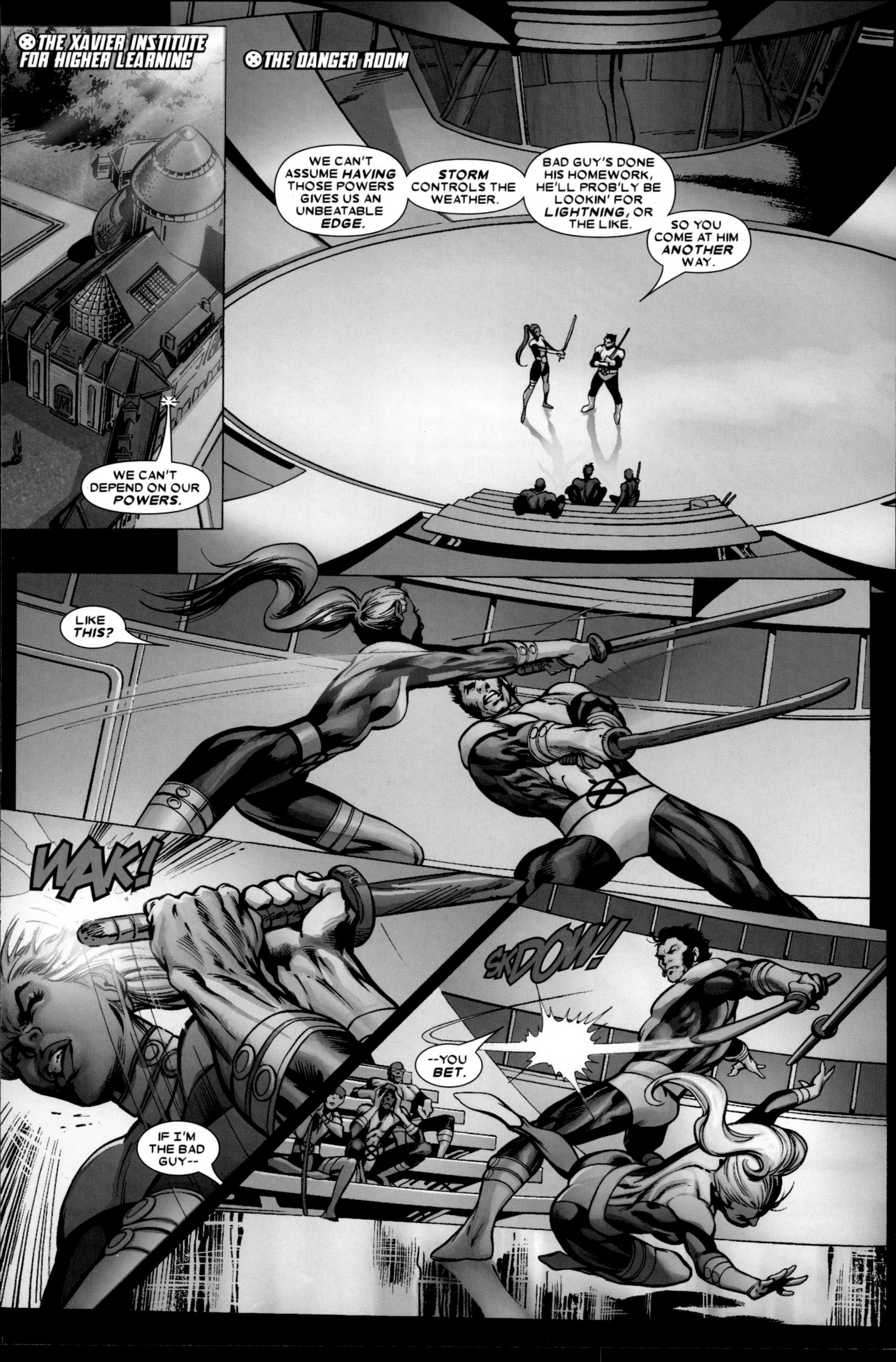
THE XAVIER INSTITUTE FOR HIGHER LEARNING
WE CAN'T DEPEND ON OUR POWERS.
THE DANGER ROOM
WE CAN'T ASSUME HAVING THOSE POWERS GIVES US AN UNBEATABLE EDGE.
STORM CONTROLS THE WEATHER.
BAD GUY'S DONE HIS HOMEWORK, HE'LL PROB'LY BE LOOKIN' FOR LIGHTNING, OR THE LIKE.
SO YOU COME AT HIM ANOTHER WAY.
LIKE THIS?
WAK!
IF I'M THE BAD GUY--
SKDOW!
--YOU BET.

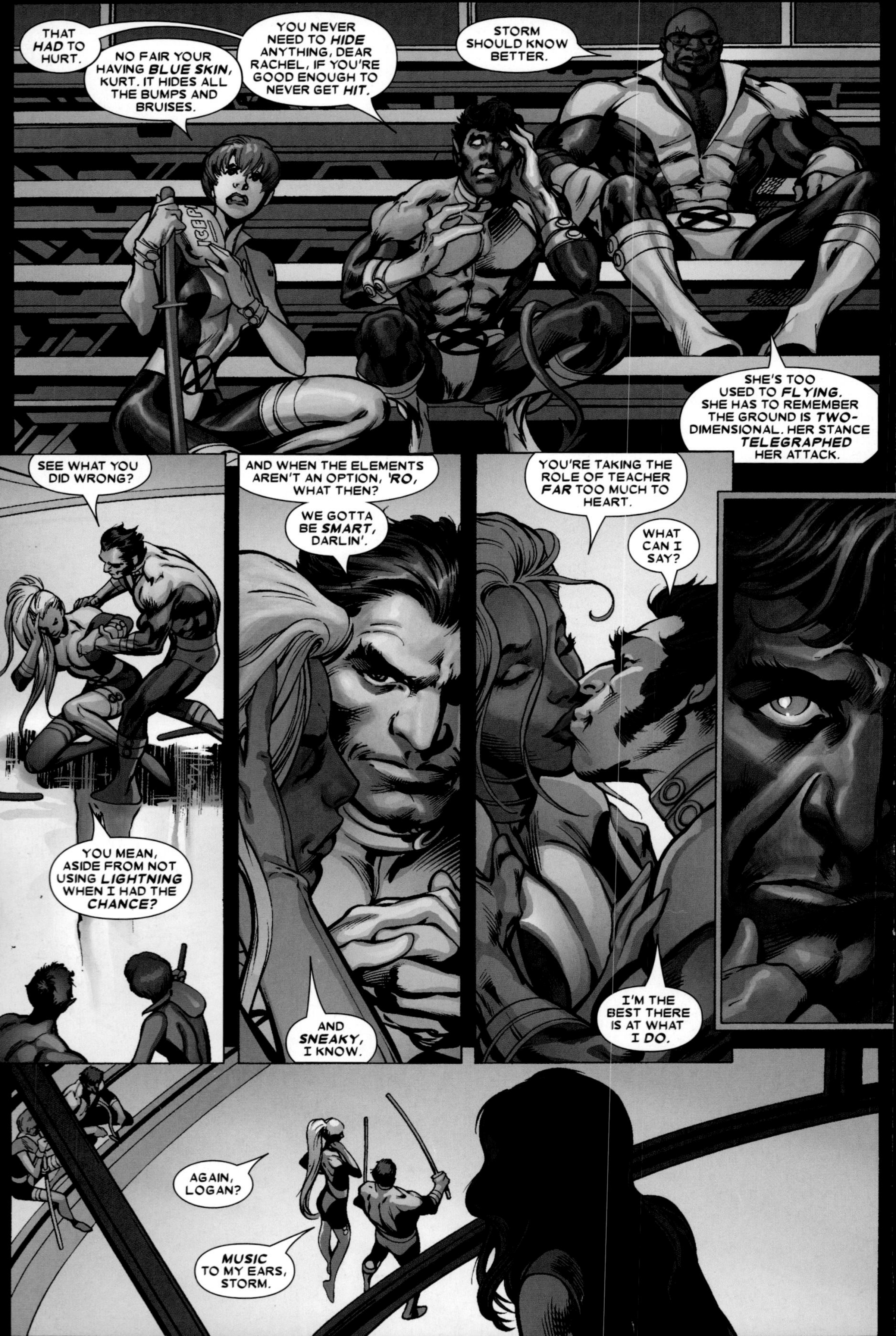
THAT HAD TO HURT.
NO FAIR YOUR HAVING BLUE SKIN, KURT. IT HIDES ALL THE BUMPS AND BRUISES.
YOU NEVER NEED TO HIDE ANYTHING, DEAR RACHEL, IF YOU'RE GOOD ENOUGH TO NEVER GET HIT.
STORM SHOULD KNOW BETTER.
SHE'S TOO USED TO FLYING. SHE HAS TO REMEMBER THE GROUND IS TWO-DIMENSIONAL. HER STANCE TELEGRAPHED HER ATTACK.
SEE WHAT YOU DID WRONG?
YOU MEAN, ASIDE FROM NOT USING LIGHTNING WHEN I HAD THE CHANCE?
AND WHEN THE ELEMENTS AREN'T AN OPTION, 'RO, WHAT THEN?
WE GOTTA BE SMART, DARLIN'.
AND SNEAKY, I KNOW.
YOU'RE TAKING THE ROLE OF TEACHER FAR TOO MUCH TO HEART.
WHAT CAN I SAY?
I'M THE BEST THERE IS AT WHAT I DO.
AGAIN, LOGAN?
MUSIC TO MY EARS, STORM.

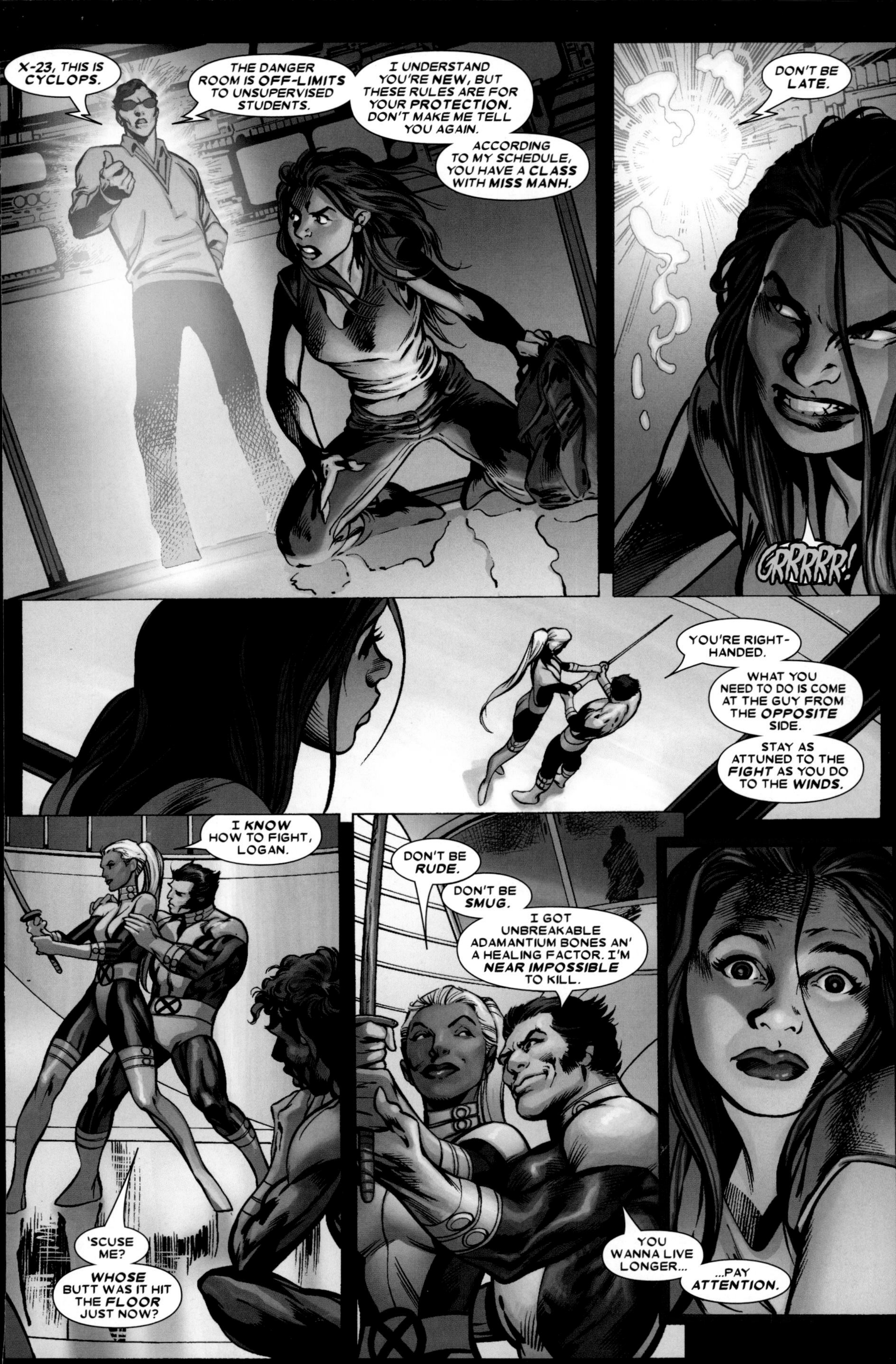
X-23, THIS IS CYCLOPS.
THE DANGER ROOM IS OFF-LIMITS TO UNSUPERVISED STUDENTS.
I UNDERSTAND YOU'RE NEW, BUT THESE RULES ARE FOR YOUR PROTECTION. DON'T MAKE ME TELL YOU AGAIN.
ACCORDING TO MY SCHEDULE, YOU HAVE A CLASS WITH MISS MANH.
DON'T BE LATE.
GRRRRR!
YOU'RE RIGHT-HANDED.
WHAT YOU NEED TO DO IS COME AT THE GUY FROM THE OPPOSITE SIDE.
STAY AS ATTUNED TO THE FIGHT AS YOU DO TO THE WINDS.
I KNOW HOW TO FIGHT, LOGAN.
'SCUSE ME?
WHOSE BUTT WAS IT HIT THE FLOOR JUST NOW?
DON'T BE RUDE.
DON'T BE SMUG.
I GOT UNBREAKABLE ADAMANTIUM BONES AN' A HEALING FACTOR. I'M NEAR IMPOSSIBLE TO KILL.
YOU WANNA LIVE LONGER...
...PAY ATTENTION.

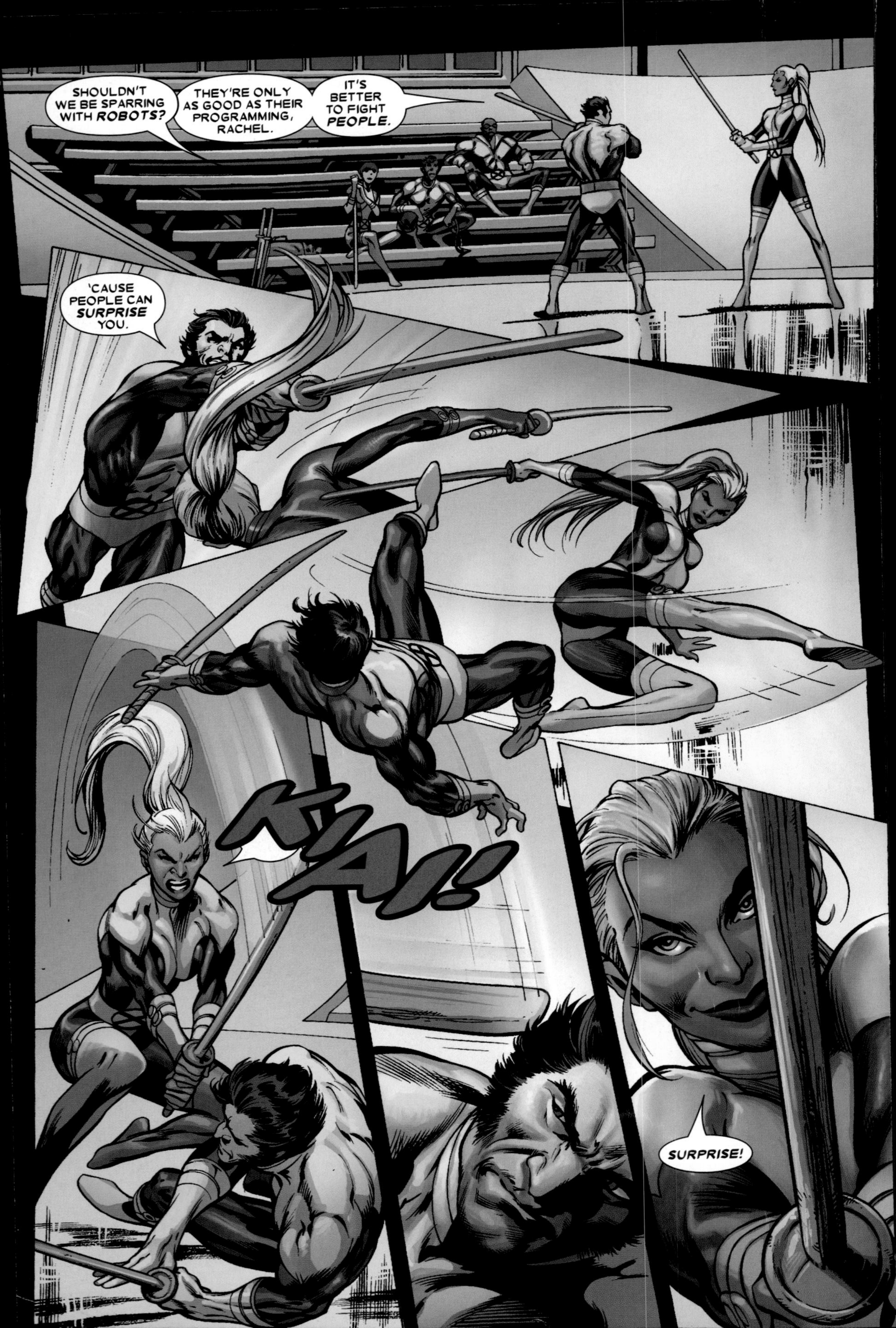
SHOULDN'T WE BE SPARRING WITH ROBOTS?
THEY'RE ONLY AS GOOD AS THEIR PROGRAMMING, RACHEL.
IT'S BETTER TO FIGHT PEOPLE.
'CAUSE PEOPLE CAN SURPRISE YOU.
KI'AI!!
SURPRISE!

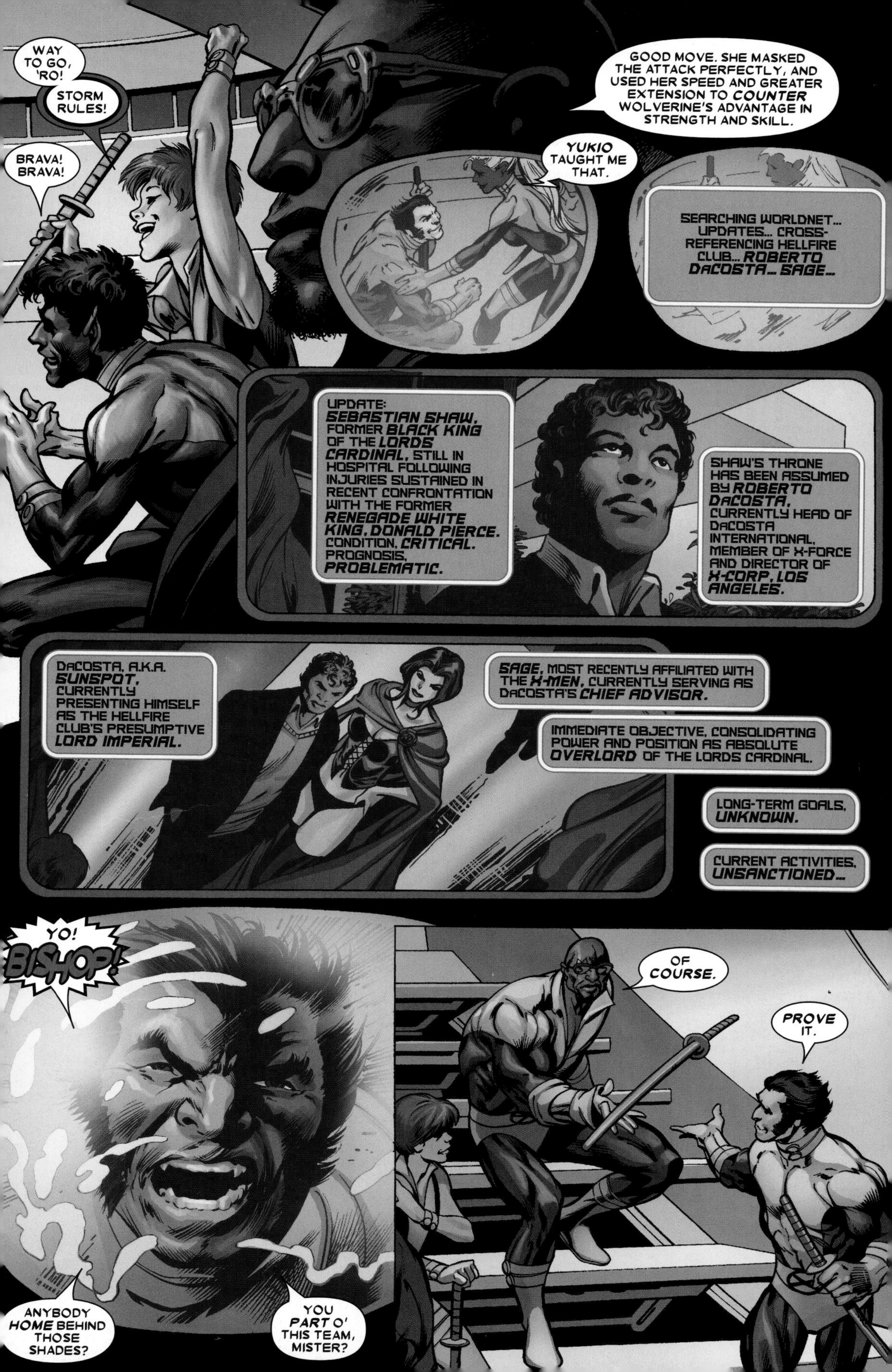

WAY TO GO, 'RO!
STORM RULES!
BRAVA! BRAVA!
GOOD MOVE. SHE MASKED THE ATTACK PERFECTLY, AND USED HER SPEED AND GREATER EXTENSION TO COUNTER WOLVERINE'S ADVANTAGE IN STRENGTH AND SKILL.
YUKIO TAUGHT ME THAT.
SEARCHING WORLDNET... UPDATES... CROSS-REFERENCING HELLFIRE CLUB... ROBERTO DACOSTA... SAGE...
UPDATE: SEBASTIAN SHAW, FORMER BLACK KING OF THE LORDS CARDINAL, STILL IN HOSPITAL FOLLOWING INJURIES SUSTAINED IN RECENT CONFRONTATION WITH THE FORMER RENEGADE WHITE KING, DONALD PIERCE. CONDITION, CRITICAL. PROGNOSIS, PROBLEMATIC.
SHAW'S THRONE HAS BEEN ASSUMED BY ROBERTO DACOSTA, CURRENTLY HEAD OF DACOSTA INTERNATIONAL, MEMBER OF X-FORCE AND DIRECTOR OF X-CORP, LOS ANGELES.
DACOSTA, A.K.A. SUNSPOT, CURRENTLY PRESENTING HIMSELF AS THE HELLFIRE CLUB'S PRESUMPTIVE LORD IMPERIAL.
SAGE, MOST RECENTLY AFFILIATED WITH THE X-MEN, CURRENTLY SERVING AS DACOSTA'S CHIEF ADVISOR.
IMMEDIATE OBJECTIVE, CONSOLIDATING POWER AND POSITION AS ABSOLUTE OVERLORD OF THE LORDS CARDINAL.
LONG-TERM GOALS, UNKNOWN.
CURRENT ACTIVITIES, UNSANCTIONED...
YO! BISHOP!
ANYBODY HOME BEHIND THOSE SHADES?
YOU PART O' THIS TEAM, MISTER?
OF COURSE.
PROVE IT.

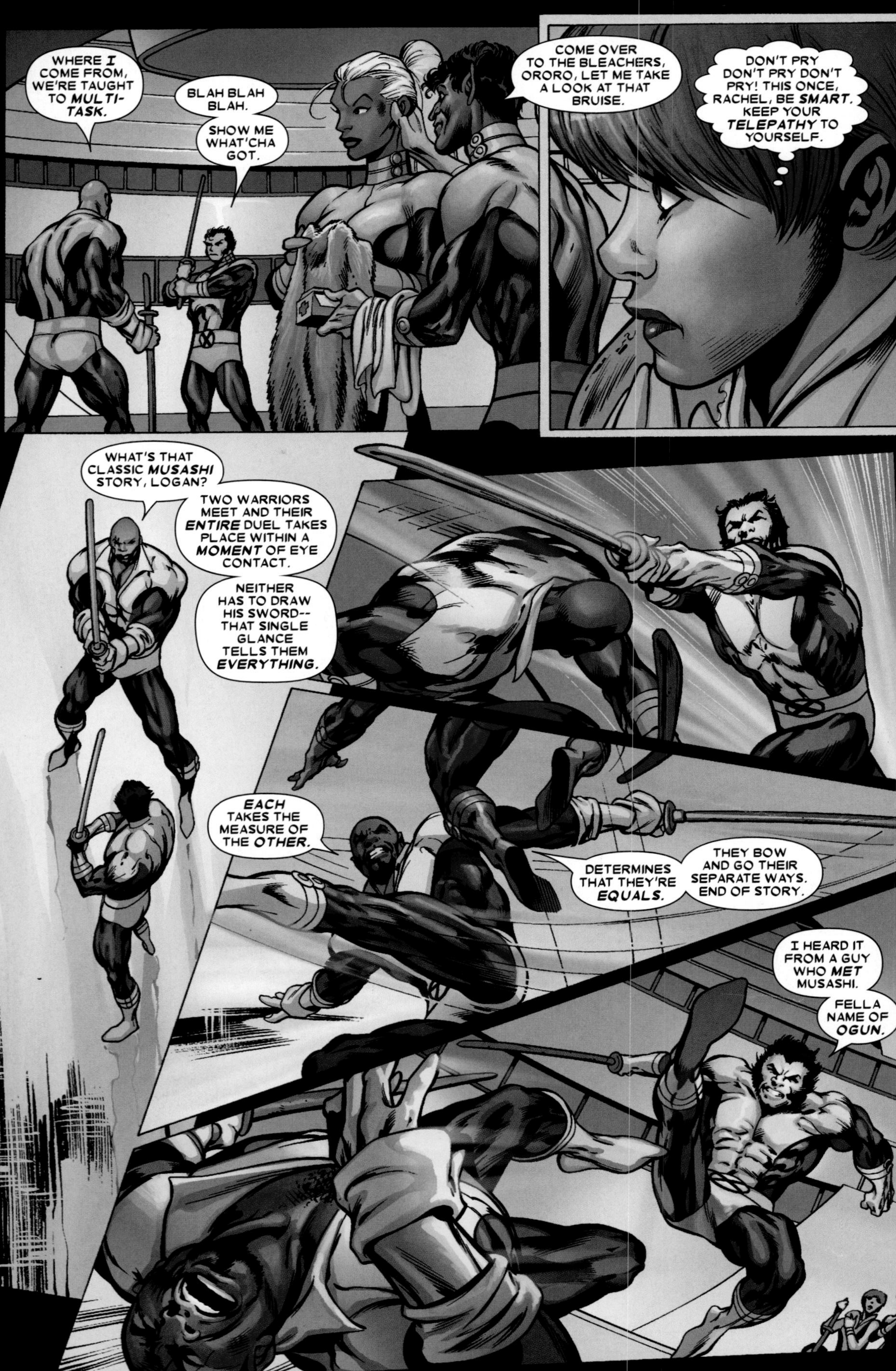

WHERE I COME FROM, WE'RE TAUGHT TO MULTI-TASK.
BLAH BLAH BLAH.
SHOW ME WHAT'CHA GOT.
COME OVER TO THE BLEACHERS, ORORO, LET ME TAKE A LOOK AT THAT BRUISE.
DON'T PRY DON'T PRY DON'T PRY! THIS ONCE, RACHEL, BE SMART. KEEP YOUR TELEPATHY TO YOURSELF.
WHAT'S THAT CLASSIC MUSASHI STORY, LOGAN?
TWO WARRIORS MEET AND THEIR ENTIRE DUEL TAKES PLACE WITHIN A MOMENT OF EYE CONTACT.
NEITHER HAS TO DRAW HIS SWORD-- THAT SINGLE GLANCE TELLS THEM EVERYTHING.
EACH TAKES THE MEASURE OF THE OTHER.
DETERMINES THAT THEY'RE EQUALS.
THEY BOW AND GO THEIR SEPARATE WAYS. END OF STORY.
I HEARD IT FROM A GUY WHO MET MUSASHI.
FELLA NAME OF OGUN.

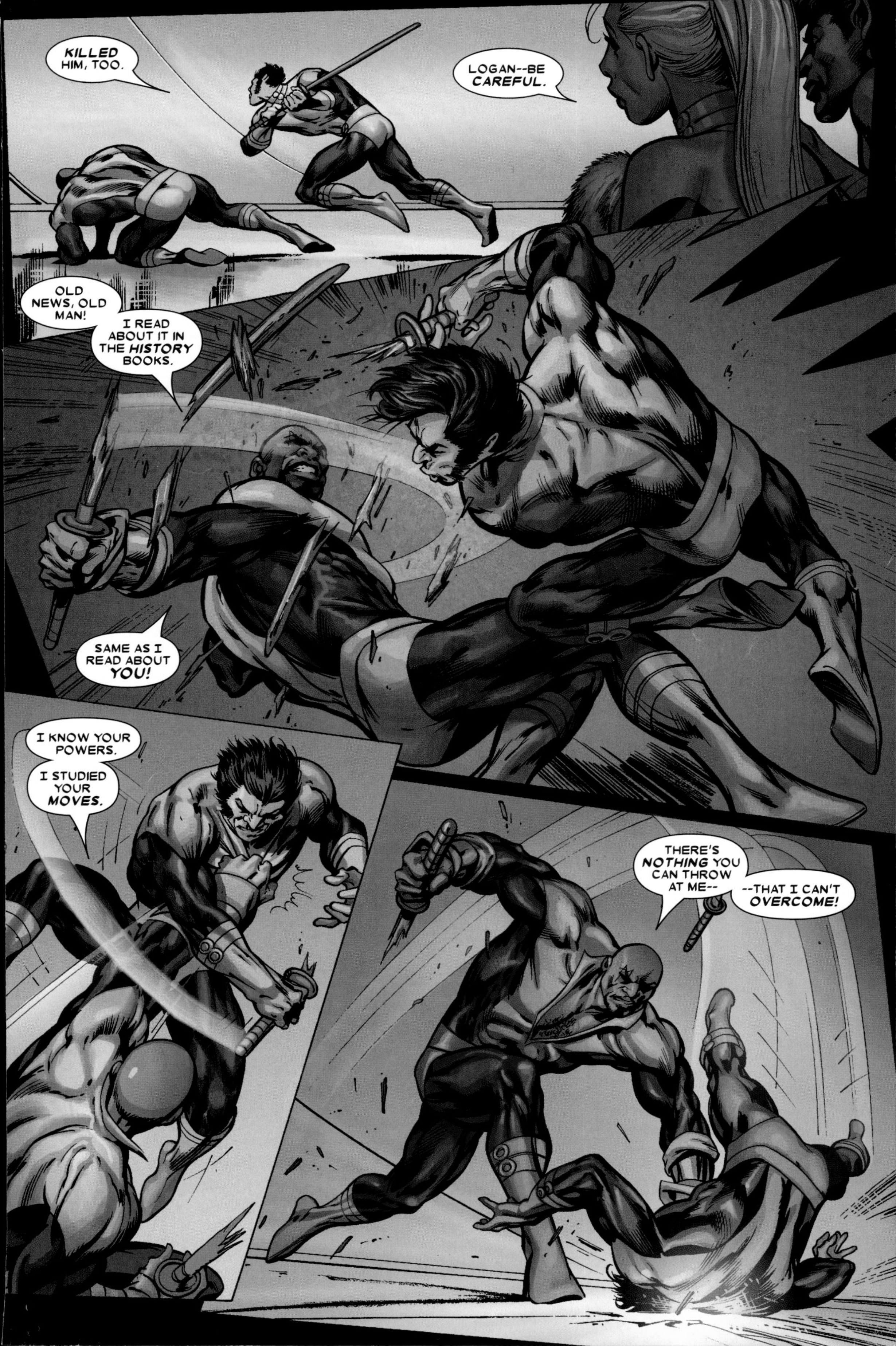

KILLED HIM, TOO.
LOGAN--BE CAREFUL.
OLD NEWS, OLD MAN!
I READ ABOUT IT IN THE HISTORY BOOKS.
SAME AS I READ ABOUT YOU!
I KNOW YOUR POWERS.
I STUDIED YOUR MOVES.
THERE'S NOTHING YOU CAN THROW AT ME--
--THAT I CAN'T OVERCOME!

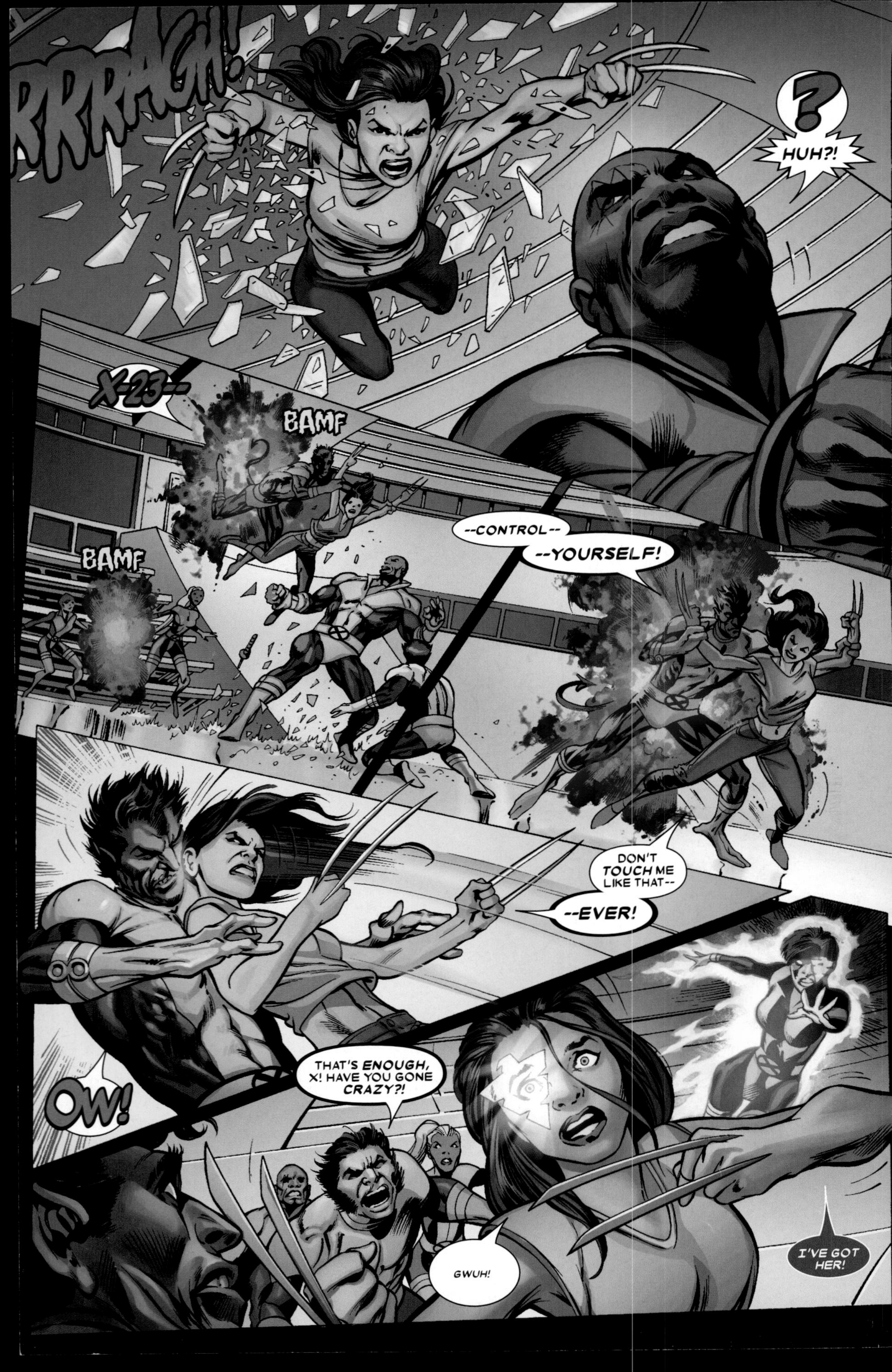
RRRAGH!
?
HUH?!
X-23--
BAMF
BAMF
--CONTROL--
--YOURSELF!
DON'T TOUCH ME LIKE THAT--
--EVER!
OW!
THAT'S ENOUGH, X! HAVE YOU GONE CRAZY?!
GWUH!
I'VE GOT HER!

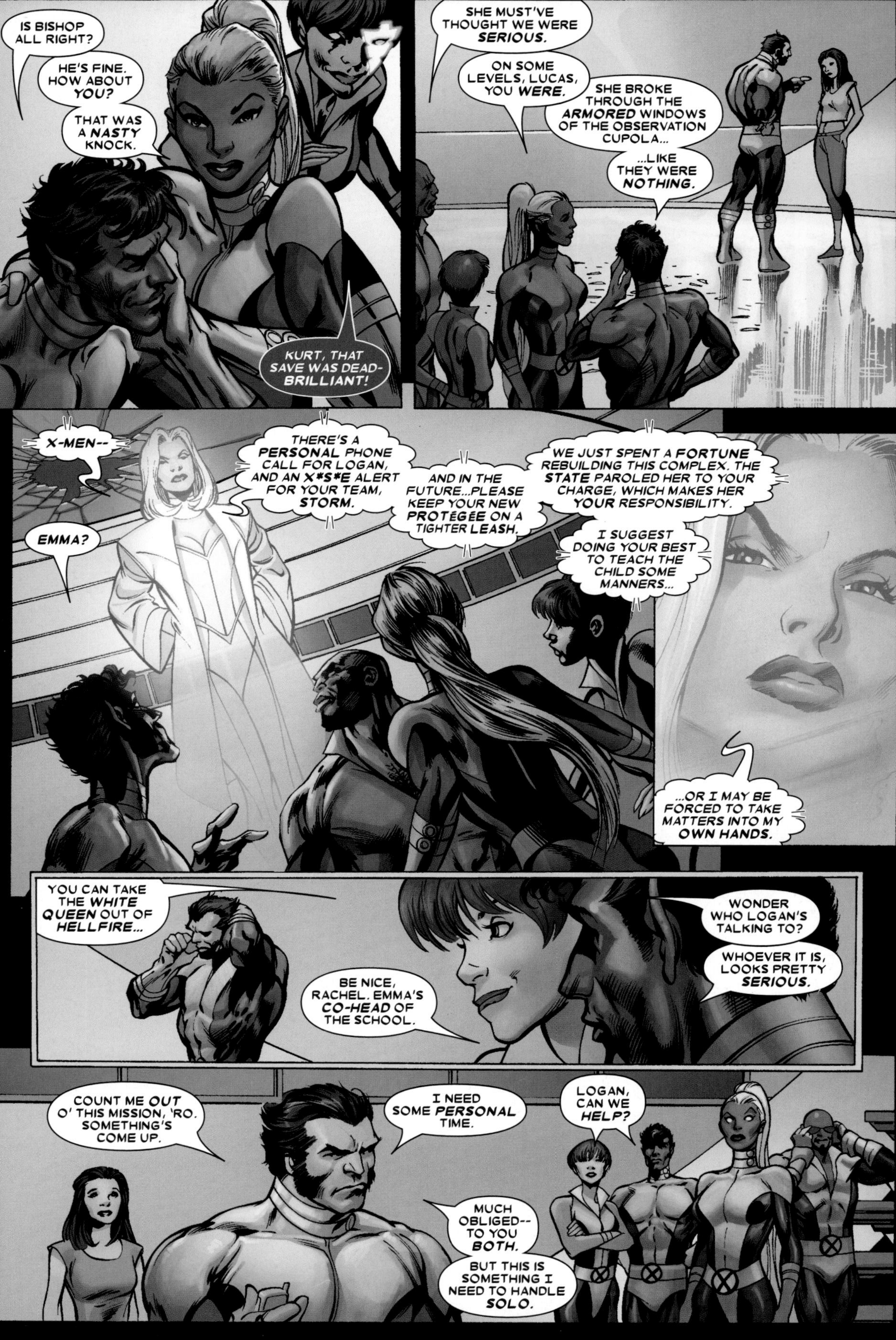
IS BISHOP ALL RIGHT?
HE'S FINE. HOW ABOUT YOU?
THAT WAS A NASTY KNOCK.
KURT, THAT SAVE WAS DEAD-BRILLIANT!
SHE MUST'VE THOUGHT WE WERE SERIOUS.
ON SOME LEVELS, LUCAS, YOU WERE.
SHE BROKE THROUGH THE ARMORED WINDOWS OF THE OBSERVATION CUPOLA...
...LIKE THEY WERE NOTHING.
X-MEN--
EMMA?
THERE'S A PERSONAL PHONE CALL FOR LOGAN, AND AN X*S*E ALERT FOR YOUR TEAM, STORM.
AND IN THE FUTURE...PLEASE KEEP YOUR NEW PROTÉGÉE ON A TIGHTER LEASH.
WE JUST SPENT A FORTUNE REBUILDING THIS COMPLEX. THE STATE PAROLED HER TO YOUR CHARGE, WHICH MAKES HER YOUR RESPONSIBILITY.
I SUGGEST DOING YOUR BEST TO TEACH THE CHILD SOME MANNERS...
...OR I MAY BE FORCED TO TAKE MATTERS INTO MY OWN HANDS.
YOU CAN TAKE THE WHITE QUEEN OUT OF HELLFIRE...
BE NICE, RACHEL. EMMA'S CO-HEAD OF THE SCHOOL.
WONDER WHO LOGAN'S TALKING TO?
WHOEVER IT IS, LOOKS PRETTY SERIOUS.
COUNT ME OUT O' THIS MISSION, 'RO. SOMETHING'S COME UP.
I NEED SOME PERSONAL TIME.
LOGAN, CAN WE HELP?
MUCH OBLIGED-- TO YOU BOTH.
BUT THIS IS SOMETHING I NEED TO HANDLE SOLO.

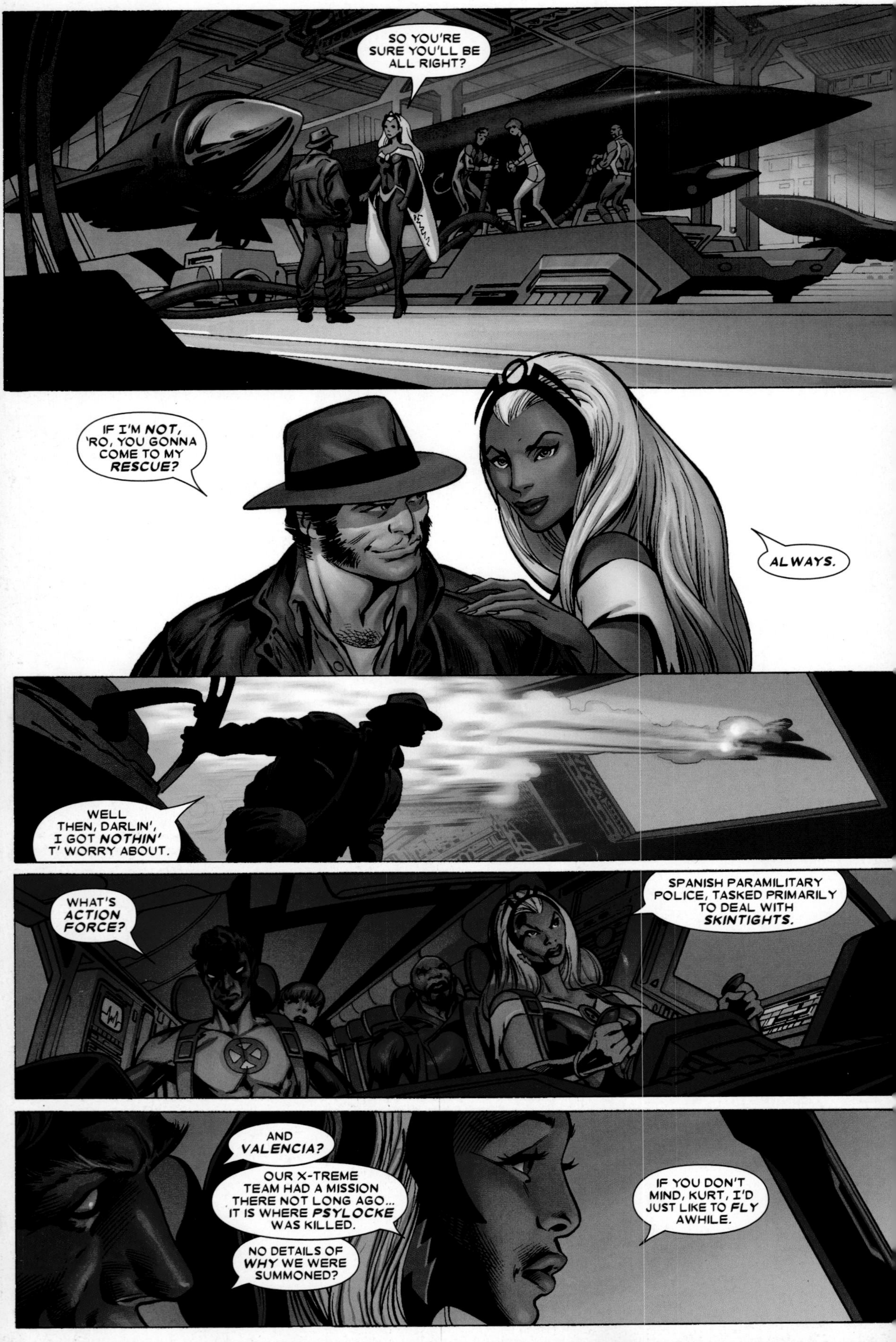
SO YOU'RE SURE YOU'LL BE ALL RIGHT?
IF I'M NOT, 'RO, YOU GONNA COME TO MY RESCUE?
ALWAYS.
WELL THEN, DARLIN', I GOT NOTHIN' T' WORRY ABOUT.
WHAT'S ACTION FORCE?
SPANISH PARAMILITARY POLICE, TASKED PRIMARILY TO DEAL WITH SKINTIGHTS.
AND VALENCIA?
OUR X-TREME TEAM HAD A MISSION THERE NOT LONG AGO... IT IS WHERE PSYLOCKE WAS KILLED.
NO DETAILS OF WHY WE WERE SUMMONED?
IF YOU DON'T MIND, KURT, I'D JUST LIKE TO FLY AWHILE.

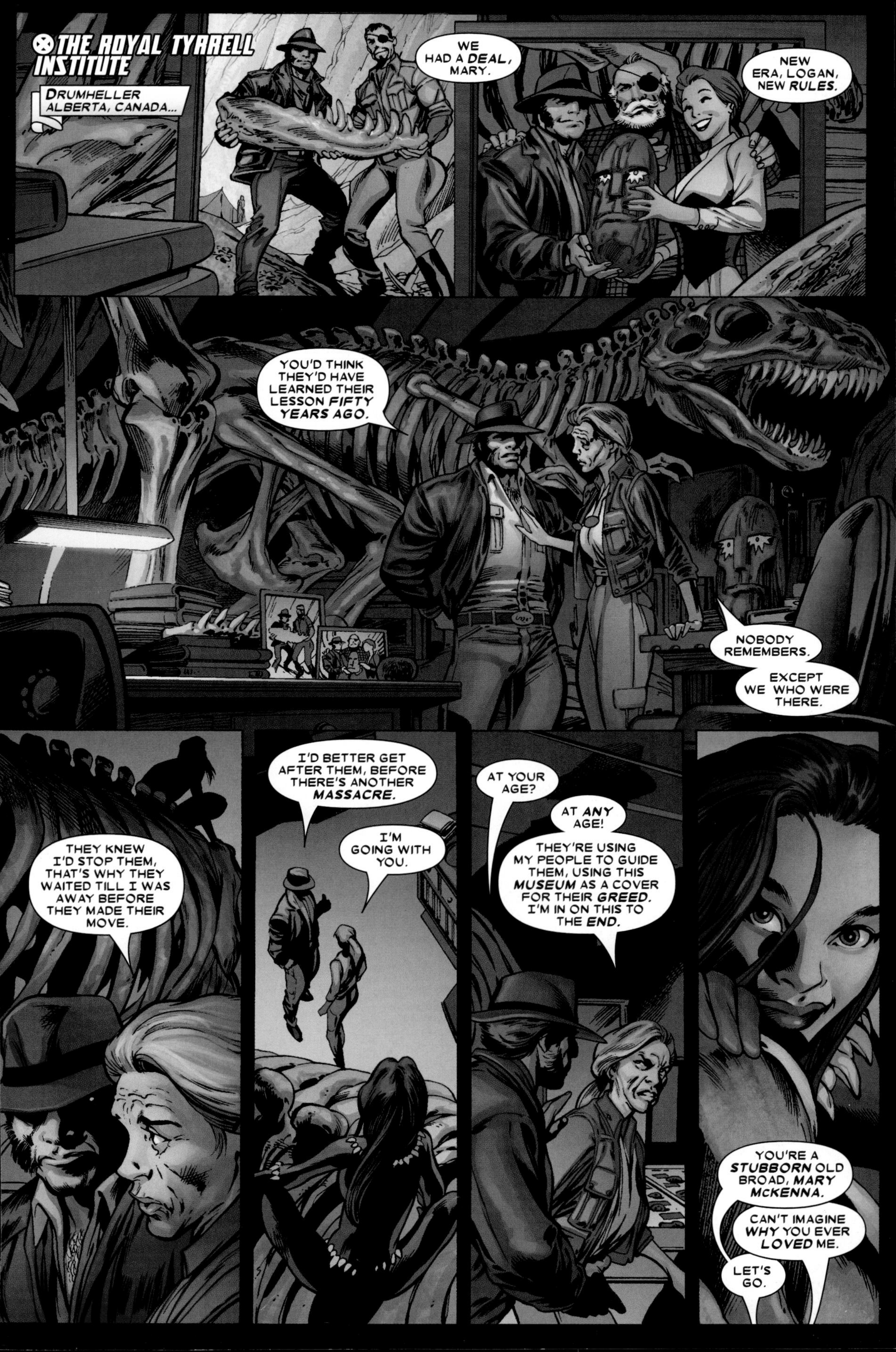
THE ROYAL TYRRELL INSTITUTE
DRUMHELLER ALBERTA, CANADA...
WE HAD A DEAL, MARY.
NEW ERA, LOGAN, NEW RULES.
YOU'D THINK THEY'D HAVE LEARNED THEIR LESSON FIFTY YEARS AGO.
NOBODY REMEMBERS.
EXCEPT WE WHO WERE THERE.
THEY KNEW I'D STOP THEM, THAT'S WHY THEY WAITED TILL I WAS AWAY BEFORE THEY MADE THEIR MOVE.
I'D BETTER GET AFTER THEM, BEFORE THERE'S ANOTHER MASSACRE.
I'M GOING WITH YOU.
AT YOUR AGE?
AT ANY AGE!
THEY'RE USING MY PEOPLE TO GUIDE THEM, USING THIS MUSEUM AS A COVER FOR THEIR GREED. I'M IN ON THIS TO THE END.
YOU'RE A STUBBORN OLD BROAD, MARY McKENNA.
CAN'T IMAGINE WHY YOU EVER LOVED ME.
LET'S GO.

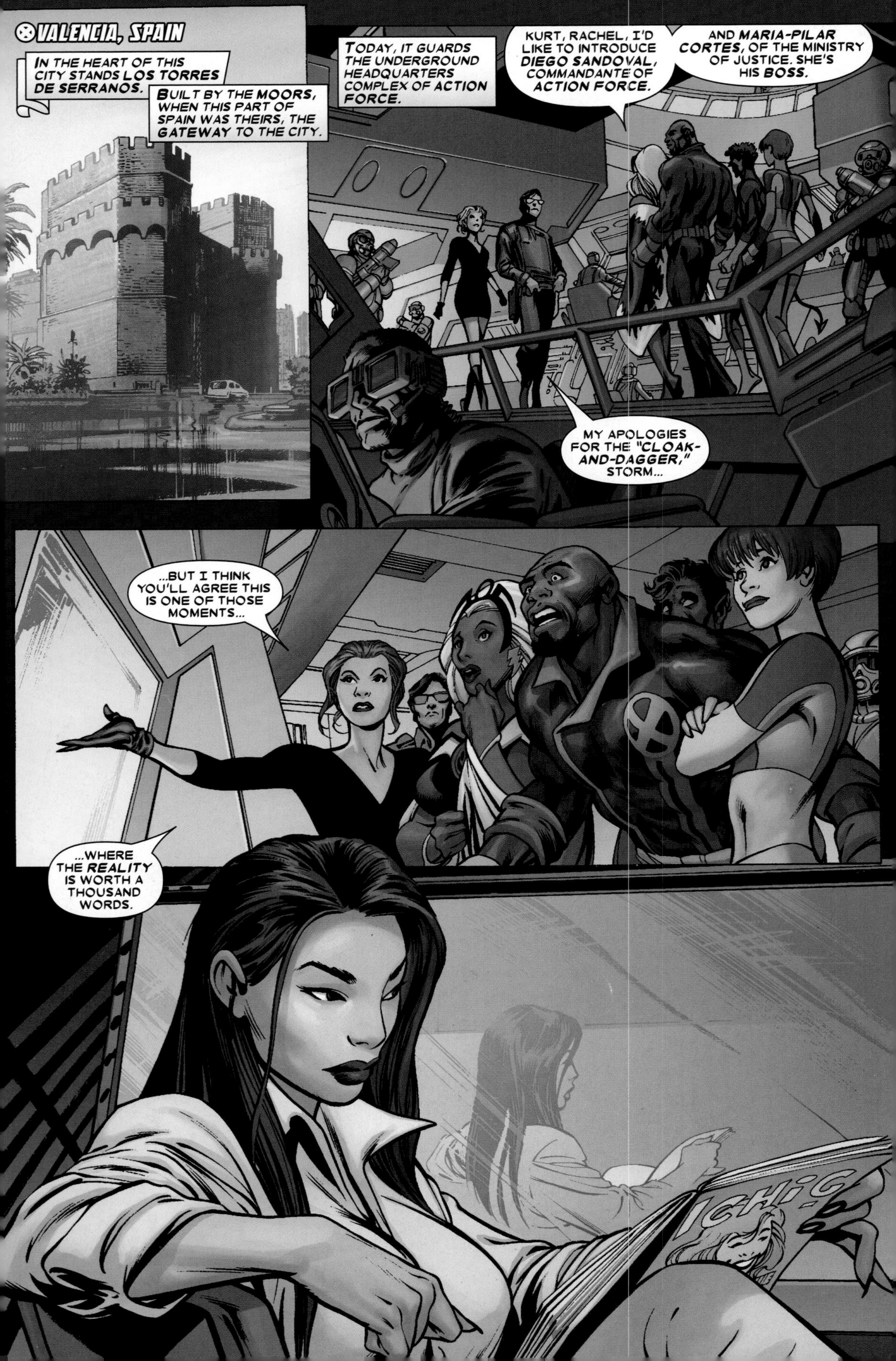
VALENCIA, SPAIN
IN THE HEART OF THIS CITY STANDS LOS TORRES DE SERRANOS.
BUILT BY THE MOORS, WHEN THIS PART OF SPAIN WAS THEIRS, THE GATEWAY TO THE CITY.
TODAY, IT GUARDS THE UNDERGROUND HEADQUARTERS COMPLEX OF ACTION FORCE.
KURT, RACHEL, I'D LIKE TO INTRODUCE DIEGO SANDOVAL, COMMANDANTE OF ACTION FORCE.
AND MARIA-PILAR CORTES, OF THE MINISTRY OF JUSTICE. SHE'S HIS BOSS.
MY APOLOGIES FOR THE "CLOAK-AND-DAGGER," STORM...
...BUT I THINK YOU'LL AGREE THIS IS ONE OF THOSE MOMENTS...
...WHERE THE REALITY IS WORTH A THOUSAND WORDS.

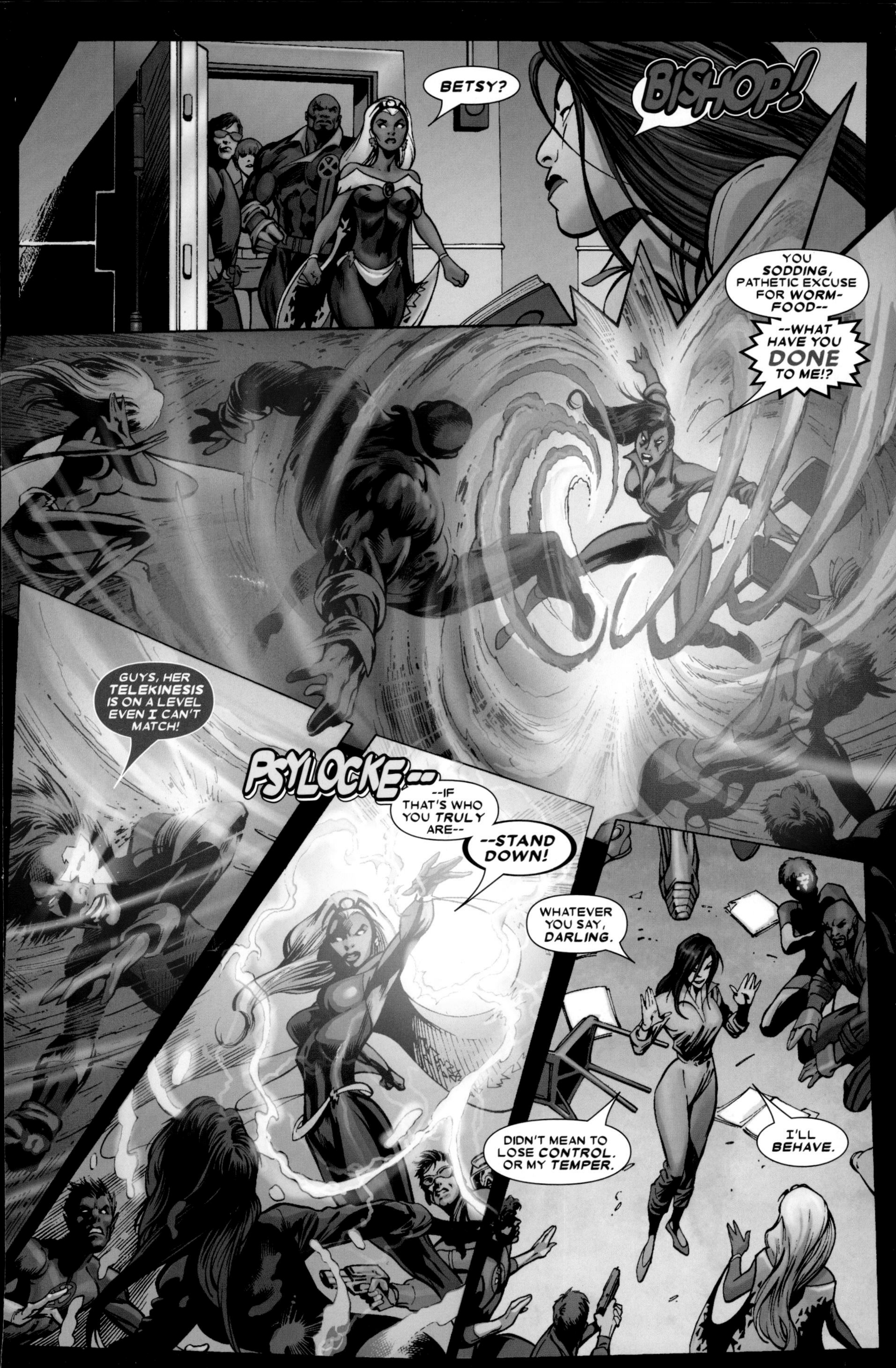
BETSY?
BISHOP!
YOU SODDING, PATHETIC EXCUSE FOR WORM-FOOD--
--WHAT HAVE YOU DONE TO ME!?
GUYS, HER TELEKINESIS IS ON A LEVEL EVEN I CAN'T MATCH!
PSYLOCKE--
--IF THAT'S WHO YOU TRULY ARE--
--STAND DOWN!
WHATEVER YOU SAY, DARLING.
DIDN'T MEAN TO LOSE CONTROL. OR MY TEMPER.
I'LL BEHAVE.

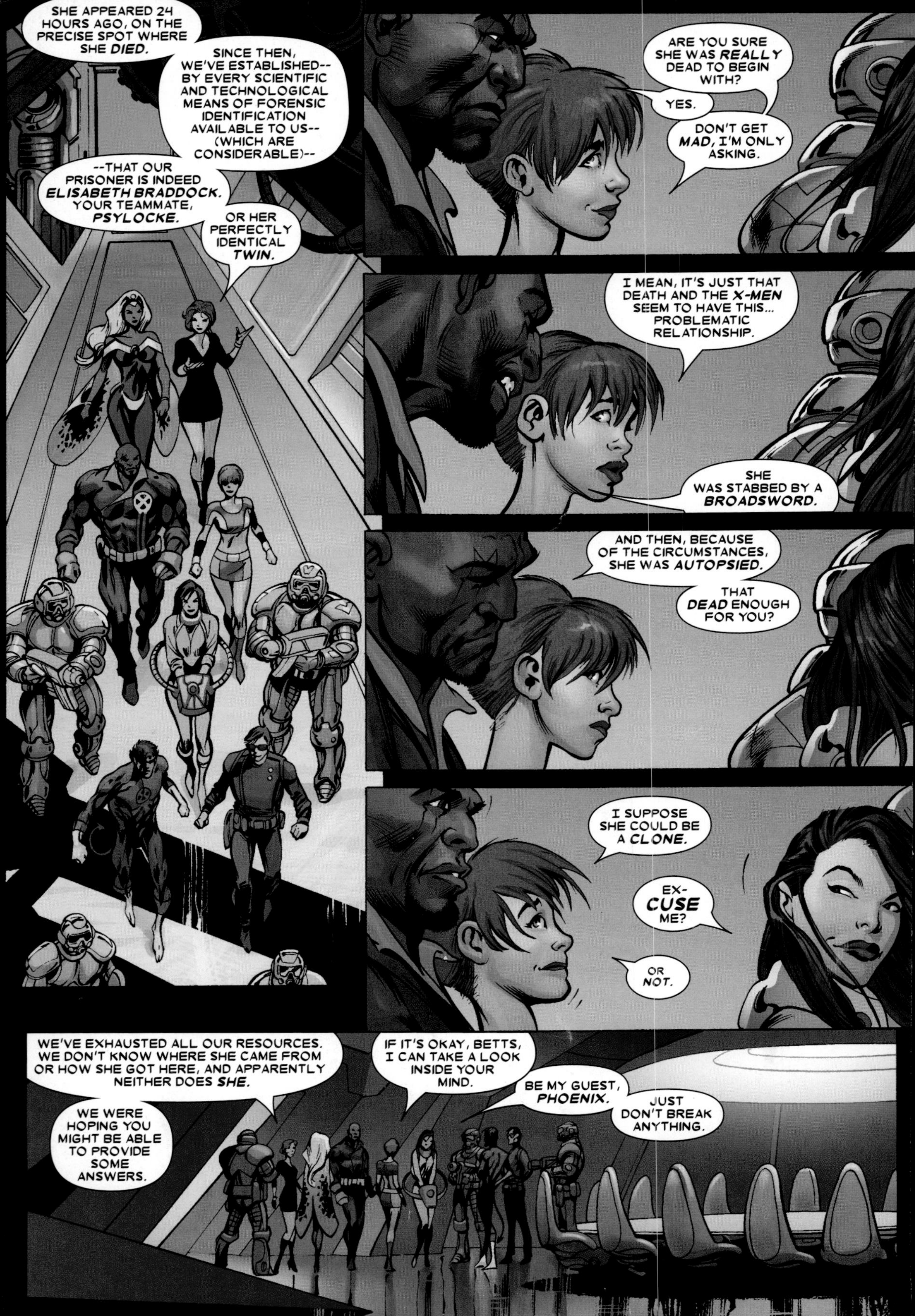
SHE APPEARED 24 HOURS AGO, ON THE PRECISE SPOT WHERE SHE *DIED.*
SINCE THEN, WE'VE ESTABLISHED-- BY EVERY SCIENTIFIC AND TECHNOLOGICAL MEANS OF FORENSIC IDENTIFICATION AVAILABLE TO US-- (WHICH ARE CONSIDERABLE)--
--THAT OUR PRISONER IS INDEED *ELISABETH BRADDOCK.* YOUR TEAMMATE, *PSYLOCKE.*
OR HER PERFECTLY IDENTICAL *TWIN.*
ARE YOU SURE SHE WAS *REALLY* DEAD TO BEGIN WITH?
YES.
DON'T GET *MAD,* I'M ONLY ASKING.
I MEAN, IT'S JUST THAT DEATH AND THE *X-MEN* SEEM TO HAVE THIS... PROBLEMATIC RELATIONSHIP.
SHE WAS STABBED BY A *BROADSWORD.*
AND THEN, BECAUSE OF THE CIRCUMSTANCES, SHE WAS *AUTOPSIED.*
THAT *DEAD* ENOUGH FOR YOU?
I SUPPOSE SHE COULD BE A *CLONE.*
EX-*CUSE* ME?
OR *NOT.*
WE'VE EXHAUSTED ALL OUR RESOURCES. WE DON'T KNOW WHERE SHE CAME FROM OR HOW SHE GOT HERE, AND APPARENTLY NEITHER DOES *SHE.*
WE WERE HOPING YOU MIGHT BE ABLE TO PROVIDE SOME ANSWERS.
IF IT'S OKAY, BETTS, I CAN TAKE A LOOK INSIDE YOUR MIND.
BE MY GUEST, *PHOENIX.*
JUST DON'T BREAK ANYTHING.

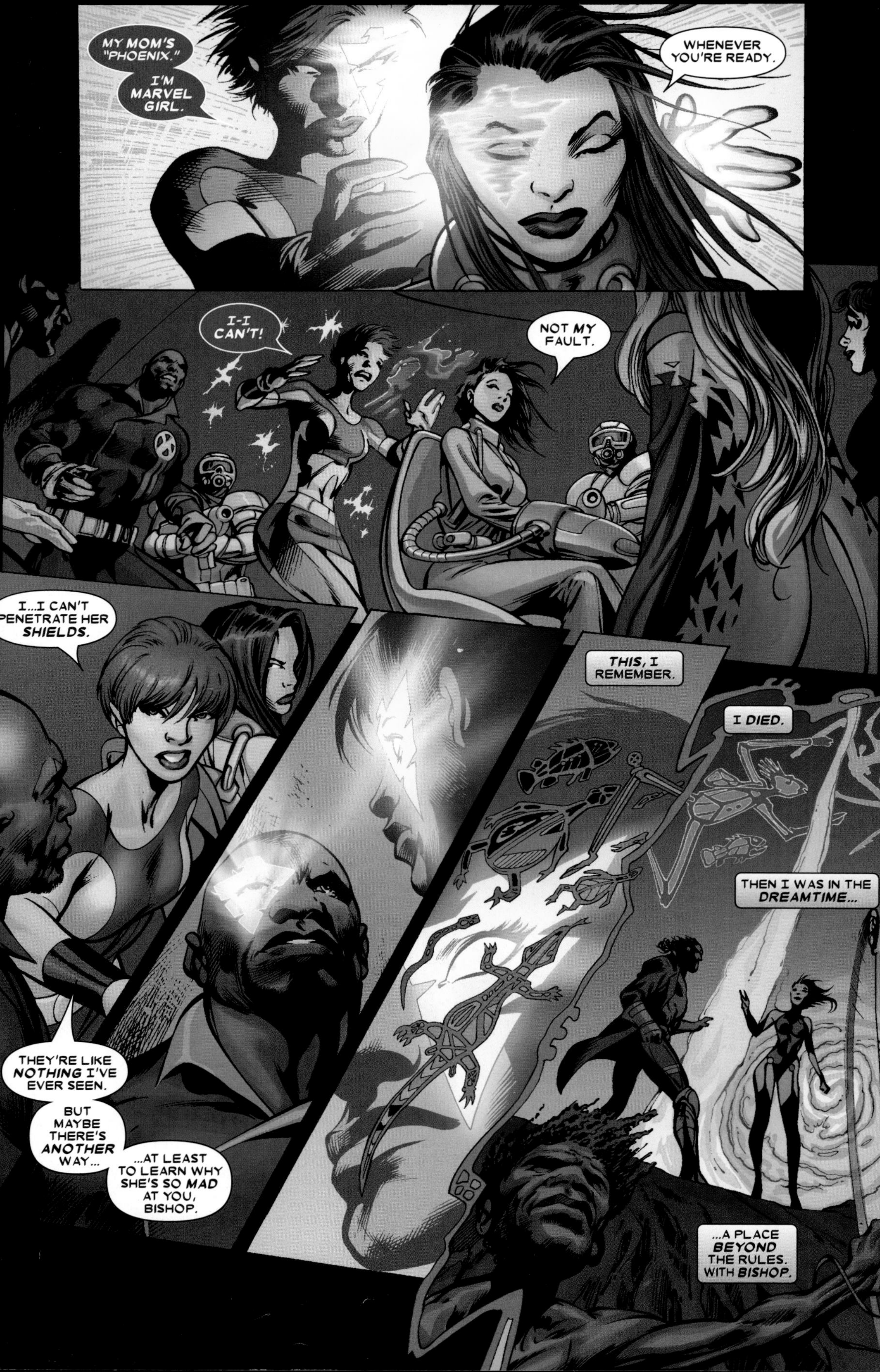

MY MOM'S "PHOENIX."
I'M MARVEL GIRL.
WHENEVER YOU'RE READY.
I-I CAN'T!
NOT MY FAULT.
I...I CAN'T PENETRATE HER SHIELDS.
THEY'RE LIKE NOTHING I'VE EVER SEEN.
BUT MAYBE THERE'S ANOTHER WAY...
...AT LEAST TO LEARN WHY SHE'S SO MAD AT YOU, BISHOP.
THIS, I REMEMBER.
I DIED.
THEN I WAS IN THE DREAMTIME...
...A PLACE BEYOND THE RULES. WITH BISHOP.

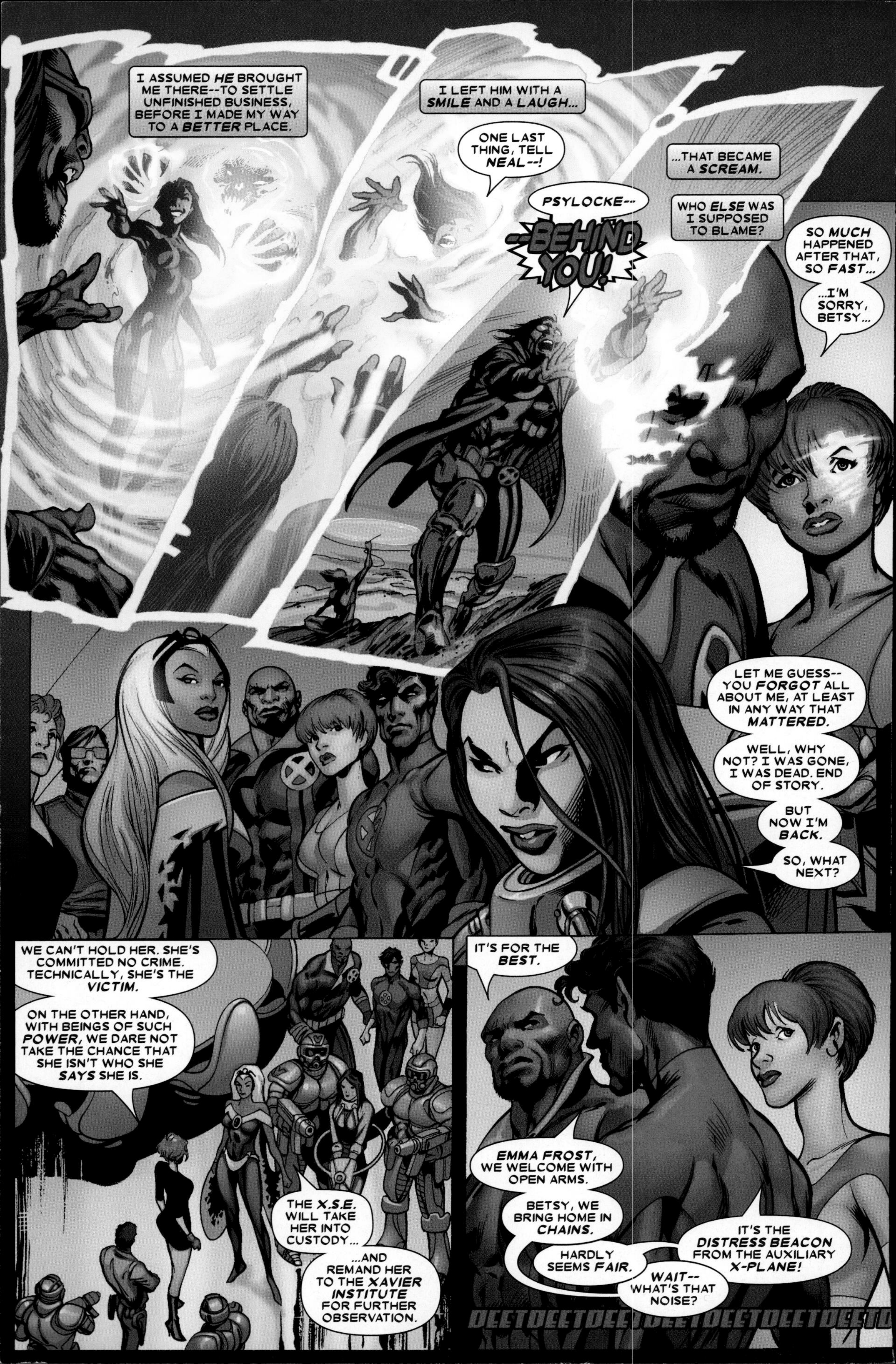
I ASSUMED HE BROUGHT ME THERE--TO SETTLE UNFINISHED BUSINESS, BEFORE I MADE MY WAY TO A BETTER PLACE.
I LEFT HIM WITH A SMILE AND A LAUGH...
ONE LAST THING, TELL NEAL--!
...THAT BECAME A SCREAM.
PSYLOCKE--
--BEHIND YOU!
WHO ELSE WAS I SUPPOSED TO BLAME?
SO MUCH HAPPENED AFTER THAT, SO FAST...
...I'M SORRY, BETSY...
LET ME GUESS-- YOU FORGOT ALL ABOUT ME, AT LEAST IN ANY WAY THAT MATTERED.
WELL, WHY NOT? I WAS GONE, I WAS DEAD. END OF STORY.
BUT NOW I'M BACK.
SO, WHAT NEXT?
WE CAN'T HOLD HER. SHE'S COMMITTED NO CRIME. TECHNICALLY, SHE'S THE VICTIM.
ON THE OTHER HAND, WITH BEINGS OF SUCH POWER, WE DARE NOT TAKE THE CHANCE THAT SHE ISN'T WHO SHE SAYS SHE IS.
THE X.S.E. WILL TAKE HER INTO CUSTODY...
...AND REMAND HER TO THE XAVIER INSTITUTE FOR FURTHER OBSERVATION.
IT'S FOR THE BEST.
EMMA FROST, WE WELCOME WITH OPEN ARMS.
BETSY, WE BRING HOME IN CHAINS.
HARDLY SEEMS FAIR.
WAIT-- WHAT'S THAT NOISE?
IT'S THE DISTRESS BEACON FROM THE AUXILIARY X-PLANE!
DEETDEETDEETDEETDEETDEETDEET

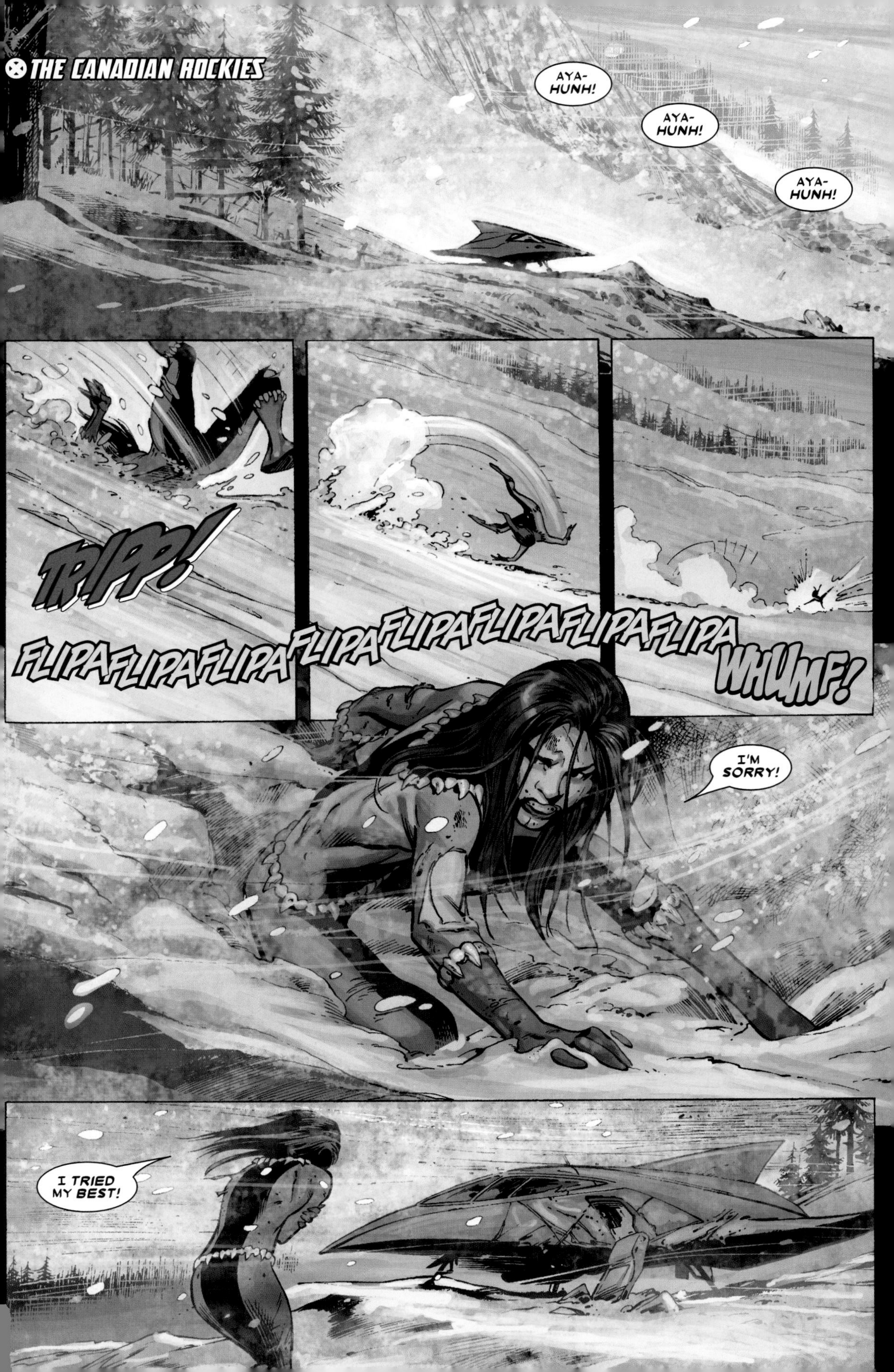
THE CANADIAN ROCKIES
AYA-HUNH!
AYA-HUNH!
AYA-HUNH!
TRIPP!
FLIPAFLIPAFLIPAFLIPAFLIPAFLIPAFLIPAFLIPAFLIPA
WHUMF!
I'M SORRY!
I TRIED MY BEST!

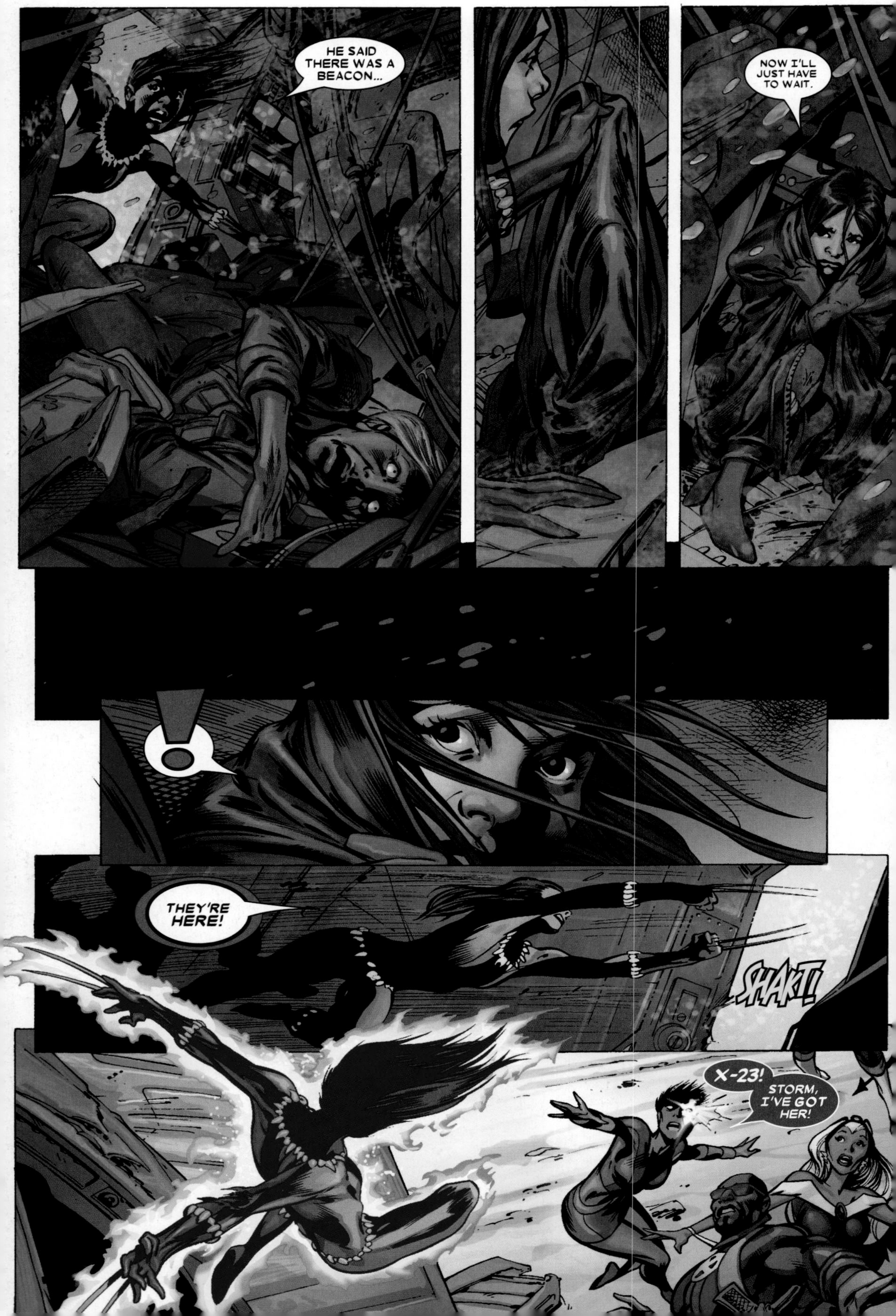
HE SAID THERE WAS A BEACON...
NOW I'LL JUST HAVE TO WAIT.
!
THEY'RE HERE!
SHAKT!
X-23!
STORM, I'VE GOT HER!

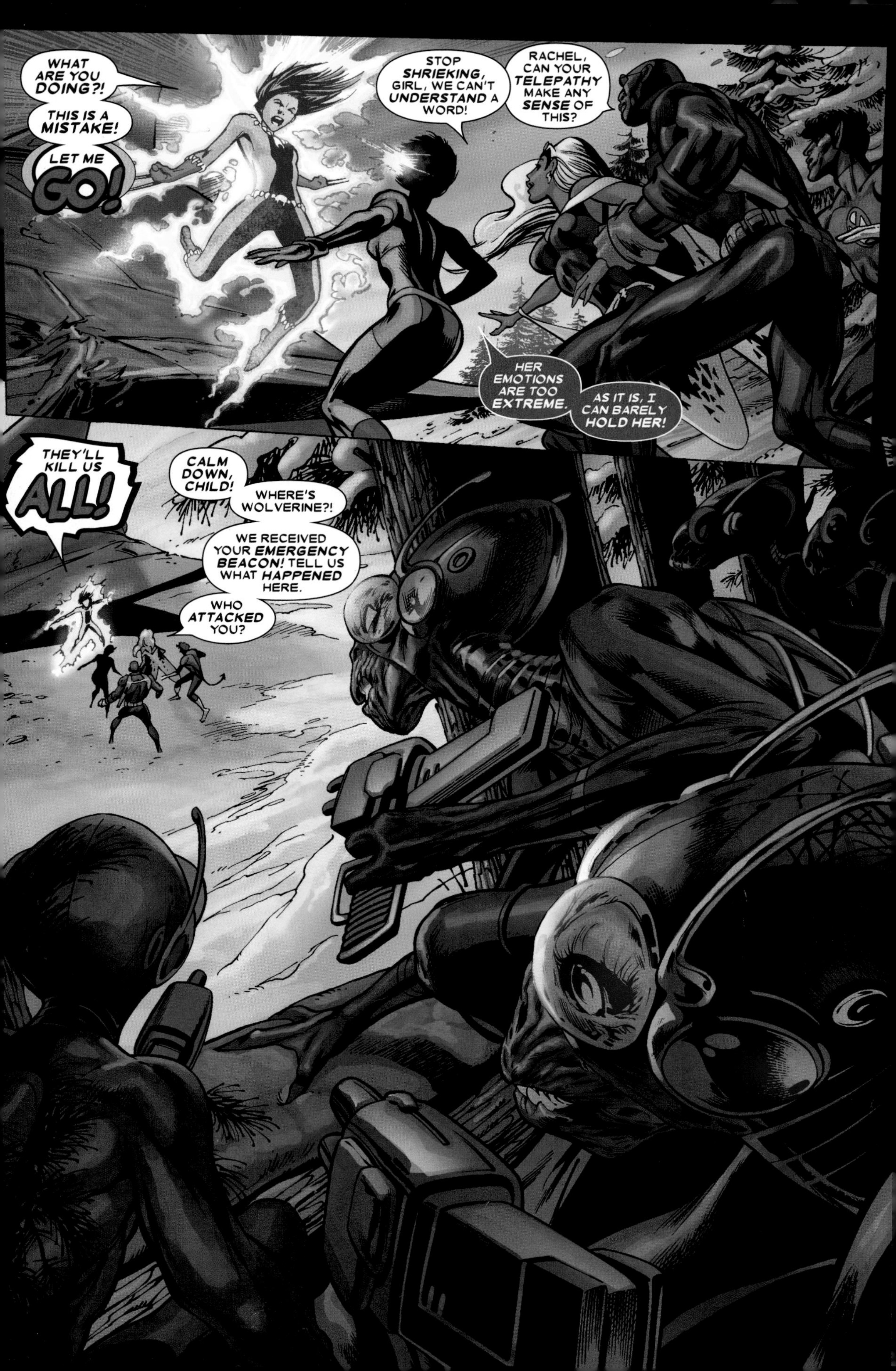
WHAT ARE YOU DOING?!
THIS IS A MISTAKE!
LET ME GO!
STOP SHRIEKING, GIRL, WE CAN'T UNDERSTAND A WORD!
RACHEL, CAN YOUR TELEPATHY MAKE ANY SENSE OF THIS?
HER EMOTIONS ARE TOO EXTREME.
AS IT IS, I CAN BARELY HOLD HER!
THEY'LL KILL US ALL!
CALM DOWN, CHILD!
WHERE'S WOLVERINE?!
WE RECEIVED YOUR EMERGENCY BEACON! TELL US WHAT HAPPENED HERE.
WHO ATTACKED YOU?

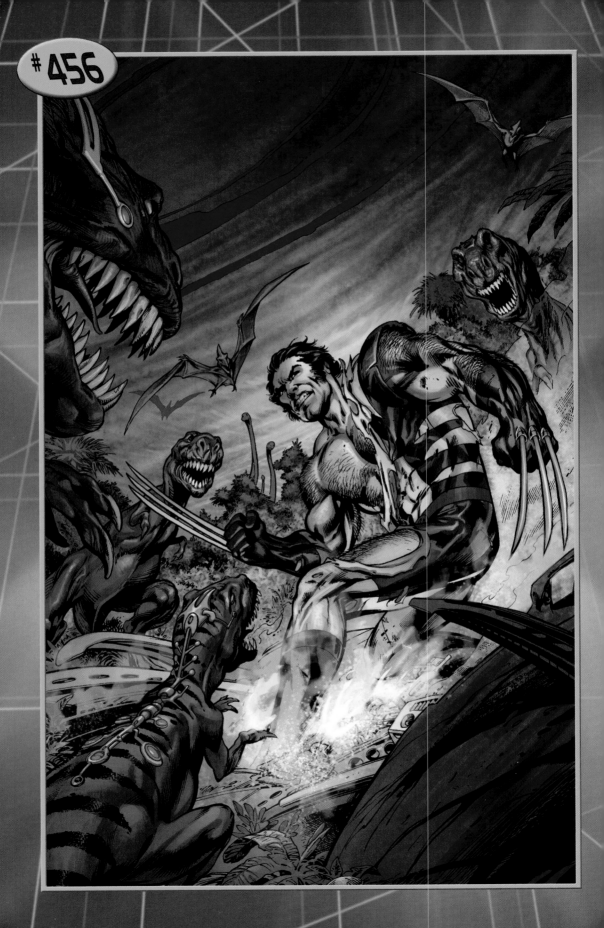

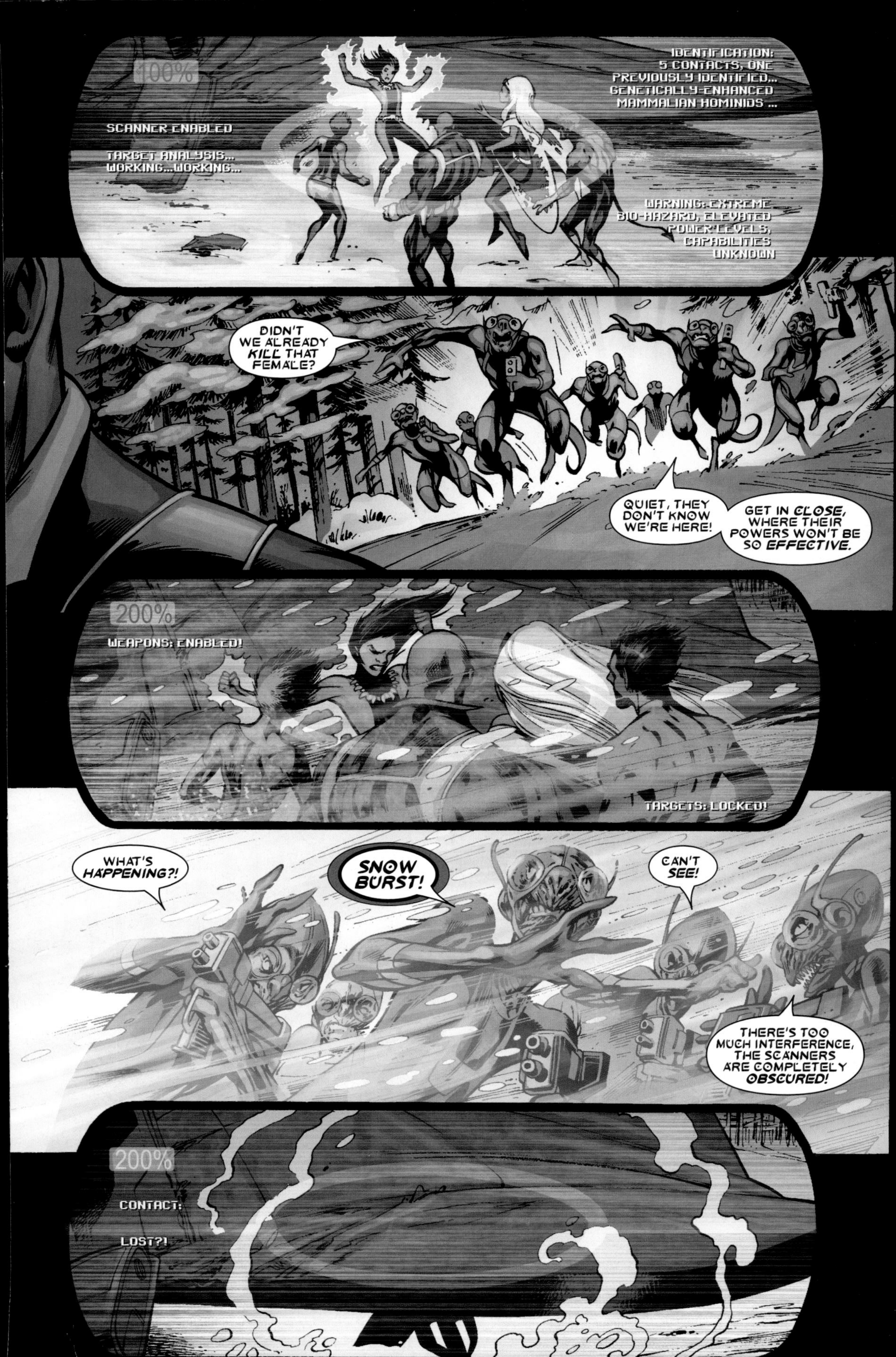
100%
SCANNER ENABLED
TARGET ANALYSIS... WORKING...WORKING...
IDENTIFICATION: 5 CONTACTS, ONE PREVIOUSLY IDENTIFIED... GENETICALLY-ENHANCED MAMMALIAN HOMINIDS ...
WARNING: EXTREME BIO-HAZARD, ELEVATED POWER LEVELS, CAPABILITIES UNKNOWN
DIDN'T WE ALREADY KILL THAT FEMALE?
QUIET, THEY DON'T KNOW WE'RE HERE!
GET IN CLOSE, WHERE THEIR POWERS WON'T BE SO EFFECTIVE.
200%
WEAPONS: ENABLED!
TARGETS: LOCKED!
WHAT'S HAPPENING?!
SNOW BURST!
CAN'T SEE!
THERE'S TOO MUCH INTERFERENCE, THE SCANNERS ARE COMPLETELY OBSCURED!
200%
CONTACT:
LOST?!

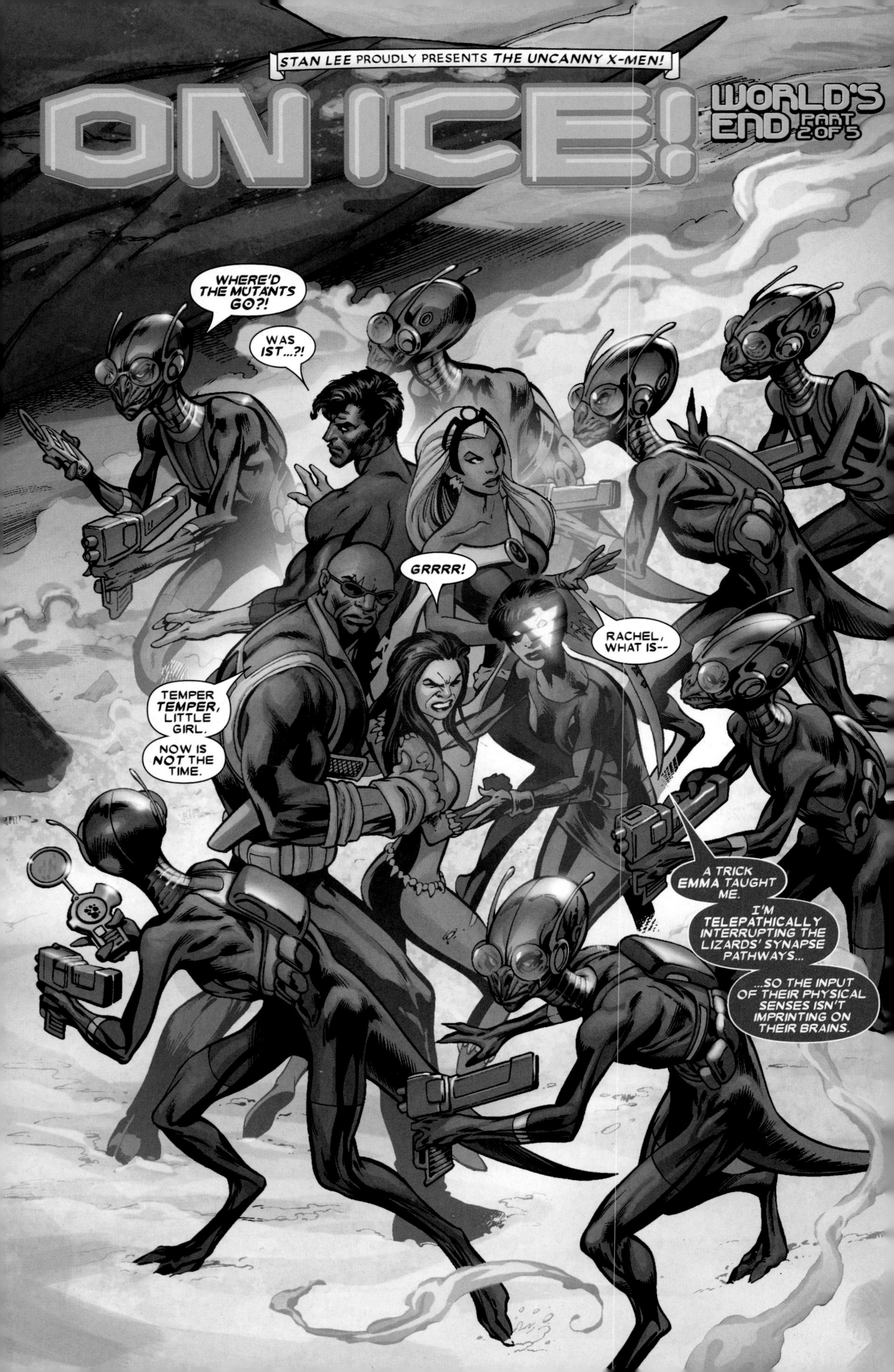

STAN LEE PROUDLY PRESENTS THE UNCANNY X-MEN!
ON ICE!
WORLD'S END PART 2 OF 5
WHERE'D THE MUTANTS GO?!
WAS IST...?!
GRRRR!
RACHEL, WHAT IS--
TEMPER TEMPER, LITTLE GIRL.
NOW IS NOT THE TIME.
A TRICK EMMA TAUGHT ME.
I'M TELEPATHICALLY INTERRUPTING THE LIZARDS' SYNAPSE PATHWAYS...
...SO THE INPUT OF THEIR PHYSICAL SENSES ISN'T IMPRINTING ON THEIR BRAINS.

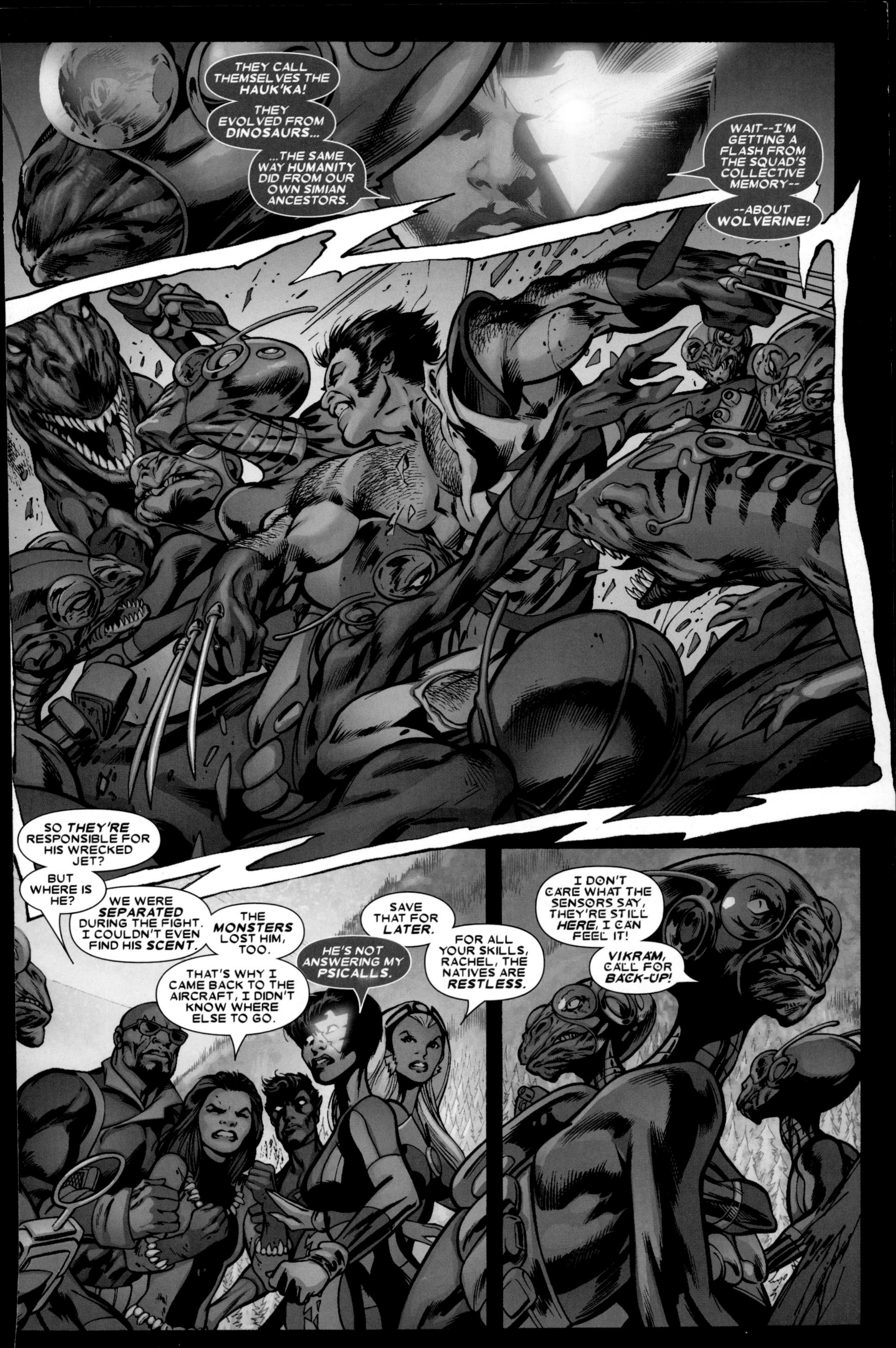
THEY CALL THEMSELVES THE HAUK'KA!
THEY EVOLVED FROM DINOSAURS...
...THE SAME WAY HUMANITY DID FROM OUR OWN SIMIAN ANCESTORS.
WAIT--I'M GETTING A FLASH FROM THE SQUAD'S COLLECTIVE MEMORY--
--ABOUT WOLVERINE!
SO THEY'RE RESPONSIBLE FOR HIS WRECKED JET?
BUT WHERE IS HE?
WE WERE SEPARATED DURING THE FIGHT. I COULDN'T EVEN FIND HIS SCENT.
THE MONSTERS LOST HIM, TOO.
THAT'S WHY I CAME BACK TO THE AIRCRAFT, I DIDN'T KNOW WHERE ELSE TO GO.
HE'S NOT ANSWERING MY PSICALLS.
SAVE THAT FOR LATER.
FOR ALL YOUR SKILLS, RACHEL, THE NATIVES ARE RESTLESS.
I DON'T CARE WHAT THE SENSORS SAY, THEY'RE STILL HERE, I CAN FEEL IT!
VIKRAM, CALL FOR BACK-UP!

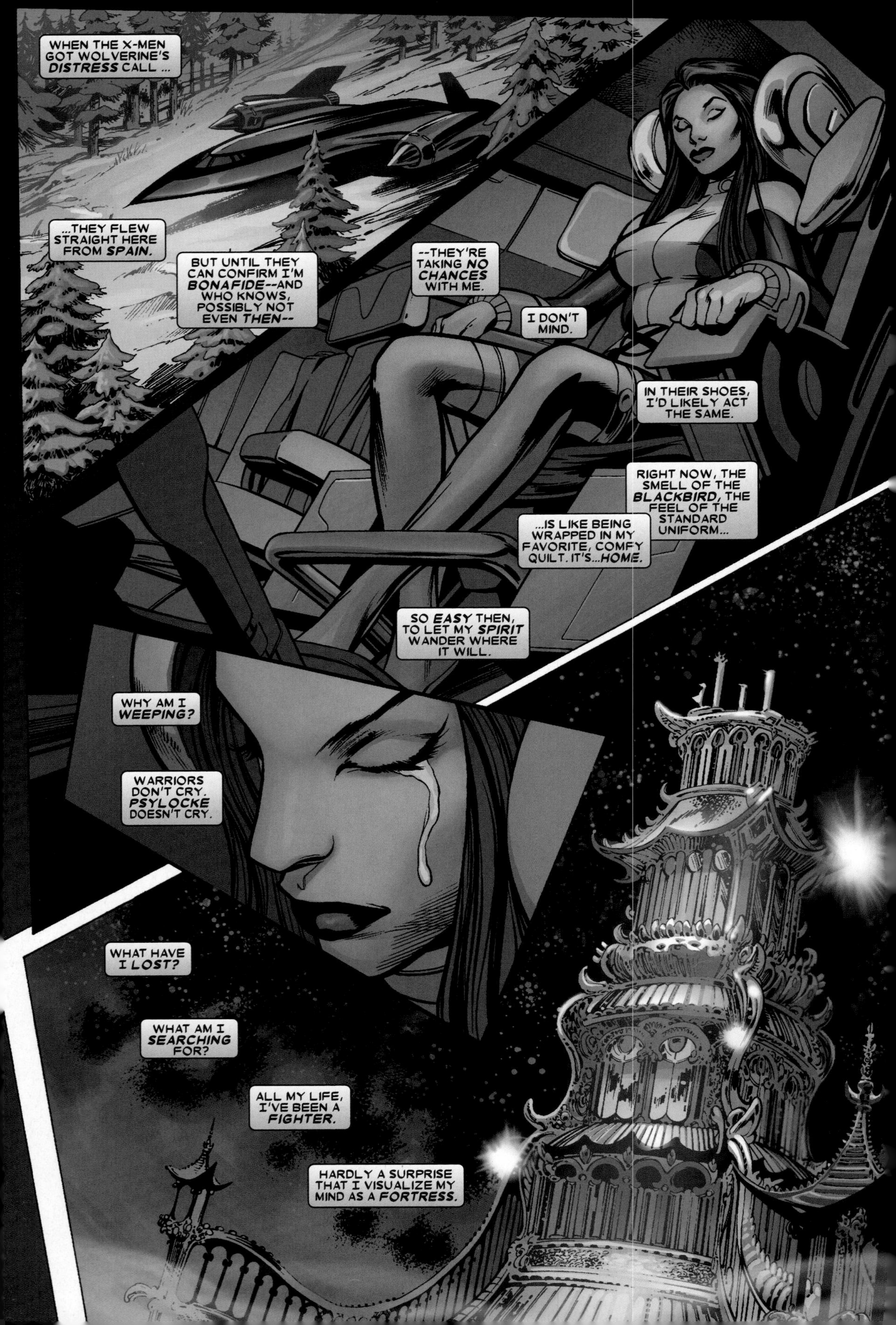
WHEN THE X-MEN GOT WOLVERINE'S *DISTRESS* CALL ...
...THEY FLEW STRAIGHT HERE FROM *SPAIN.*
BUT UNTIL THEY CAN CONFIRM I'M *BONAFIDE*--AND WHO KNOWS, POSSIBLY NOT EVEN *THEN*--
--THEY'RE TAKING *NO CHANCES* WITH ME.
I DON'T MIND.
IN THEIR SHOES, I'D LIKELY ACT THE SAME.
RIGHT NOW, THE SMELL OF THE *BLACKBIRD,* THE FEEL OF THE STANDARD UNIFORM...
...IS LIKE BEING WRAPPED IN MY FAVORITE, COMFY QUILT. IT'S...*HOME.*
SO *EASY* THEN, TO LET MY *SPIRIT* WANDER WHERE IT WILL.
WHY AM I *WEEPING?*
WARRIORS DON'T CRY. *PSYLOCKE* DOESN'T CRY.
WHAT HAVE I *LOST?*
WHAT AM I *SEARCHING* FOR?
ALL MY LIFE, I'VE BEEN A *FIGHTER.*
HARDLY A SURPRISE THAT I VISUALIZE MY MIND AS A *FORTRESS.*

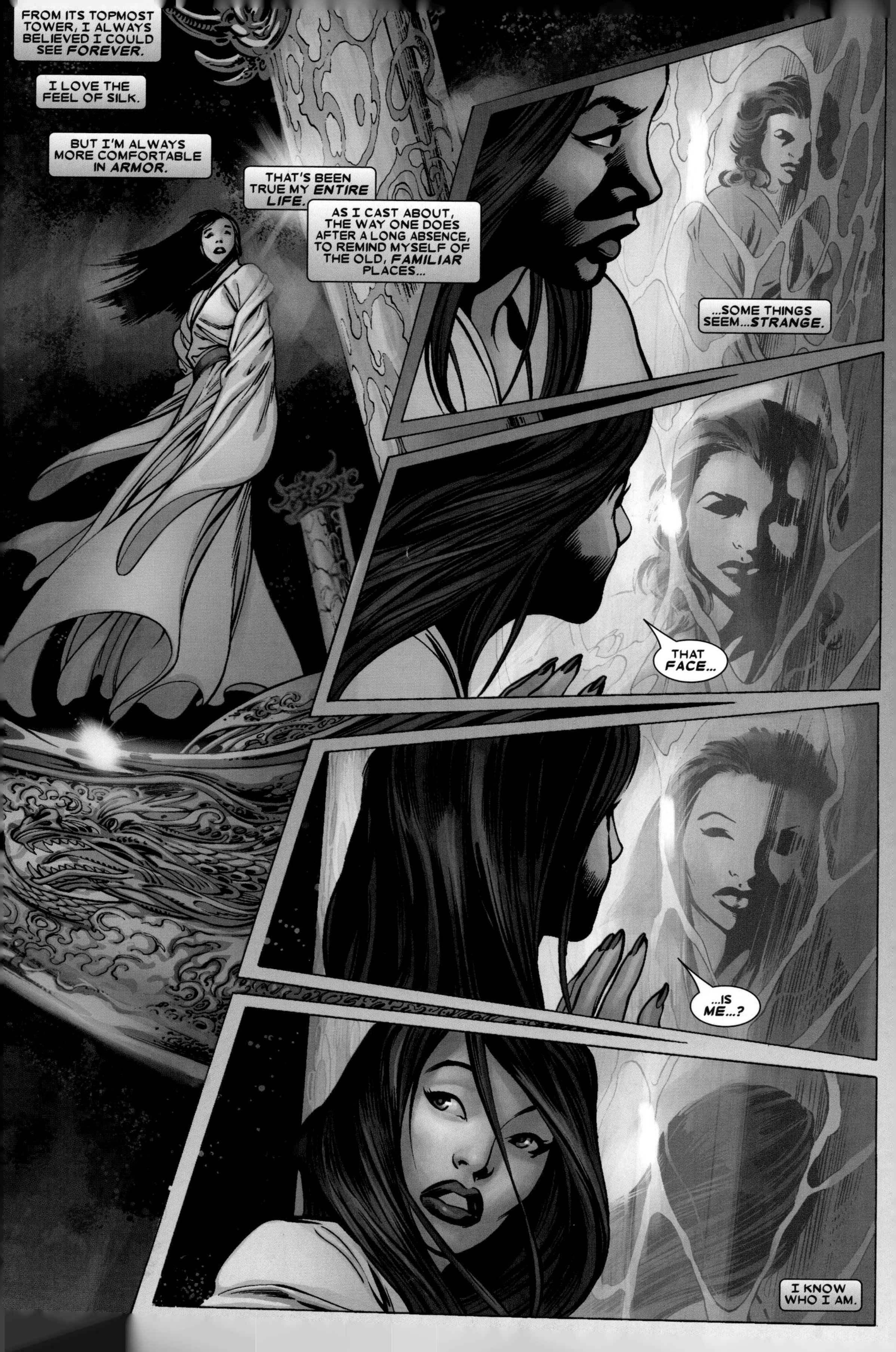
FROM ITS TOPMOST TOWER, I ALWAYS BELIEVED I COULD SEE FOREVER.
I LOVE THE FEEL OF SILK.
BUT I'M ALWAYS MORE COMFORTABLE IN ARMOR.
THAT'S BEEN TRUE MY ENTIRE LIFE.
AS I CAST ABOUT, THE WAY ONE DOES AFTER A LONG ABSENCE, TO REMIND MYSELF OF THE OLD, FAMILIAR PLACES...
...SOME THINGS SEEM...STRANGE.
THAT FACE...
...IS ME...?
I KNOW WHO I AM.

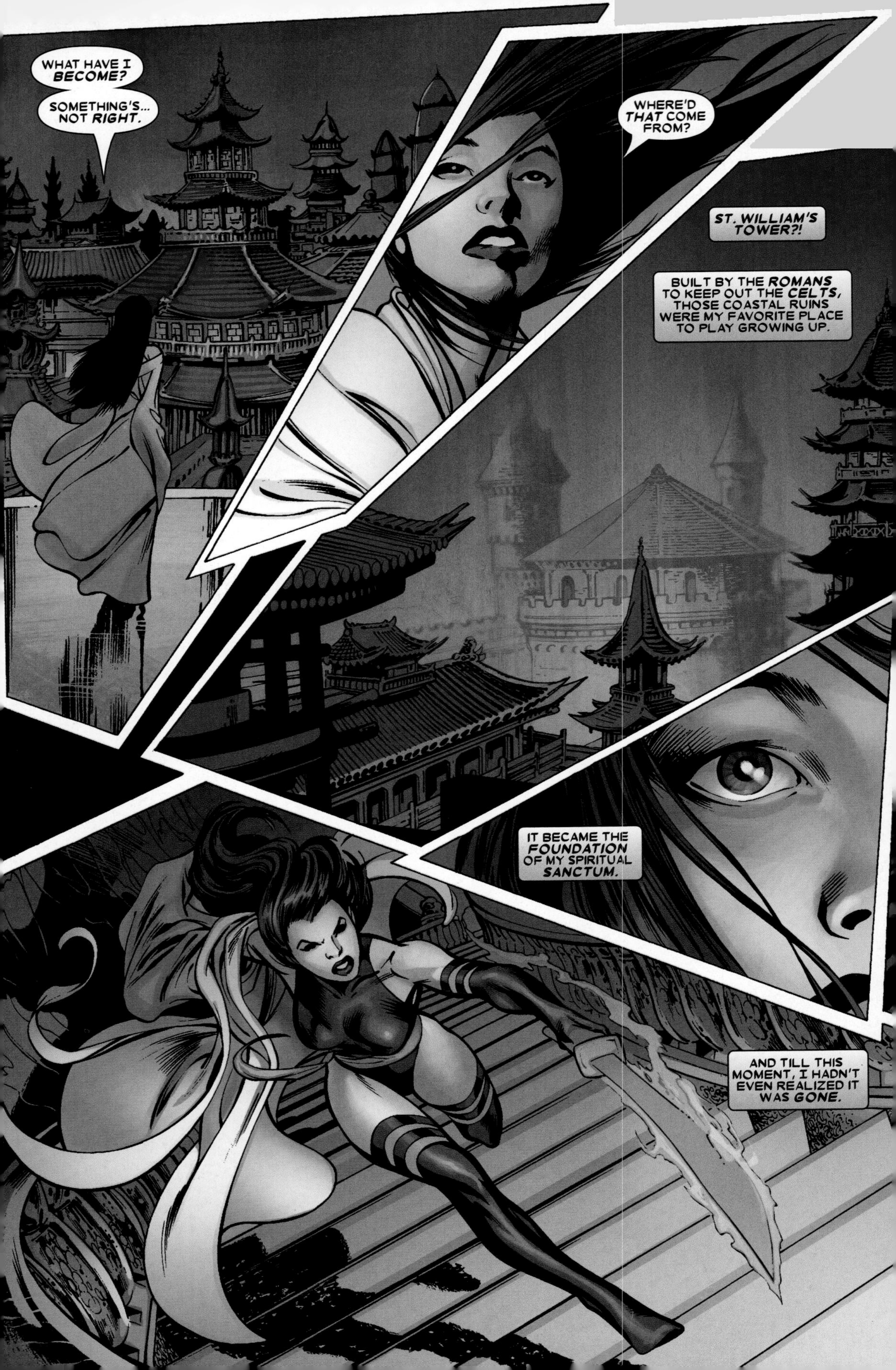
WHAT HAVE I BECOME?
SOMETHING'S... NOT RIGHT.
WHERE'D THAT COME FROM?
ST. WILLIAM'S TOWER?!
BUILT BY THE ROMANS TO KEEP OUT THE CELTS, THOSE COASTAL RUINS WERE MY FAVORITE PLACE TO PLAY GROWING UP.
IT BECAME THE FOUNDATION OF MY SPIRITUAL SANCTUM.
AND TILL THIS MOMENT, I HADN'T EVEN REALIZED IT WAS GONE.

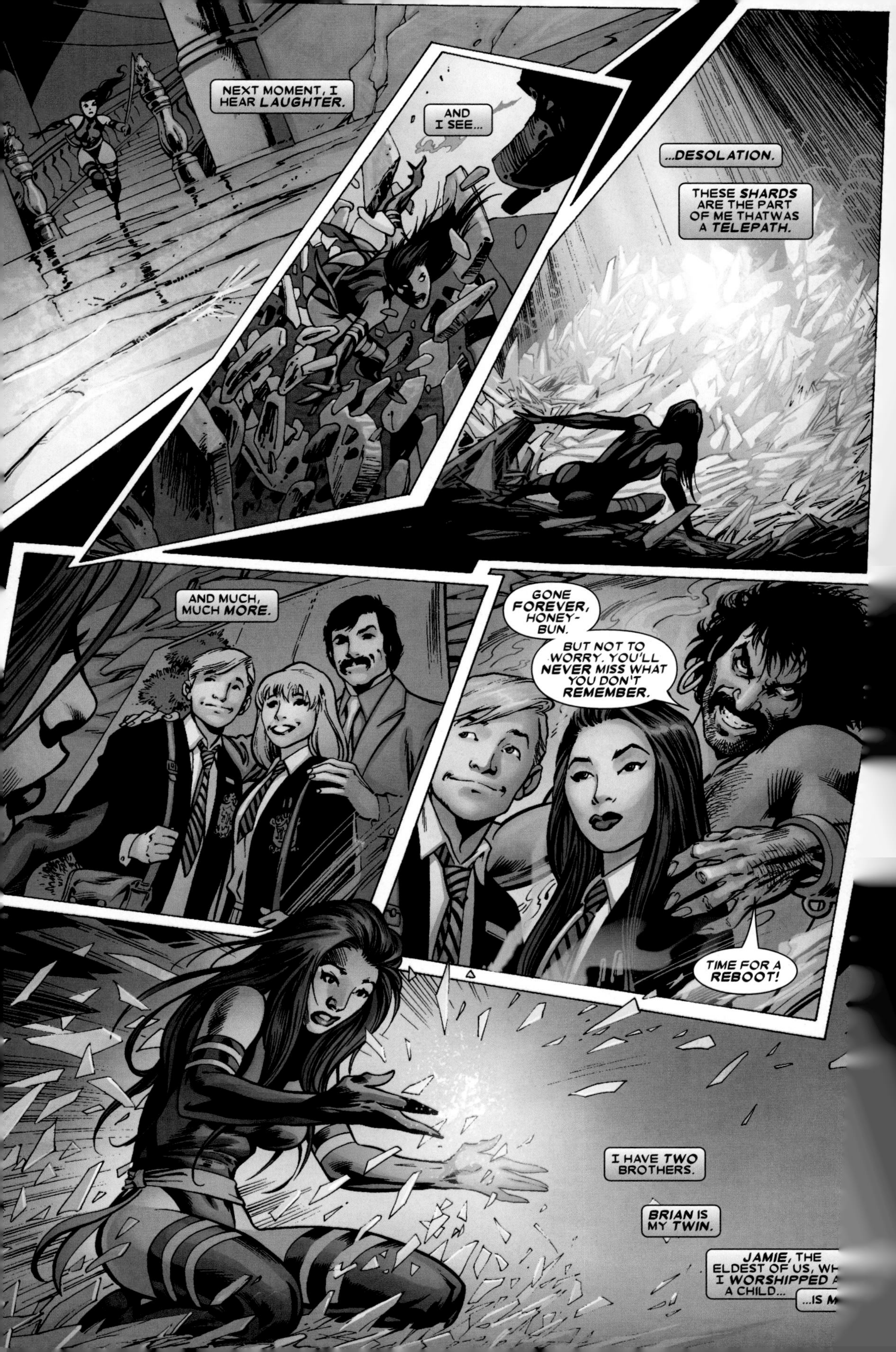
NEXT MOMENT, I HEAR LAUGHTER.
AND I SEE...
...DESOLATION.
THESE SHARDS ARE THE PART OF ME THATWAS A TELEPATH.
AND MUCH, MUCH MORE.
GONE FOREVER, HONEY-BUN.
BUT NOT TO WORRY. YOU'LL NEVER MISS WHAT YOU DON'T REMEMBER.
TIME FOR A REBOOT!
I HAVE TWO BROTHERS.
BRIAN IS MY TWIN.
JAMIE, THE ELDEST OF US, WH
I WORSHIPPED A
A CHILD...
...IS M

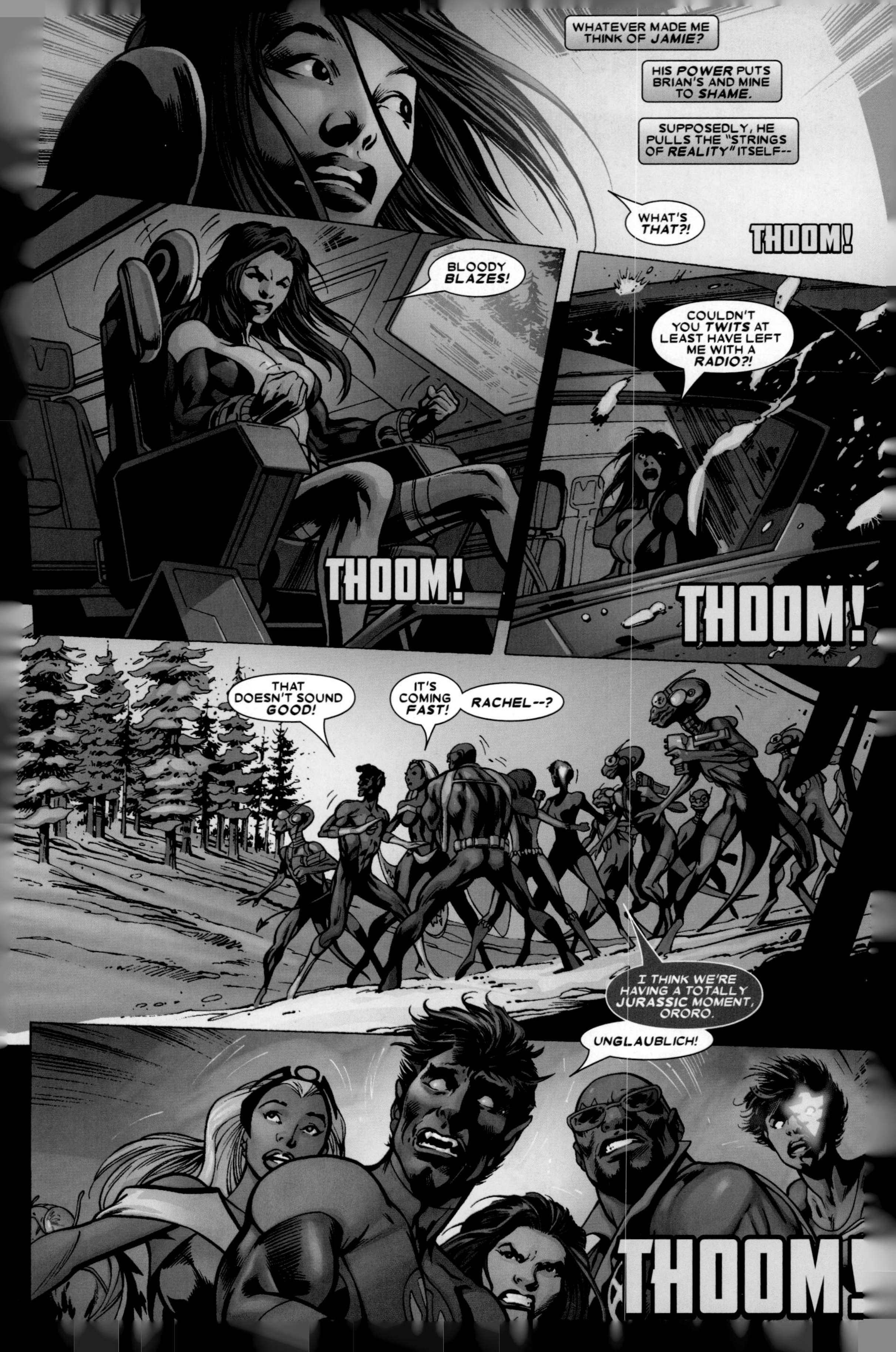
WHATEVER MADE ME THINK OF JAMIE?
HIS POWER PUTS BRIAN'S AND MINE TO SHAME.
SUPPOSEDLY, HE PULLS THE "STRINGS OF REALITY" ITSELF--
WHAT'S THAT?!
THOOM!
BLOODY BLAZES!
THOOM!
COULDN'T YOU TWITS AT LEAST HAVE LEFT ME WITH A RADIO?!
THOOM!
THAT DOESN'T SOUND GOOD!
IT'S COMING FAST!
RACHEL--?
I THINK WE'RE HAVING A TOTALLY JURASSIC MOMENT, ORORO.
UNGLAUBLICH!
THOOM!

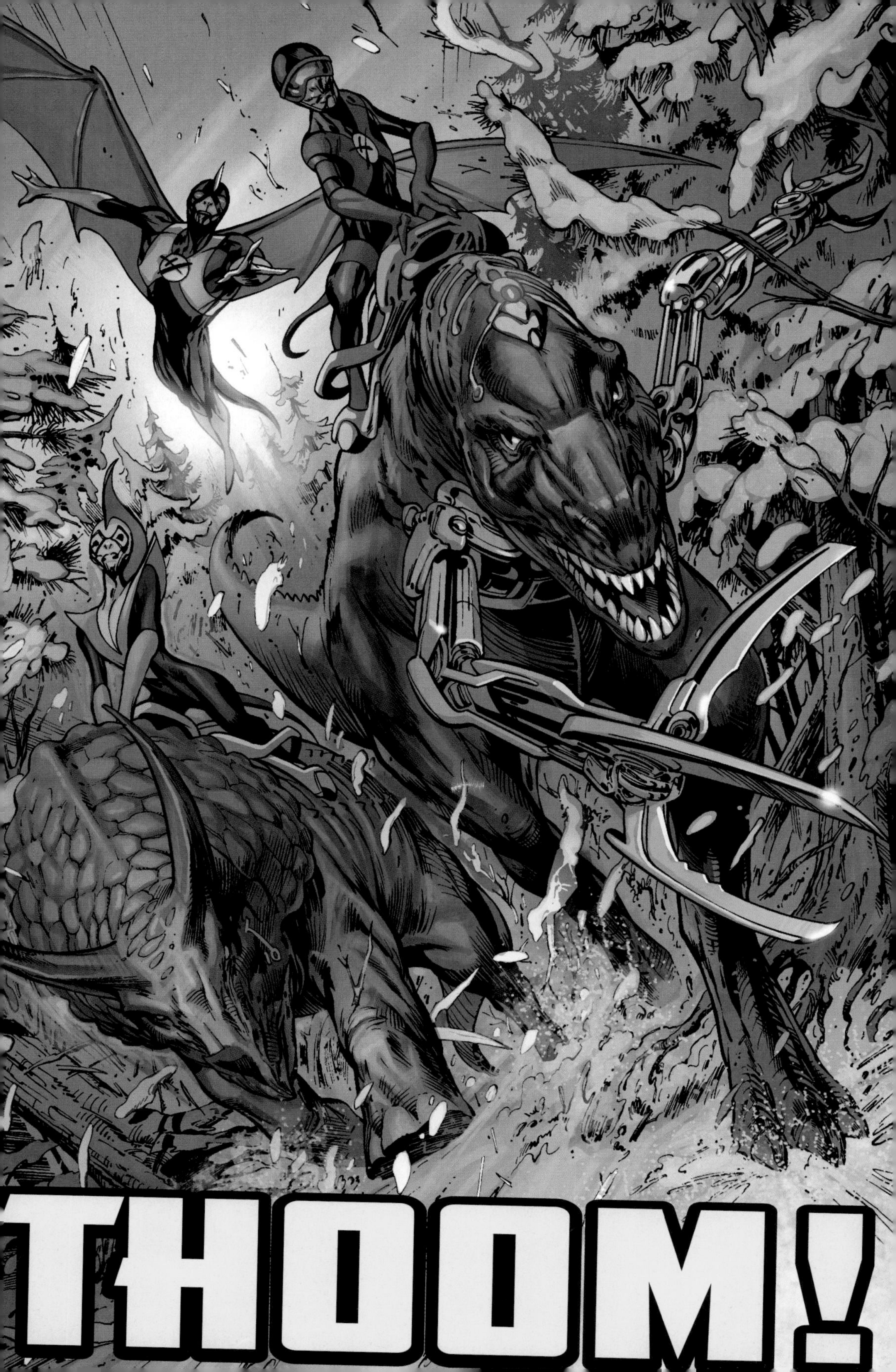
THOOM!

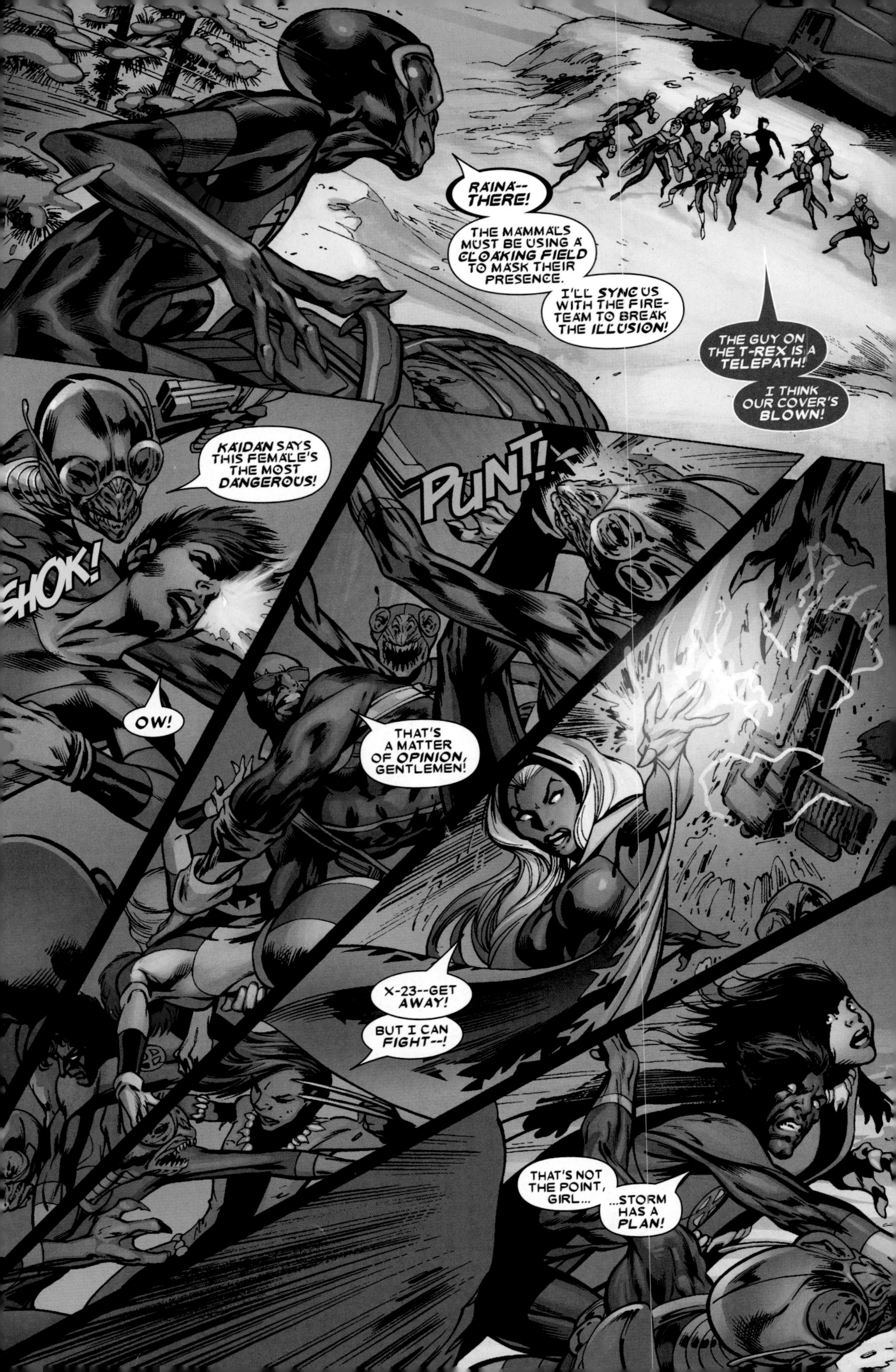
RAINA--THERE!
THE MAMMALS MUST BE USING A CLOAKING FIELD TO MASK THEIR PRESENCE.
I'LL SYNC US WITH THE FIRE-TEAM TO BREAK THE ILLUSION!
THE GUY ON THE T-REX IS A TELEPATH!
I THINK OUR COVER'S BLOWN!
KAIDAN SAYS THIS FEMALE'S THE MOST DANGEROUS!
SHOK!
OW!
PUNT!
THAT'S A MATTER OF OPINION, GENTLEMEN!
X-23--GET AWAY!
BUT I CAN FIGHT--!
THAT'S NOT THE POINT, GIRL...
...STORM HAS A PLAN!

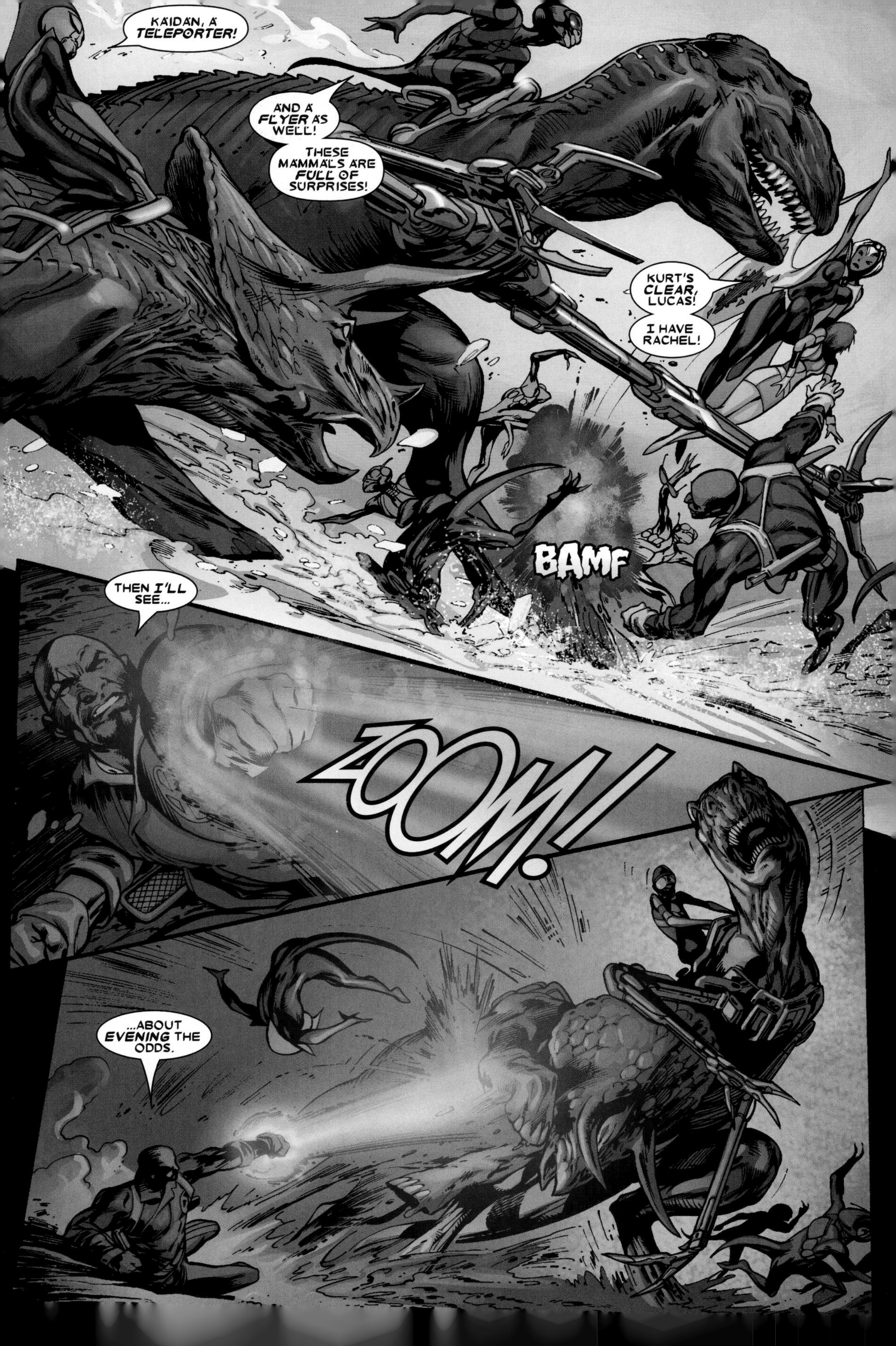
KAIDAN, A TELEPORTER!
AND A FLYER AS WELL!
THESE MAMMALS ARE FULL OF SURPRISES!
KURT'S CLEAR, LUCAS!
I HAVE RACHEL!
BAMF
THEN I'LL SEE...
ZOOM!
...ABOUT EVENING THE ODDS.

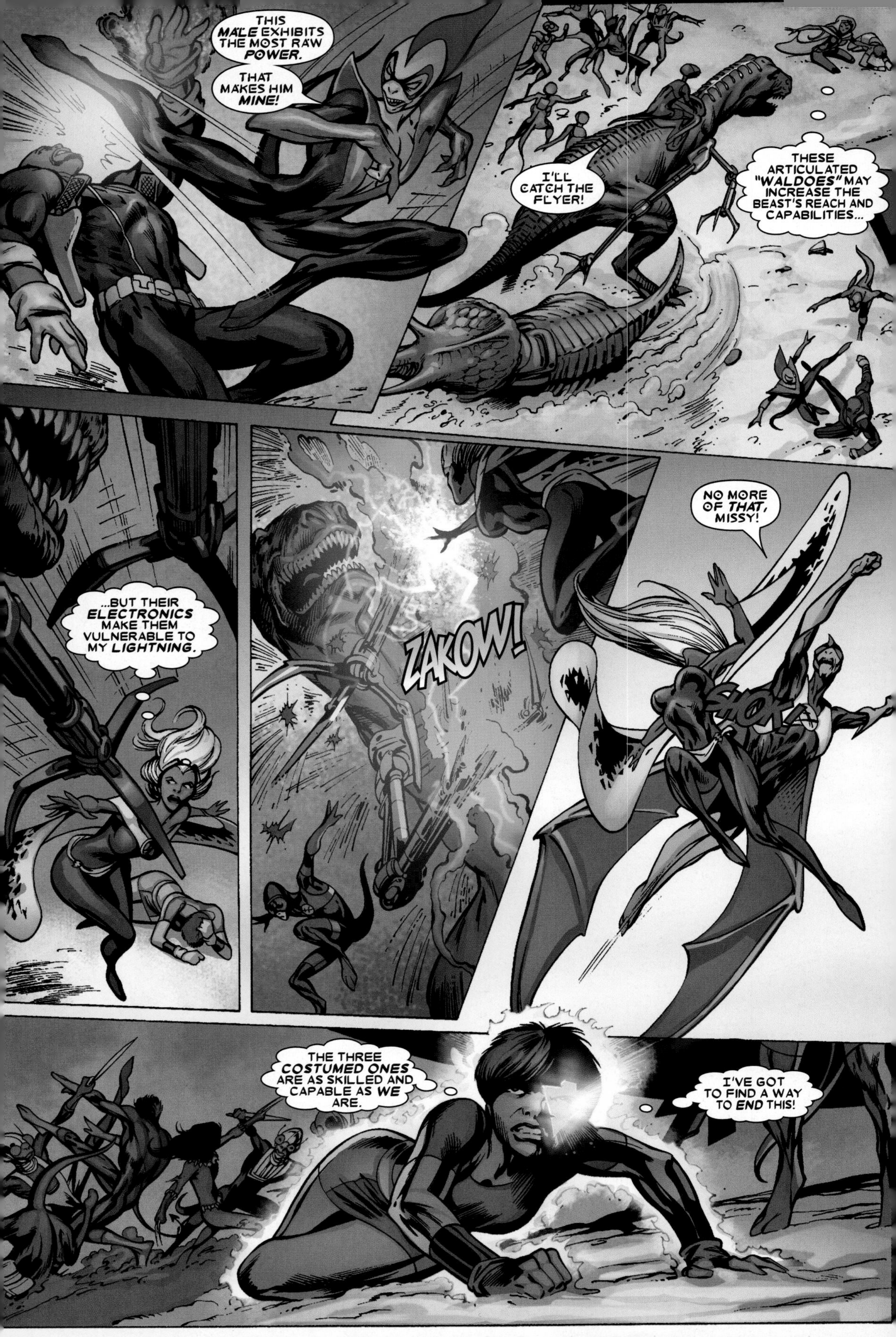
THIS MALE EXHIBITS THE MOST RAW POWER.
THAT MAKES HIM MINE!
I'LL CATCH THE FLYER!
THESE ARTICULATED "WALDOES" MAY INCREASE THE BEAST'S REACH AND CAPABILITIES...
...BUT THEIR ELECTRONICS MAKE THEM VULNERABLE TO MY LIGHTNING.
ZAKOW!
NO MORE OF THAT, MISSY!
CHOK
THE THREE COSTUMED ONES ARE AS SKILLED AND CAPABLE AS WE ARE.
I'VE GOT TO FIND A WAY TO END THIS!

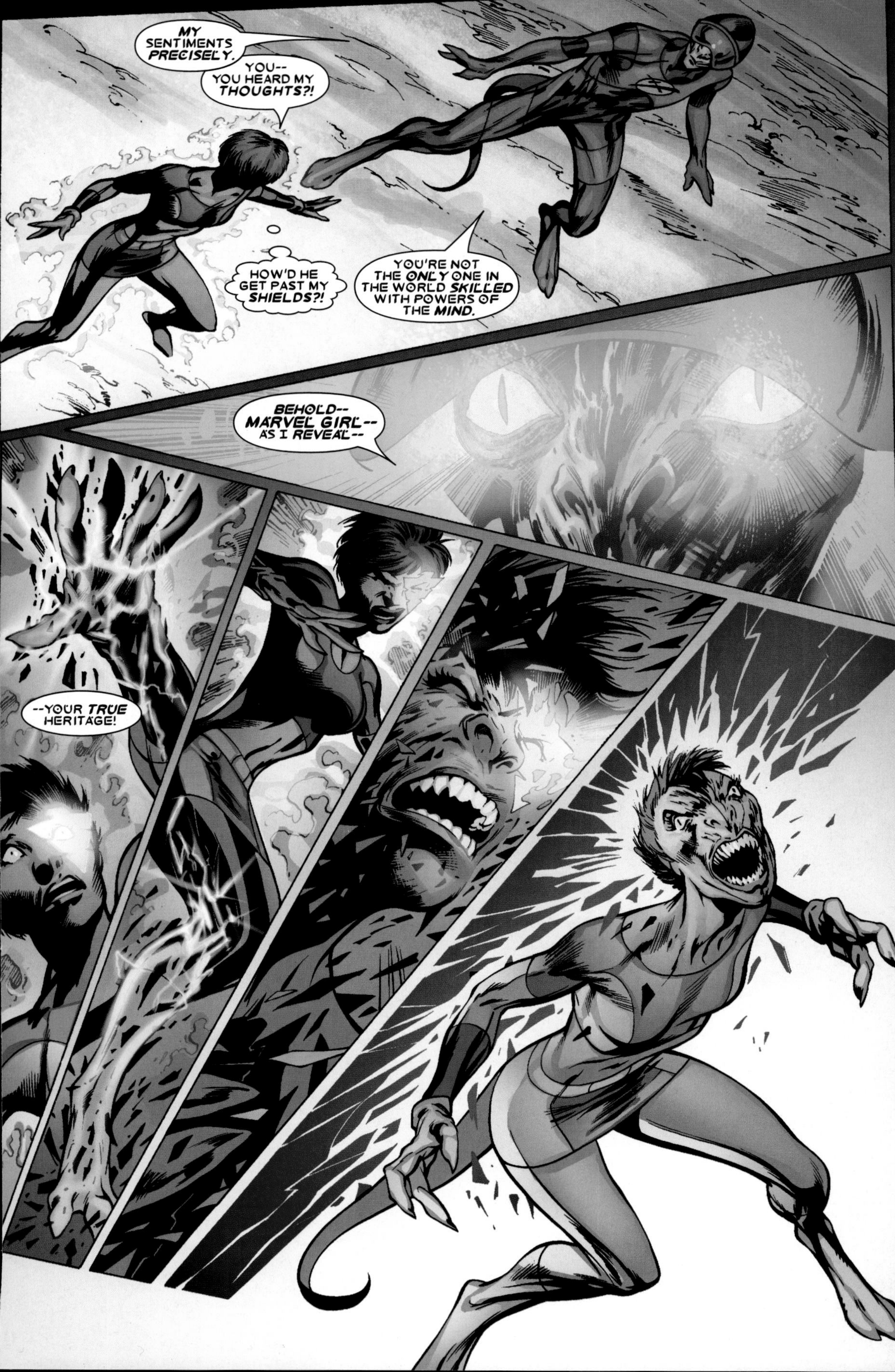
MY SENTIMENTS PRECISELY.
YOU-- YOU HEARD MY THOUGHTS?!
HOW'D HE GET PAST MY SHIELDS?!
YOU'RE NOT THE ONLY ONE IN THE WORLD SKILLED WITH POWERS OF THE MIND.
BEHOLD-- MARVEL GIRL-- AS I REVEAL--
--YOUR TRUE HERITAGE!

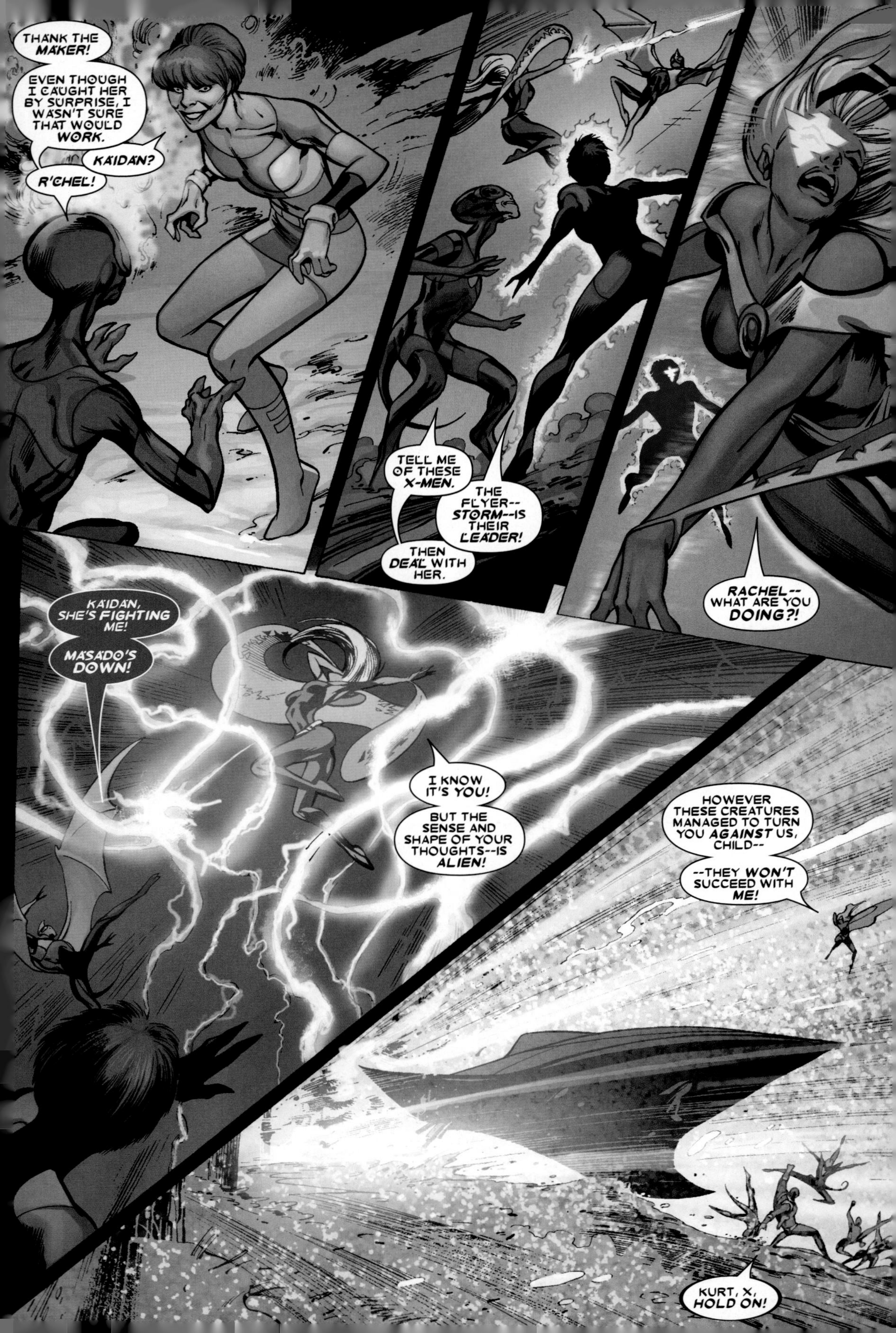
THANK THE MAKER!
EVEN THOUGH I CAUGHT HER BY SURPRISE, I WASN'T SURE THAT WOULD WORK.
KAIDAN?
R'CHEL!
TELL ME OF THESE X-MEN.
THE FLYER--STORM--IS THEIR LEADER!
THEN DEAL WITH HER.
RACHEL--WHAT ARE YOU DOING?!
KAIDAN, SHE'S FIGHTING ME!
MASADO'S DOWN!
I KNOW IT'S YOU!
BUT THE SENSE AND SHAPE OF YOUR THOUGHTS--IS ALIEN!
HOWEVER THESE CREATURES MANAGED TO TURN YOU AGAINST US, CHILD--
--THEY WON'T SUCCEED WITH ME!
KURT, X, HOLD ON!

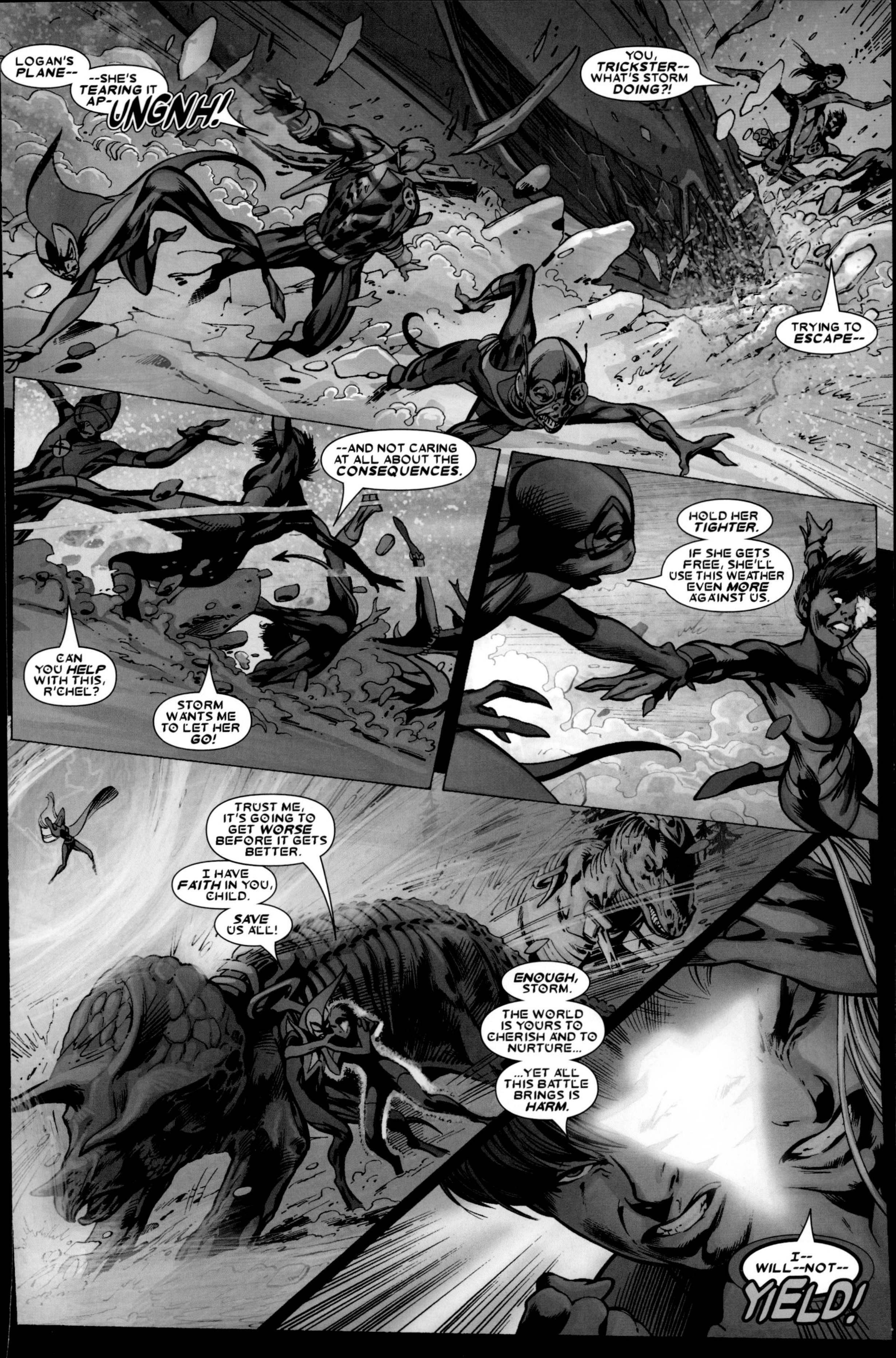

LOGAN'S PLANE--
--SHE'S TEARING IT AP-UNGNH!
YOU, TRICKSTER-- WHAT'S STORM DOING?!
TRYING TO ESCAPE--
--AND NOT CARING AT ALL ABOUT THE CONSEQUENCES.
CAN YOU HELP WITH THIS, R'CHEL?
STORM WANTS ME TO LET HER GO!
HOLD HER TIGHTER.
IF SHE GETS FREE, SHE'LL USE THIS WEATHER EVEN MORE AGAINST US.
TRUST ME, IT'S GOING TO GET WORSE BEFORE IT GETS BETTER.
I HAVE FAITH IN YOU, CHILD.
SAVE US ALL!
ENOUGH, STORM.
THE WORLD IS YOURS TO CHERISH AND TO NURTURE...
...YET ALL THIS BATTLE BRINGS IS HARM.
I-- WILL--NOT-- YIELD!

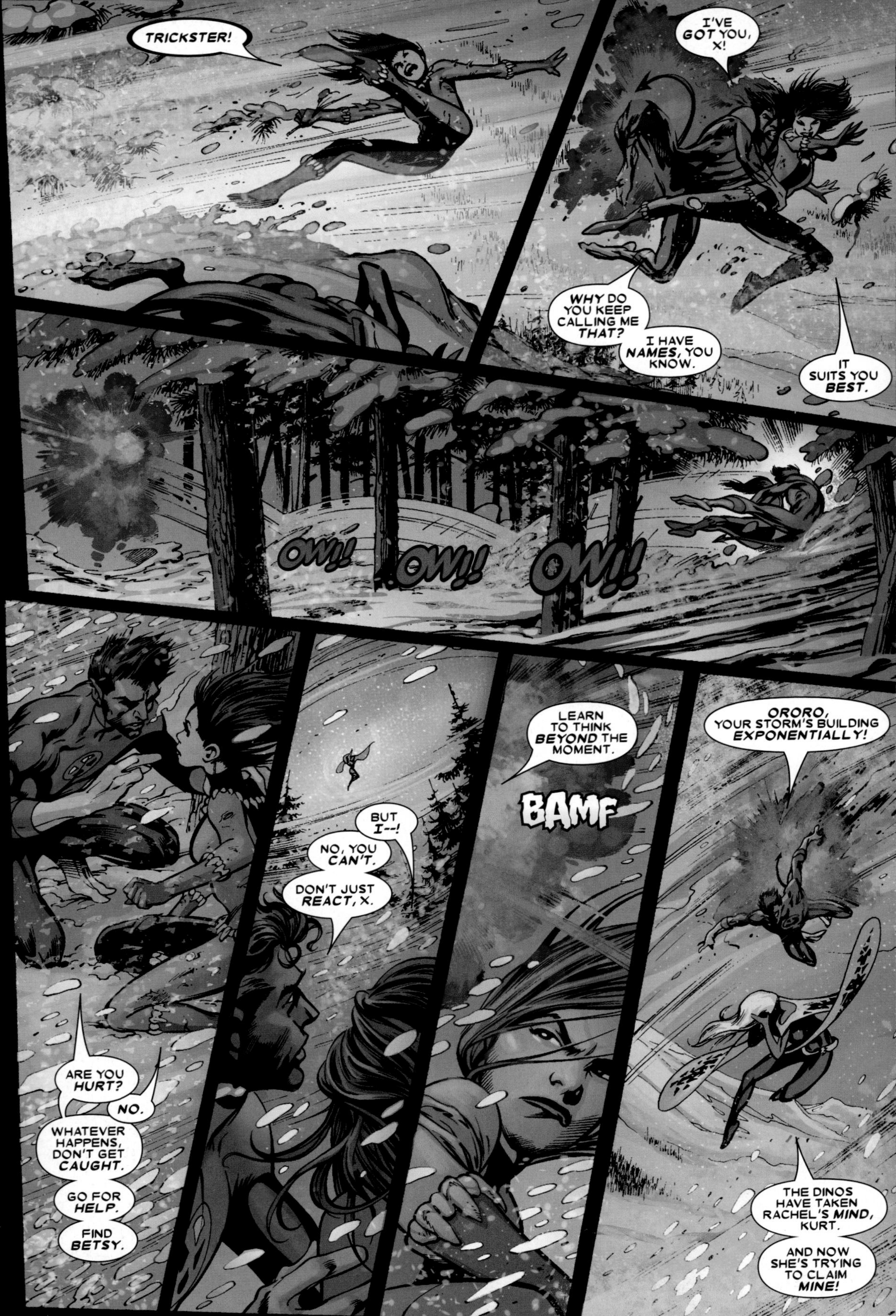

TRICKSTER!
I'VE GOT YOU, X!
WHY DO YOU KEEP CALLING ME THAT?
I HAVE NAMES, YOU KNOW.
IT SUITS YOU BEST.
OW!! OW!! OW!!
ARE YOU HURT?
NO.
WHATEVER HAPPENS, DON'T GET CAUGHT.
GO FOR HELP.
FIND BETSY.
BUT I--!
NO, YOU CAN'T.
DON'T JUST REACT, X.
LEARN TO THINK BEYOND THE MOMENT.
BAMF
ORORO, YOUR STORM'S BUILDING EXPONENTIALLY!
THE DINOS HAVE TAKEN RACHEL'S MIND, KURT.
AND NOW SHE'S TRYING TO CLAIM MINE!

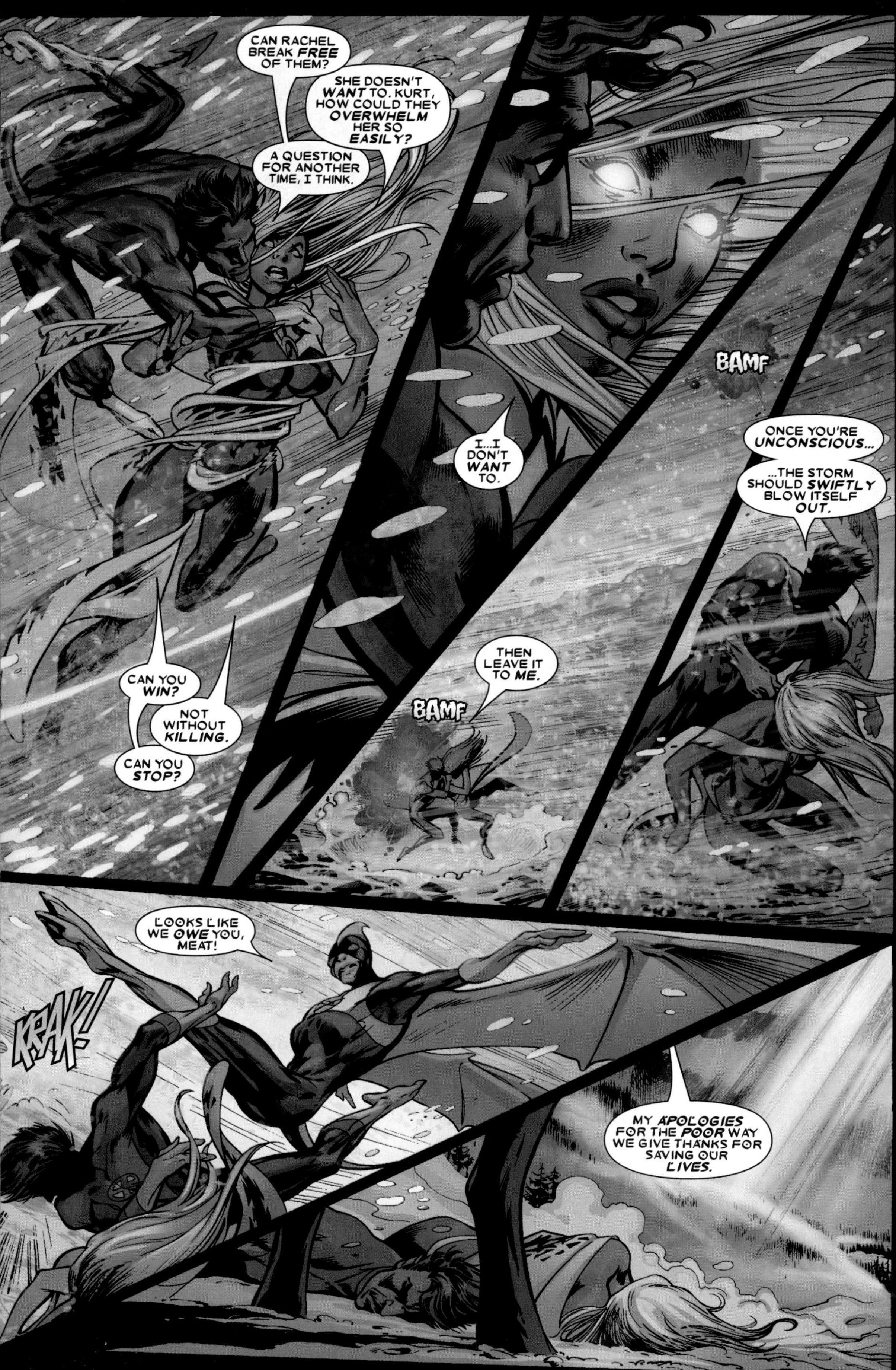
CAN RACHEL BREAK FREE OF THEM?
SHE DOESN'T WANT TO. KURT, HOW COULD THEY OVERWHELM HER SO EASILY?
A QUESTION FOR ANOTHER TIME, I THINK.
CAN YOU WIN?
NOT WITHOUT KILLING.
CAN YOU STOP?
I...I DON'T WANT TO.
THEN LEAVE IT TO ME.
BAMF
BAMF
ONCE YOU'RE UNCONSCIOUS...
...THE STORM SHOULD SWIFTLY BLOW ITSELF OUT.
LOOKS LIKE WE OWE YOU, MEAT!
KRAAK!
MY APOLOGIES FOR THE POOR WAY WE GIVE THANKS FOR SAVING OUR LIVES.

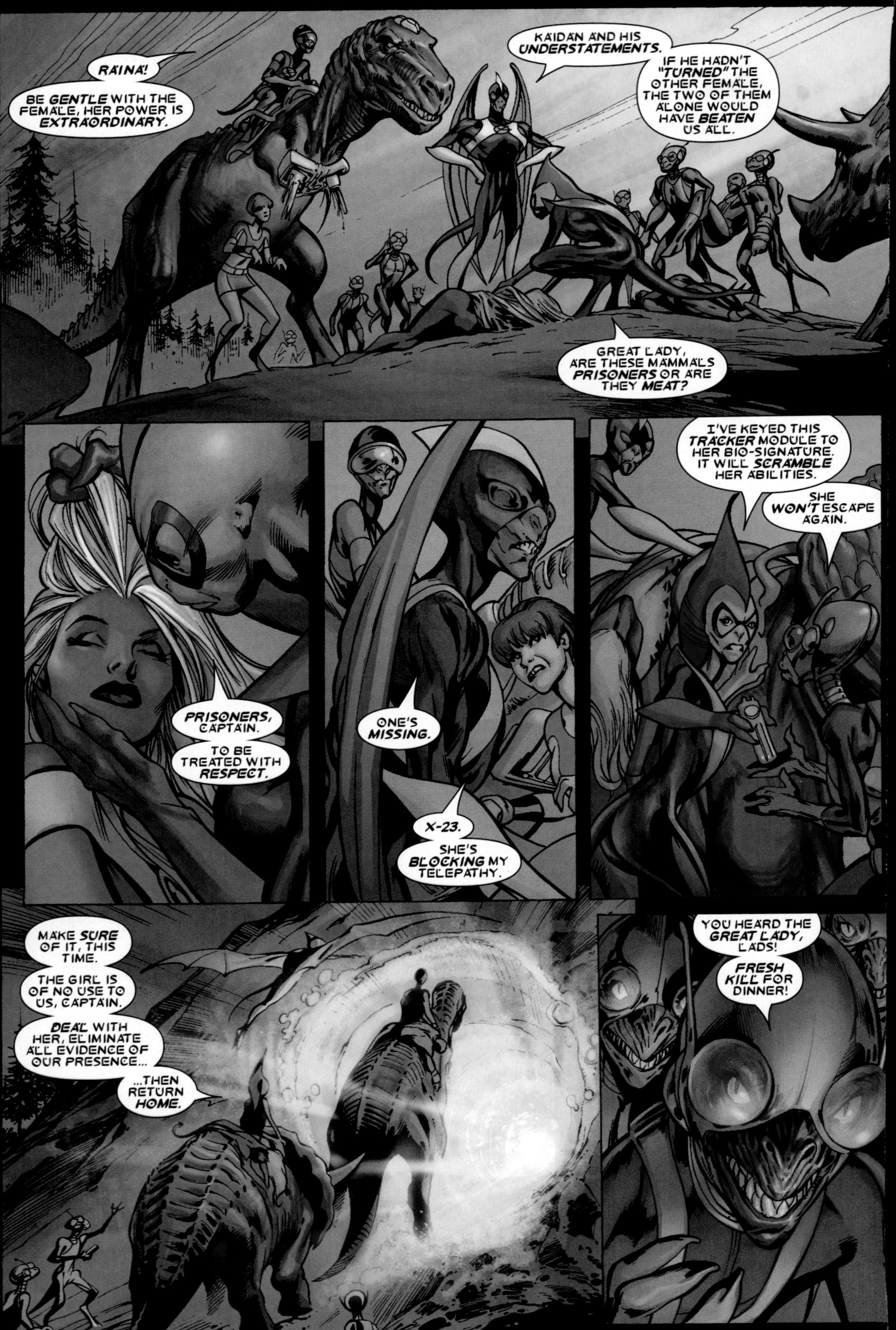

RAINA!
BE GENTLE WITH THE FEMALE, HER POWER IS EXTRAORDINARY.
KAIDAN AND HIS UNDERSTATEMENTS.
IF HE HADN'T "TURNED" THE OTHER FEMALE, THE TWO OF THEM ALONE WOULD HAVE BEATEN US ALL.
GREAT LADY, ARE THESE MAMMALS PRISONERS OR ARE THEY MEAT?
PRISONERS, CAPTAIN.
TO BE TREATED WITH RESPECT.
ONE'S MISSING.
X-23.
SHE'S BLOCKING MY TELEPATHY.
I'VE KEYED THIS TRACKER MODULE TO HER BIO-SIGNATURE. IT WILL SCRAMBLE HER ABILITIES.
SHE WON'T ESCAPE AGAIN.
MAKE SURE OF IT, THIS TIME.
THE GIRL IS OF NO USE TO US, CAPTAIN.
DEAL WITH HER, ELIMINATE ALL EVIDENCE OF OUR PRESENCE...
...THEN RETURN HOME.
YOU HEARD THE GREAT LADY, LADS!
FRESH KILL FOR DINNER!

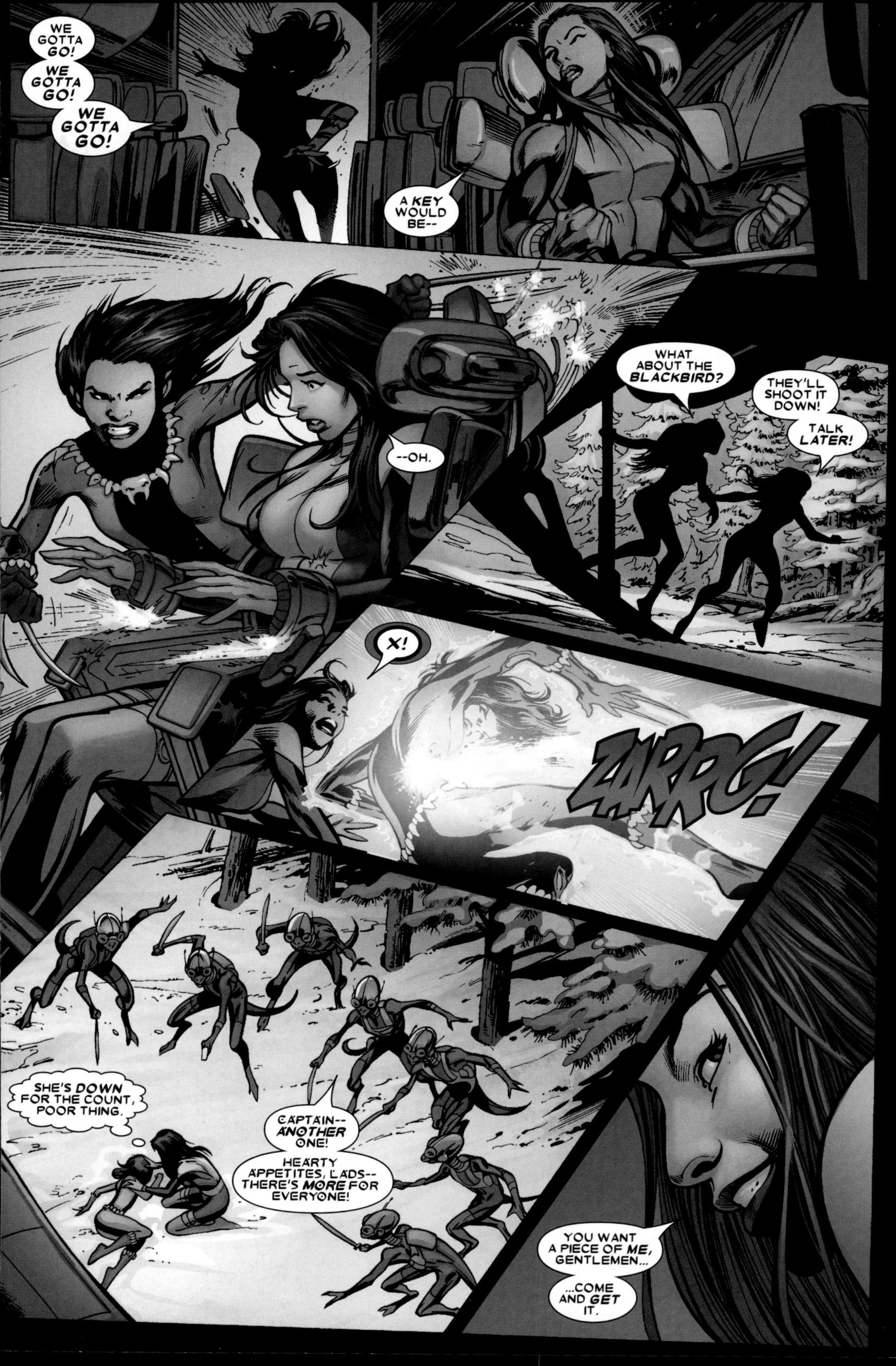
WE GOTTA GO!
WE GOTTA GO!
WE GOTTA GO!
A KEY WOULD BE--
--OH.
WHAT ABOUT THE BLACKBIRD?
THEY'LL SHOOT IT DOWN!
TALK LATER!
X!
ZARRG!
SHE'S DOWN FOR THE COUNT, POOR THING.
CAPTAIN-- ANOTHER ONE!
HEARTY APPETITES, LADS-- THERE'S MORE FOR EVERYONE!
YOU WANT A PIECE OF ME, GENTLEMEN...
...COME AND GET IT.

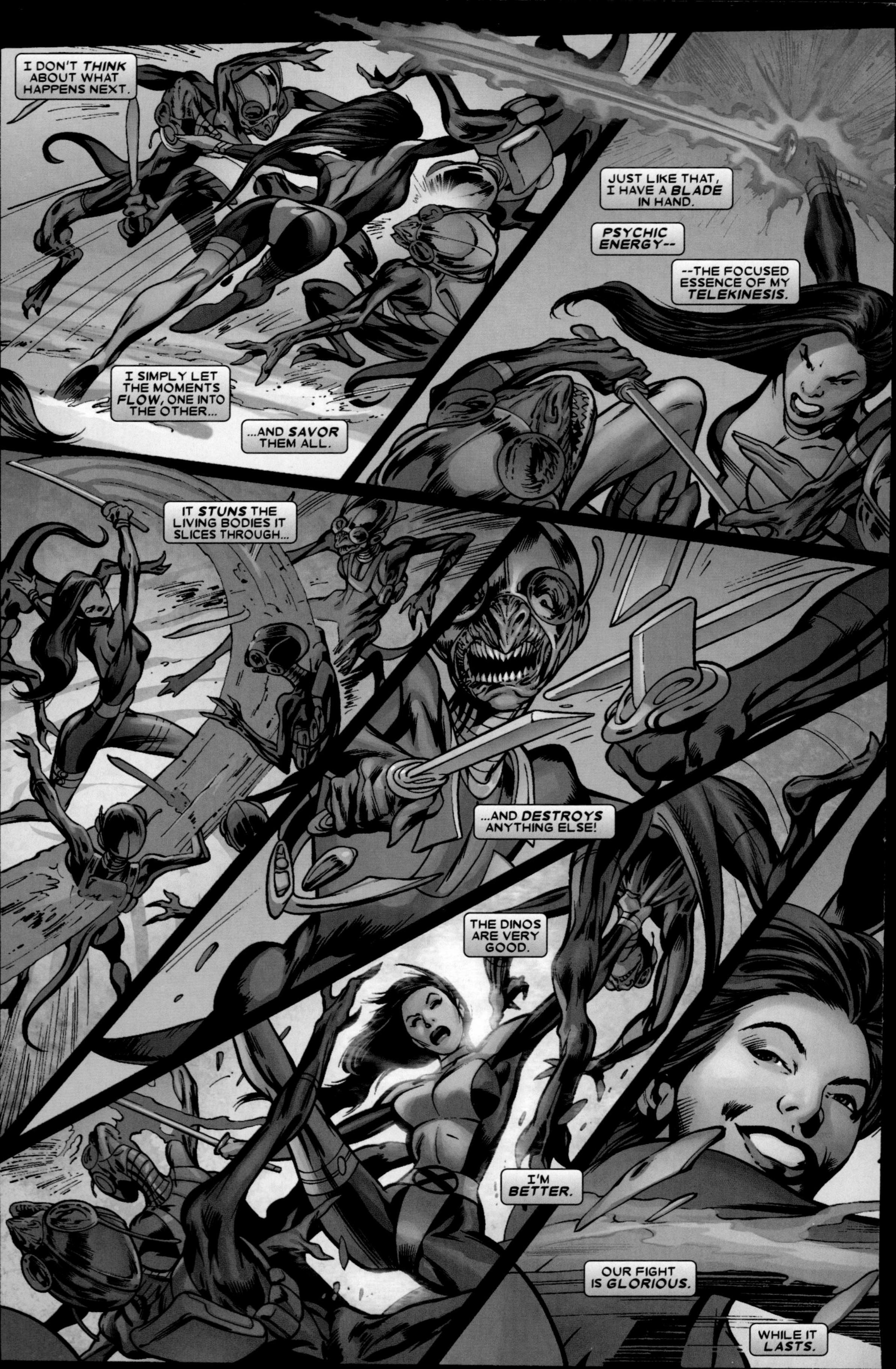
I DON'T THINK ABOUT WHAT HAPPENS NEXT.
I SIMPLY LET THE MOMENTS FLOW, ONE INTO THE OTHER...
...AND SAVOR THEM ALL.
JUST LIKE THAT, I HAVE A BLADE IN HAND.
PSYCHIC ENERGY--
--THE FOCUSED ESSENCE OF MY TELEKINESIS.
IT STUNS THE LIVING BODIES IT SLICES THROUGH...
...AND DESTROYS ANYTHING ELSE!
THE DINOS ARE VERY GOOD.
I'M BETTER.
OUR FIGHT IS GLORIOUS.
WHILE IT LASTS.

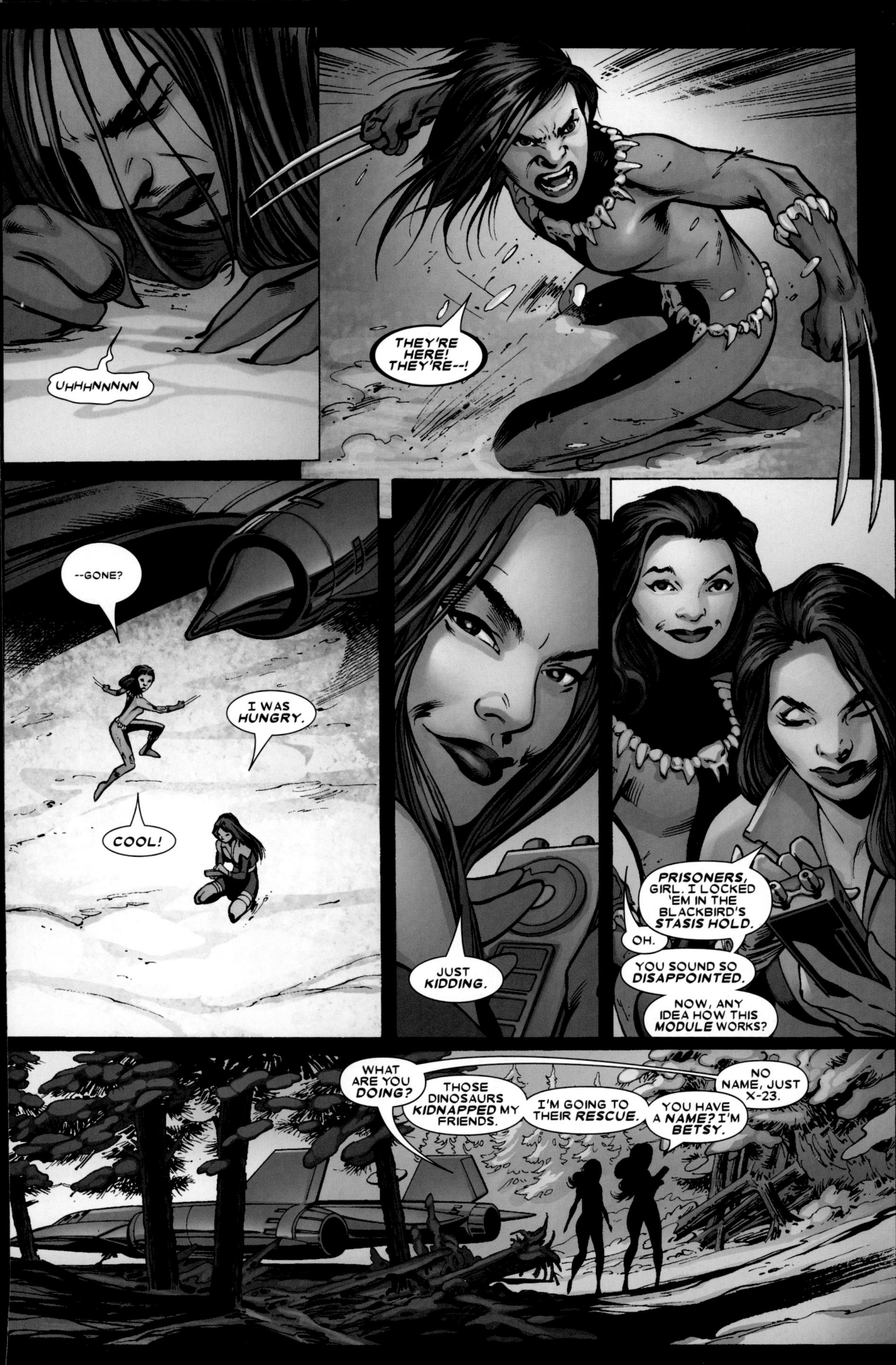
UHHHNNNNN
THEY'RE HERE! THEY'RE--!
--GONE?
I WAS HUNGRY.
COOL!
JUST KIDDING.
PRISONERS, GIRL. I LOCKED 'EM IN THE BLACKBIRD'S STASIS HOLD.
OH.
YOU SOUND SO DISAPPOINTED.
NOW, ANY IDEA HOW THIS MODULE WORKS?
WHAT ARE YOU DOING?
THOSE DINOSAURS KIDNAPPED MY FRIENDS.
I'M GOING TO THEIR RESCUE.
YOU HAVE A NAME? I'M BETSY.
NO NAME, JUST X-23.

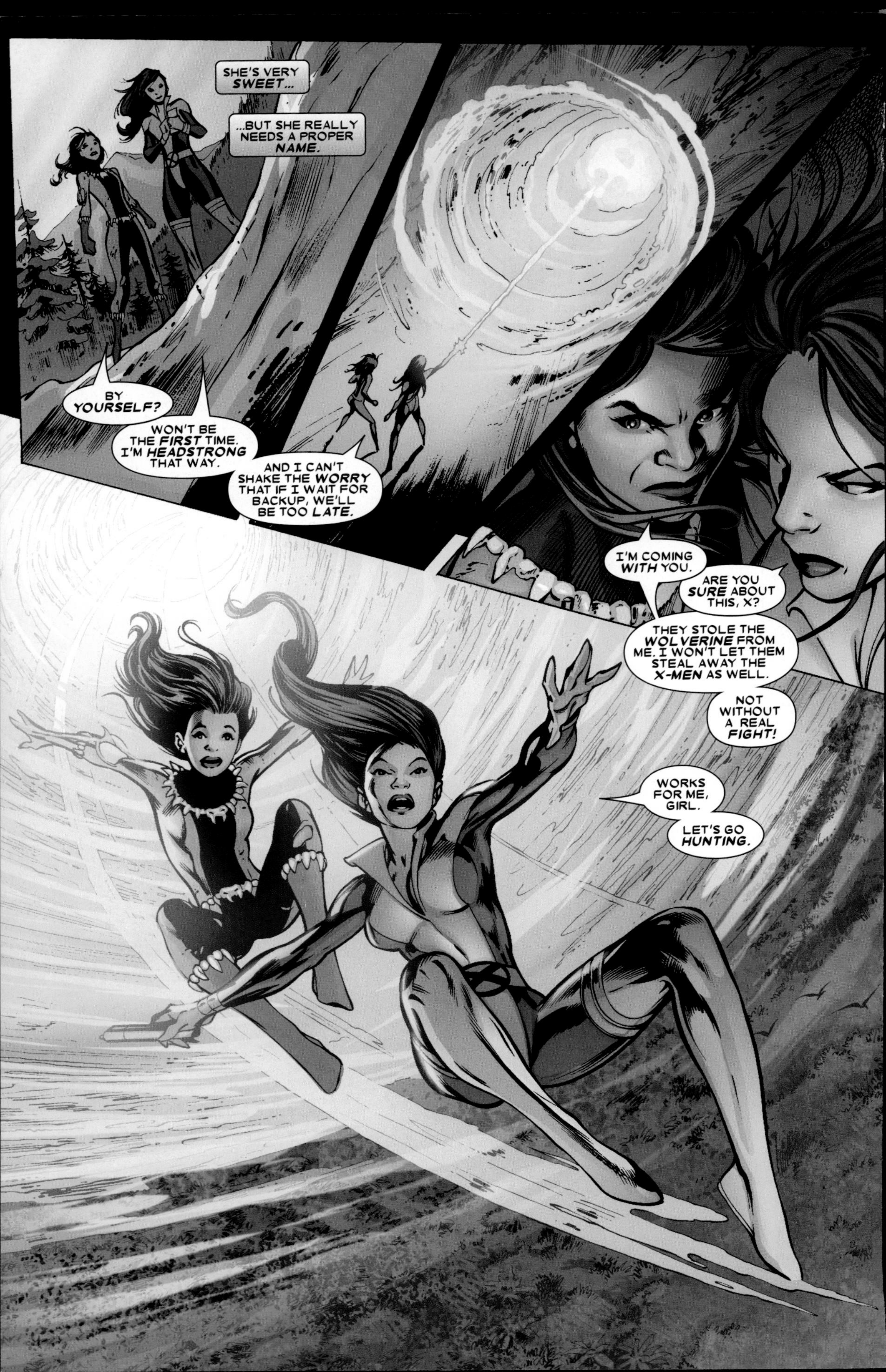

SHE'S VERY SWEET...
...BUT SHE REALLY NEEDS A PROPER NAME.
BY YOURSELF?
WON'T BE THE FIRST TIME. I'M HEADSTRONG THAT WAY.
AND I CAN'T SHAKE THE WORRY THAT IF I WAIT FOR BACKUP, WE'LL BE TOO LATE.
I'M COMING WITH YOU.
ARE YOU SURE ABOUT THIS, X?
THEY STOLE THE WOLVERINE FROM ME. I WON'T LET THEM STEAL AWAY THE X-MEN AS WELL.
NOT WITHOUT A REAL FIGHT!
WORKS FOR ME, GIRL.
LET'S GO HUNTING.

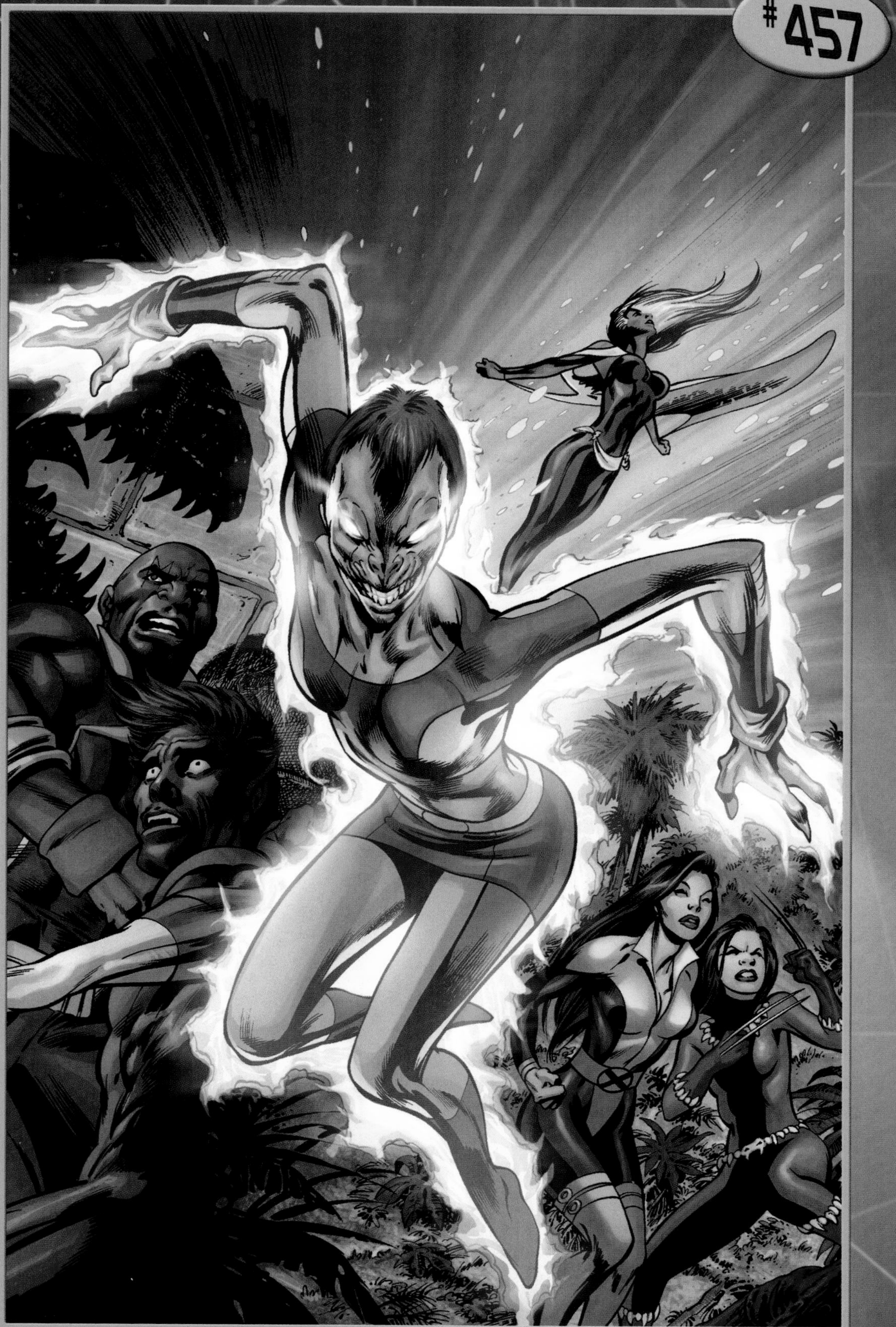
#457

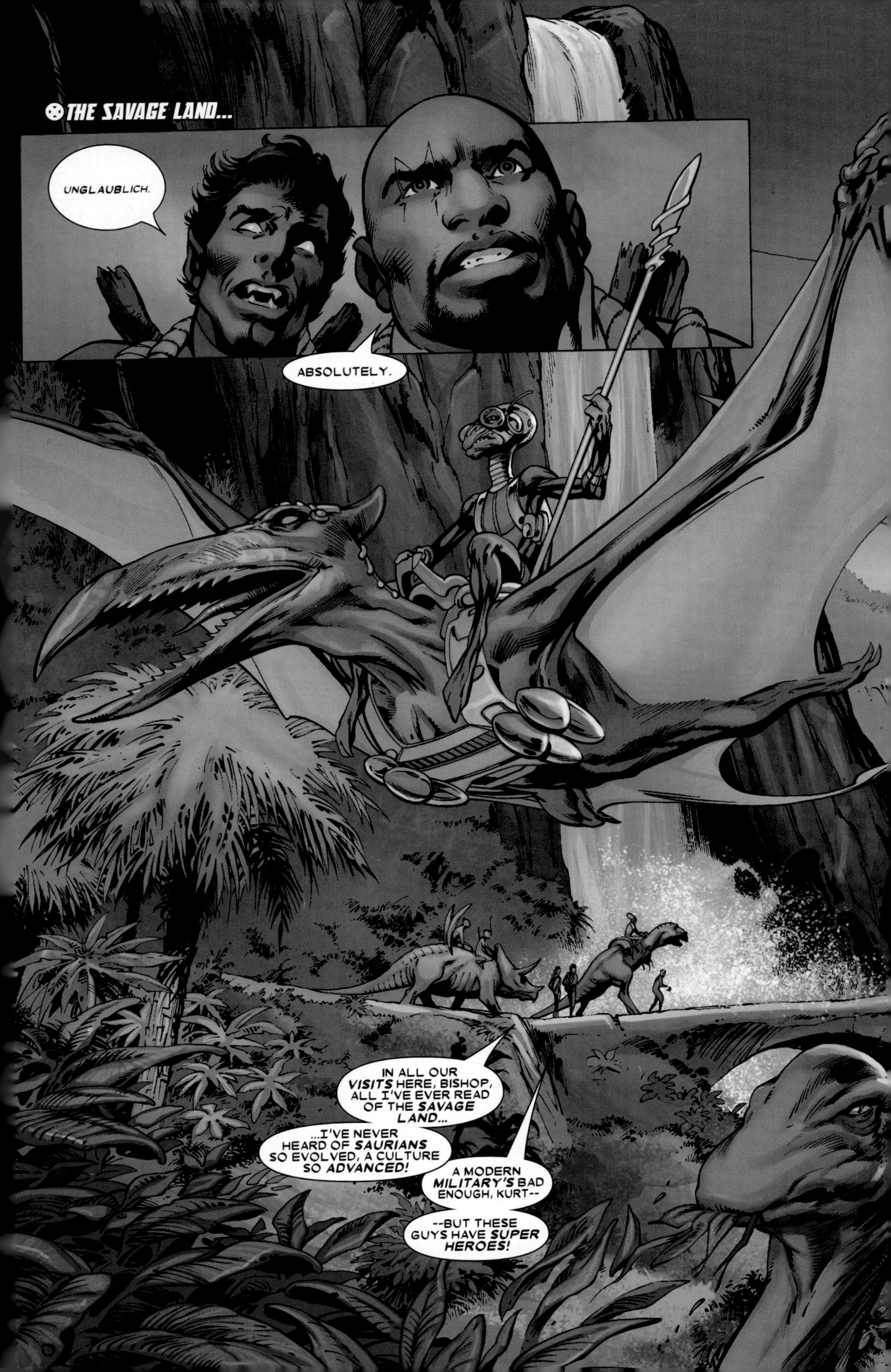
THE SAVAGE LAND...
UNGLAUBLICH.
ABSOLUTELY.
IN ALL OUR VISITS HERE, BISHOP, ALL I'VE EVER READ OF THE SAVAGE LAND...
...I'VE NEVER HEARD OF SAURIANS SO EVOLVED, A CULTURE SO ADVANCED!
A MODERN MILITARY'S BAD ENOUGH, KURT--
--BUT THESE GUYS HAVE SUPER HEROES!

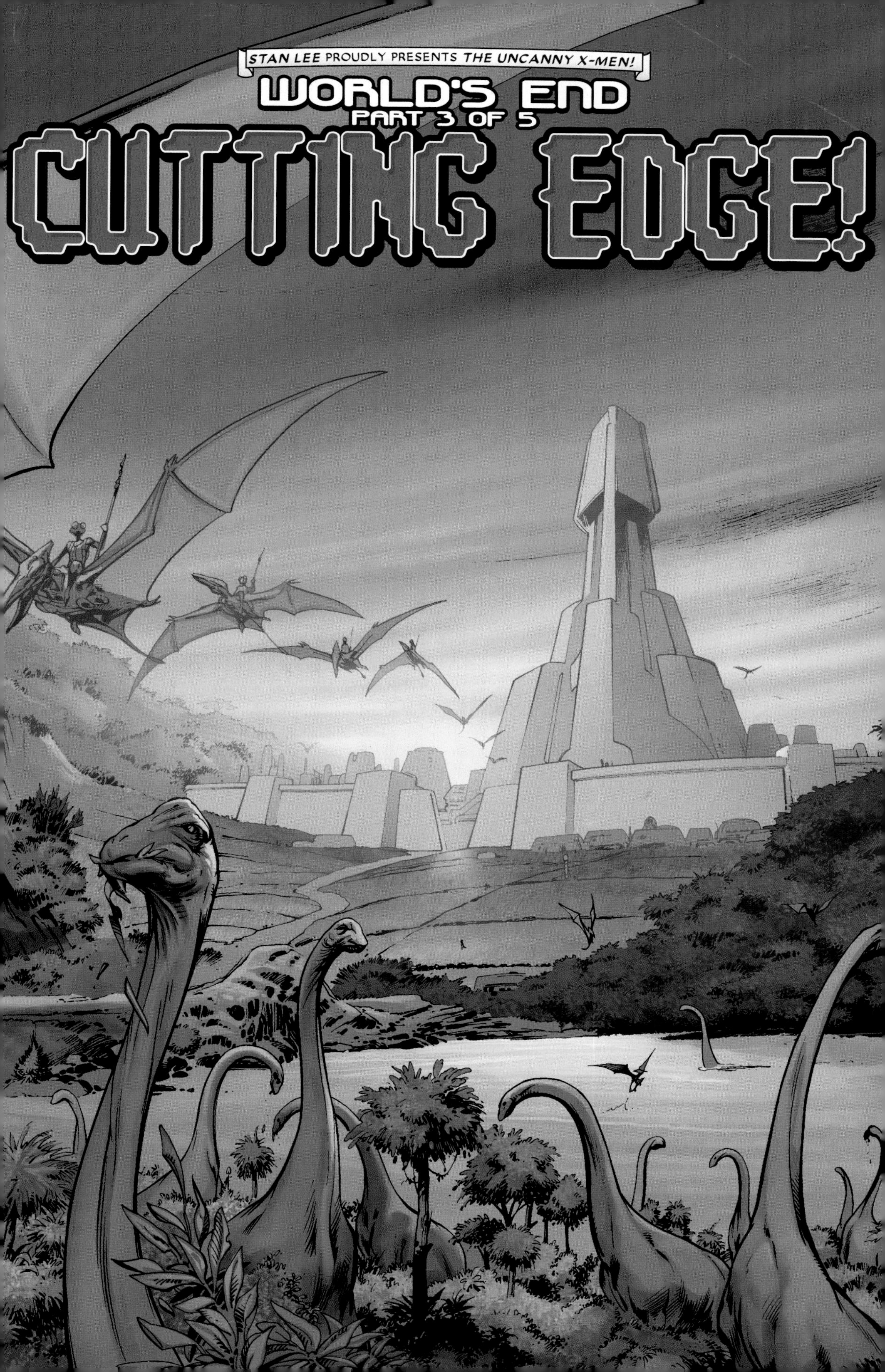
STAN LEE PROUDLY PRESENTS THE UNCANNY X-MEN!
WORLD'S END
PART 3 OF 5
CUTTING EDGE!

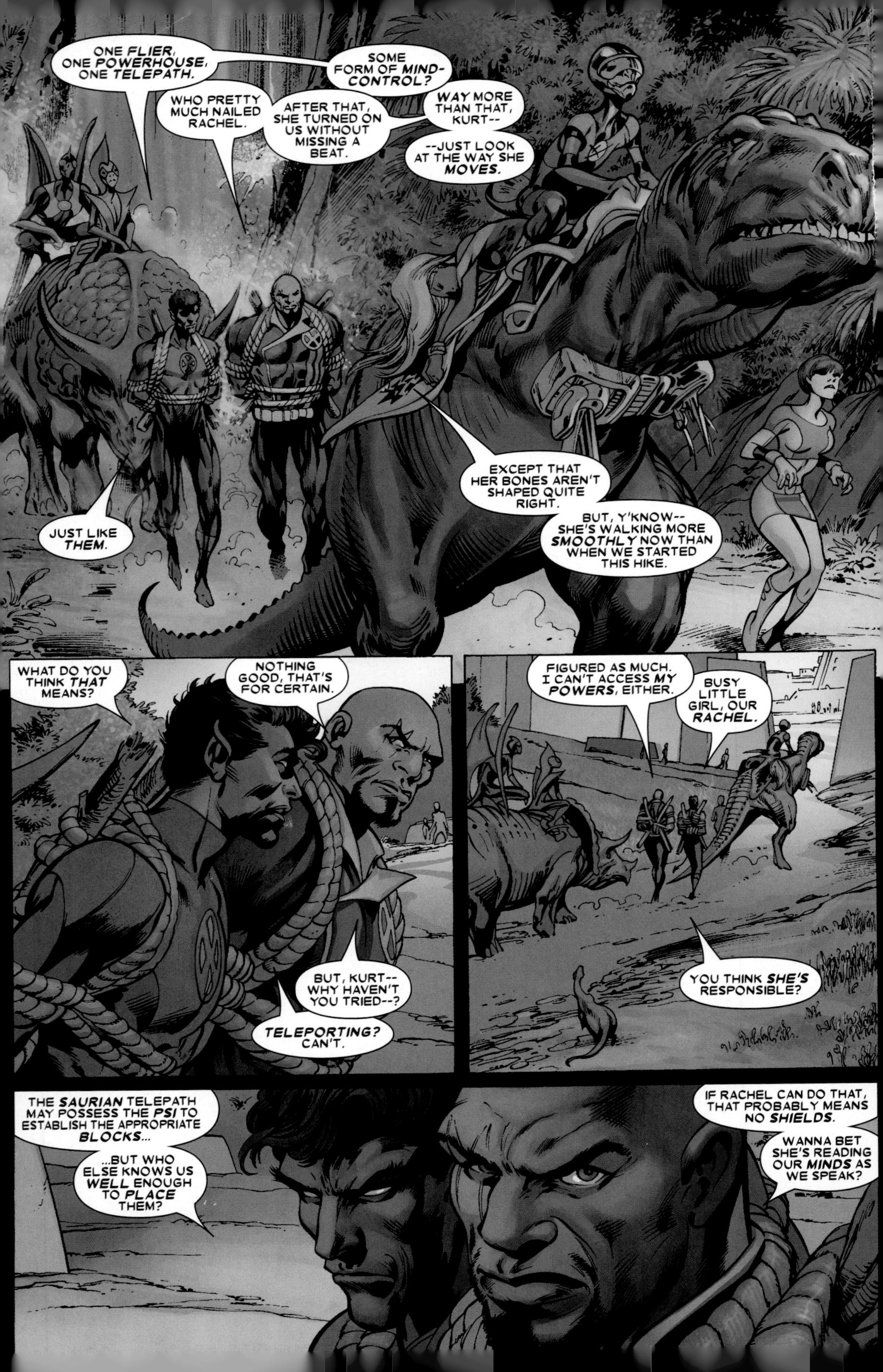
ONE FLIER, ONE POWERHOUSE, ONE TELEPATH.
SOME FORM OF MIND-CONTROL?
WHO PRETTY MUCH NAILED RACHEL.
AFTER THAT, SHE TURNED ON US WITHOUT MISSING A BEAT.
WAY MORE THAN THAT, KURT--
--JUST LOOK AT THE WAY SHE MOVES.
JUST LIKE THEM.
EXCEPT THAT HER BONES AREN'T SHAPED QUITE RIGHT.
BUT, Y'KNOW-- SHE'S WALKING MORE SMOOTHLY NOW THAN WHEN WE STARTED THIS HIKE.
WHAT DO YOU THINK THAT MEANS?
NOTHING GOOD, THAT'S FOR CERTAIN.
BUT, KURT-- WHY HAVEN'T YOU TRIED--?
TELEPORTING? CAN'T.
FIGURED AS MUCH. I CAN'T ACCESS MY POWERS, EITHER.
BUSY LITTLE GIRL, OUR RACHEL.
YOU THINK SHE'S RESPONSIBLE?
THE SAURIAN TELEPATH MAY POSSESS THE PSI TO ESTABLISH THE APPROPRIATE BLOCKS...
...BUT WHO ELSE KNOWS US WELL ENOUGH TO PLACE THEM?
IF RACHEL CAN DO THAT, THAT PROBABLY MEANS NO SHIELDS.
WANNA BET SHE'S READING OUR MINDS AS WE SPEAK?

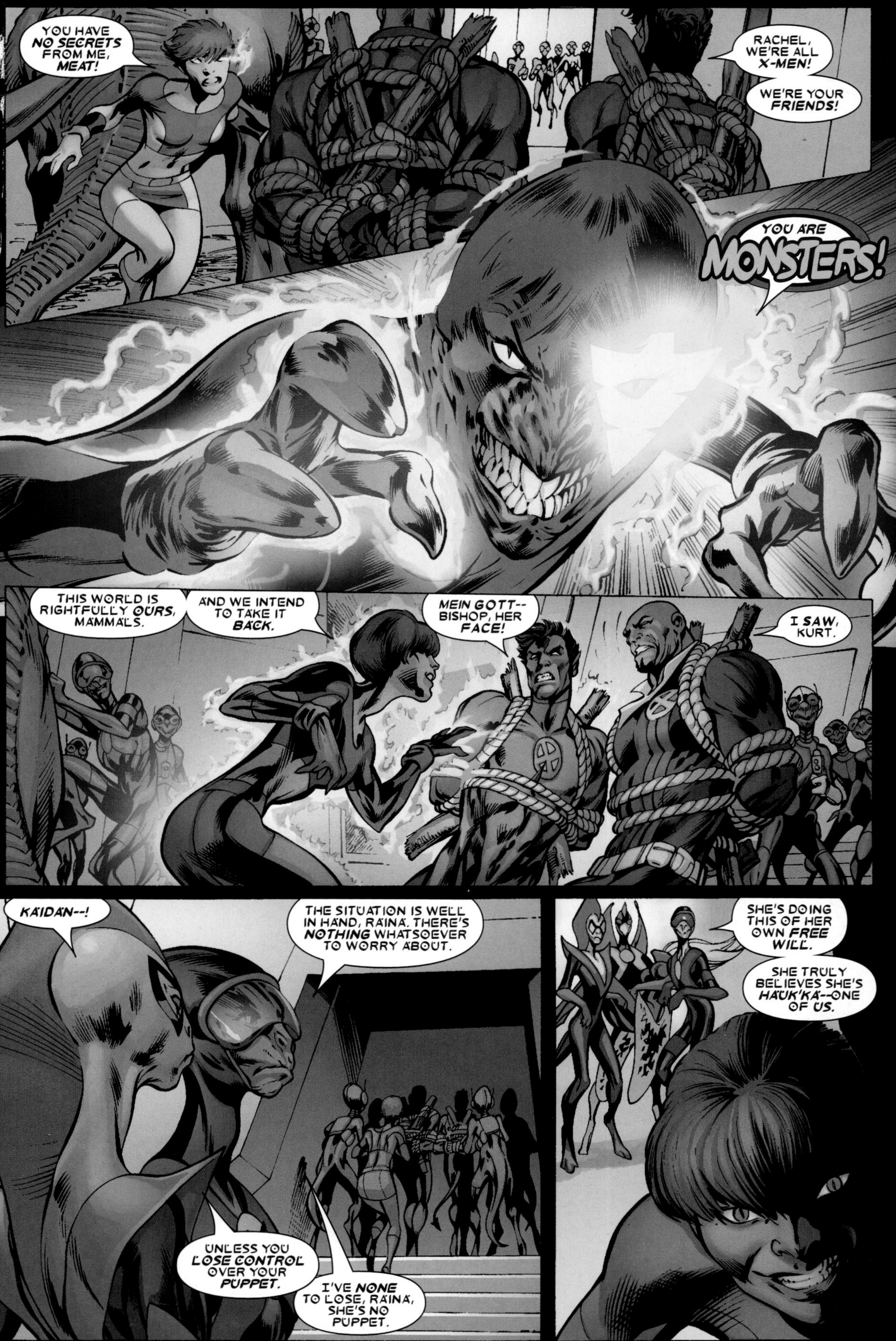
YOU HAVE NO SECRETS FROM ME, MEAT!
RACHEL, WE'RE ALL X-MEN!
WE'RE YOUR FRIENDS!
YOU ARE MONSTERS!
THIS WORLD IS RIGHTFULLY OURS, MAMMALS.
AND WE INTEND TO TAKE IT BACK.
MEIN GOTT-- BISHOP, HER FACE!
I SAW, KURT.
KAIDAN--!
THE SITUATION IS WELL IN HAND, RAINA. THERE'S NOTHING WHATSOEVER TO WORRY ABOUT.
UNLESS YOU LOSE CONTROL OVER YOUR PUPPET.
I'VE NONE TO LOSE, RAINA, SHE'S NO PUPPET.
SHE'S DOING THIS OF HER OWN FREE WILL.
SHE TRULY BELIEVES SHE'S HAUK'KA--ONE OF US.

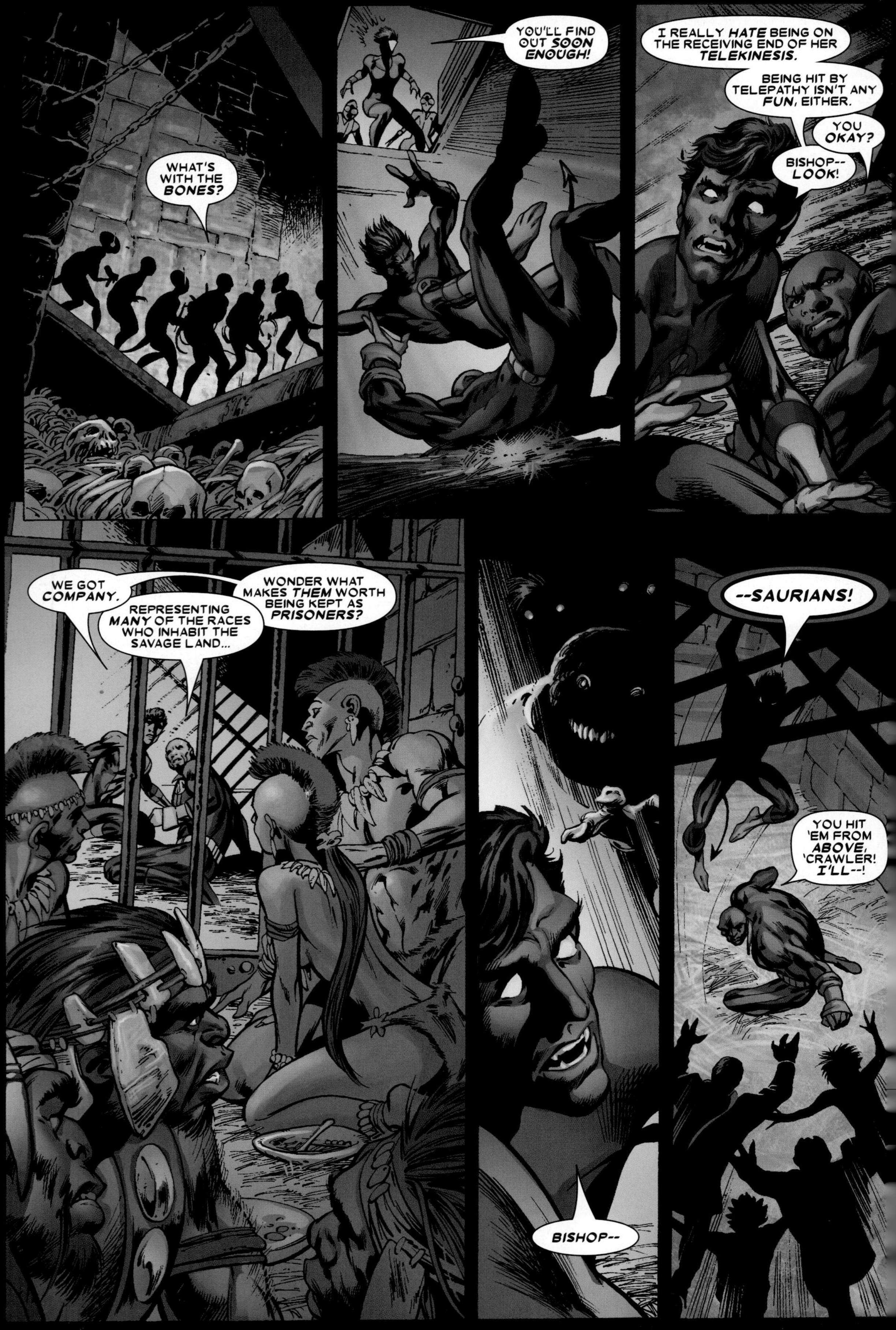
WHAT'S WITH THE BONES?
YOU'LL FIND OUT SOON ENOUGH!
I REALLY HATE BEING ON THE RECEIVING END OF HER TELEKINESIS.
BEING HIT BY TELEPATHY ISN'T ANY FUN, EITHER.
YOU OKAY?
BISHOP-- LOOK!
WE GOT COMPANY.
REPRESENTING MANY OF THE RACES WHO INHABIT THE SAVAGE LAND...
WONDER WHAT MAKES THEM WORTH BEING KEPT AS PRISONERS?
BISHOP--
--SAURIANS!
YOU HIT 'EM FROM ABOVE, 'CRAWLER! I'LL--!

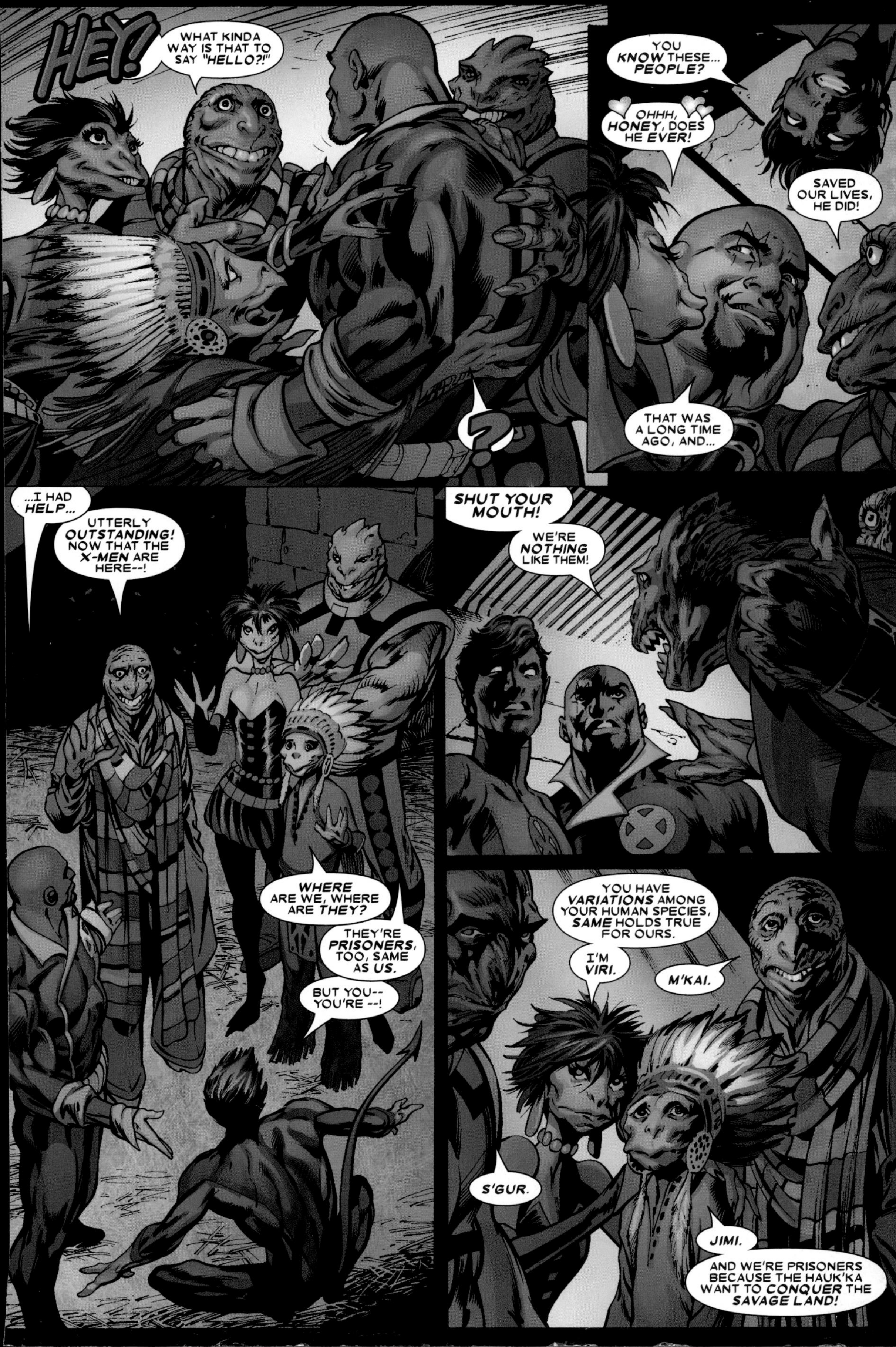
HEY!
WHAT KINDA WAY IS THAT TO SAY "HELLO?!"
?
YOU KNOW THESE... PEOPLE?
OHHH, HONEY, DOES HE EVER!
SAVED OUR LIVES, HE DID!
THAT WAS A LONG TIME AGO, AND...
...I HAD HELP...
UTTERLY OUTSTANDING! NOW THAT THE X-MEN ARE HERE--!
WHERE ARE WE, WHERE ARE THEY?
THEY'RE PRISONERS, TOO, SAME AS US.
BUT YOU-- YOU'RE --!
SHUT YOUR MOUTH!
WE'RE NOTHING LIKE THEM!
YOU HAVE VARIATIONS AMONG YOUR HUMAN SPECIES, SAME HOLDS TRUE FOR OURS.
I'M VIRI.
M'KAI.
S'GUR.
JIMI.
AND WE'RE PRISONERS BECAUSE THE HAUK'KA WANT TO CONQUER THE SAVAGE LAND!

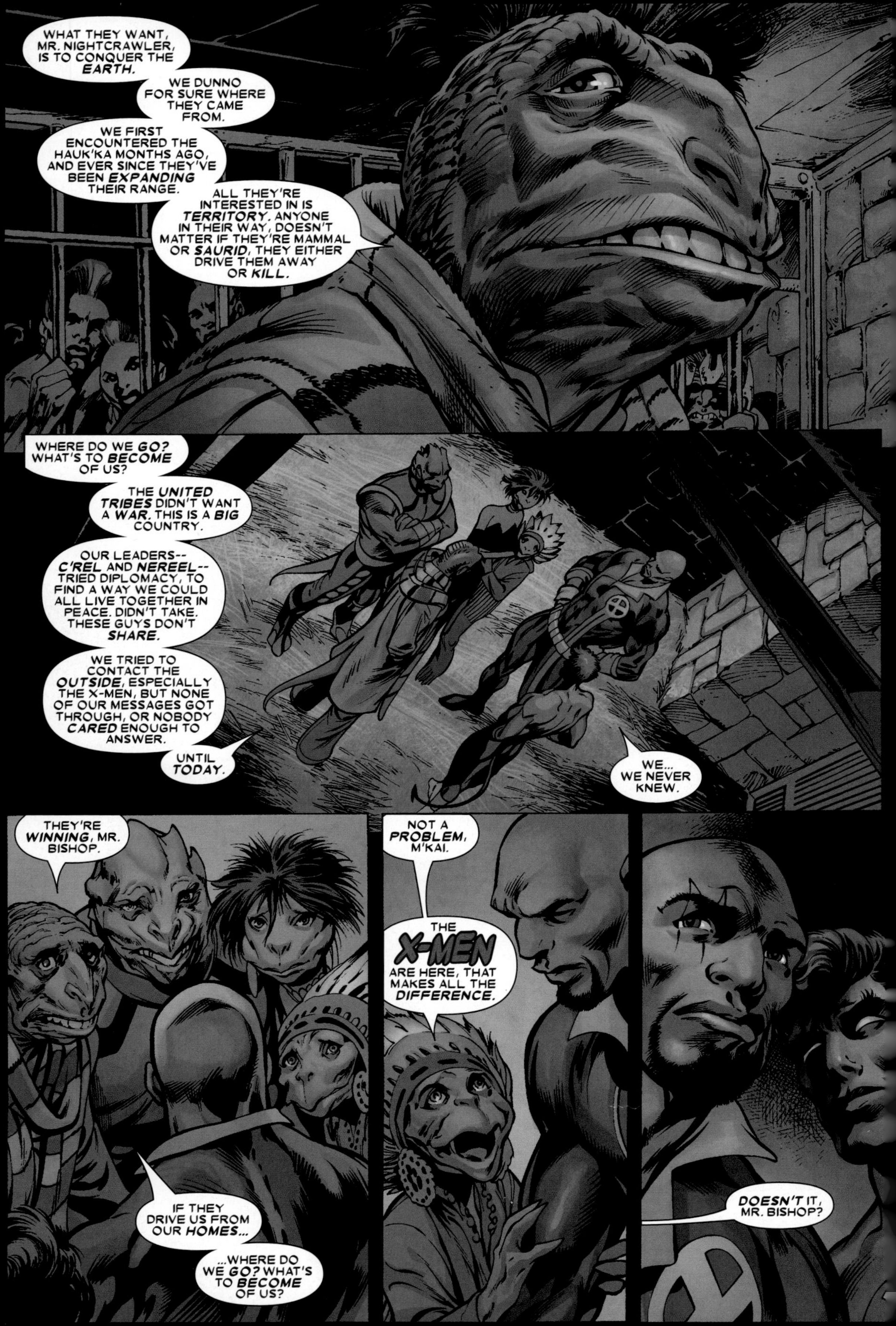
WHAT THEY WANT, MR. NIGHTCRAWLER, IS TO CONQUER THE EARTH.
WE DUNNO FOR SURE WHERE THEY CAME FROM.
WE FIRST ENCOUNTERED THE HAUK'KA MONTHS AGO, AND EVER SINCE THEY'VE BEEN EXPANDING THEIR RANGE.
ALL THEY'RE INTERESTED IN IS TERRITORY. ANYONE IN THEIR WAY, DOESN'T MATTER IF THEY'RE MAMMAL OR SAURID, THEY EITHER DRIVE THEM AWAY OR KILL.
WHERE DO WE GO? WHAT'S TO BECOME OF US?
THE UNITED TRIBES DIDN'T WANT A WAR. THIS IS A BIG COUNTRY.
OUR LEADERS-- C'REL AND NEREEL-- TRIED DIPLOMACY, TO FIND A WAY WE COULD ALL LIVE TOGETHER IN PEACE. DIDN'T TAKE. THESE GUYS DON'T SHARE.
WE TRIED TO CONTACT THE OUTSIDE, ESPECIALLY THE X-MEN, BUT NONE OF OUR MESSAGES GOT THROUGH, OR NOBODY CARED ENOUGH TO ANSWER.
UNTIL TODAY.
WE... WE NEVER KNEW.
THEY'RE WINNING, MR. BISHOP.
IF THEY DRIVE US FROM OUR HOMES...
...WHERE DO WE GO? WHAT'S TO BECOME OF US?
NOT A PROBLEM, M'KAI.
THE X-MEN ARE HERE, THAT MAKES ALL THE DIFFERENCE.
DOESN'T IT, MR. BISHOP?

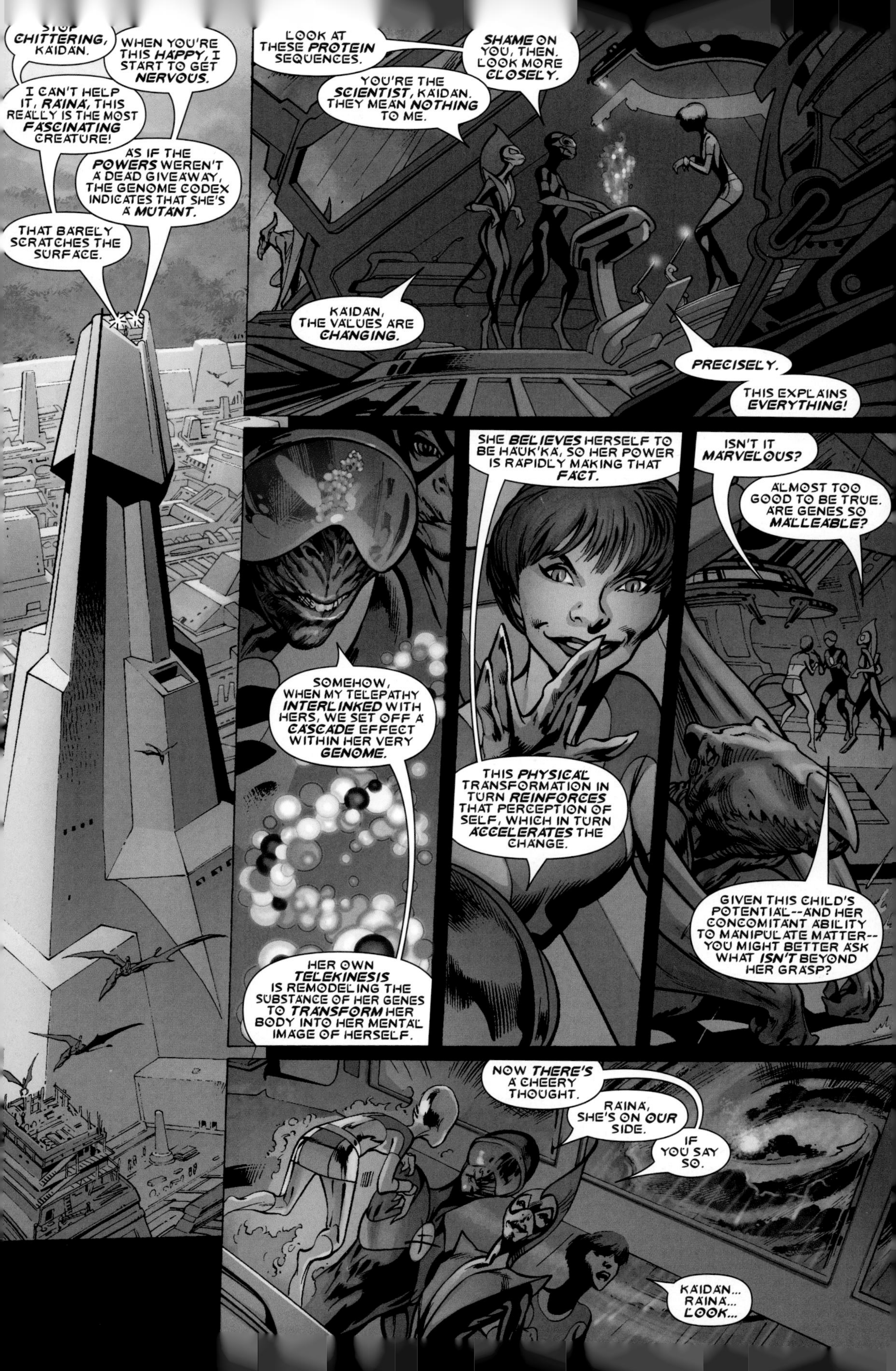

STOP CHITTERING, KAIDAN.
WHEN YOU'RE THIS HAPPY, I START TO GET NERVOUS.
I CAN'T HELP IT, RAINA, THIS REALLY IS THE MOST FASCINATING CREATURE!
AS IF THE POWERS WEREN'T A DEAD GIVEAWAY, THE GENOME CODEX INDICATES THAT SHE'S A MUTANT.
THAT BARELY SCRATCHES THE SURFACE.
LOOK AT THESE PROTEIN SEQUENCES.
YOU'RE THE SCIENTIST, KAIDAN. THEY MEAN NOTHING TO ME.
SHAME ON YOU, THEN. LOOK MORE CLOSELY.
KAIDAN, THE VALUES ARE CHANGING.
PRECISELY.
THIS EXPLAINS EVERYTHING!
SOMEHOW, WHEN MY TELEPATHY INTERLINKED WITH HERS, WE SET OFF A CASCADE EFFECT WITHIN HER VERY GENOME.
HER OWN TELEKINESIS IS REMODELING THE SUBSTANCE OF HER GENES TO TRANSFORM HER BODY INTO HER MENTAL IMAGE OF HERSELF.
SHE BELIEVES HERSELF TO BE HAUK'KA, SO HER POWER IS RAPIDLY MAKING THAT FACT.
THIS PHYSICAL TRANSFORMATION IN TURN REINFORCES THAT PERCEPTION OF SELF, WHICH IN TURN ACCELERATES THE CHANGE.
ISN'T IT MARVELOUS?
ALMOST TOO GOOD TO BE TRUE. ARE GENES SO MALLEABLE?
GIVEN THIS CHILD'S POTENTIAL--AND HER CONCOMITANT ABILITY TO MANIPULATE MATTER--YOU MIGHT BETTER ASK WHAT ISN'T BEYOND HER GRASP?
NOW THERE'S A CHEERY THOUGHT.
RAINA, SHE'S ON OUR SIDE.
IF YOU SAY SO.
KAIDAN... RAINA... LOOK...

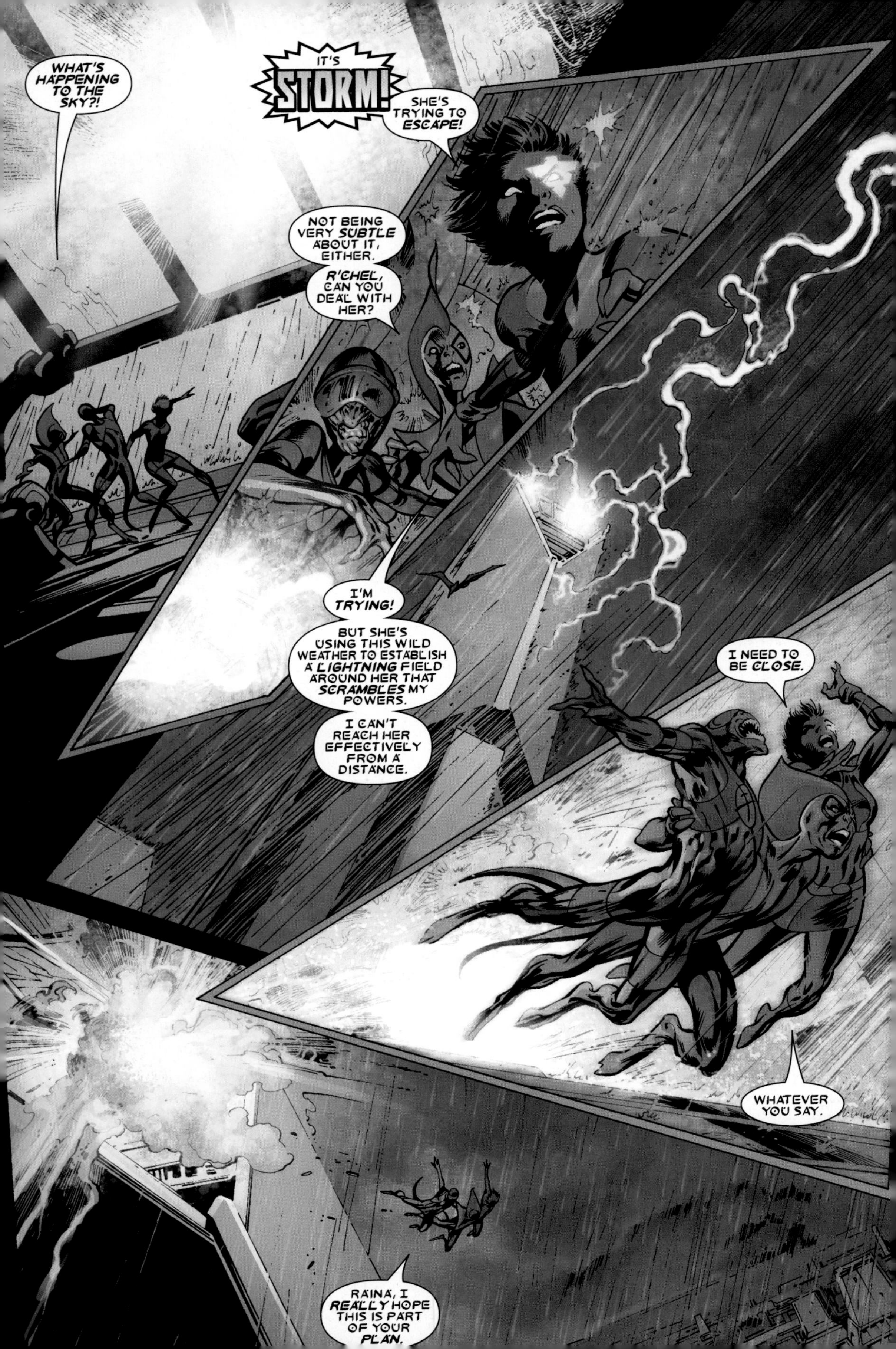
WHAT'S HAPPENING TO THE SKY?!
IT'S STORM!
SHE'S TRYING TO ESCAPE!
NOT BEING VERY SUBTLE ABOUT IT, EITHER.
R'CHEL, CAN YOU DEAL WITH HER?
I'M TRYING!
BUT SHE'S USING THIS WILD WEATHER TO ESTABLISH A LIGHTNING FIELD AROUND HER THAT SCRAMBLES MY POWERS.
I CAN'T REACH HER EFFECTIVELY FROM A DISTANCE.
I NEED TO BE CLOSE.
WHATEVER YOU SAY.
RAINA, I REALLY HOPE THIS IS PART OF YOUR PLAN.

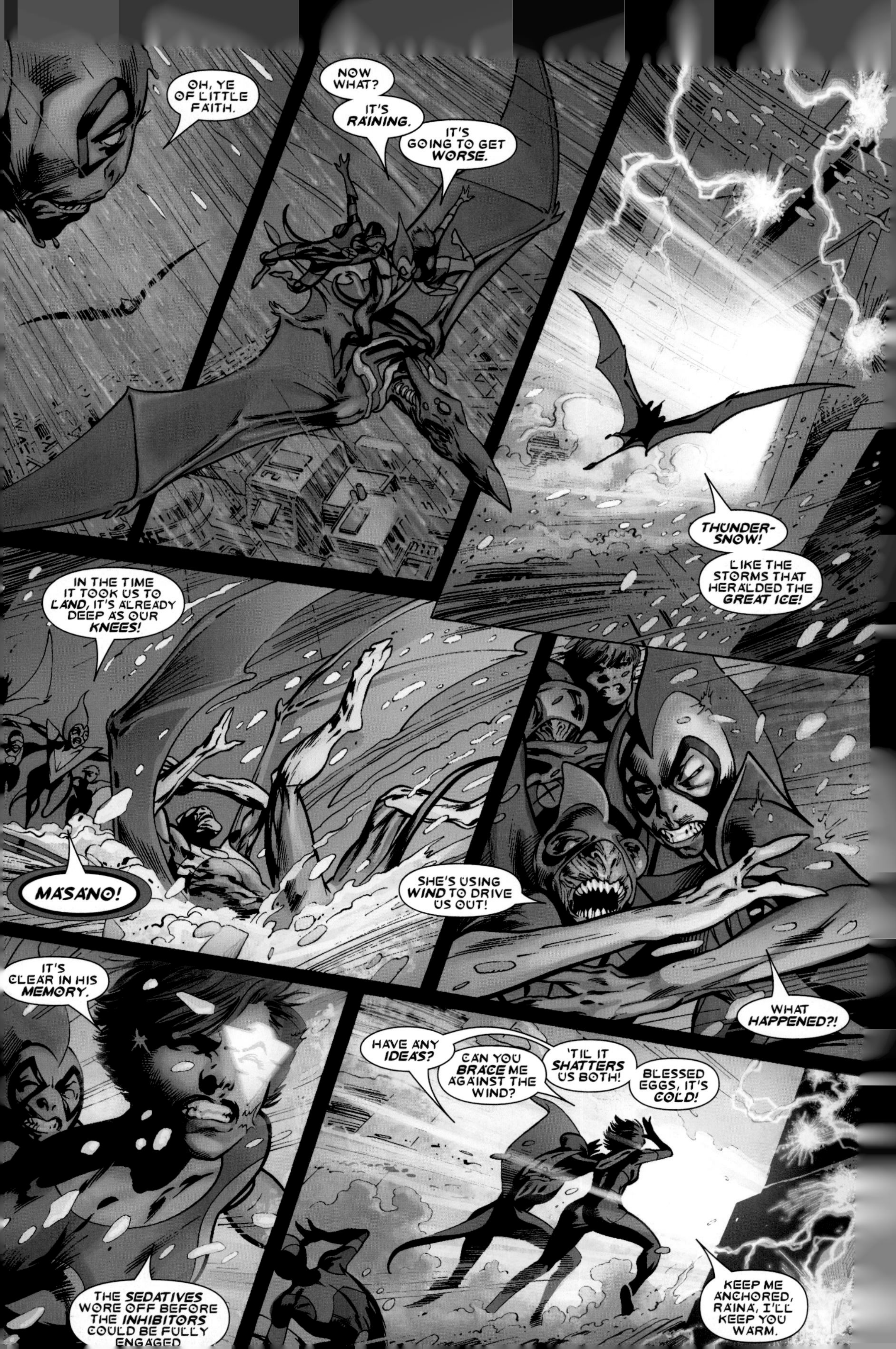
OH, YE OF LITTLE FAITH.
NOW WHAT?
IT'S RAINING.
IT'S GOING TO GET WORSE.
THUNDER-SNOW!
LIKE THE STORMS THAT HERALDED THE GREAT ICE!
IN THE TIME IT TOOK US TO LAND, IT'S ALREADY DEEP AS OUR KNEES!
MASANO!
SHE'S USING WIND TO DRIVE US OUT!
WHAT HAPPENED?!
IT'S CLEAR IN HIS MEMORY.
THE SEDATIVES WORE OFF BEFORE THE INHIBITORS COULD BE FULLY ENGAGED
HAVE ANY IDEAS?
CAN YOU BRACE ME AGAINST THE WIND?
'TIL IT SHATTERS US BOTH!
BLESSED EGGS, IT'S COLD!
KEEP ME ANCHORED, RAINA, I'LL KEEP YOU WARM.

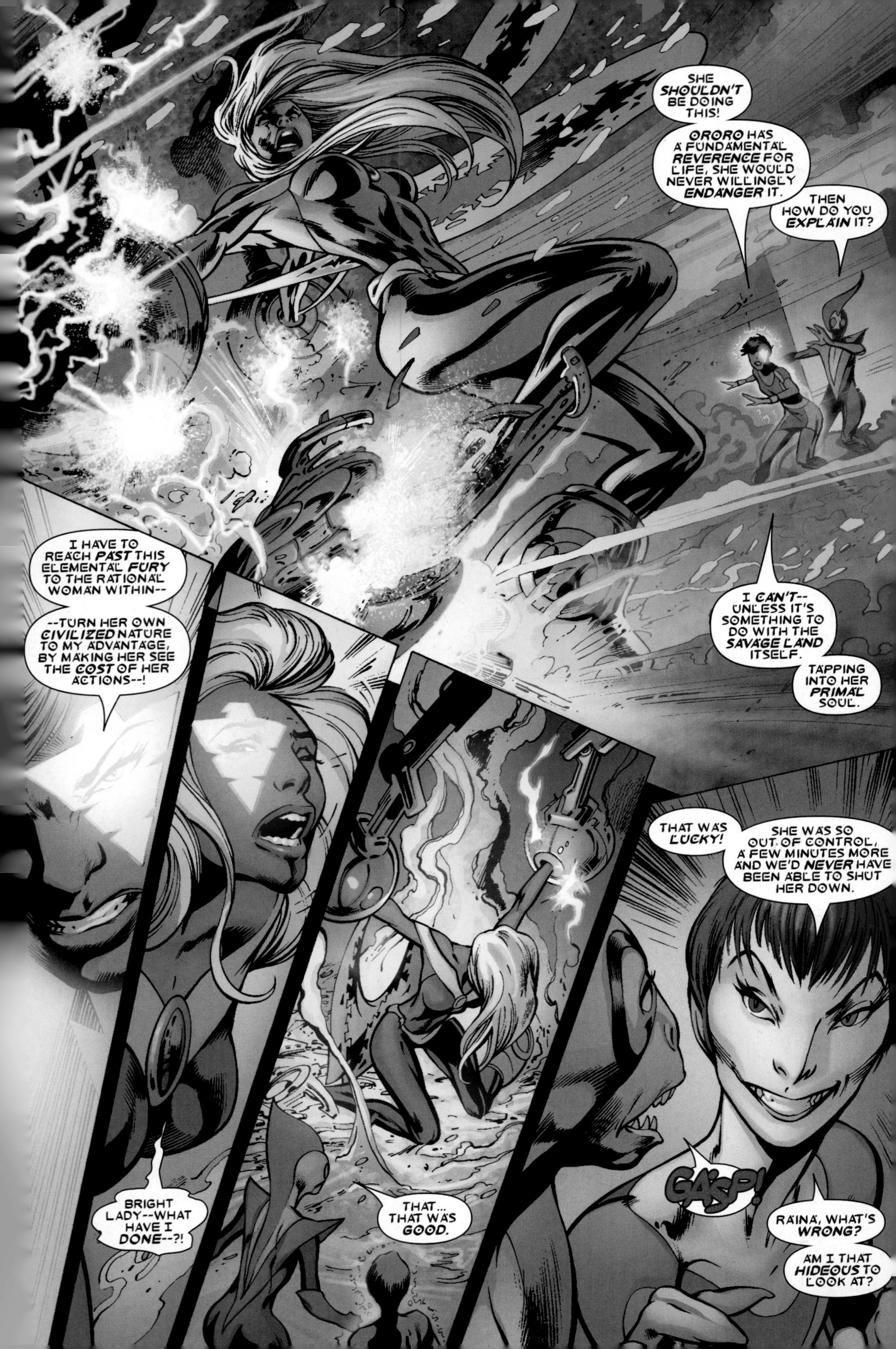
SHE SHOULDN'T BE DOING THIS!
ORORO HAS A FUNDAMENTAL REVERENCE FOR LIFE, SHE WOULD NEVER WILLINGLY ENDANGER IT.
THEN HOW DO YOU EXPLAIN IT?
I CAN'T--UNLESS IT'S SOMETHING TO DO WITH THE SAVAGE LAND ITSELF.
TAPPING INTO HER PRIMAL SOUL.
I HAVE TO REACH PAST THIS ELEMENTAL FURY TO THE RATIONAL WOMAN WITHIN--
--TURN HER OWN CIVILIZED NATURE TO MY ADVANTAGE, BY MAKING HER SEE THE COST OF HER ACTIONS--!
BRIGHT LADY--WHAT HAVE I DONE--?!
THAT... THAT WAS GOOD.
THAT WAS LUCKY!
SHE WAS SO OUT OF CONTROL, A FEW MINUTES MORE AND WE'D NEVER HAVE BEEN ABLE TO SHUT HER DOWN.
GASP!
RAINA, WHAT'S WRONG?
AM I THAT HIDEOUS TO LOOK AT?

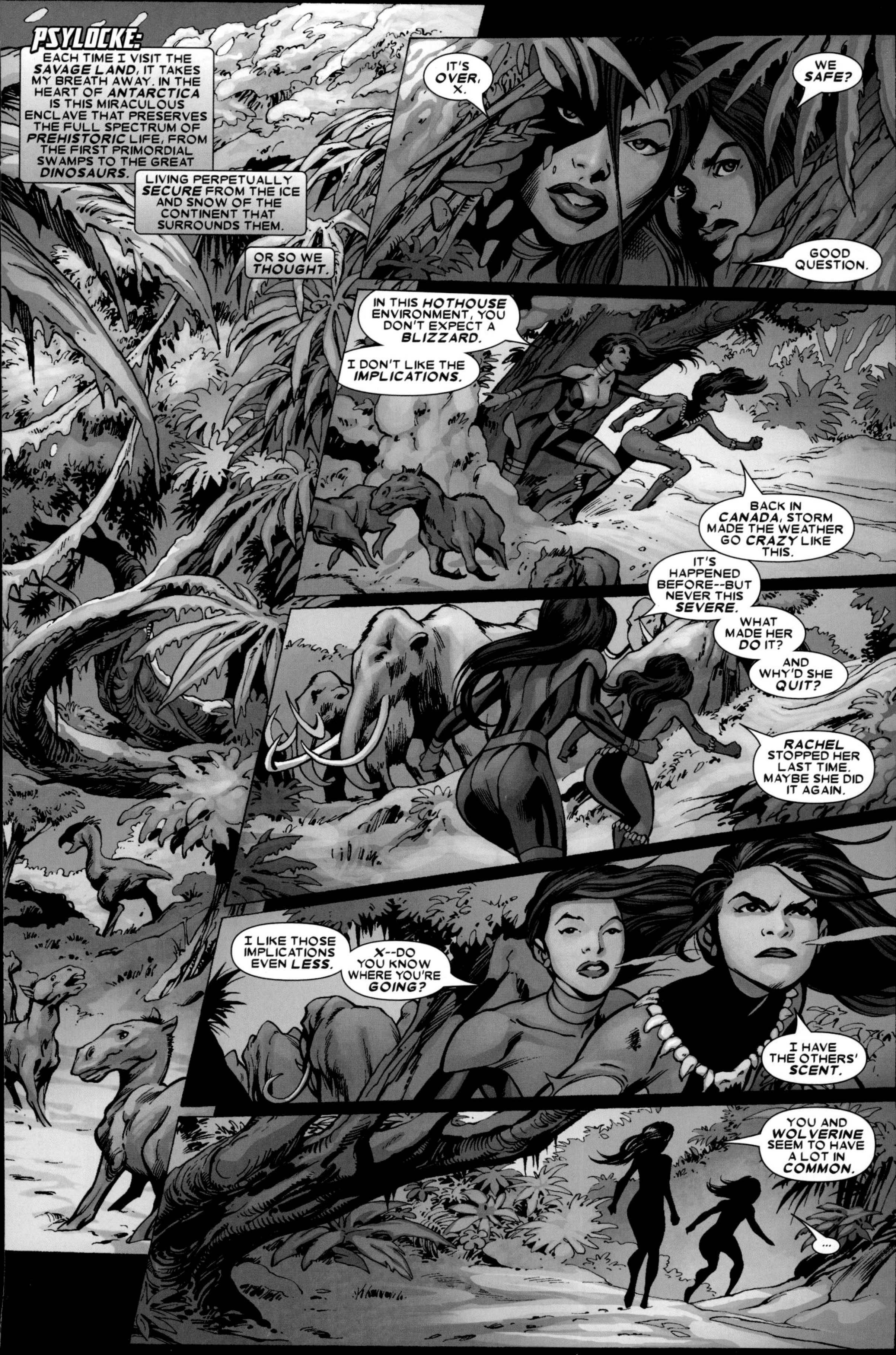
PSYLOCKE:
EACH TIME I VISIT THE SAVAGE LAND, IT TAKES MY BREATH AWAY. IN THE HEART OF ANTARCTICA IS THIS MIRACULOUS ENCLAVE THAT PRESERVES THE FULL SPECTRUM OF PREHISTORIC LIFE, FROM THE FIRST PRIMORDIAL SWAMPS TO THE GREAT DINOSAURS.
LIVING PERPETUALLY SECURE FROM THE ICE AND SNOW OF THE CONTINENT THAT SURROUNDS THEM.
OR SO WE THOUGHT.
IT'S OVER, X.
WE SAFE?
GOOD QUESTION.
IN THIS HOTHOUSE ENVIRONMENT, YOU DON'T EXPECT A BLIZZARD.
I DON'T LIKE THE IMPLICATIONS.
BACK IN CANADA, STORM MADE THE WEATHER GO CRAZY LIKE THIS.
IT'S HAPPENED BEFORE--BUT NEVER THIS SEVERE.
WHAT MADE HER DO IT?
AND WHY'D SHE QUIT?
RACHEL STOPPED HER LAST TIME. MAYBE SHE DID IT AGAIN.
I LIKE THOSE IMPLICATIONS EVEN LESS.
X--DO YOU KNOW WHERE YOU'RE GOING?
I HAVE THE OTHERS' SCENT.
YOU AND WOLVERINE SEEM TO HAVE A LOT IN COMMON.
...

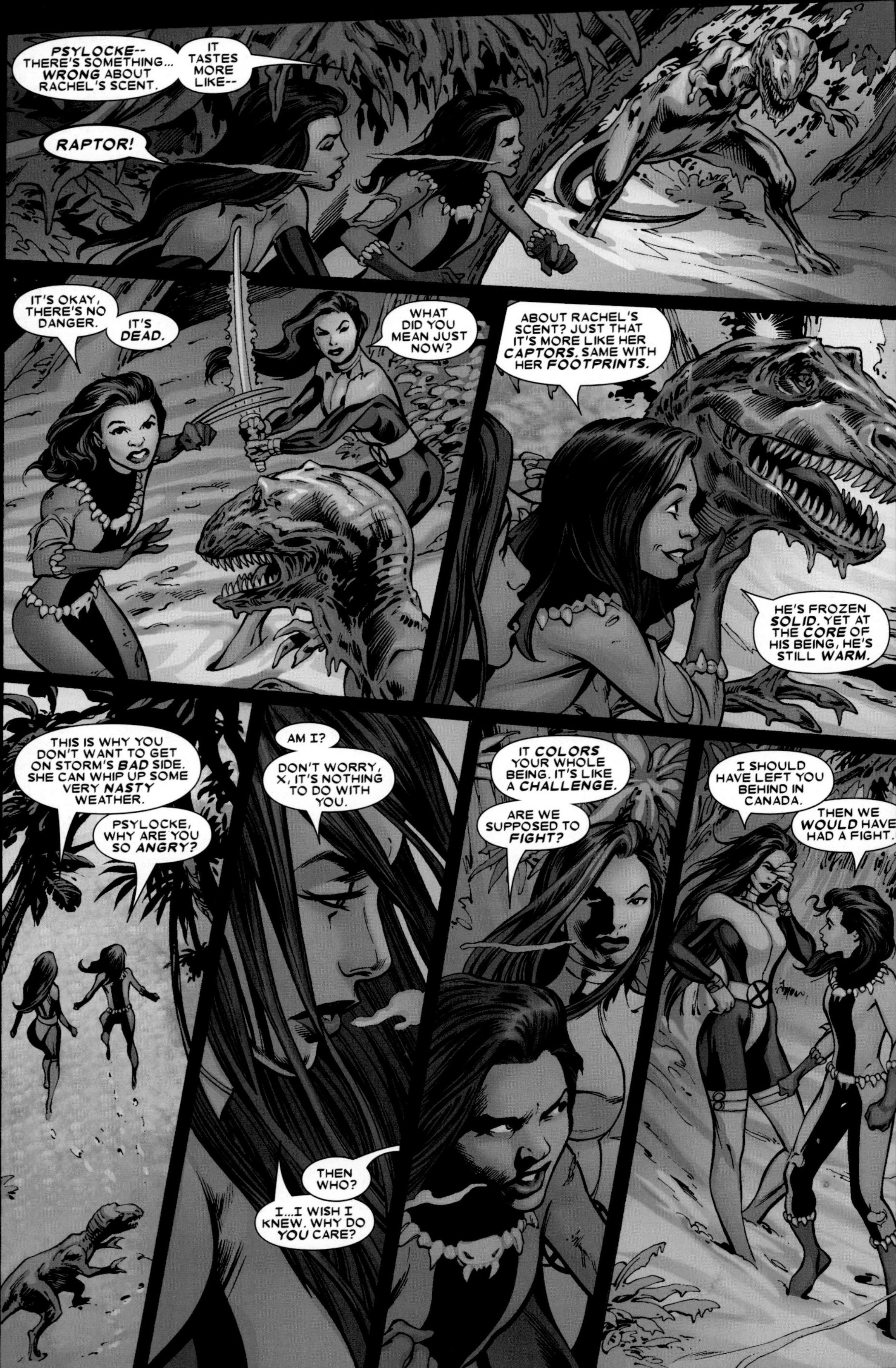
PSYLOCKE-- THERE'S SOMETHING... WRONG ABOUT RACHEL'S SCENT.
IT TASTES MORE LIKE--
RAPTOR!
IT'S OKAY, THERE'S NO DANGER.
IT'S DEAD.
WHAT DID YOU MEAN JUST NOW?
ABOUT RACHEL'S SCENT? JUST THAT IT'S MORE LIKE HER CAPTORS. SAME WITH HER FOOTPRINTS.
HE'S FROZEN SOLID. YET AT THE CORE OF HIS BEING, HE'S STILL WARM.
THIS IS WHY YOU DON'T WANT TO GET ON STORM'S BAD SIDE. SHE CAN WHIP UP SOME VERY NASTY WEATHER.
PSYLOCKE, WHY ARE YOU SO ANGRY?
AM I?
DON'T WORRY, X, IT'S NOTHING TO DO WITH YOU.
THEN WHO?
I...I WISH I KNEW. WHY DO YOU CARE?
IT COLORS YOUR WHOLE BEING. IT'S LIKE A CHALLENGE.
ARE WE SUPPOSED TO FIGHT?
I SHOULD HAVE LEFT YOU BEHIND IN CANADA.
THEN WE WOULD HAVE HAD A FIGHT.

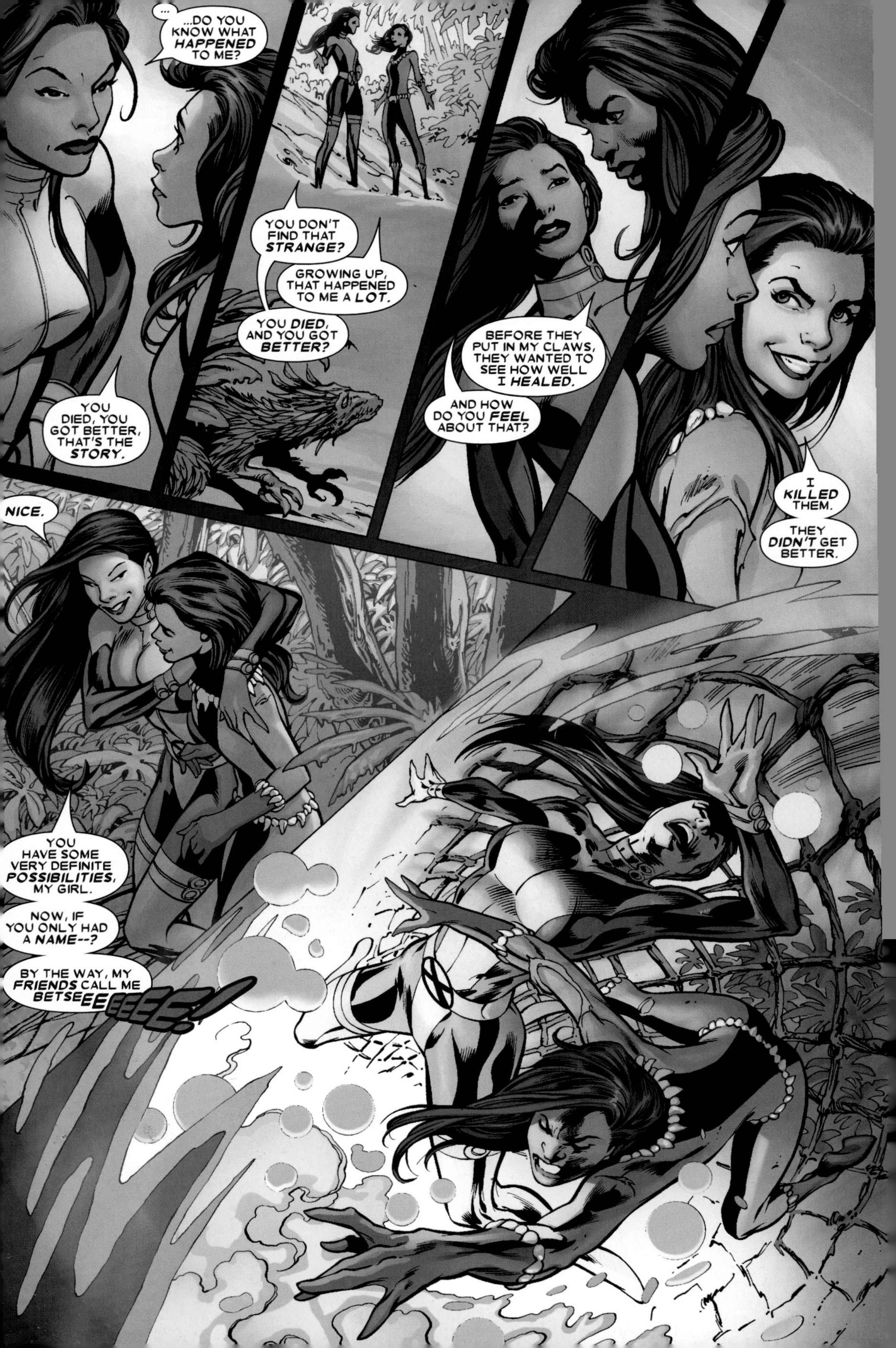
...
...DO YOU KNOW WHAT HAPPENED TO ME?
YOU DIED, YOU GOT BETTER, THAT'S THE STORY.
YOU DON'T FIND THAT STRANGE?
GROWING UP, THAT HAPPENED TO ME A LOT.
YOU DIED, AND YOU GOT BETTER?
BEFORE THEY PUT IN MY CLAWS, THEY WANTED TO SEE HOW WELL I HEALED.
AND HOW DO YOU FEEL ABOUT THAT?
I KILLED THEM.
THEY DIDN'T GET BETTER.
NICE.
YOU HAVE SOME VERY DEFINITE POSSIBILITIES, MY GIRL.
NOW, IF YOU ONLY HAD A NAME--?
BY THE WAY, MY FRIENDS CALL ME BETSEEEEEE!

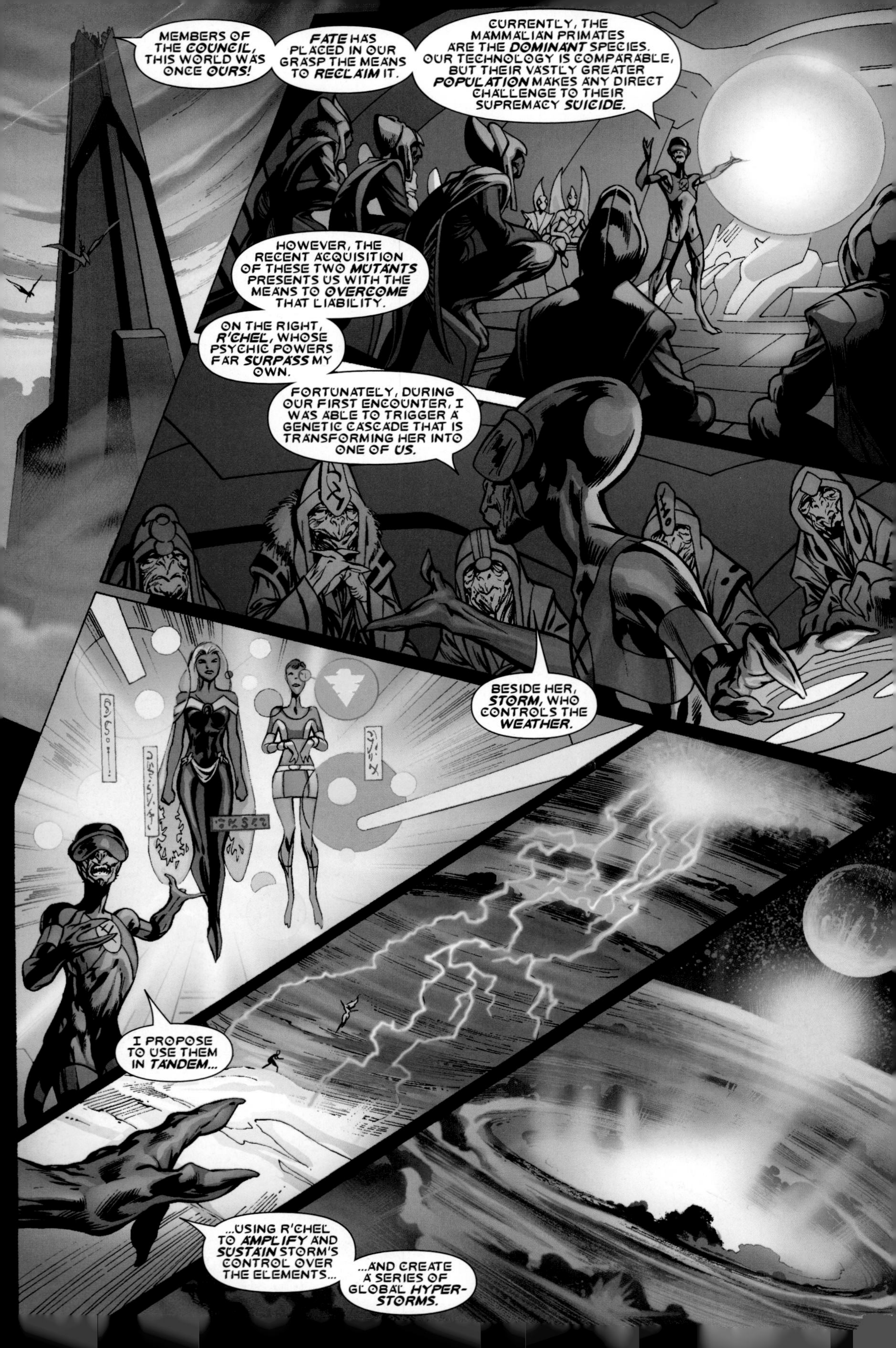
MEMBERS OF THE COUNCIL, THIS WORLD WAS ONCE OURS!
FATE HAS PLACED IN OUR GRASP THE MEANS TO RECLAIM IT.
CURRENTLY, THE MAMMALIAN PRIMATES ARE THE DOMINANT SPECIES. OUR TECHNOLOGY IS COMPARABLE, BUT THEIR VASTLY GREATER POPULATION MAKES ANY DIRECT CHALLENGE TO THEIR SUPREMACY SUICIDE.
HOWEVER, THE RECENT ACQUISITION OF THESE TWO MUTANTS PRESENTS US WITH THE MEANS TO OVERCOME THAT LIABILITY.
ON THE RIGHT, R'CHEL, WHOSE PSYCHIC POWERS FAR SURPASS MY OWN.
FORTUNATELY, DURING OUR FIRST ENCOUNTER, I WAS ABLE TO TRIGGER A GENETIC CASCADE THAT IS TRANSFORMING HER INTO ONE OF US.
BESIDE HER, STORM, WHO CONTROLS THE WEATHER.
I PROPOSE TO USE THEM IN TANDEM...
...USING R'CHEL TO AMPLIFY AND SUSTAIN STORM'S CONTROL OVER THE ELEMENTS...
...AND CREATE A SERIES OF GLOBAL HYPER-STORMS.

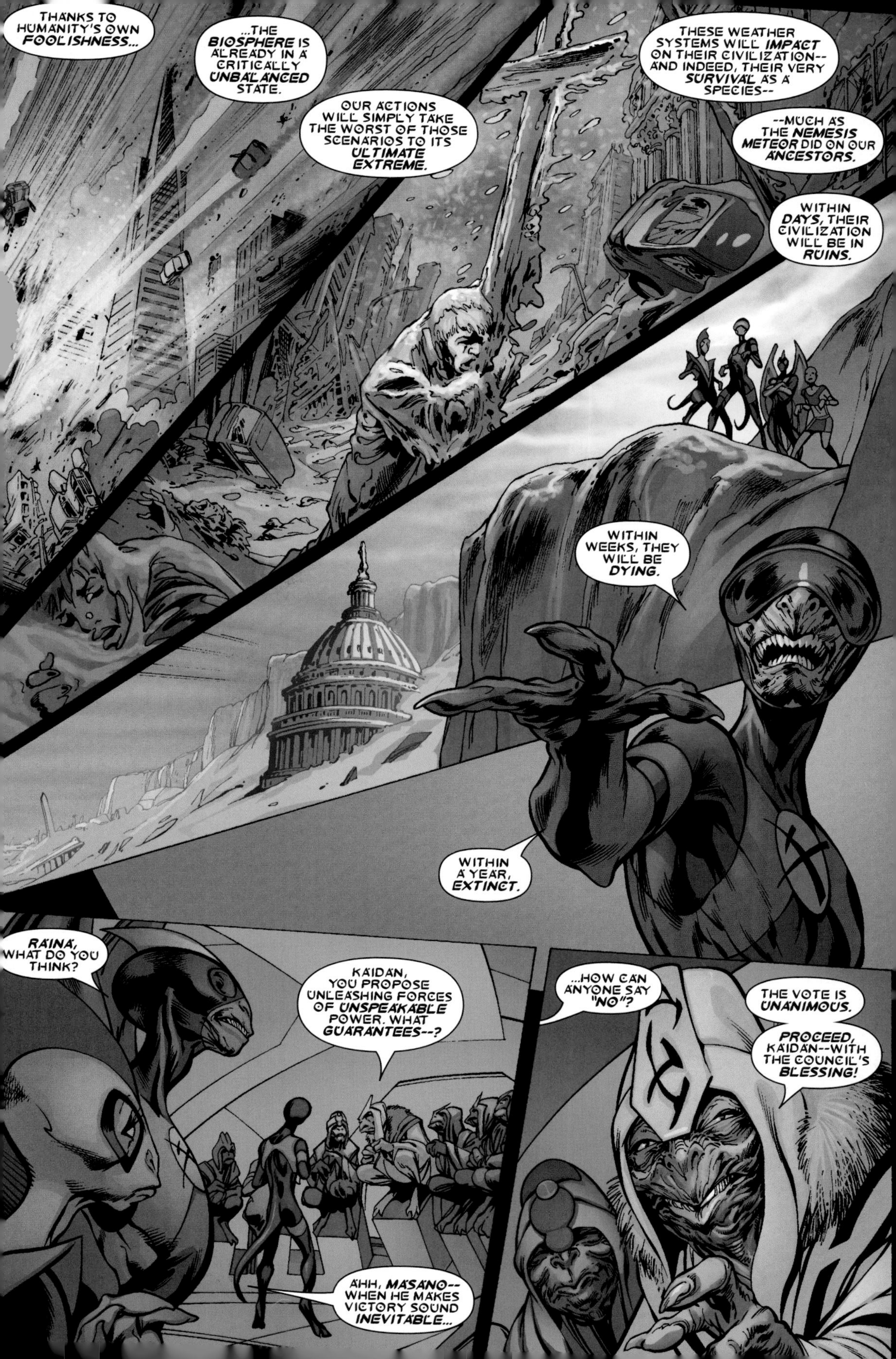
THANKS TO HUMANITY'S OWN FOOLISHNESS...
...THE BIOSPHERE IS ALREADY IN A CRITICALLY UNBALANCED STATE.
OUR ACTIONS WILL SIMPLY TAKE THE WORST OF THOSE SCENARIOS TO ITS ULTIMATE EXTREME.
THESE WEATHER SYSTEMS WILL IMPACT ON THEIR CIVILIZATION-- AND INDEED, THEIR VERY SURVIVAL AS A SPECIES--
--MUCH AS THE NEMESIS METEOR DID ON OUR ANCESTORS.
WITHIN DAYS, THEIR CIVILIZATION WILL BE IN RUINS.
WITHIN WEEKS, THEY WILL BE DYING.
WITHIN A YEAR, EXTINCT.
RAINA, WHAT DO YOU THINK?
KAIDAN, YOU PROPOSE UNLEASHING FORCES OF UNSPEAKABLE POWER. WHAT GUARANTEES--?
AHH, MASANO-- WHEN HE MAKES VICTORY SOUND INEVITABLE...
...HOW CAN ANYONE SAY "NO"?
THE VOTE IS UNANIMOUS.
PROCEED, KAIDAN--WITH THE COUNCIL'S BLESSING!

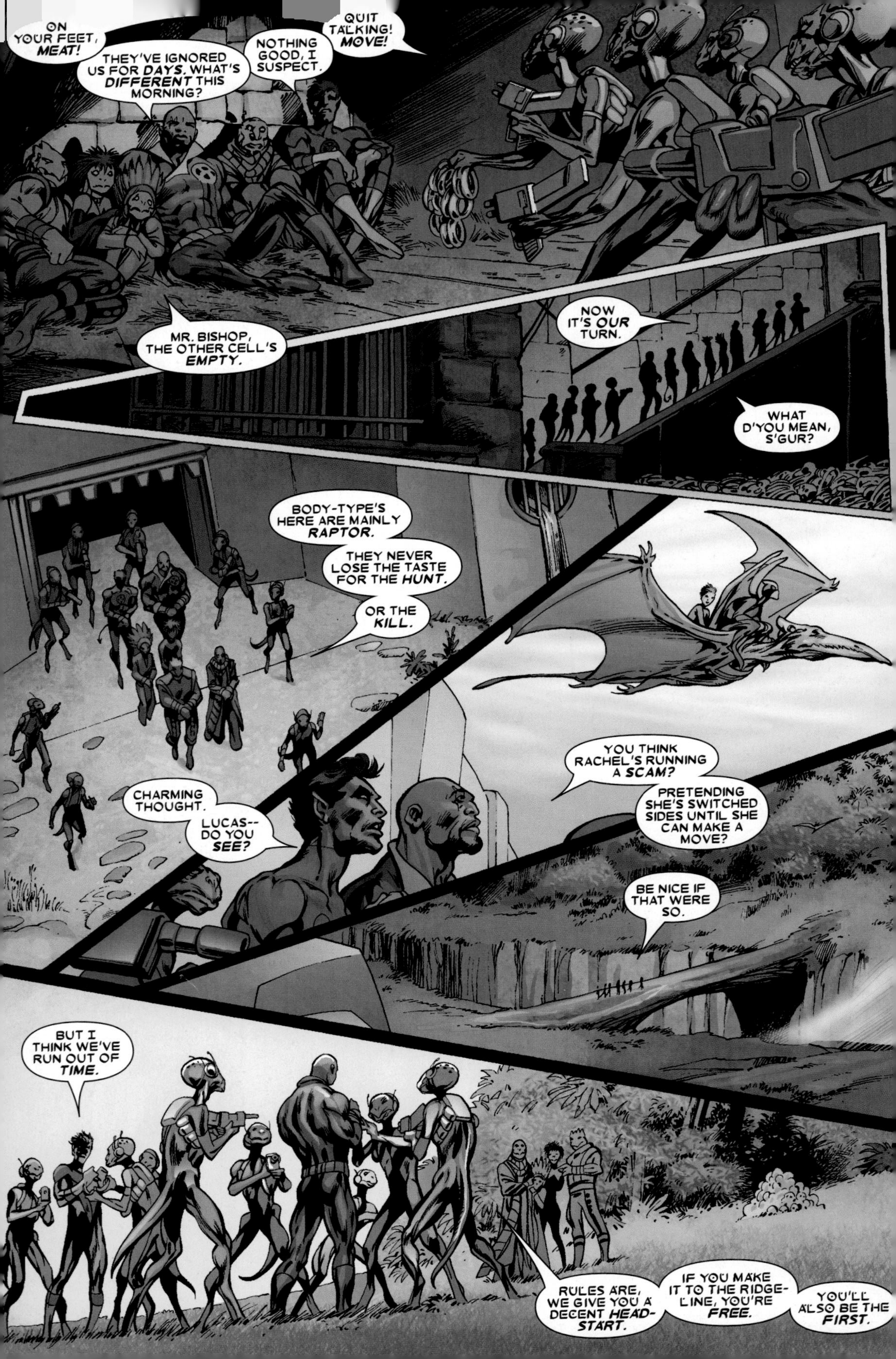

ON YOUR FEET, MEAT!
THEY'VE IGNORED US FOR DAYS. WHAT'S DIFFERENT THIS MORNING?
NOTHING GOOD, I SUSPECT.
QUIT TALKING! MOVE!
MR. BISHOP, THE OTHER CELL'S EMPTY.
NOW IT'S OUR TURN.
WHAT D'YOU MEAN, S'GUR?
BODY-TYPE'S HERE ARE MAINLY RAPTOR.
THEY NEVER LOSE THE TASTE FOR THE HUNT.
OR THE KILL.
CHARMING THOUGHT.
LUCAS-- DO YOU SEE?
YOU THINK RACHEL'S RUNNING A SCAM?
PRETENDING SHE'S SWITCHED SIDES UNTIL SHE CAN MAKE A MOVE?
BE NICE IF THAT WERE SO.
BUT I THINK WE'VE RUN OUT OF TIME.
RULES ARE, WE GIVE YOU A DECENT HEAD-START.
IF YOU MAKE IT TO THE RIDGE-LINE, YOU'RE FREE.
YOU'LL ALSO BE THE FIRST.

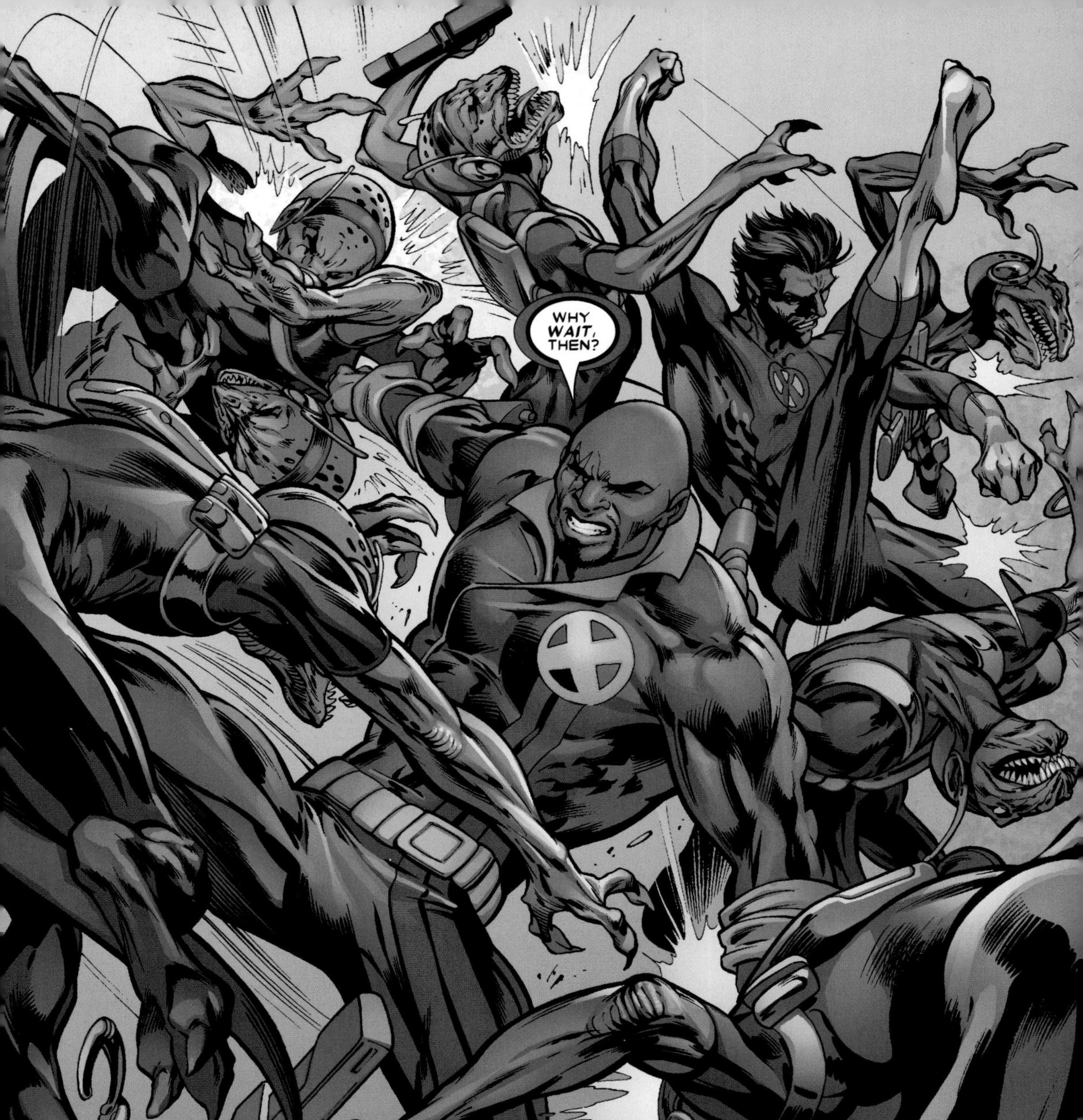
WHY WAIT, THEN?

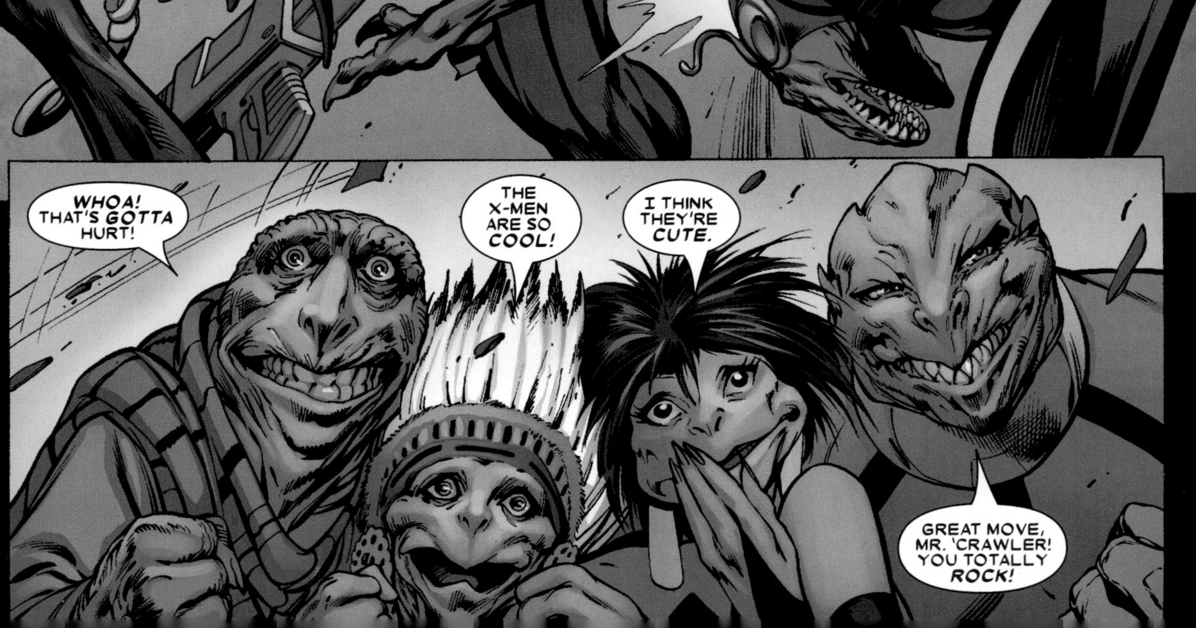
WHOA! THAT'S GOTTA HURT!
THE X-MEN ARE SO COOL!
I THINK THEY'RE CUTE.
GREAT MOVE, MR. 'CRAWLER! YOU TOTALLY ROCK!

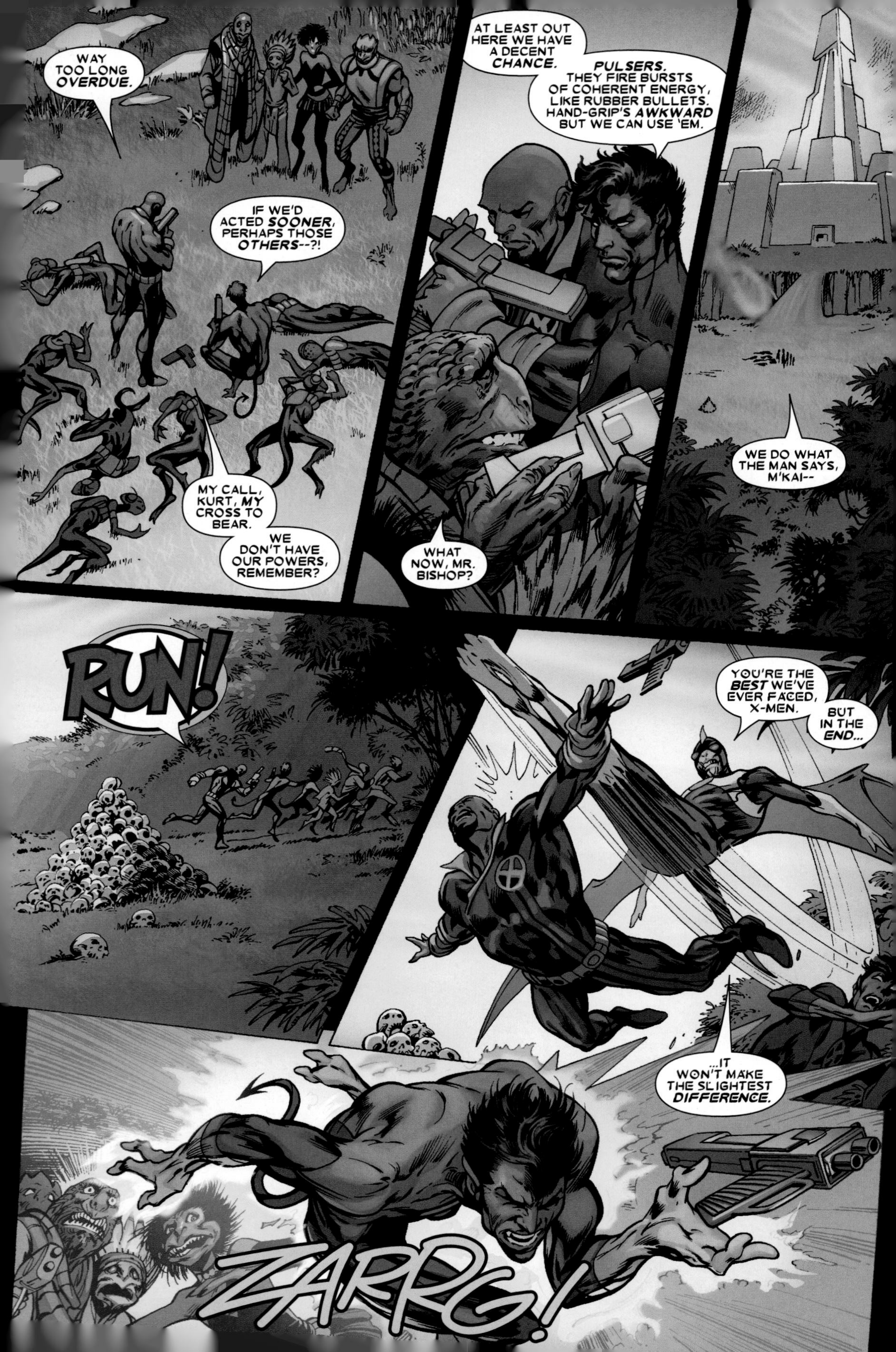
WAY TOO LONG OVERDUE.
IF WE'D ACTED SOONER, PERHAPS THOSE OTHERS--?!
MY CALL, KURT, MY CROSS TO BEAR.
WE DON'T HAVE OUR POWERS, REMEMBER?
AT LEAST OUT HERE WE HAVE A DECENT CHANCE.
PULSERS. THEY FIRE BURSTS OF COHERENT ENERGY, LIKE RUBBER BULLETS. HAND-GRIP'S AWKWARD BUT WE CAN USE 'EM.
WHAT NOW, MR. BISHOP?
WE DO WHAT THE MAN SAYS, M'KAI--
RUN!
YOU'RE THE BEST WE'VE EVER FACED, X-MEN.
BUT IN THE END...
...IT WON'T MAKE THE SLIGHTEST DIFFERENCE.
ZARRG!

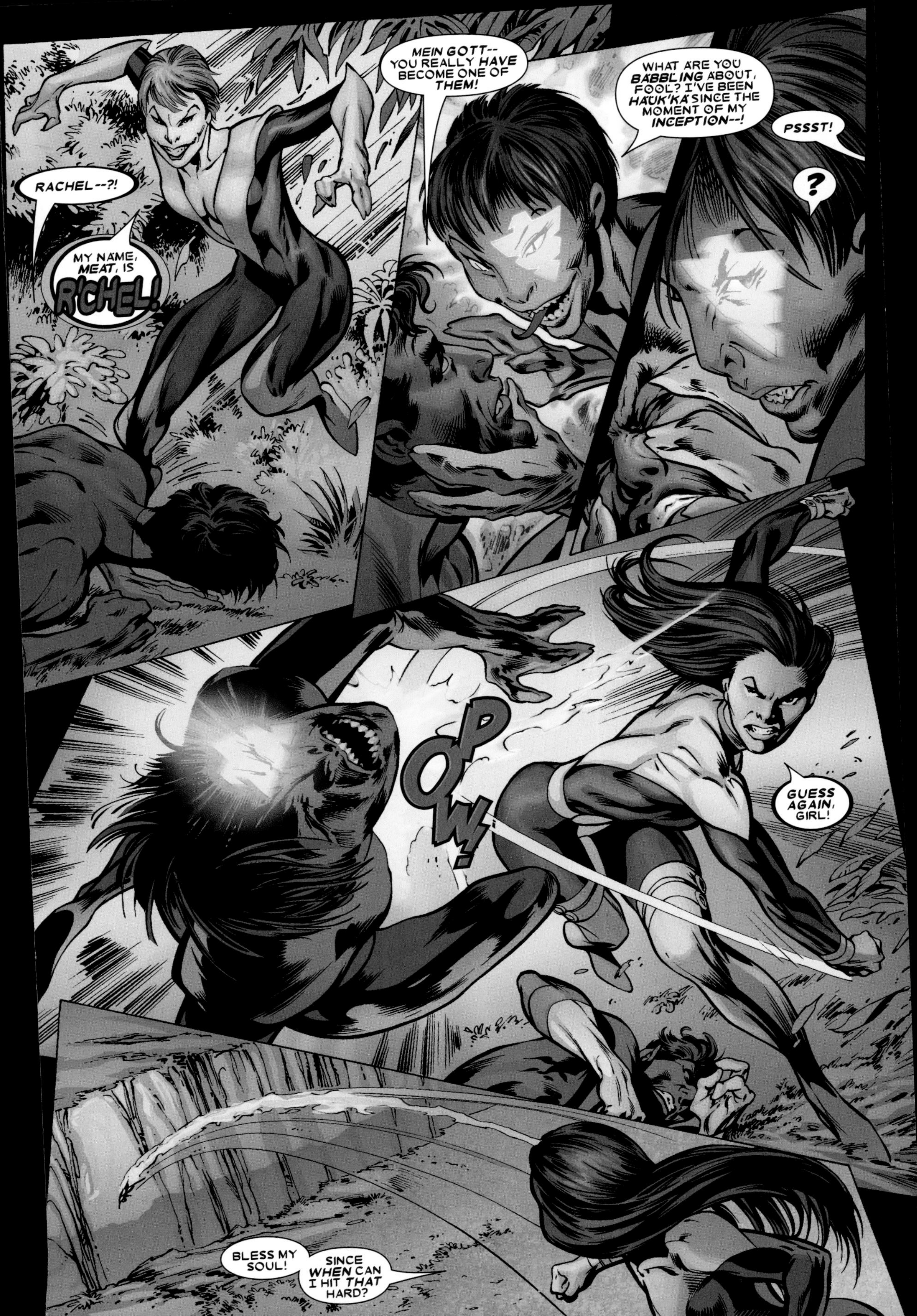

RACHEL--?!
MY NAME, MEAT, IS
R'CHEL!
MEIN GOTT-- YOU REALLY HAVE BECOME ONE OF THEM!
WHAT ARE YOU BABBLING ABOUT, FOOL? I'VE BEEN HAUK'KA SINCE THE MOMENT OF MY INCEPTION--!
PSSST!
?
POW!
GUESS AGAIN, GIRL!
BLESS MY SOUL!
SINCE WHEN CAN I HIT THAT HARD?

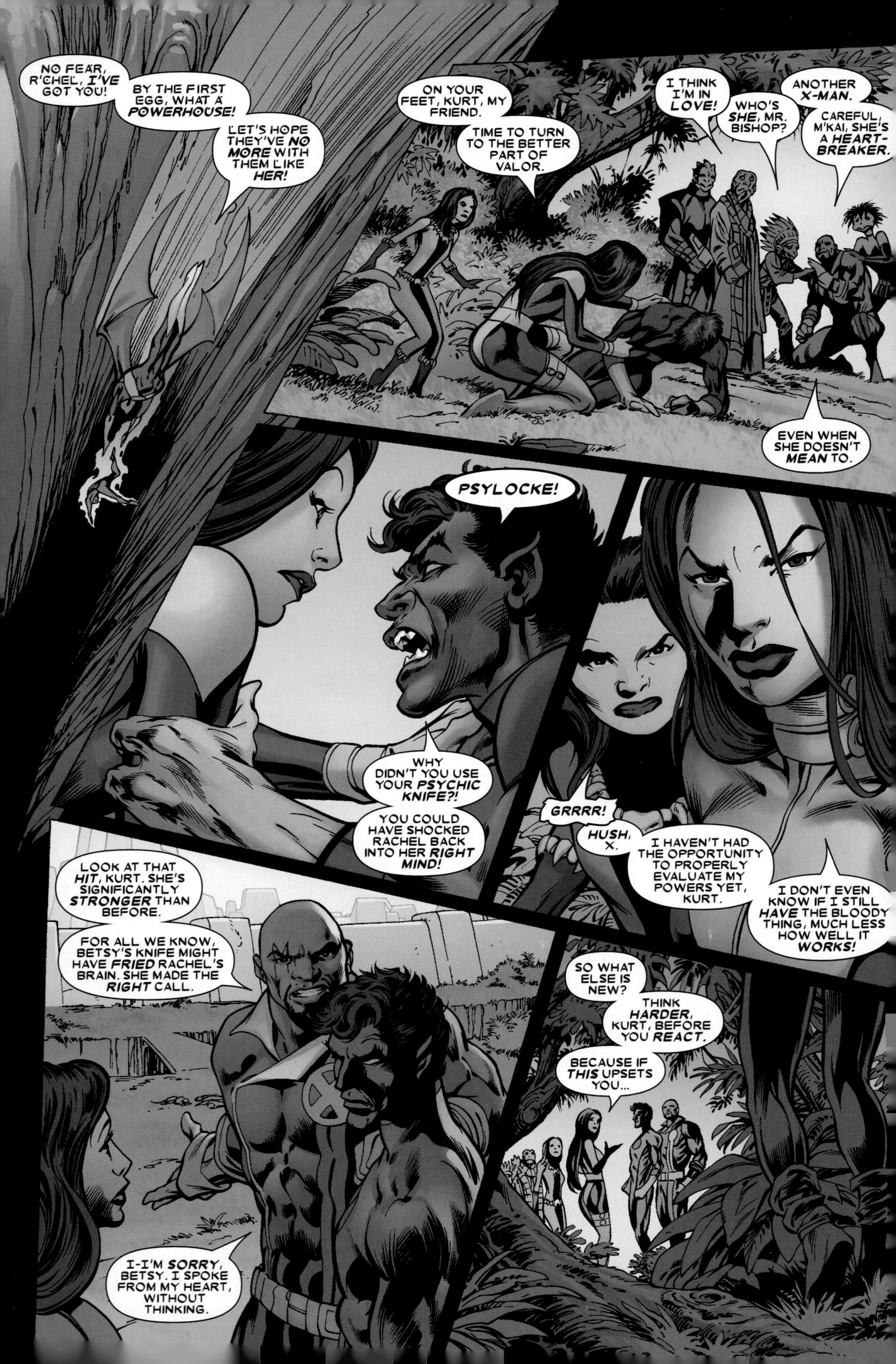

NO FEAR, R'CHEL, I'VE GOT YOU!
BY THE FIRST EGG, WHAT A POWERHOUSE!
LET'S HOPE THEY'VE NO MORE WITH THEM LIKE HER!
ON YOUR FEET, KURT, MY FRIEND.
TIME TO TURN TO THE BETTER PART OF VALOR.
I THINK I'M IN LOVE!
WHO'S SHE, MR. BISHOP?
ANOTHER X-MAN.
CAREFUL, M'KAI, SHE'S A HEART-BREAKER.
EVEN WHEN SHE DOESN'T MEAN TO.
PSYLOCKE!
WHY DIDN'T YOU USE YOUR PSYCHIC KNIFE?!
YOU COULD HAVE SHOCKED RACHEL BACK INTO HER RIGHT MIND!
GRRRR!
HUSH, X.
I HAVEN'T HAD THE OPPORTUNITY TO PROPERLY EVALUATE MY POWERS YET, KURT.
I DON'T EVEN KNOW IF I STILL HAVE THE BLOODY THING, MUCH LESS HOW WELL IT WORKS!
LOOK AT THAT HIT, KURT. SHE'S SIGNIFICANTLY STRONGER THAN BEFORE.
FOR ALL WE KNOW, BETSY'S KNIFE MIGHT HAVE FRIED RACHEL'S BRAIN. SHE MADE THE RIGHT CALL.
I-I'M SORRY, BETSY. I SPOKE FROM MY HEART, WITHOUT THINKING.
SO WHAT ELSE IS NEW?
THINK HARDER, KURT, BEFORE YOU REACT.
BECAUSE IF THIS UPSETS YOU...

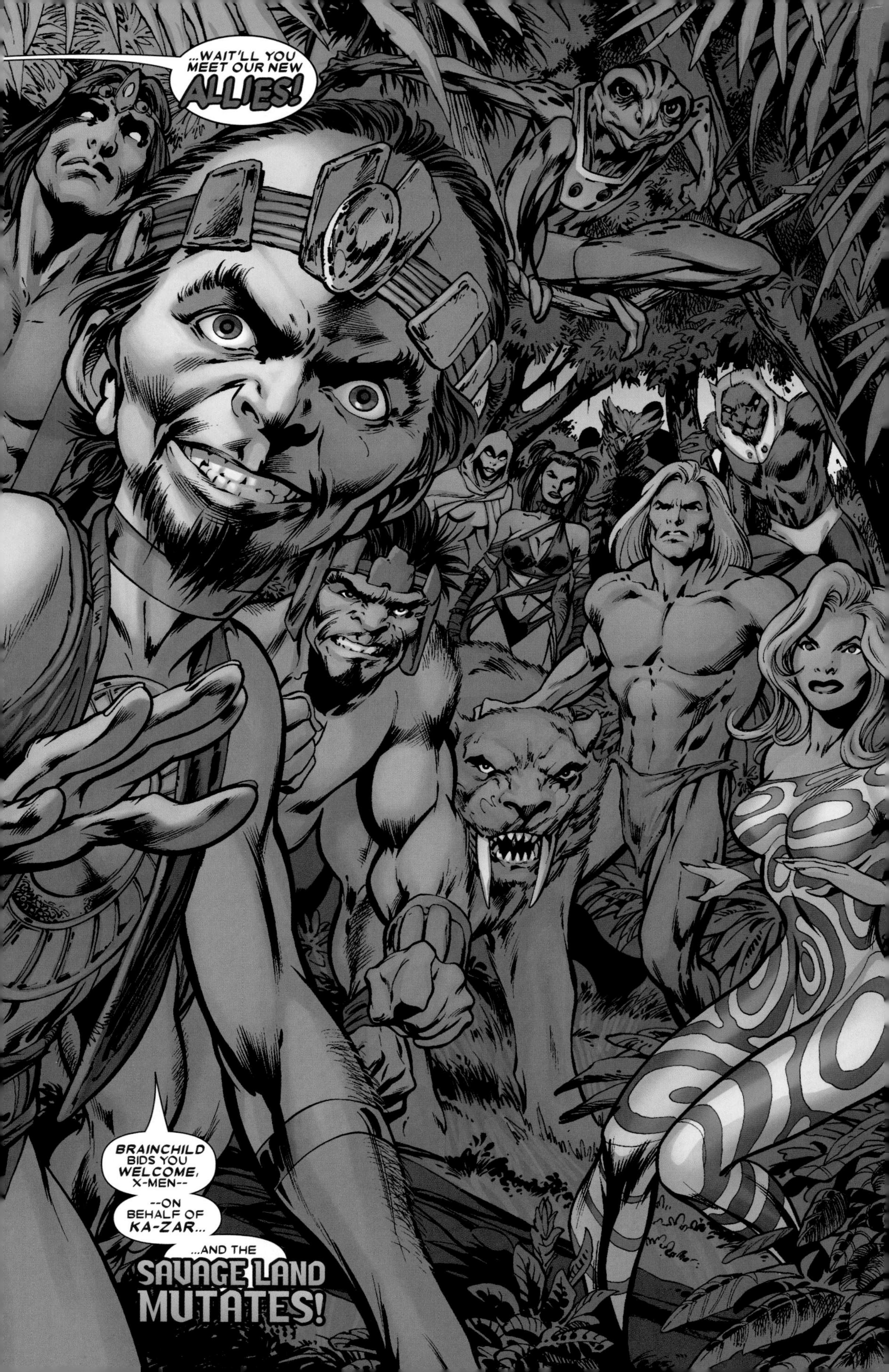
...WAIT'LL YOU MEET OUR NEW ALLIES!
BRAINCHILD BIDS YOU WELCOME, X-MEN--
--ON BEHALF OF KA-ZAR...
...AND THE
SAVAGE LAND MUTATES!

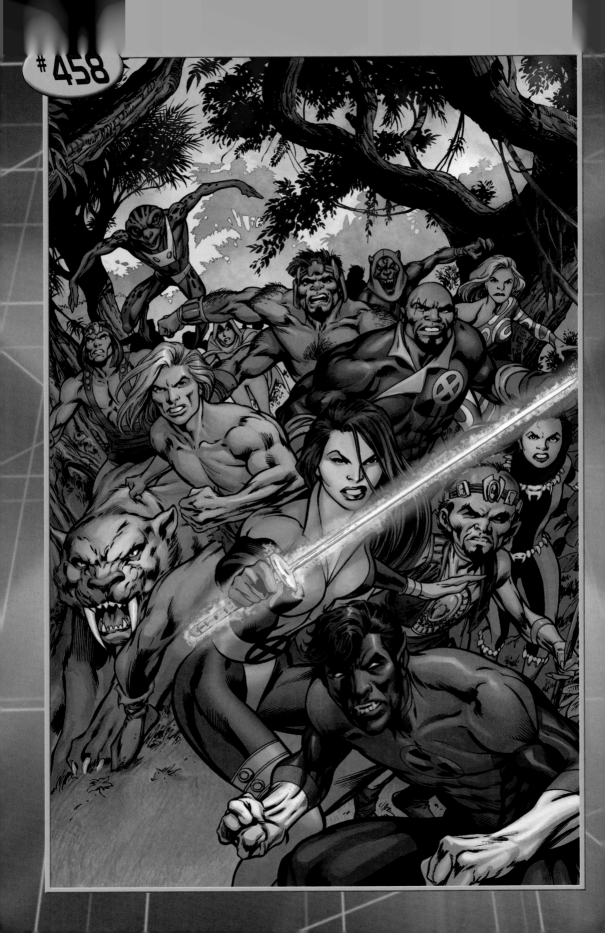

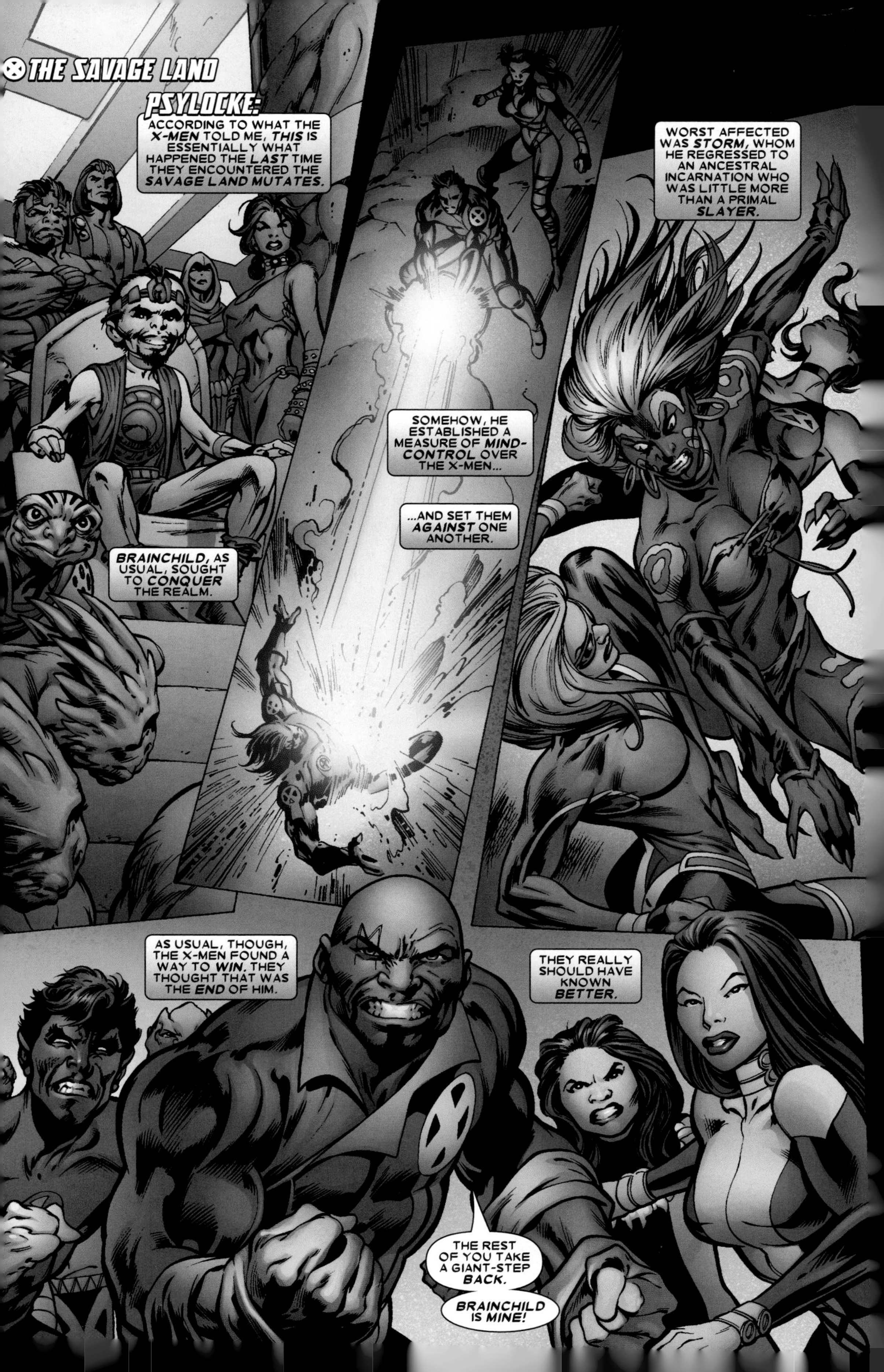
THE SAVAGE LAND
PSYLOCKE:
ACCORDING TO WHAT THE X-MEN TOLD ME, THIS IS ESSENTIALLY WHAT HAPPENED THE LAST TIME THEY ENCOUNTERED THE SAVAGE LAND MUTATES.
BRAINCHILD, AS USUAL, SOUGHT TO CONQUER THE REALM.
SOMEHOW, HE ESTABLISHED A MEASURE OF MIND-CONTROL OVER THE X-MEN...
...AND SET THEM AGAINST ONE ANOTHER.
WORST AFFECTED WAS STORM, WHOM HE REGRESSED TO AN ANCESTRAL INCARNATION WHO WAS LITTLE MORE THAN A PRIMAL SLAYER.
AS USUAL, THOUGH, THE X-MEN FOUND A WAY TO WIN. THEY THOUGHT THAT WAS THE END OF HIM.
THEY REALLY SHOULD HAVE KNOWN BETTER.
THE REST OF YOU TAKE A GIANT-STEP BACK.
BRAINCHILD IS MINE!

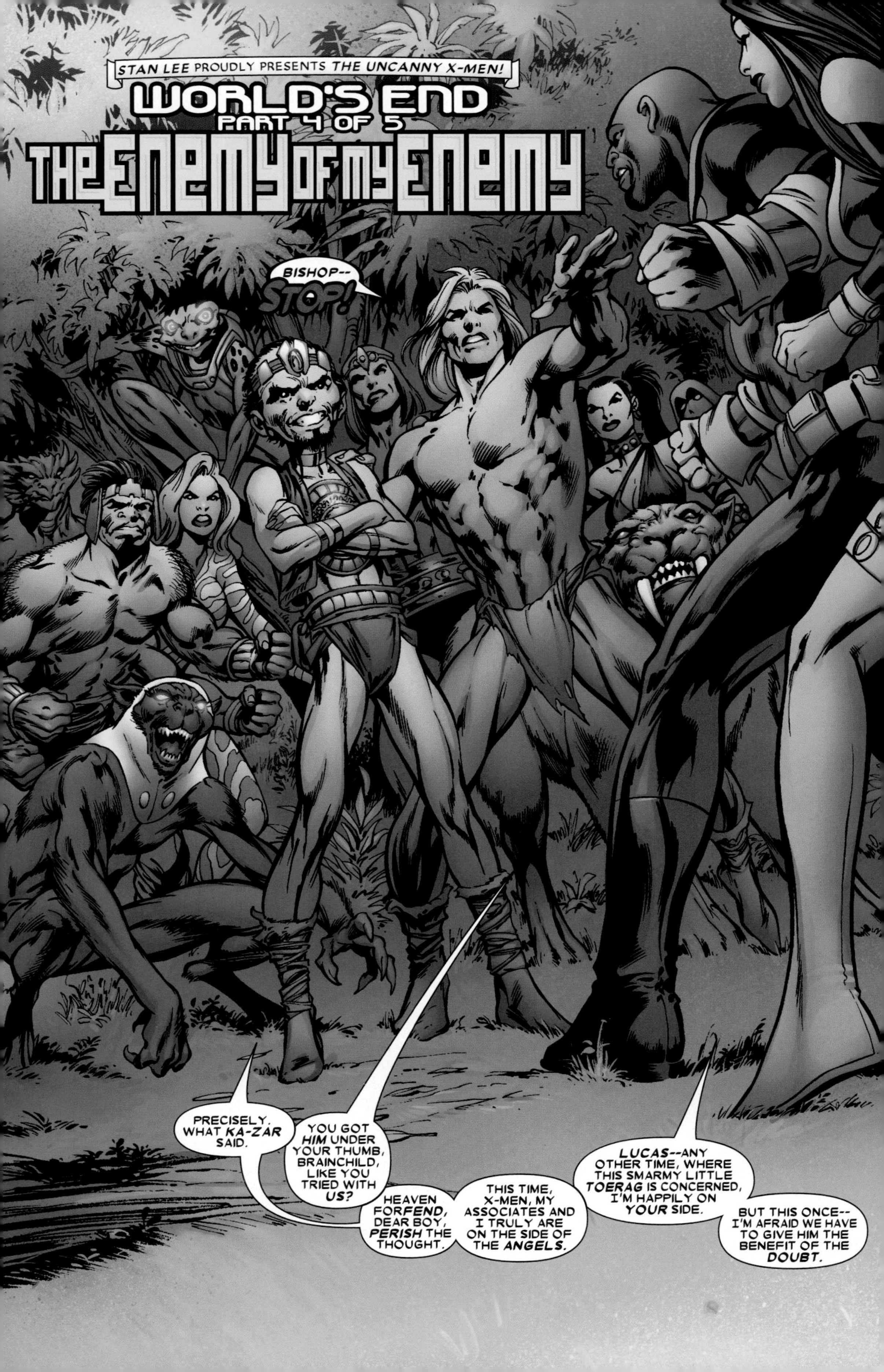
STAN LEE PROUDLY PRESENTS THE UNCANNY X-MEN!
WORLD'S END
PART 4 OF 5
THE ENEMY OF MY ENEMY
BISHOP-- STOP!
PRECISELY. WHAT KA-ZAR SAID.
YOU GOT HIM UNDER YOUR THUMB, BRAINCHILD, LIKE YOU TRIED WITH US?
HEAVEN FORFEND, DEAR BOY, PERISH THE THOUGHT.
THIS TIME, X-MEN, MY ASSOCIATES AND I TRULY ARE ON THE SIDE OF THE ANGELS.
LUCAS--ANY OTHER TIME, WHERE THIS SMARMY LITTLE TOERAG IS CONCERNED, I'M HAPPILY ON YOUR SIDE.
BUT THIS ONCE-- I'M AFRAID WE HAVE TO GIVE HIM THE BENEFIT OF THE DOUBT.

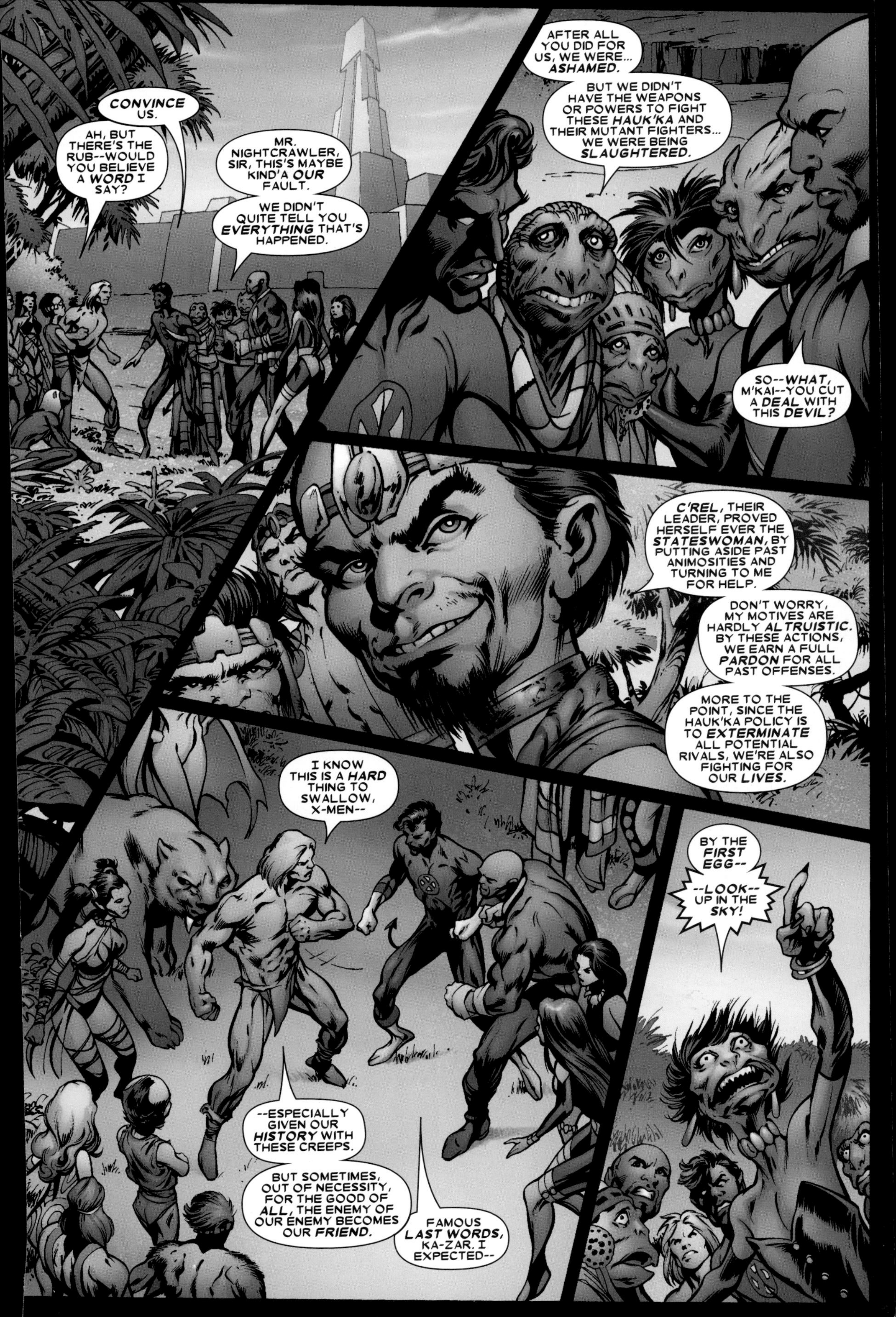
CONVINCE US.
AH, BUT THERE'S THE RUB--WOULD YOU BELIEVE A WORD I SAY?
MR. NIGHTCRAWLER, SIR, THIS'S MAYBE KIND'A OUR FAULT.
WE DIDN'T QUITE TELL YOU EVERYTHING THAT'S HAPPENED.
AFTER ALL YOU DID FOR US, WE WERE... ASHAMED.
BUT WE DIDN'T HAVE THE WEAPONS OR POWERS TO FIGHT THESE HAUK'KA AND THEIR MUTANT FIGHTERS... WE WERE BEING SLAUGHTERED.
SO--WHAT, M'KAI--YOU CUT A DEAL WITH THIS DEVIL?
C'REL, THEIR LEADER, PROVED HERSELF EVER THE STATESWOMAN, BY PUTTING ASIDE PAST ANIMOSITIES AND TURNING TO ME FOR HELP.
DON'T WORRY, MY MOTIVES ARE HARDLY ALTRUISTIC. BY THESE ACTIONS, WE EARN A FULL PARDON FOR ALL PAST OFFENSES.
MORE TO THE POINT, SINCE THE HAUK'KA POLICY IS TO EXTERMINATE ALL POTENTIAL RIVALS, WE'RE ALSO FIGHTING FOR OUR LIVES.
I KNOW THIS IS A HARD THING TO SWALLOW, X-MEN--
--ESPECIALLY GIVEN OUR HISTORY WITH THESE CREEPS.
BUT SOMETIMES, OUT OF NECESSITY, FOR THE GOOD OF ALL, THE ENEMY OF OUR ENEMY BECOMES OUR FRIEND.
FAMOUS LAST WORDS, KA-ZAR. I EXPECTED--
BY THE FIRST EGG--
--LOOK-- UP IN THE SKY!

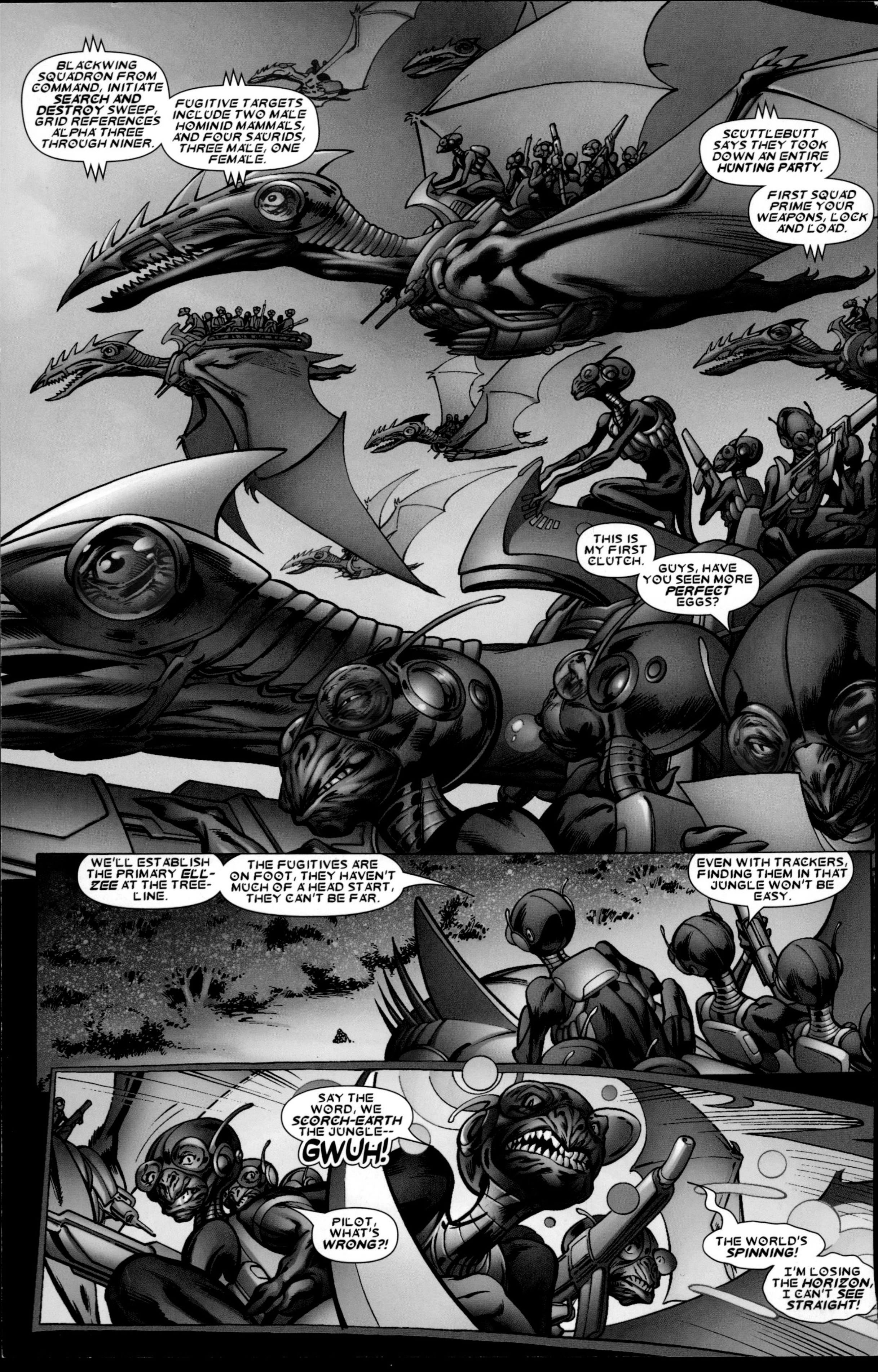
BLACKWING SQUADRON FROM COMMAND, INITIATE SEARCH AND DESTROY SWEEP, GRID REFERENCES ALPHA THREE THROUGH NINER.
FUGITIVE TARGETS INCLUDE TWO MALE HOMINID MAMMALS, AND FOUR SAURIDS, THREE MALE, ONE FEMALE.
SCUTTLEBUTT SAYS THEY TOOK DOWN AN ENTIRE HUNTING PARTY.
FIRST SQUAD PRIME YOUR WEAPONS, LOCK AND LOAD.
THIS IS MY FIRST CLUTCH.
GUYS, HAVE YOU SEEN MORE PERFECT EGGS?
WE'LL ESTABLISH THE PRIMARY ELL-ZEE AT THE TREE-LINE.
THE FUGITIVES ARE ON FOOT, THEY HAVEN'T MUCH OF A HEAD START, THEY CAN'T BE FAR.
EVEN WITH TRACKERS, FINDING THEM IN THAT JUNGLE WON'T BE EASY.
SAY THE WORD, WE SCORCH-EARTH THE JUNGLE--
GWUH!
PILOT, WHAT'S WRONG?!
THE WORLD'S SPINNING!
I'M LOSING THE HORIZON, I CAN'T SEE STRAIGHT!

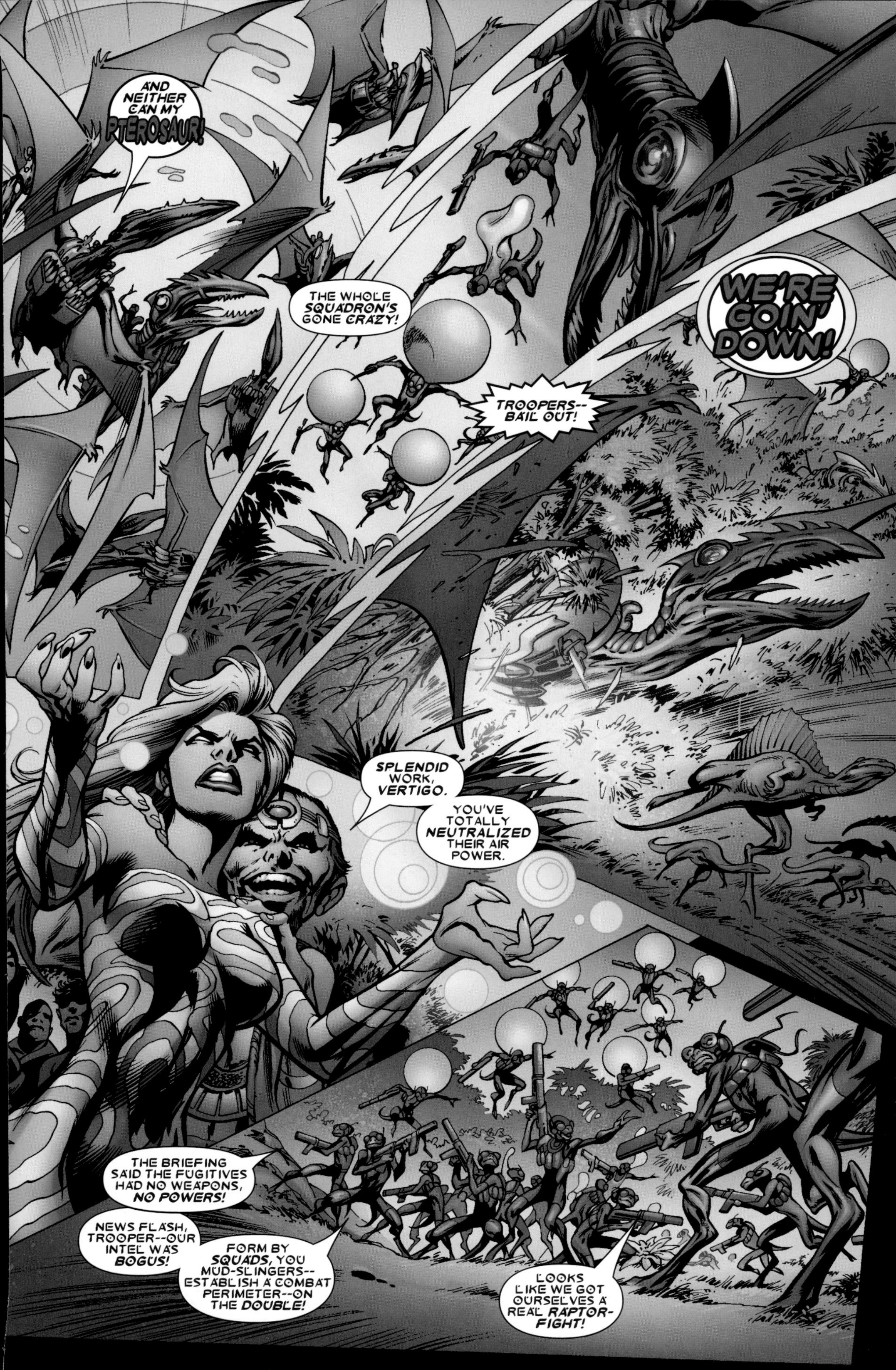
AND NEITHER CAN MY PTEROSAUR!
THE WHOLE SQUADRON'S GONE CRAZY!
WE'RE GOIN' DOWN!
TROOPERS-- BAIL OUT!
SPLENDID WORK, VERTIGO.
YOU'VE TOTALLY NEUTRALIZED THEIR AIR POWER.
THE BRIEFING SAID THE FUGITIVES HAD NO WEAPONS, NO POWERS!
NEWS FLASH, TROOPER--OUR INTEL WAS BOGUS!
FORM BY SQUADS, YOU MUD-SLINGERS-- ESTABLISH A COMBAT PERIMETER--ON THE DOUBLE!
LOOKS LIKE WE GOT OURSELVES A REAL RAPTOR-FIGHT!

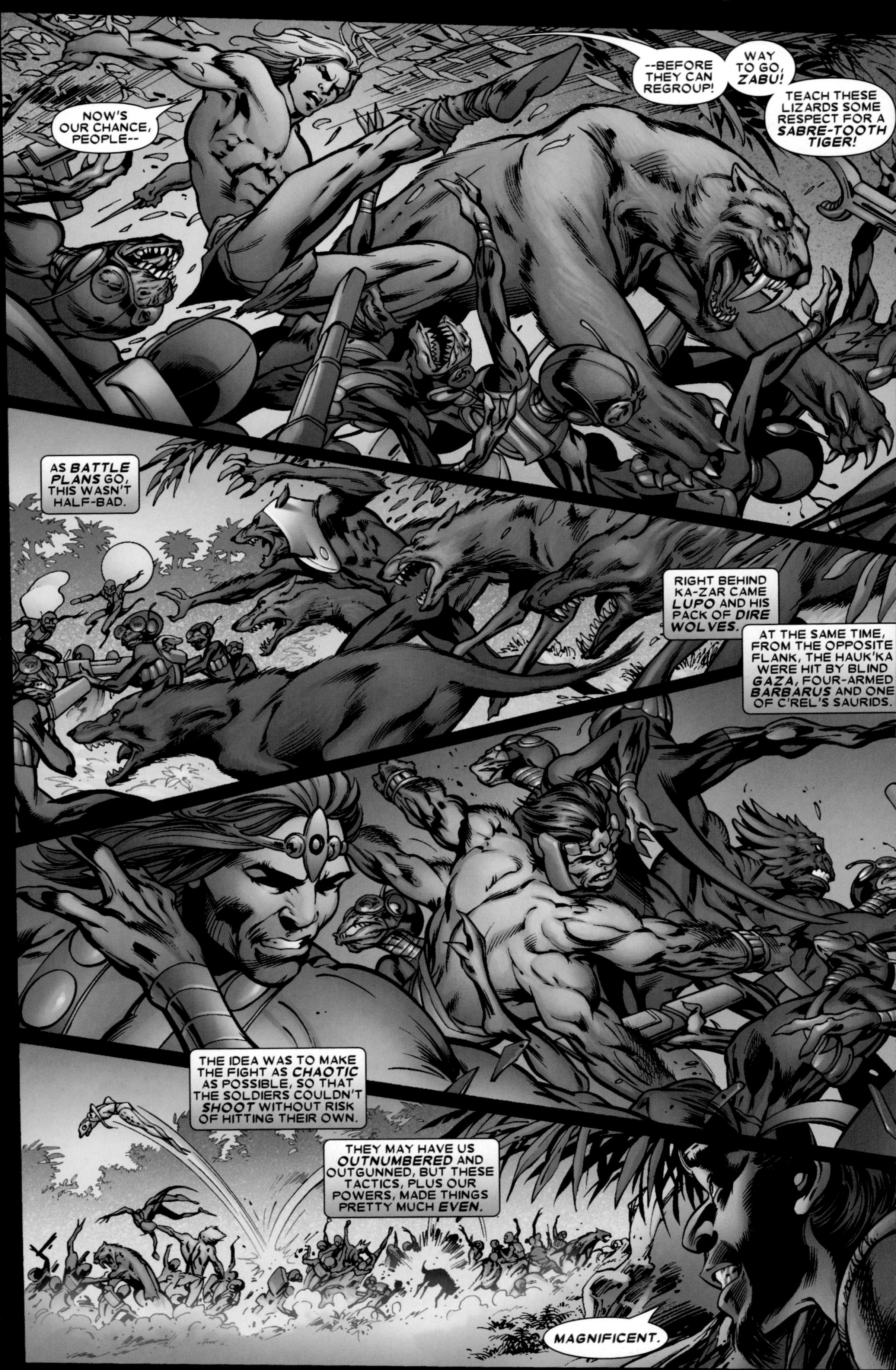
NOW'S OUR CHANCE, PEOPLE--
--BEFORE THEY CAN REGROUP!
WAY TO GO, ZABU!
TEACH THESE LIZARDS SOME RESPECT FOR A SABRE-TOOTH TIGER!
AS BATTLE PLANS GO, THIS WASN'T HALF-BAD.
RIGHT BEHIND KA-ZAR CAME LUPO AND HIS PACK OF DIRE WOLVES.
AT THE SAME TIME, FROM THE OPPOSITE FLANK, THE HAUK'KA WERE HIT BY BLIND GAZA, FOUR-ARMED BARBARUS AND ONE OF C'REL'S SAURIDS.
THE IDEA WAS TO MAKE THE FIGHT AS CHAOTIC AS POSSIBLE, SO THAT THE SOLDIERS COULDN'T SHOOT WITHOUT RISK OF HITTING THEIR OWN.
THEY MAY HAVE US OUTNUMBERED AND OUTGUNNED, BUT THESE TACTICS, PLUS OUR POWERS, MADE THINGS PRETTY MUCH EVEN.
MAGNIFICENT.

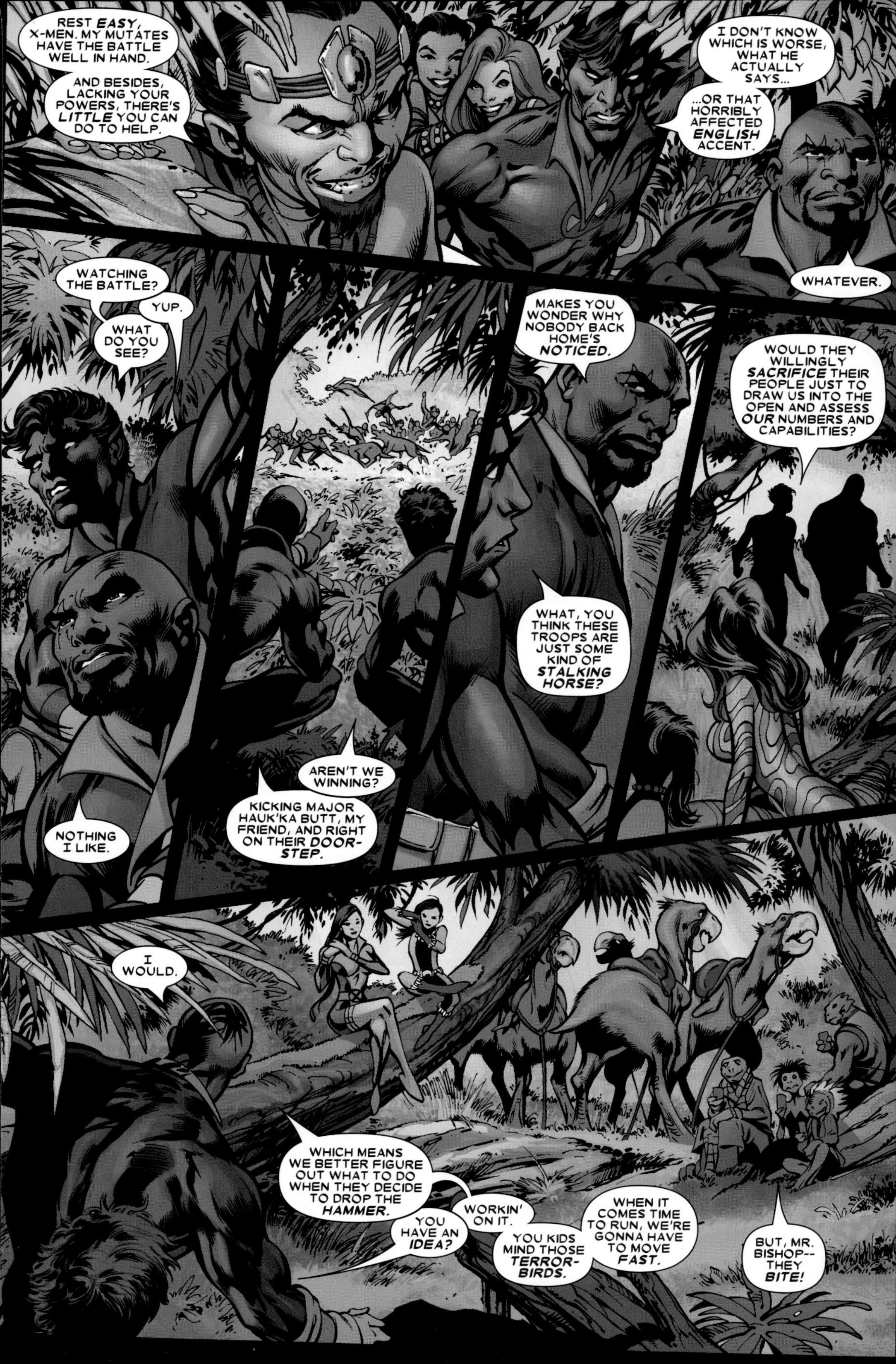
REST EASY, X-MEN. MY MUTATES HAVE THE BATTLE WELL IN HAND.
AND BESIDES, LACKING YOUR POWERS, THERE'S LITTLE YOU CAN DO TO HELP.
I DON'T KNOW WHICH IS WORSE, WHAT HE ACTUALLY SAYS...
...OR THAT HORRIBLY AFFECTED ENGLISH ACCENT.
WHATEVER.
WATCHING THE BATTLE?
YUP.
WHAT DO YOU SEE?
NOTHING I LIKE.
AREN'T WE WINNING?
KICKING MAJOR HAUK'KA BUTT, MY FRIEND, AND RIGHT ON THEIR DOOR-STEP.
MAKES YOU WONDER WHY NOBODY BACK HOME'S NOTICED.
WHAT, YOU THINK THESE TROOPS ARE JUST SOME KIND OF STALKING HORSE?
WOULD THEY WILLINGLY SACRIFICE THEIR PEOPLE JUST TO DRAW US INTO THE OPEN AND ASSESS OUR NUMBERS AND CAPABILITIES?
I WOULD.
WHICH MEANS WE BETTER FIGURE OUT WHAT TO DO WHEN THEY DECIDE TO DROP THE HAMMER.
YOU HAVE AN IDEA?
WORKIN' ON IT.
YOU KIDS MIND THOSE TERROR-BIRDS.
WHEN IT COMES TIME TO RUN, WE'RE GONNA HAVE TO MOVE FAST.
BUT, MR. BISHOP-- THEY BITE!

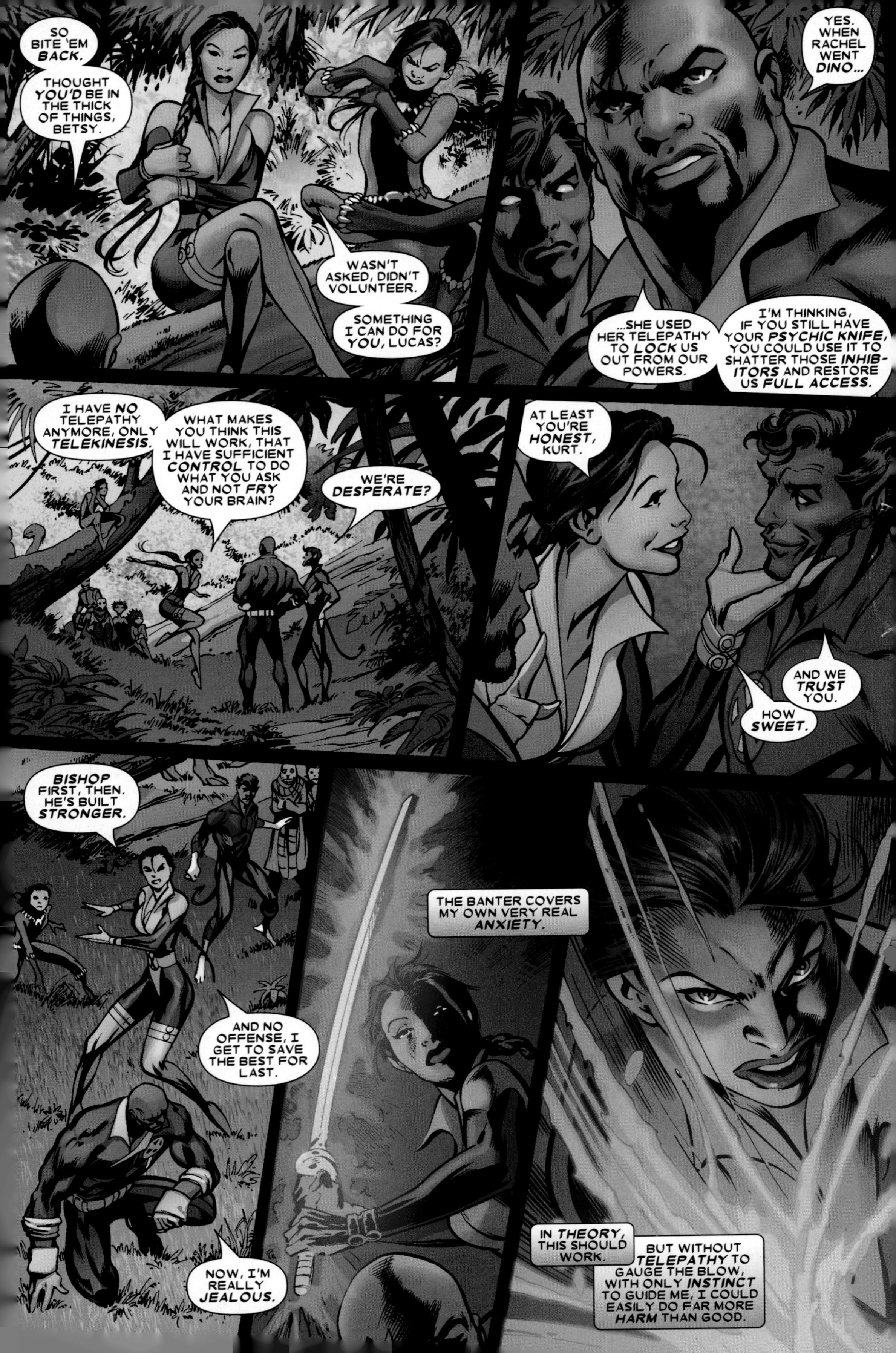
SO BITE 'EM BACK.
THOUGHT YOU'D BE IN THE THICK OF THINGS, BETSY.
WASN'T ASKED, DIDN'T VOLUNTEER.
SOMETHING I CAN DO FOR YOU, LUCAS?
YES. WHEN RACHEL WENT DINO...
...SHE USED HER TELEPATHY TO LOCK US OUT FROM OUR POWERS.
I'M THINKING, IF YOU STILL HAVE YOUR PSYCHIC KNIFE, YOU COULD USE IT TO SHATTER THOSE INHIBITORS AND RESTORE US FULL ACCESS.
I HAVE NO TELEPATHY ANYMORE, ONLY TELEKINESIS.
WHAT MAKES YOU THINK THIS WILL WORK, THAT I HAVE SUFFICIENT CONTROL TO DO WHAT YOU ASK AND NOT FRY YOUR BRAIN?
WE'RE DESPERATE?
AT LEAST YOU'RE HONEST, KURT.
AND WE TRUST YOU.
HOW SWEET.
BISHOP FIRST, THEN. HE'S BUILT STRONGER.
AND NO OFFENSE, I GET TO SAVE THE BEST FOR LAST.
NOW, I'M REALLY JEALOUS.
THE BANTER COVERS MY OWN VERY REAL ANXIETY.
IN THEORY, THIS SHOULD WORK.
BUT WITHOUT TELEPATHY TO GAUGE THE BLOW, WITH ONLY INSTINCT TO GUIDE ME, I COULD EASILY DO FAR MORE HARM THAN GOOD.

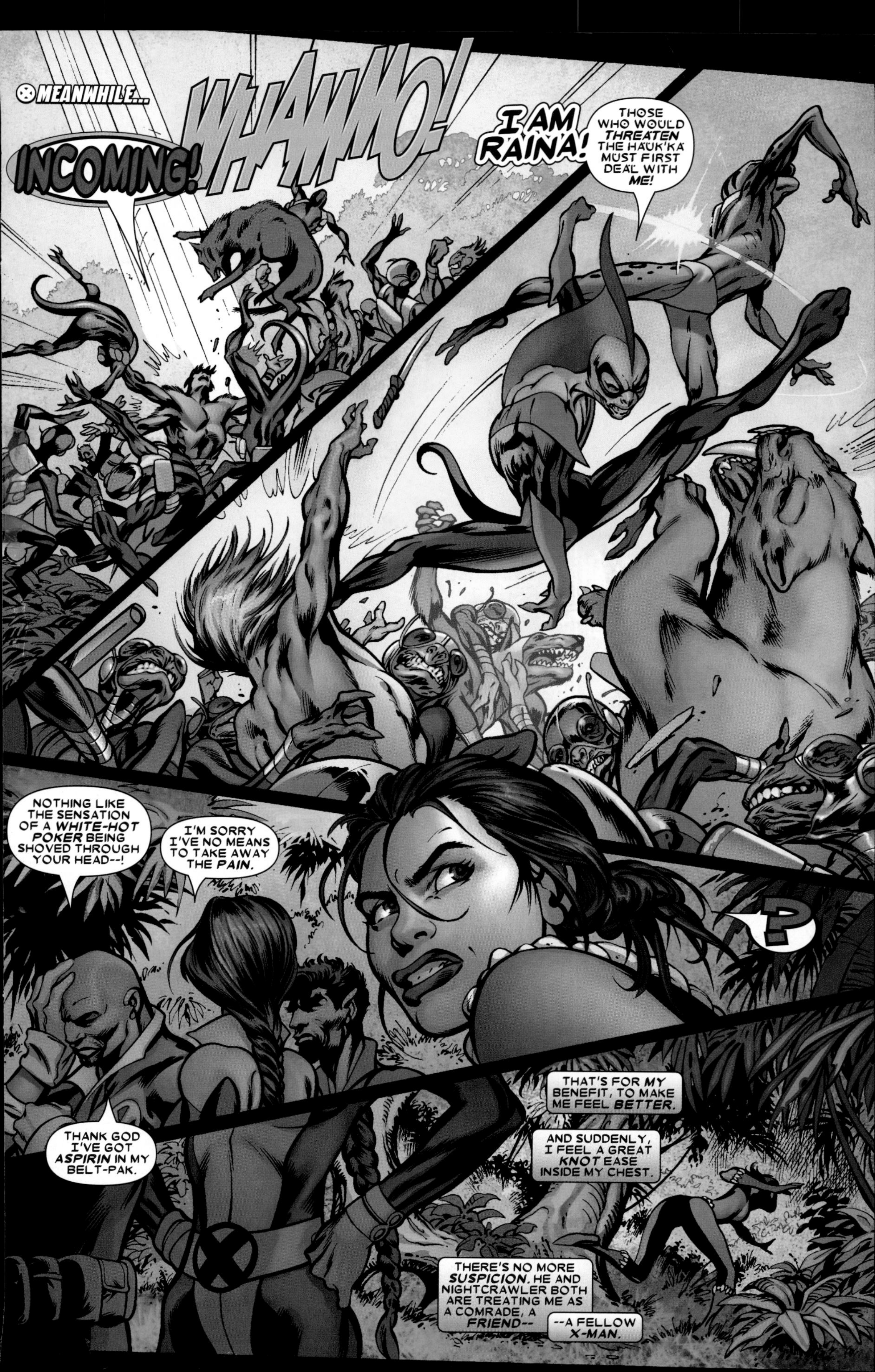
MEANWHILE...
INCOMING!
WHAMMO!
I AM RAINA!
THOSE WHO WOULD THREATEN THE HAUK'KA MUST FIRST DEAL WITH ME!
NOTHING LIKE THE SENSATION OF A WHITE-HOT POKER BEING SHOVED THROUGH YOUR HEAD--!
I'M SORRY I'VE NO MEANS TO TAKE AWAY THE PAIN.
?
THANK GOD I'VE GOT ASPIRIN IN MY BELT-PAK.
THAT'S FOR MY BENEFIT, TO MAKE ME FEEL BETTER.
AND SUDDENLY, I FEEL A GREAT KNOT EASE INSIDE MY CHEST.
THERE'S NO MORE SUSPICION. HE AND NIGHTCRAWLER BOTH ARE TREATING ME AS A COMRADE, A FRIEND--
--A FELLOW X-MAN.

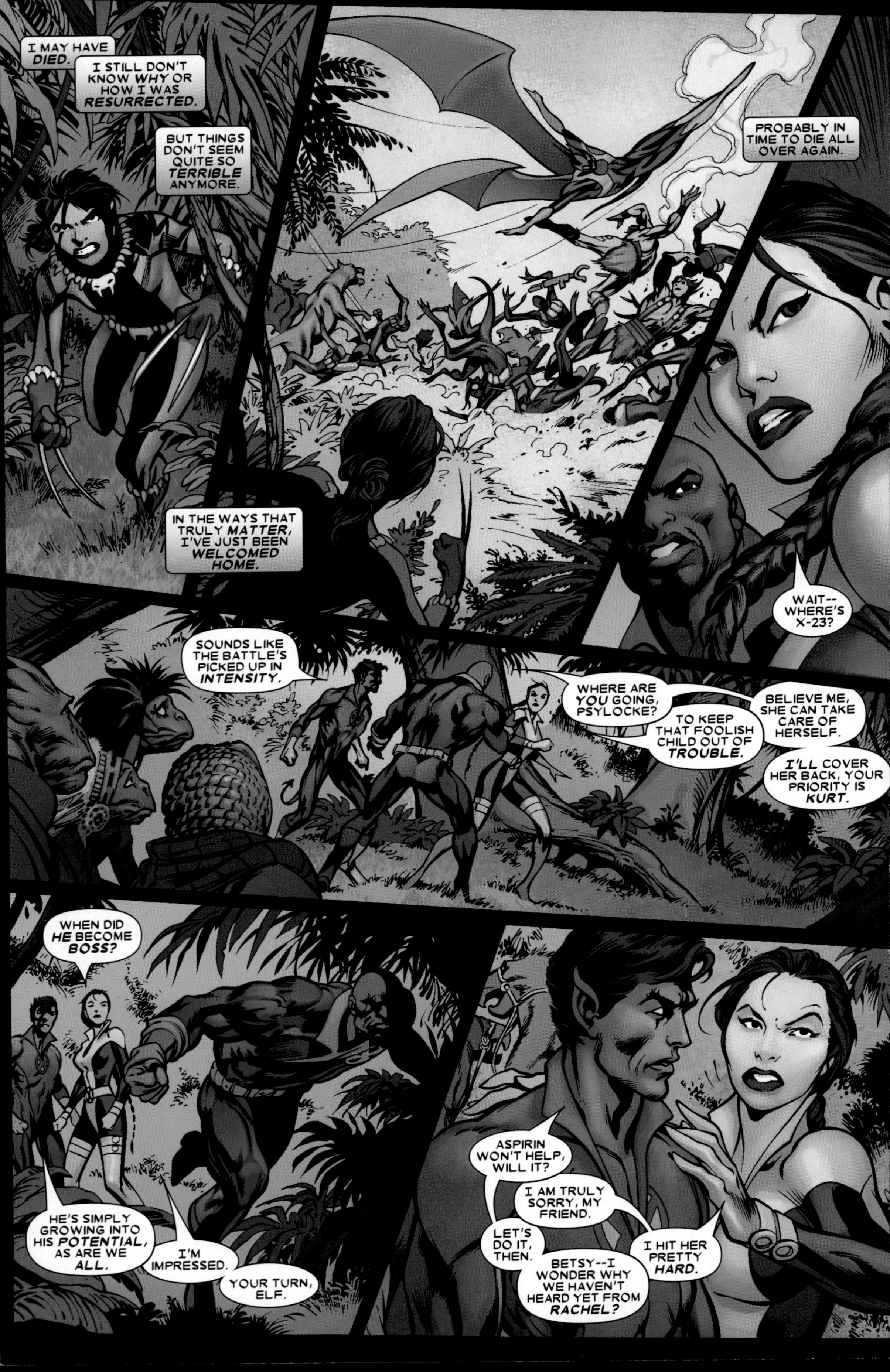
I MAY HAVE DIED.
I STILL DON'T KNOW WHY OR HOW I WAS RESURRECTED.
BUT THINGS DON'T SEEM QUITE SO TERRIBLE ANYMORE.
IN THE WAYS THAT TRULY MATTER, I'VE JUST BEEN WELCOMED HOME.
PROBABLY IN TIME TO DIE ALL OVER AGAIN.
WAIT-- WHERE'S X-23?
SOUNDS LIKE THE BATTLE'S PICKED UP IN INTENSITY.
WHERE ARE YOU GOING, PSYLOCKE?
TO KEEP THAT FOOLISH CHILD OUT OF TROUBLE.
BELIEVE ME, SHE CAN TAKE CARE OF HERSELF.
I'LL COVER HER BACK, YOUR PRIORITY IS KURT.
WHEN DID HE BECOME BOSS?
HE'S SIMPLY GROWING INTO HIS POTENTIAL, AS ARE WE ALL.
I'M IMPRESSED.
YOUR TURN, ELF.
ASPIRIN WON'T HELP, WILL IT?
I AM TRULY SORRY, MY FRIEND.
LET'S DO IT, THEN.
I HIT HER PRETTY HARD.
BETSY--I WONDER WHY WE HAVEN'T HEARD YET FROM RACHEL?

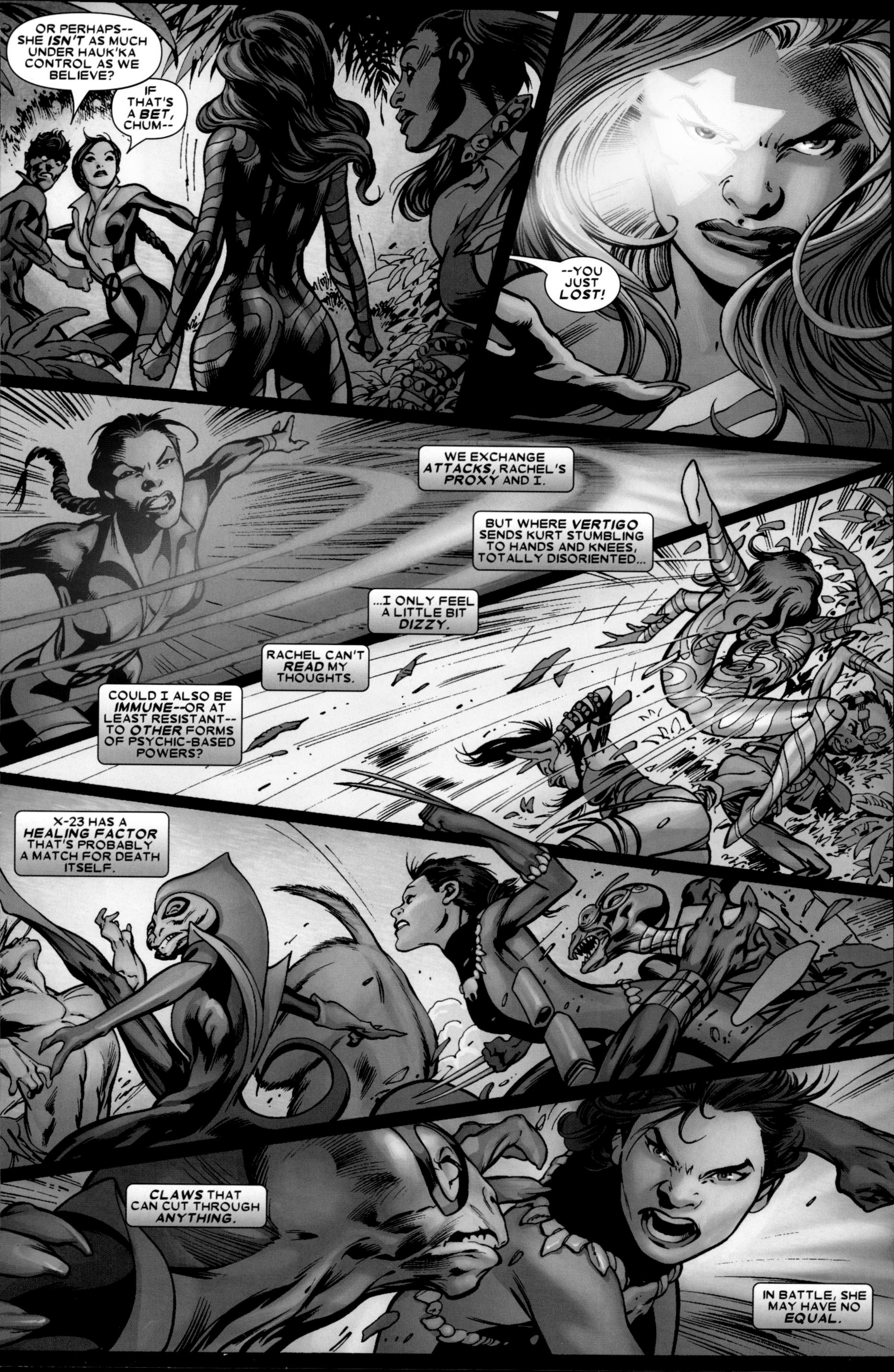
OR PERHAPS-- SHE ISN'T AS MUCH UNDER HAUK'KA CONTROL AS WE BELIEVE?
IF THAT'S A BET, CHUM--
--YOU JUST LOST!
WE EXCHANGE ATTACKS, RACHEL'S PROXY AND I.
BUT WHERE VERTIGO SENDS KURT STUMBLING TO HANDS AND KNEES, TOTALLY DISORIENTED...
...I ONLY FEEL A LITTLE BIT DIZZY.
RACHEL CAN'T READ MY THOUGHTS.
COULD I ALSO BE IMMUNE--OR AT LEAST RESISTANT-- TO OTHER FORMS OF PSYCHIC-BASED POWERS?
X-23 HAS A HEALING FACTOR THAT'S PROBABLY A MATCH FOR DEATH ITSELF.
CLAWS THAT CAN CUT THROUGH ANYTHING.
IN BATTLE, SHE MAY HAVE NO EQUAL.

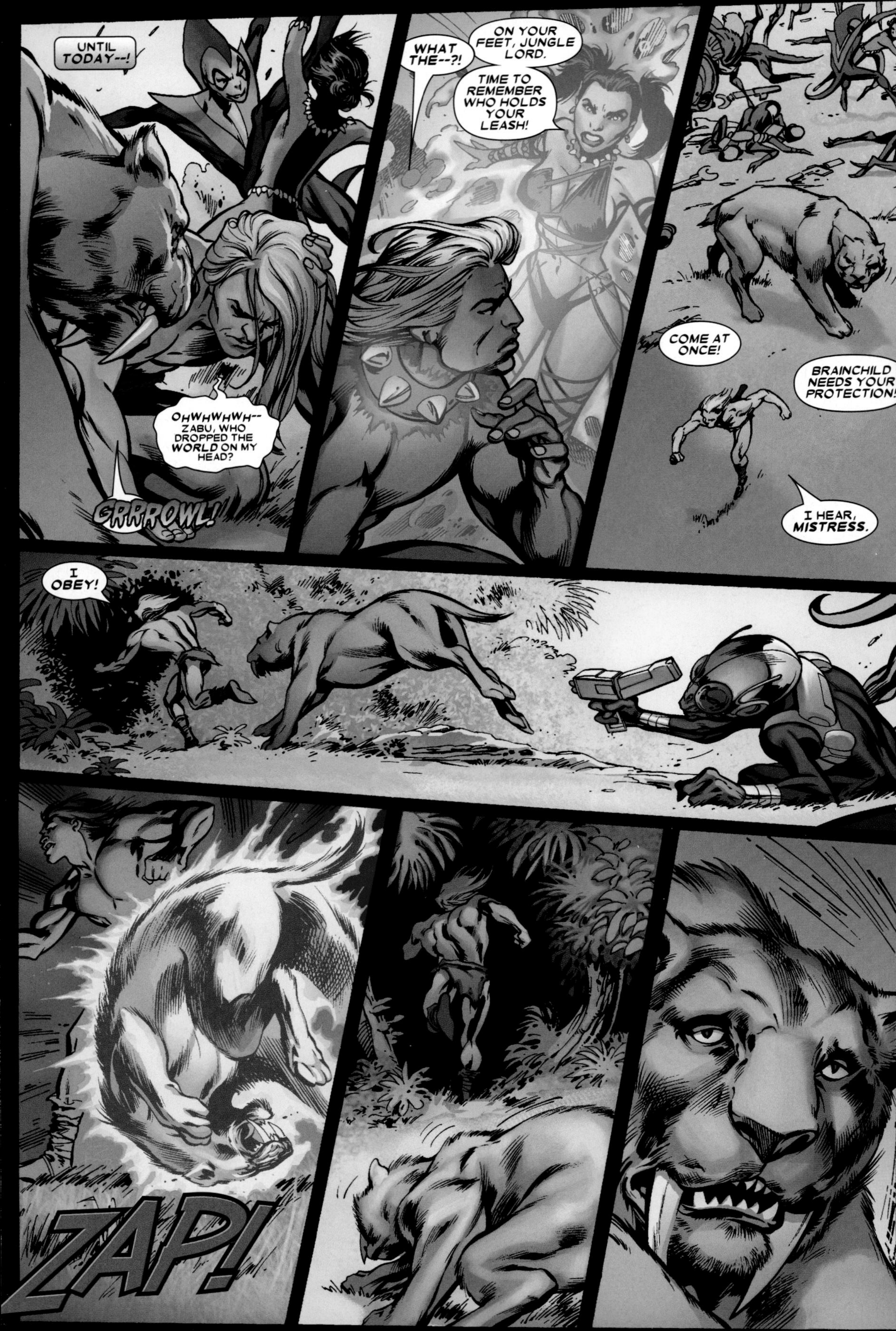

UNTIL TODAY--!
OHWHWHWH-- ZABU, WHO DROPPED THE WORLD ON MY HEAD?
GRRROWL!
WHAT THE--?!
ON YOUR FEET, JUNGLE LORD.
TIME TO REMEMBER WHO HOLDS YOUR LEASH!
COME AT ONCE!
BRAINCHILD NEEDS YOUR PROTECTION!
I HEAR, MISTRESS.
I OBEY!
ZAP!

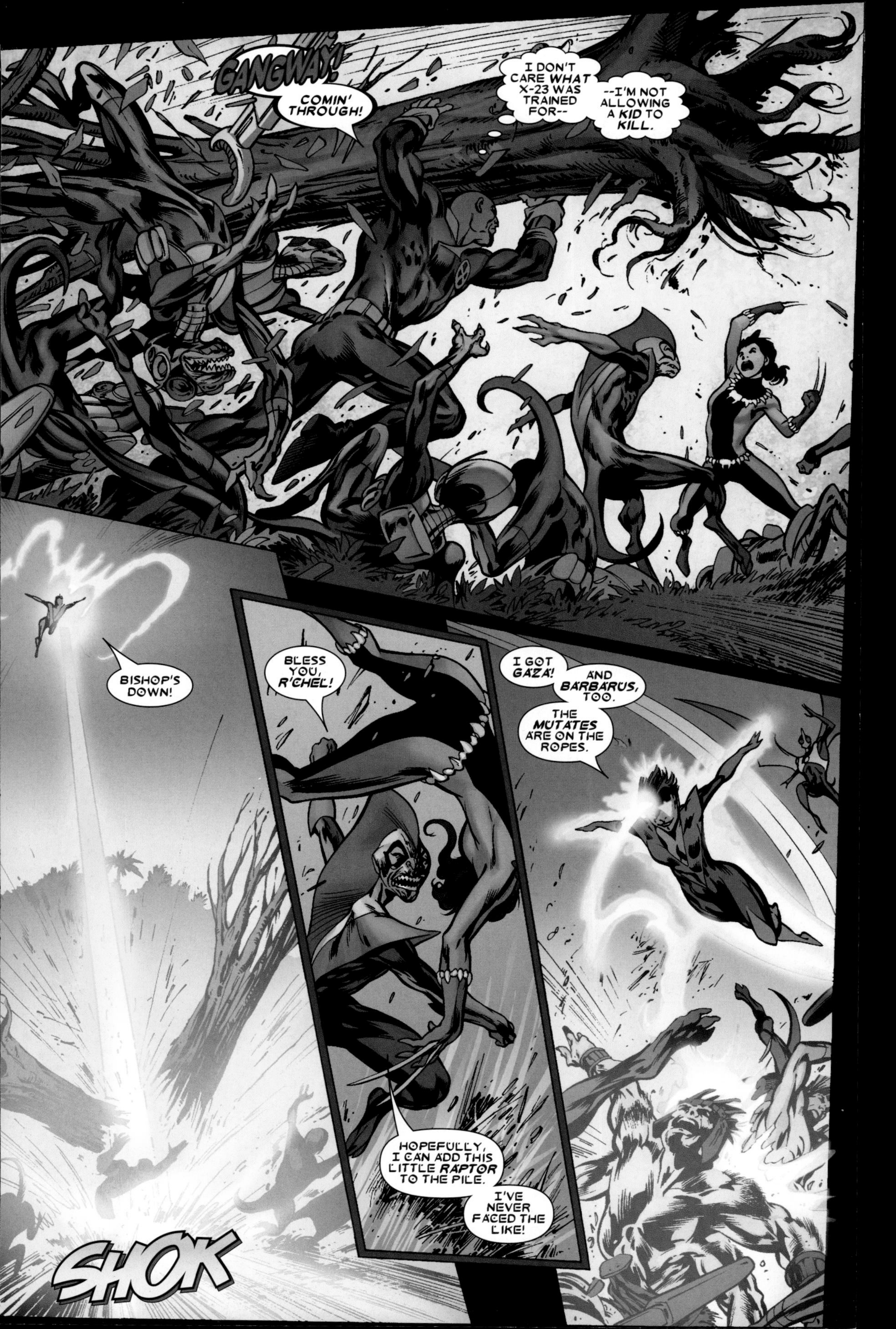
GANGWAY!
COMIN' THROUGH!
I DON'T CARE WHAT X-23 WAS TRAINED FOR--
--I'M NOT ALLOWING A KID TO KILL.
BISHOP'S DOWN!
BLESS YOU, R'CHEL!
I GOT GAZA!
AND BARBARUS, TOO.
THE MUTATES ARE ON THE ROPES.
HOPEFULLY, I CAN ADD THIS LITTLE RAPTOR TO THE PILE.
I'VE NEVER FACED THE LIKE!
SHOK

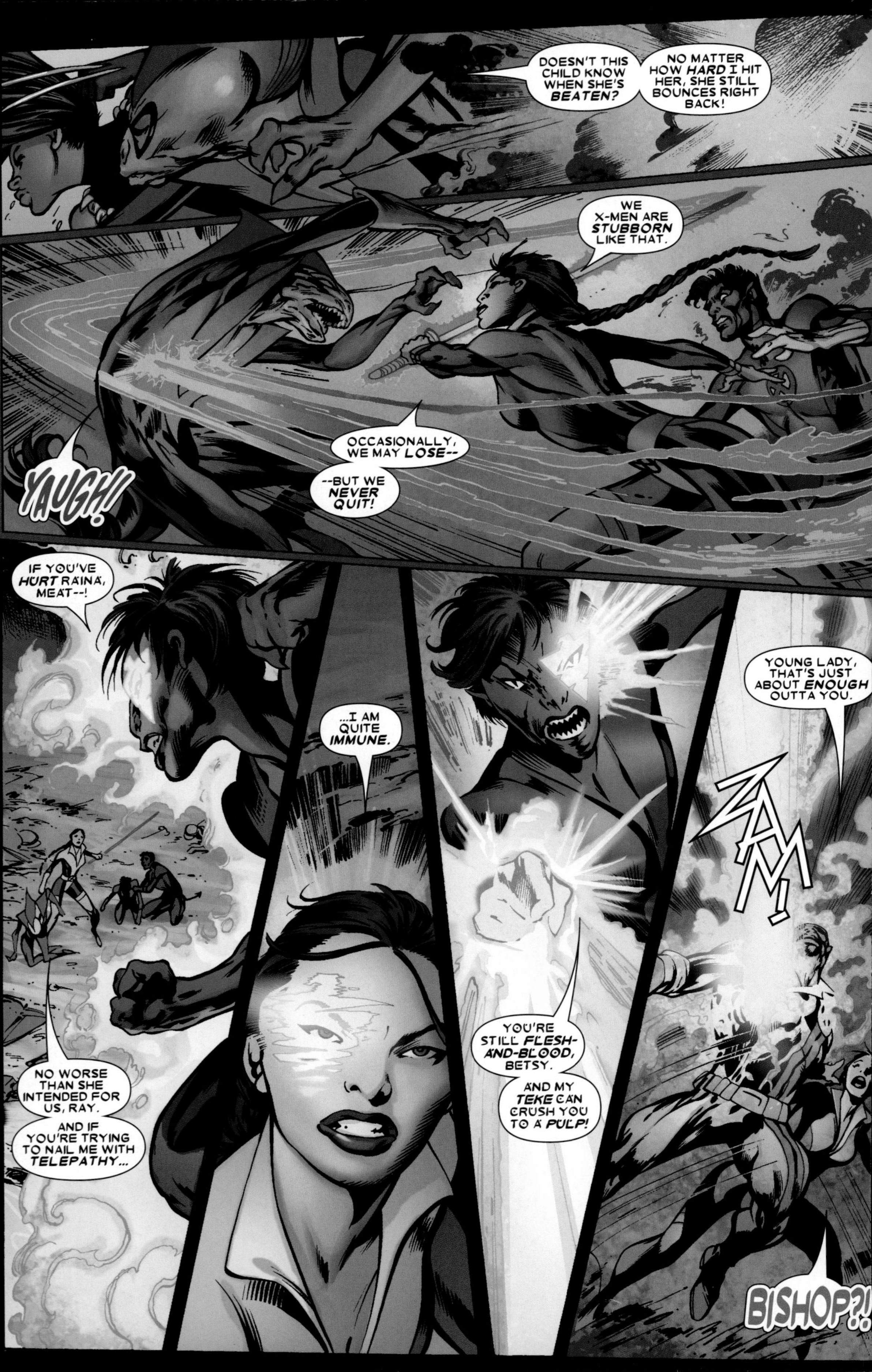
DOESN'T THIS CHILD KNOW WHEN SHE'S BEATEN?
NO MATTER HOW HARD I HIT HER, SHE STILL BOUNCES RIGHT BACK!
WE X-MEN ARE STUBBORN LIKE THAT.
OCCASIONALLY, WE MAY LOSE--
--BUT WE NEVER QUIT!
YAUGH!!
IF YOU'VE HURT RAINA, MEAT--!
NO WORSE THAN SHE INTENDED FOR US, RAY.
AND IF YOU'RE TRYING TO NAIL ME WITH TELEPATHY...
...I AM QUITE IMMUNE.
YOU'RE STILL FLESH-AND-BLOOD, BETSY.
AND MY TEKE CAN CRUSH YOU TO A PULP!
YOUNG LADY, THAT'S JUST ABOUT ENOUGH OUTTA YOU.
ZZAM!
BISHOP?!

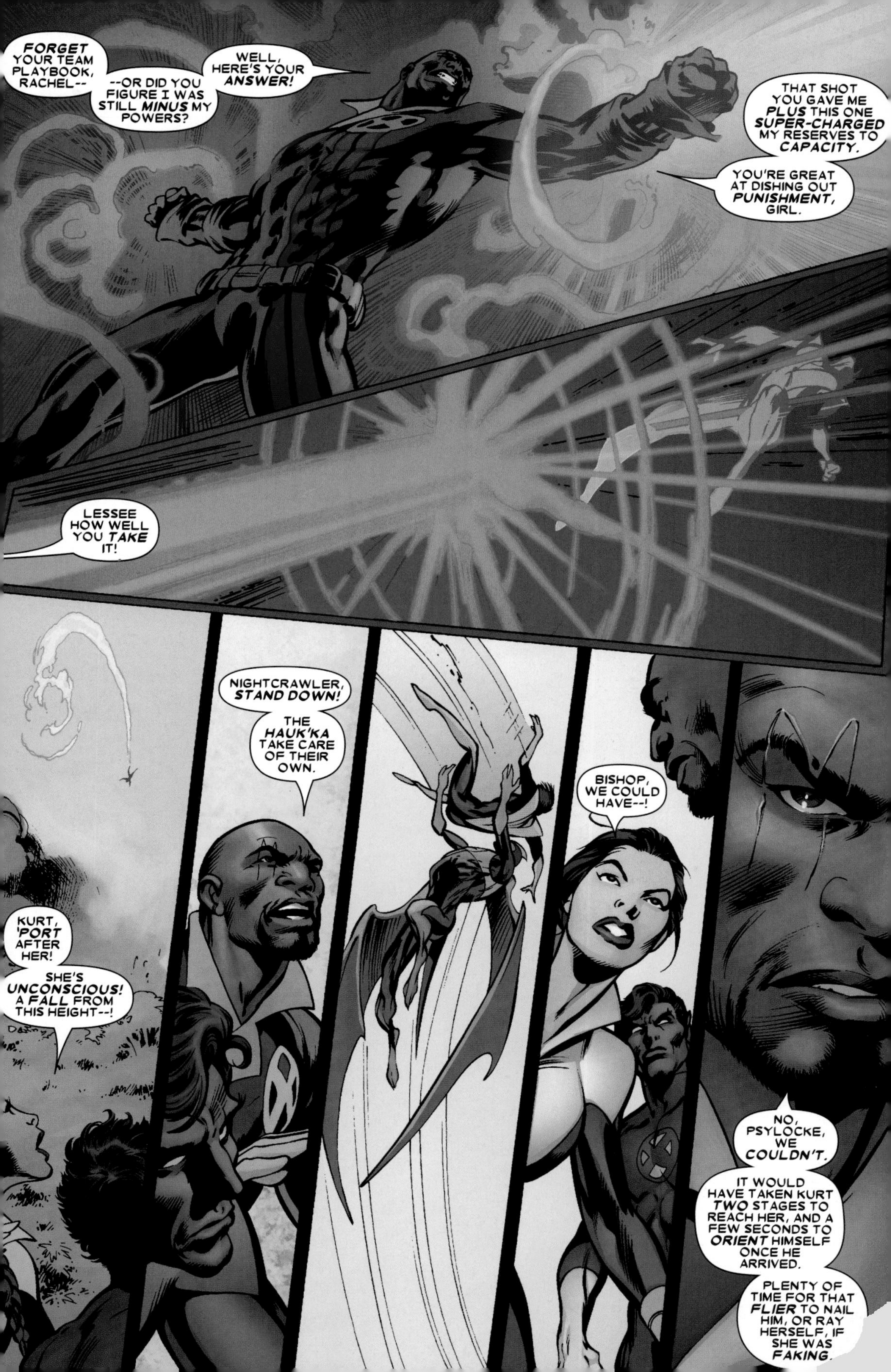
FORGET YOUR TEAM PLAYBOOK, RACHEL--
--OR DID YOU FIGURE I WAS STILL MINUS MY POWERS?
WELL, HERE'S YOUR ANSWER!
THAT SHOT YOU GAVE ME PLUS THIS ONE SUPER-CHARGED MY RESERVES TO CAPACITY.
YOU'RE GREAT AT DISHING OUT PUNISHMENT, GIRL.
LESSEE HOW WELL YOU TAKE IT!
KURT, 'PORT AFTER HER!
SHE'S UNCONSCIOUS! A FALL FROM THIS HEIGHT--!
NIGHTCRAWLER, STAND DOWN!
THE HAUK'KA TAKE CARE OF THEIR OWN.
BISHOP, WE COULD HAVE--!
NO, PSYLOCKE, WE COULDN'T.
IT WOULD HAVE TAKEN KURT TWO STAGES TO REACH HER, AND A FEW SECONDS TO ORIENT HIMSELF ONCE HE ARRIVED.
PLENTY OF TIME FOR THAT FLIER TO NAIL HIM, OR RAY HERSELF, IF SHE WAS FAKING.

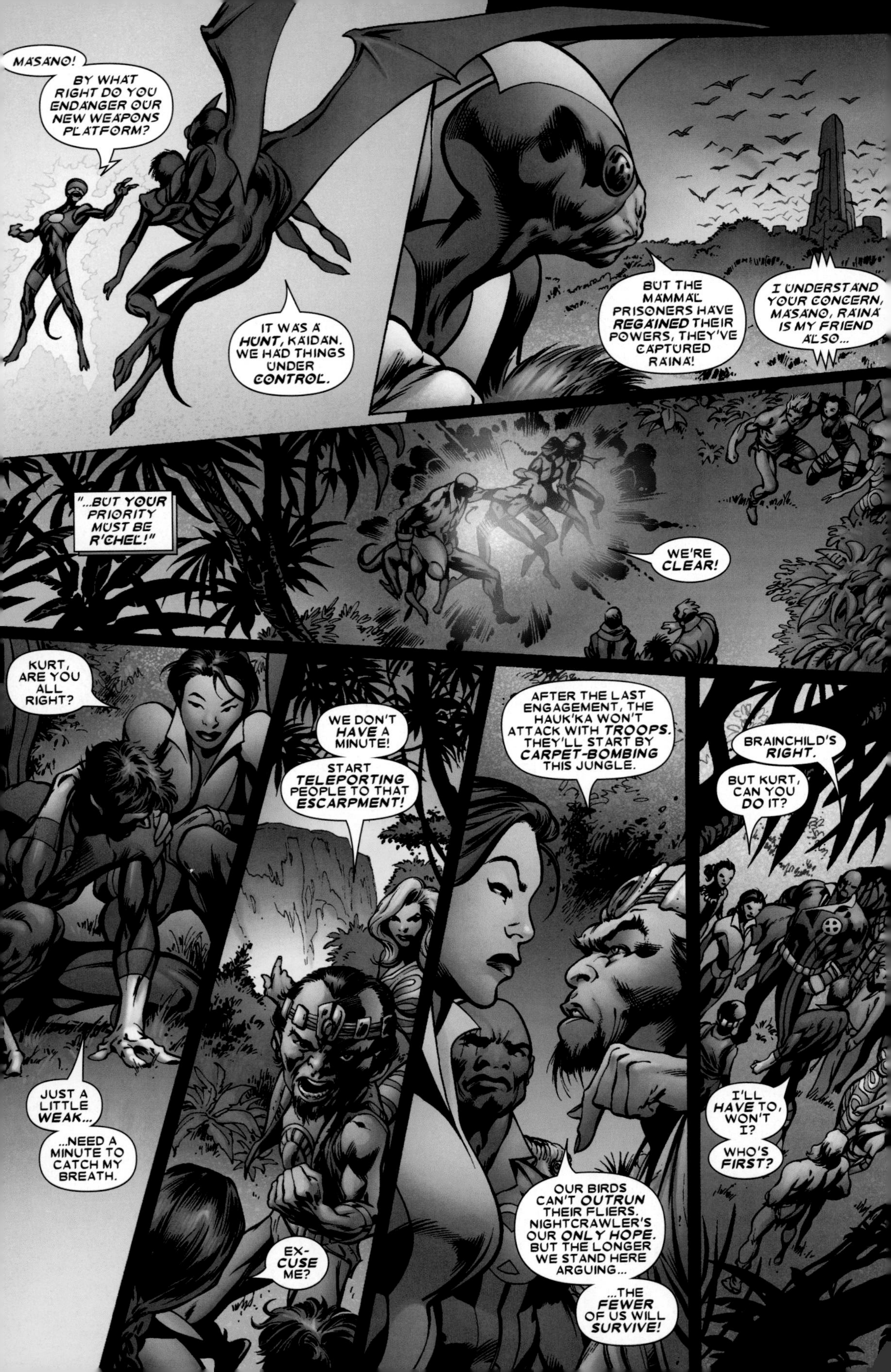
MASANO!
BY WHAT RIGHT DO YOU ENDANGER OUR NEW WEAPONS PLATFORM?
IT WAS A HUNT, KAIDAN. WE HAD THINGS UNDER CONTROL.
BUT THE MAMMAL PRISONERS HAVE REGAINED THEIR POWERS, THEY'VE CAPTURED RAINA!
I UNDERSTAND YOUR CONCERN, MASANO. RAINA IS MY FRIEND ALSO...
"...BUT YOUR PRIORITY MUST BE R'CHEL!"
WE'RE CLEAR!
KURT, ARE YOU ALL RIGHT?
JUST A LITTLE WEAK...
...NEED A MINUTE TO CATCH MY BREATH.
WE DON'T HAVE A MINUTE!
START TELEPORTING PEOPLE TO THAT ESCARPMENT!
EX-CUSE ME?
AFTER THE LAST ENGAGEMENT, THE HAUK'KA WON'T ATTACK WITH TROOPS. THEY'LL START BY CARPET-BOMBING THIS JUNGLE.
OUR BIRDS CAN'T OUTRUN THEIR FLIERS. NIGHTCRAWLER'S OUR ONLY HOPE. BUT THE LONGER WE STAND HERE ARGUING...
...THE FEWER OF US WILL SURVIVE!
BRAINCHILD'S RIGHT.
BUT KURT, CAN YOU DO IT?
I'LL HAVE TO, WON'T I?
WHO'S FIRST?

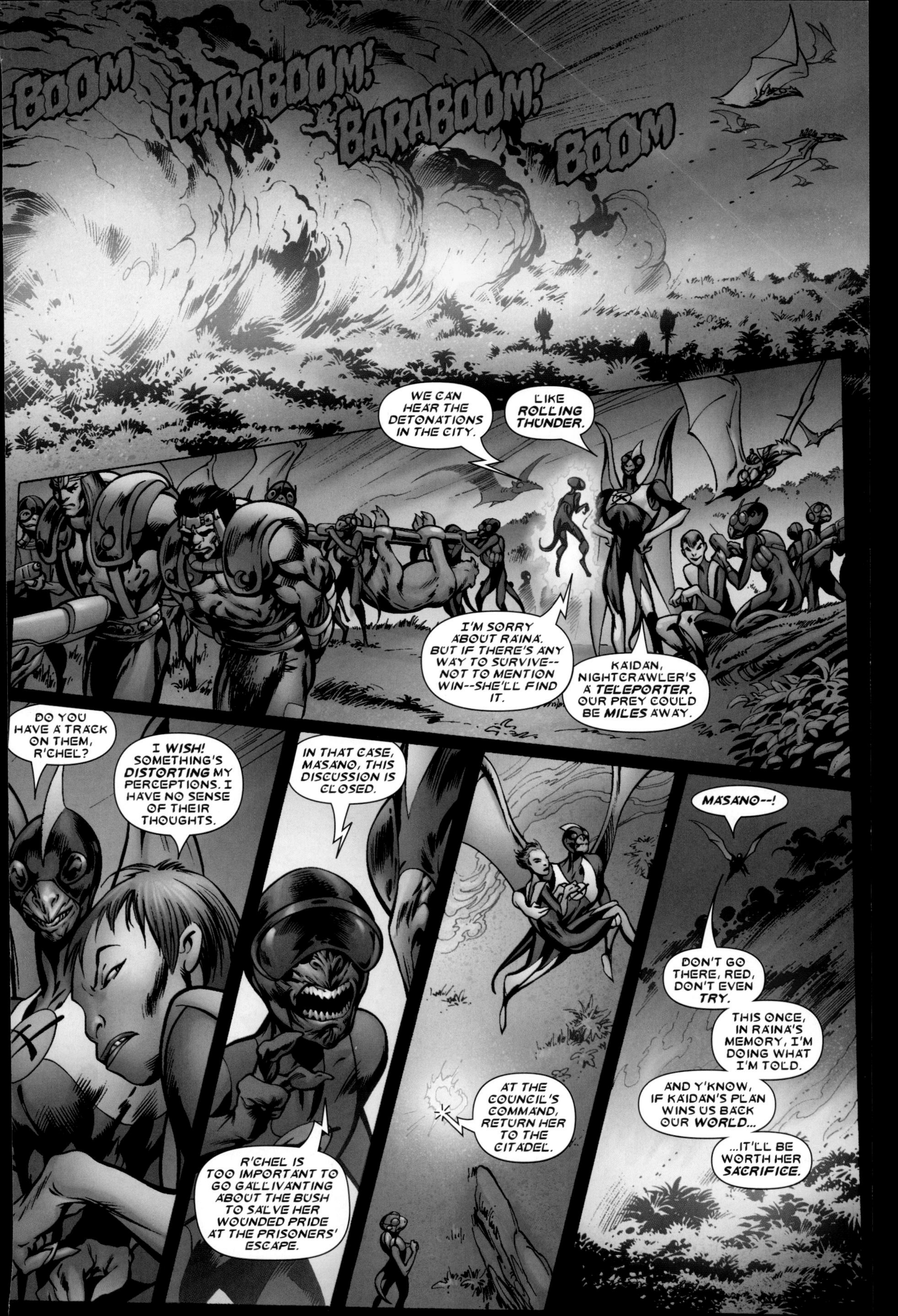
BOOM
BARABOOM!
BARABOOM!
BOOM
WE CAN HEAR THE DETONATIONS IN THE CITY.
LIKE ROLLING THUNDER.
I'M SORRY ABOUT RAINA. BUT IF THERE'S ANY WAY TO SURVIVE-- NOT TO MENTION WIN--SHE'LL FIND IT.
KAIDAN, NIGHTCRAWLER'S A TELEPORTER. OUR PREY COULD BE MILES AWAY.
DO YOU HAVE A TRACK ON THEM, R'CHEL?
I WISH! SOMETHING'S DISTORTING MY PERCEPTIONS. I HAVE NO SENSE OF THEIR THOUGHTS.
IN THAT CASE, MASANO, THIS DISCUSSION IS CLOSED.
R'CHEL IS TOO IMPORTANT TO GO GALLIVANTING ABOUT THE BUSH TO SALVE HER WOUNDED PRIDE AT THE PRISONERS' ESCAPE.
AT THE COUNCIL'S COMMAND, RETURN HER TO THE CITADEL.
MASANO--!
DON'T GO THERE, RED, DON'T EVEN TRY.
THIS ONCE, IN RAINA'S MEMORY, I'M DOING WHAT I'M TOLD.
AND Y'KNOW, IF KAIDAN'S PLAN WINS US BACK OUR WORLD...
...IT'LL BE WORTH HER SACRIFICE.

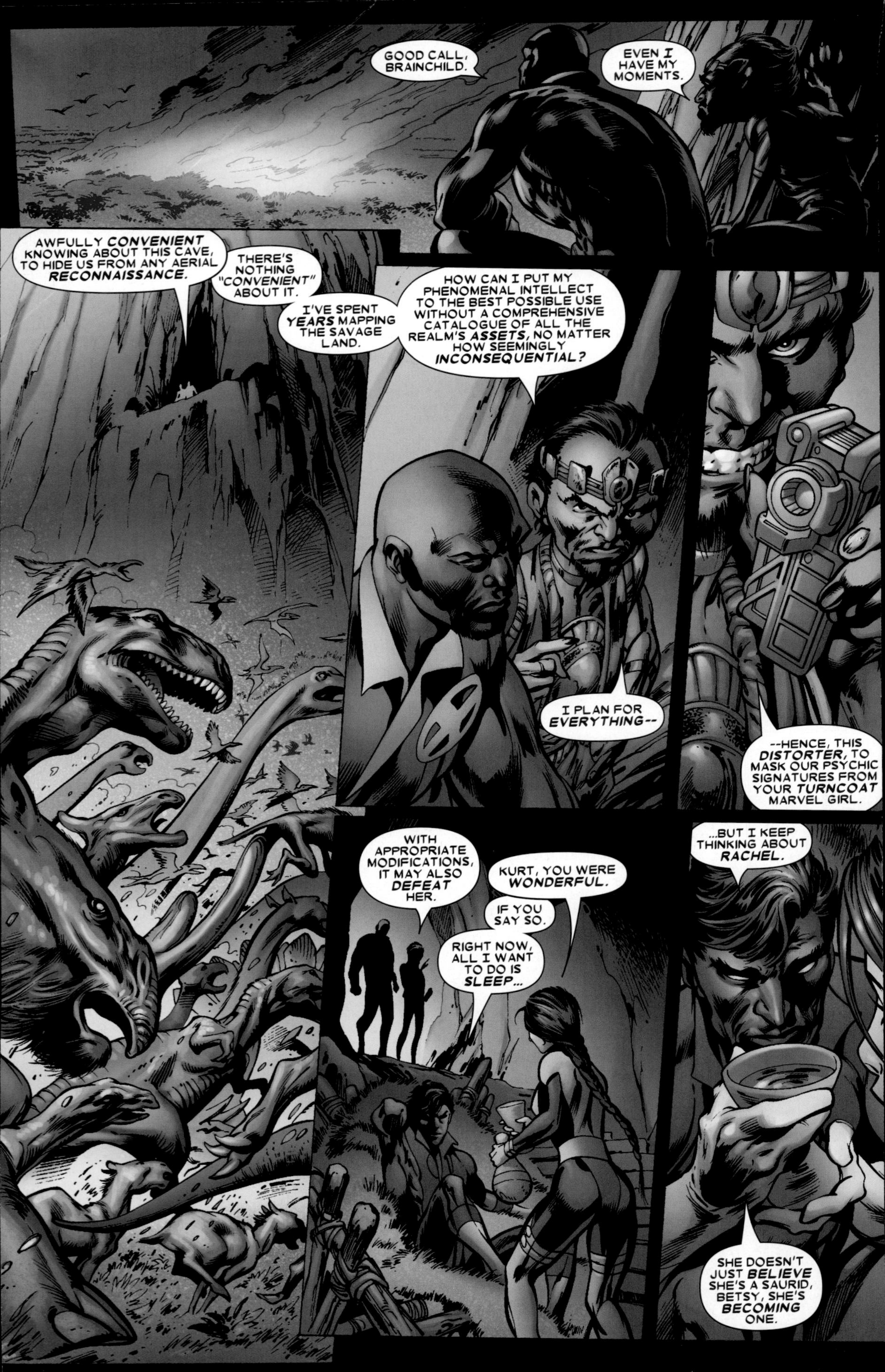
GOOD CALL, BRAINCHILD.
EVEN I HAVE MY MOMENTS.
AWFULLY CONVENIENT KNOWING ABOUT THIS CAVE, TO HIDE US FROM ANY AERIAL RECONNAISSANCE.
THERE'S NOTHING "CONVENIENT" ABOUT IT.
I'VE SPENT YEARS MAPPING THE SAVAGE LAND.
HOW CAN I PUT MY PHENOMENAL INTELLECT TO THE BEST POSSIBLE USE WITHOUT A COMPREHENSIVE CATALOGUE OF ALL THE REALM'S ASSETS, NO MATTER HOW SEEMINGLY INCONSEQUENTIAL?
I PLAN FOR EVERYTHING--
--HENCE, THIS DISTORTER, TO MASK OUR PSYCHIC SIGNATURES FROM YOUR TURNCOAT MARVEL GIRL.
WITH APPROPRIATE MODIFICATIONS, IT MAY ALSO DEFEAT HER.
KURT, YOU WERE WONDERFUL.
IF YOU SAY SO.
RIGHT NOW, ALL I WANT TO DO IS SLEEP...
...BUT I KEEP THINKING ABOUT RACHEL.
SHE DOESN'T JUST BELIEVE SHE'S A SAURID, BETSY, SHE'S BECOMING ONE.

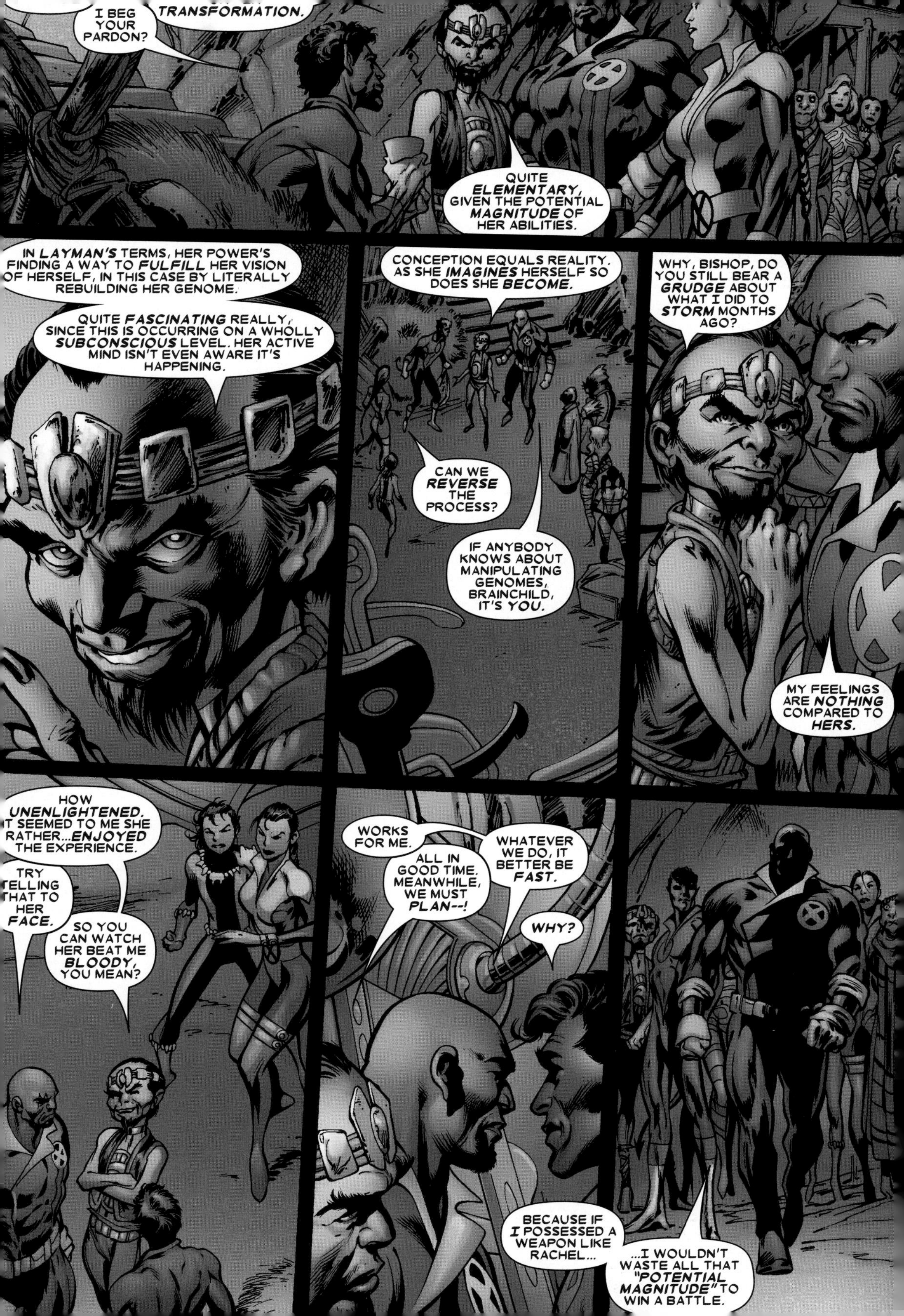

I BEG YOUR PARDON?
TRANSFORMATION.
QUITE ELEMENTARY, GIVEN THE POTENTIAL MAGNITUDE OF HER ABILITIES.
IN LAYMAN'S TERMS, HER POWER'S FINDING A WAY TO FULFILL HER VISION OF HERSELF, IN THIS CASE BY LITERALLY REBUILDING HER GENOME.
QUITE FASCINATING REALLY, SINCE THIS IS OCCURRING ON A WHOLLY SUBCONSCIOUS LEVEL. HER ACTIVE MIND ISN'T EVEN AWARE IT'S HAPPENING.
CONCEPTION EQUALS REALITY. AS SHE IMAGINES HERSELF SO DOES SHE BECOME.
CAN WE REVERSE THE PROCESS?
IF ANYBODY KNOWS ABOUT MANIPULATING GENOMES, BRAINCHILD, IT'S YOU.
WHY, BISHOP, DO YOU STILL BEAR A GRUDGE ABOUT WHAT I DID TO STORM MONTHS AGO?
MY FEELINGS ARE NOTHING COMPARED TO HERS.
HOW UNENLIGHTENED. IT SEEMED TO ME SHE RATHER...ENJOYED THE EXPERIENCE.
TRY TELLING THAT TO HER FACE.
SO YOU CAN WATCH HER BEAT ME BLOODY, YOU MEAN?
WORKS FOR ME.
ALL IN GOOD TIME. MEANWHILE, WE MUST PLAN--!
WHATEVER WE DO, IT BETTER BE FAST.
WHY?
BECAUSE IF I POSSESSED A WEAPON LIKE RACHEL...
...I WOULDN'T WASTE ALL THAT "POTENTIAL MAGNITUDE" TO WIN A BATTLE.

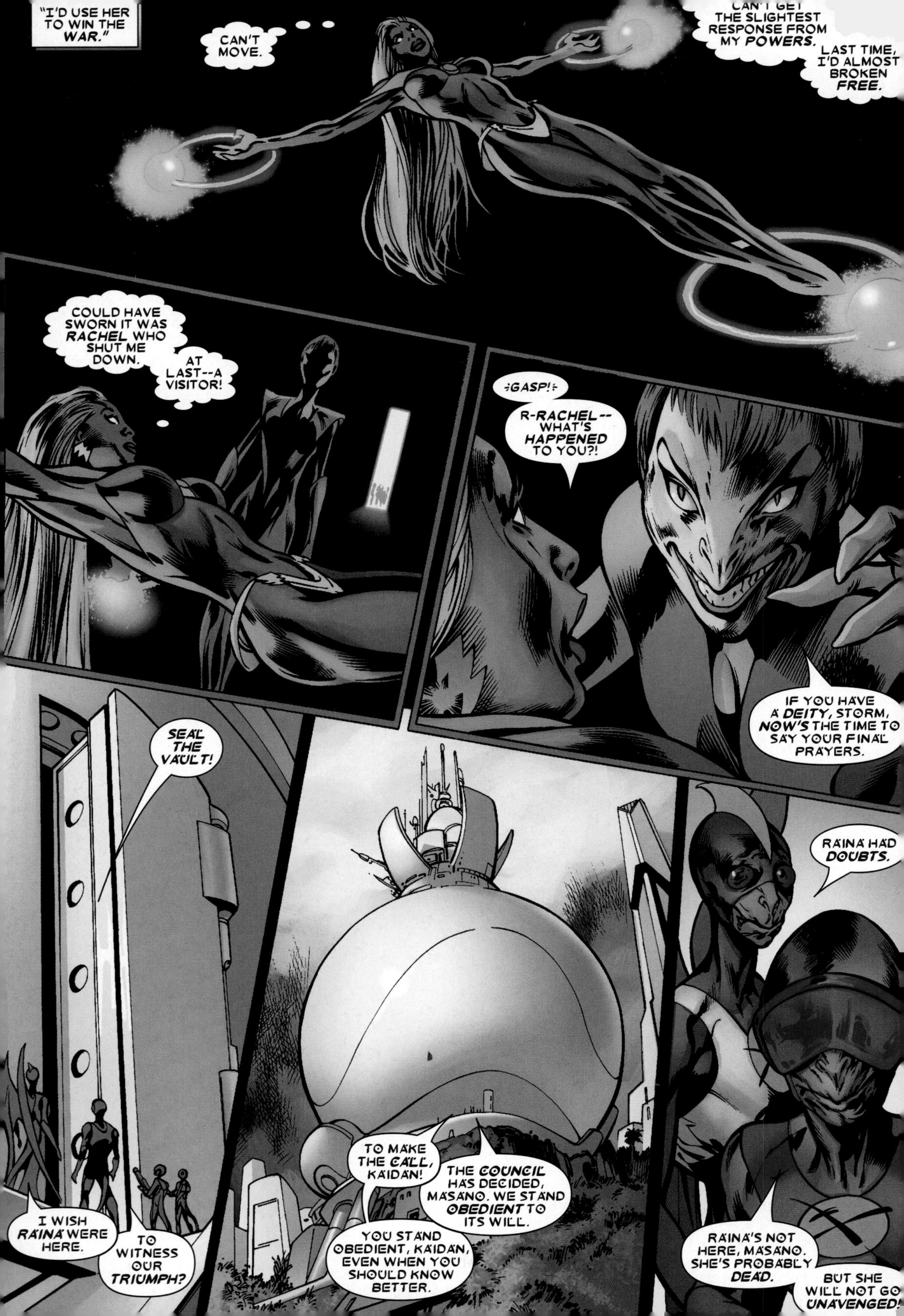
"I'D USE HER TO WIN THE WAR."
CAN'T MOVE.
CAN'T GET THE SLIGHTEST RESPONSE FROM MY POWERS.
LAST TIME, I'D ALMOST BROKEN FREE.
COULD HAVE SWORN IT WAS RACHEL WHO SHUT ME DOWN.
AT LAST--A VISITOR!
GASP!
R-RACHEL-- WHAT'S HAPPENED TO YOU?!
IF YOU HAVE A DEITY, STORM, NOW'S THE TIME TO SAY YOUR FINAL PRAYERS.
SEAL THE VAULT!
I WISH RAINA WERE HERE.
TO WITNESS OUR TRIUMPH?
TO MAKE THE CALL, KAIDAN!
THE COUNCIL HAS DECIDED, MASANO. WE STAND OBEDIENT TO ITS WILL.
YOU STAND OBEDIENT, KAIDAN, EVEN WHEN YOU SHOULD KNOW BETTER.
RAINA HAD DOUBTS.
RAINA'S NOT HERE, MASANO. SHE'S PROBABLY DEAD.
BUT SHE WILL NOT GO UNAVENGED!

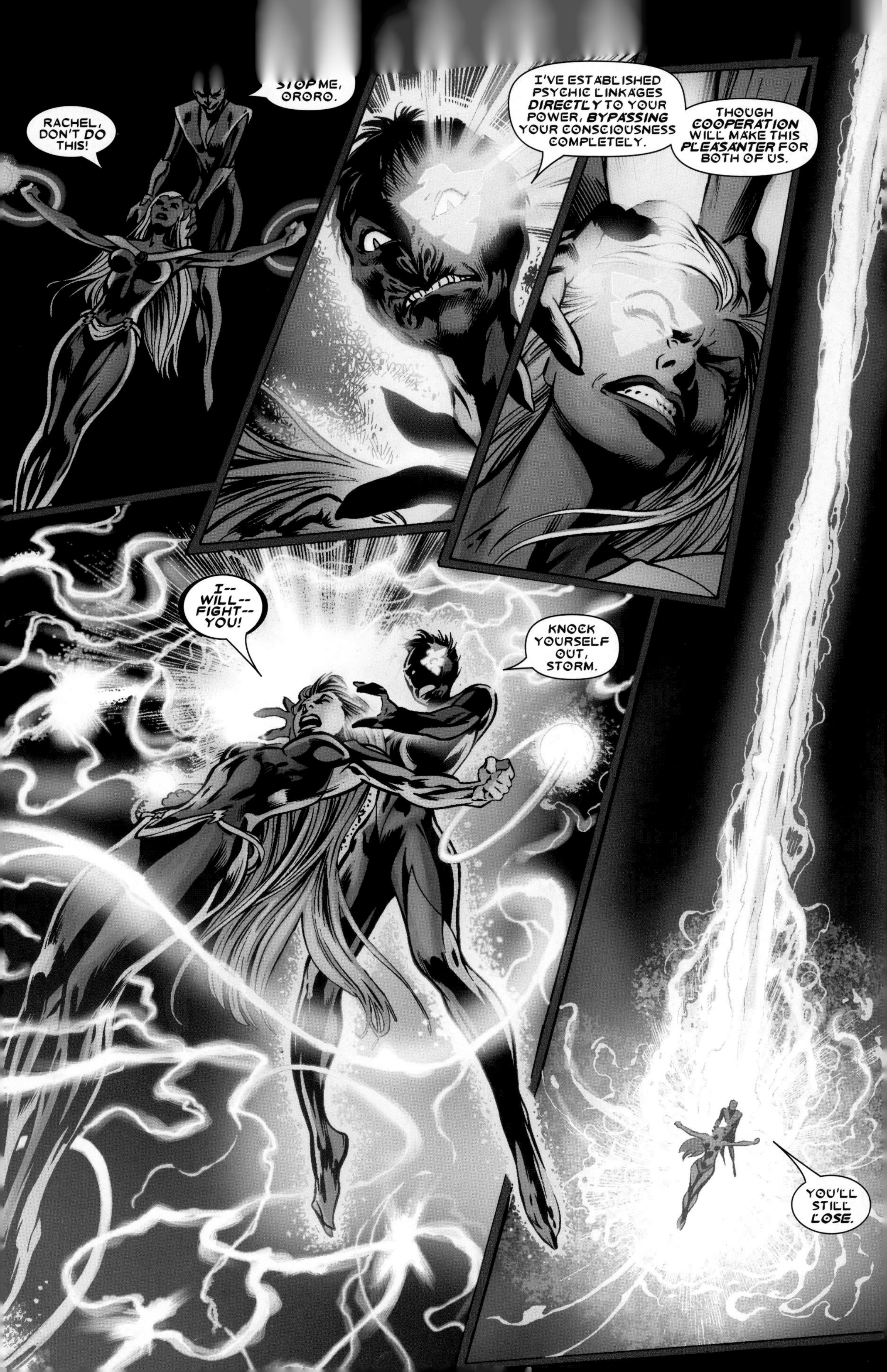
RACHEL, DON'T DO THIS!
STOP ME, ORORO.
I'VE ESTABLISHED PSYCHIC LINKAGES DIRECTLY TO YOUR POWER, BYPASSING YOUR CONSCIOUSNESS COMPLETELY.
THOUGH COOPERATION WILL MAKE THIS PLEASANTER FOR BOTH OF US.
I-- WILL-- FIGHT-- YOU!
KNOCK YOURSELF OUT, STORM.
YOU'LL STILL LOSE.

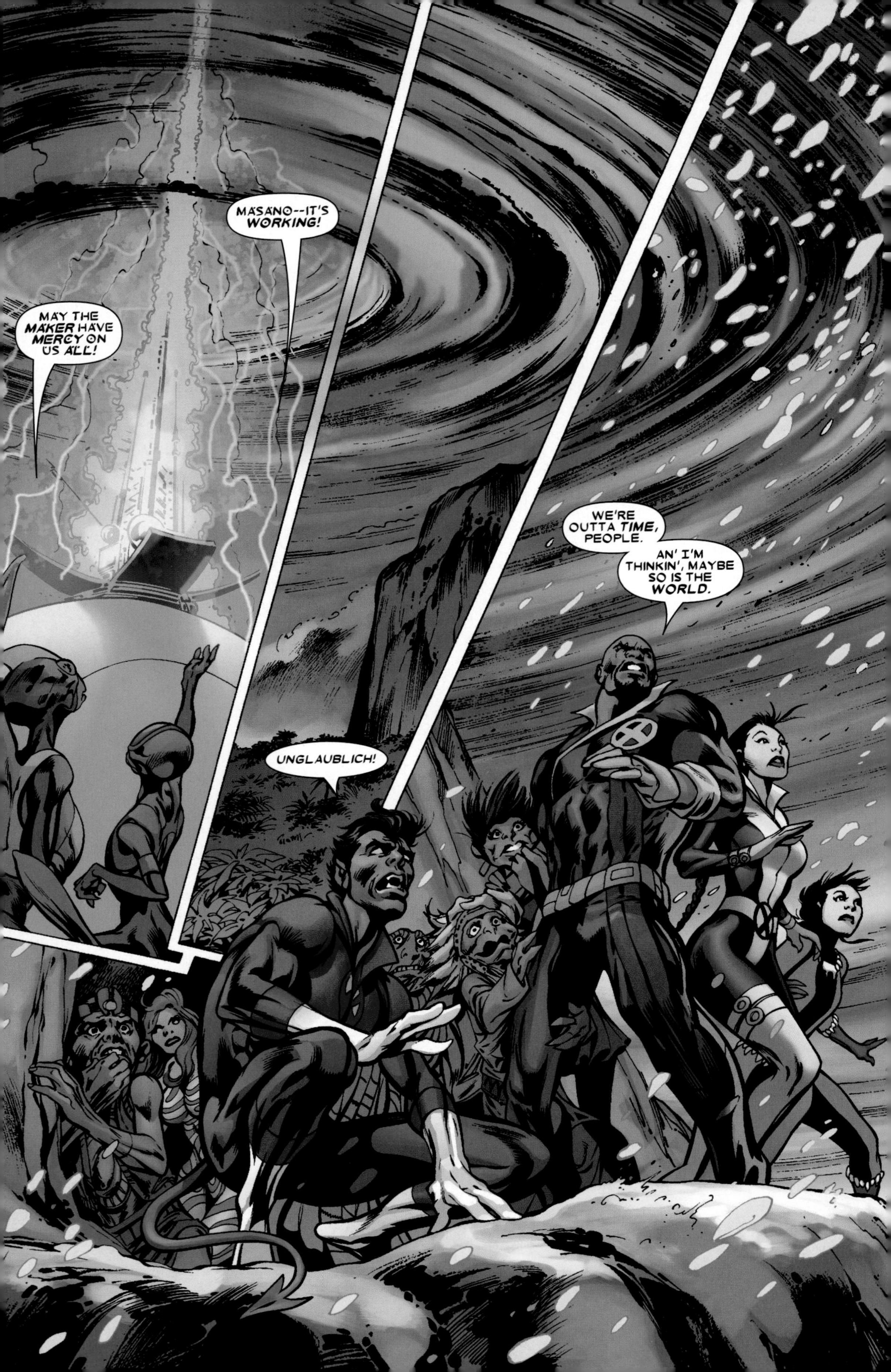
MAY THE MAKER HAVE MERCY ON US ALL!
MASANO--IT'S WORKING!
WE'RE OUTTA TIME, PEOPLE.
AN' I'M THINKIN', MAYBE SO IS THE WORLD.
UNGLAUBLICH!

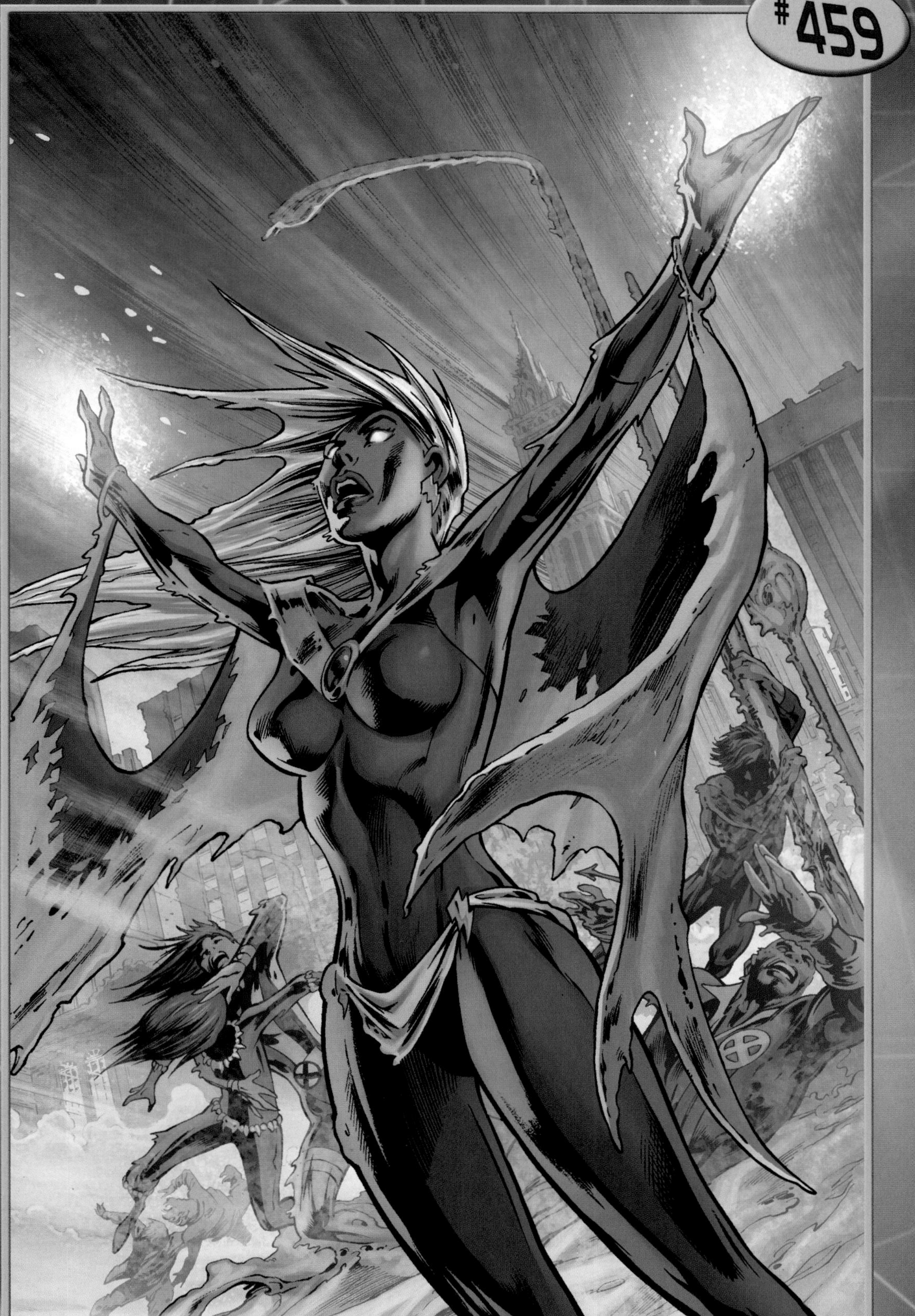
#459

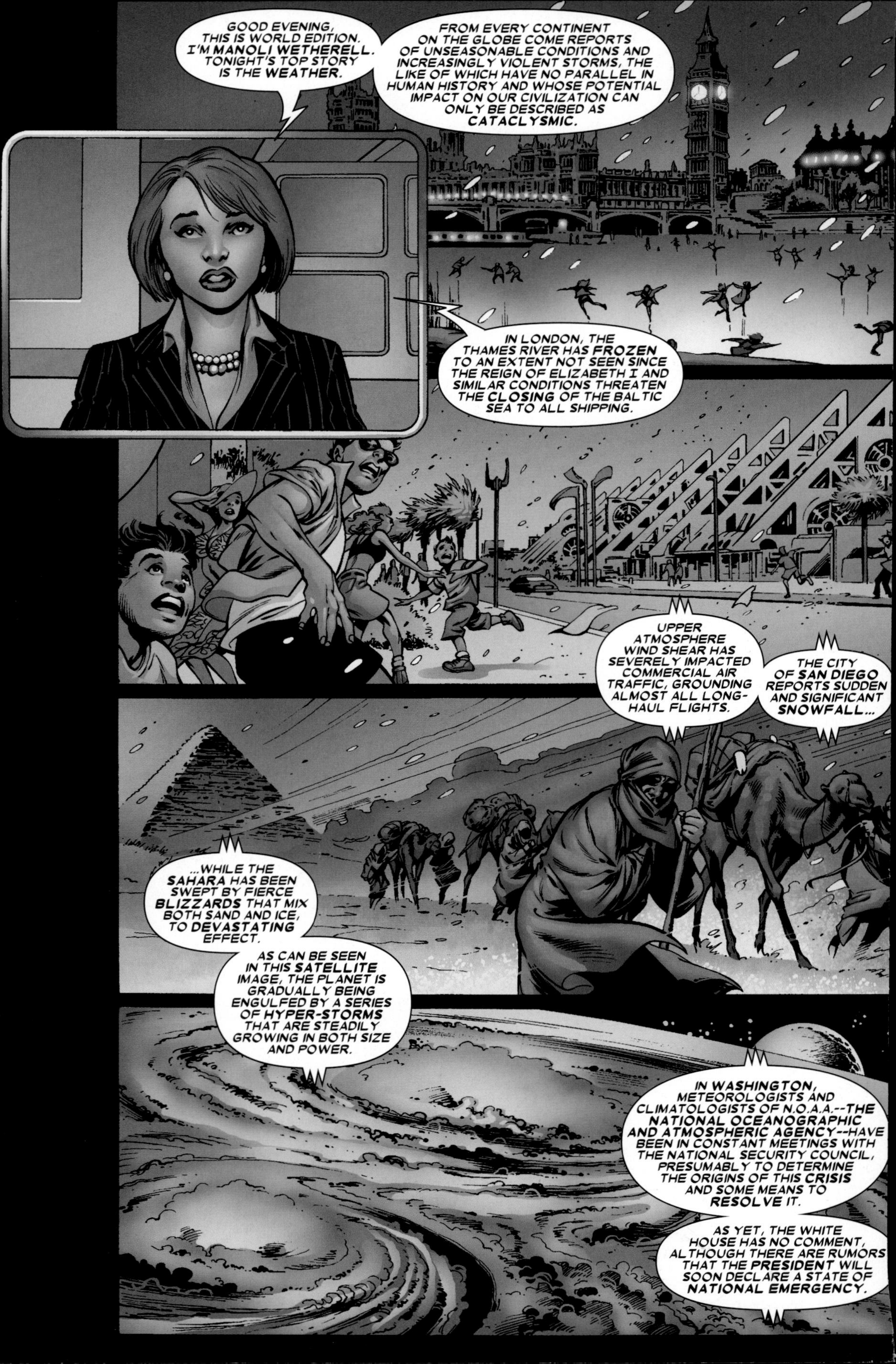
GOOD EVENING, THIS IS WORLD EDITION. I'M MANOLI WETHERELL. TONIGHT'S TOP STORY IS THE WEATHER.
FROM EVERY CONTINENT ON THE GLOBE COME REPORTS OF UNSEASONABLE CONDITIONS AND INCREASINGLY VIOLENT STORMS, THE LIKE OF WHICH HAVE NO PARALLEL IN HUMAN HISTORY AND WHOSE POTENTIAL IMPACT ON OUR CIVILIZATION CAN ONLY BE DESCRIBED AS CATACLYSMIC.
IN LONDON, THE THAMES RIVER HAS FROZEN TO AN EXTENT NOT SEEN SINCE THE REIGN OF ELIZABETH I AND SIMILAR CONDITIONS THREATEN THE CLOSING OF THE BALTIC SEA TO ALL SHIPPING.
UPPER ATMOSPHERE WIND SHEAR HAS SEVERELY IMPACTED COMMERCIAL AIR TRAFFIC, GROUNDING ALMOST ALL LONG-HAUL FLIGHTS.
THE CITY OF SAN DIEGO REPORTS SUDDEN AND SIGNIFICANT SNOWFALL...
...WHILE THE SAHARA HAS BEEN SWEPT BY FIERCE BLIZZARDS THAT MIX BOTH SAND AND ICE, TO DEVASTATING EFFECT.
AS CAN BE SEEN IN THIS SATELLITE IMAGE, THE PLANET IS GRADUALLY BEING ENGULFED BY A SERIES OF HYPER-STORMS THAT ARE STEADILY GROWING IN BOTH SIZE AND POWER.
IN WASHINGTON, METEOROLOGISTS AND CLIMATOLOGISTS OF N.O.A.A.--THE NATIONAL OCEANOGRAPHIC AND ATMOSPHERIC AGENCY--HAVE BEEN IN CONSTANT MEETINGS WITH THE NATIONAL SECURITY COUNCIL, PRESUMABLY TO DETERMINE THE ORIGINS OF THIS CRISIS AND SOME MEANS TO RESOLVE IT.
AS YET, THE WHITE HOUSE HAS NO COMMENT, ALTHOUGH THERE ARE RUMORS THAT THE PRESIDENT WILL SOON DECLARE A STATE OF NATIONAL EMERGENCY.

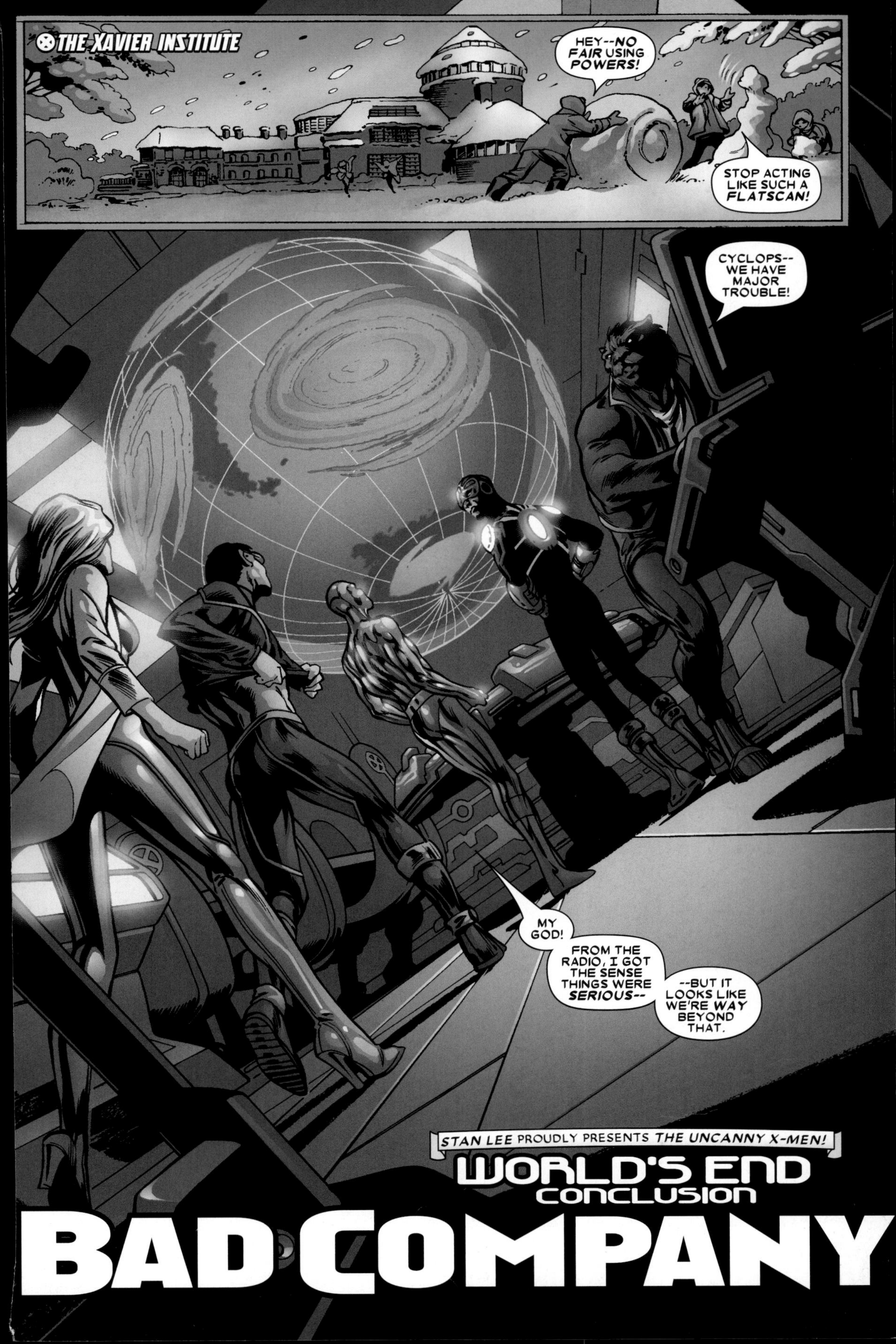
THE XAVIER INSTITUTE
HEY--NO FAIR USING POWERS!
STOP ACTING LIKE SUCH A FLATSCAN!
CYCLOPS--WE HAVE MAJOR TROUBLE!
MY GOD!
FROM THE RADIO, I GOT THE SENSE THINGS WERE SERIOUS--
--BUT IT LOOKS LIKE WE'RE WAY BEYOND THAT.
STAN LEE PROUDLY PRESENTS THE UNCANNY X-MEN!
WORLD'S END CONCLUSION
BAD COMPANY

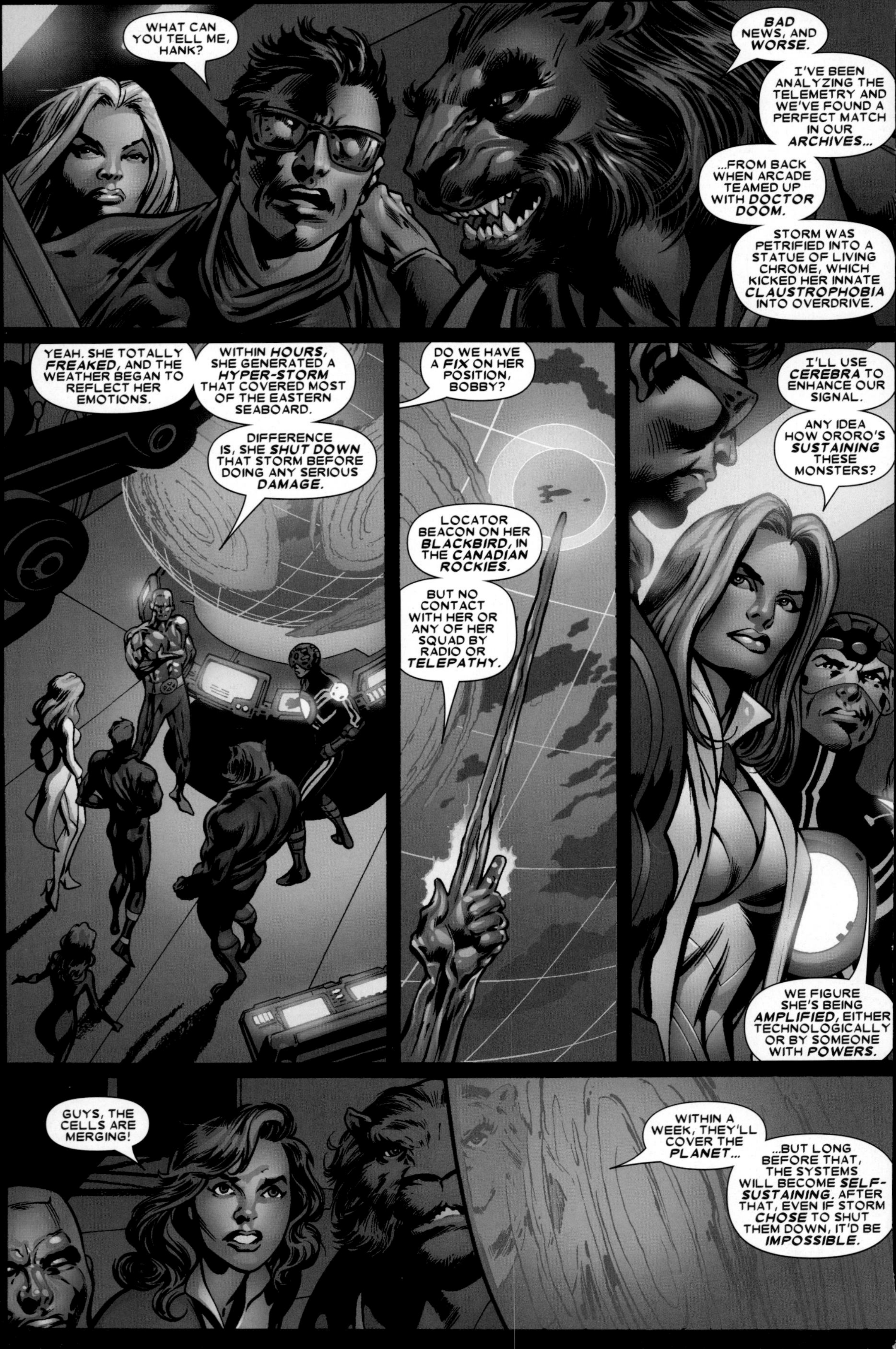
WHAT CAN YOU TELL ME, HANK?
BAD NEWS, AND WORSE.
I'VE BEEN ANALYZING THE TELEMETRY AND WE'VE FOUND A PERFECT MATCH IN OUR ARCHIVES...
...FROM BACK WHEN ARCADE TEAMED UP WITH DOCTOR DOOM.
STORM WAS PETRIFIED INTO A STATUE OF LIVING CHROME, WHICH KICKED HER INNATE CLAUSTROPHOBIA INTO OVERDRIVE.
YEAH. SHE TOTALLY FREAKED, AND THE WEATHER BEGAN TO REFLECT HER EMOTIONS.
WITHIN HOURS, SHE GENERATED A HYPER-STORM THAT COVERED MOST OF THE EASTERN SEABOARD.
DIFFERENCE IS, SHE SHUT DOWN THAT STORM BEFORE DOING ANY SERIOUS DAMAGE.
DO WE HAVE A FIX ON HER POSITION, BOBBY?
LOCATOR BEACON ON HER BLACKBIRD, IN THE CANADIAN ROCKIES.
BUT NO CONTACT WITH HER OR ANY OF HER SQUAD BY RADIO OR TELEPATHY.
I'LL USE CEREBRA TO ENHANCE OUR SIGNAL.
ANY IDEA HOW ORORO'S SUSTAINING THESE MONSTERS?
WE FIGURE SHE'S BEING AMPLIFIED, EITHER TECHNOLOGICALLY OR BY SOMEONE WITH POWERS.
GUYS, THE CELLS ARE MERGING!
WITHIN A WEEK, THEY'LL COVER THE PLANET...
...BUT LONG BEFORE THAT, THE SYSTEMS WILL BECOME SELF-SUSTAINING. AFTER THAT, EVEN IF STORM CHOSE TO SHUT THEM DOWN, IT'D BE IMPOSSIBLE.

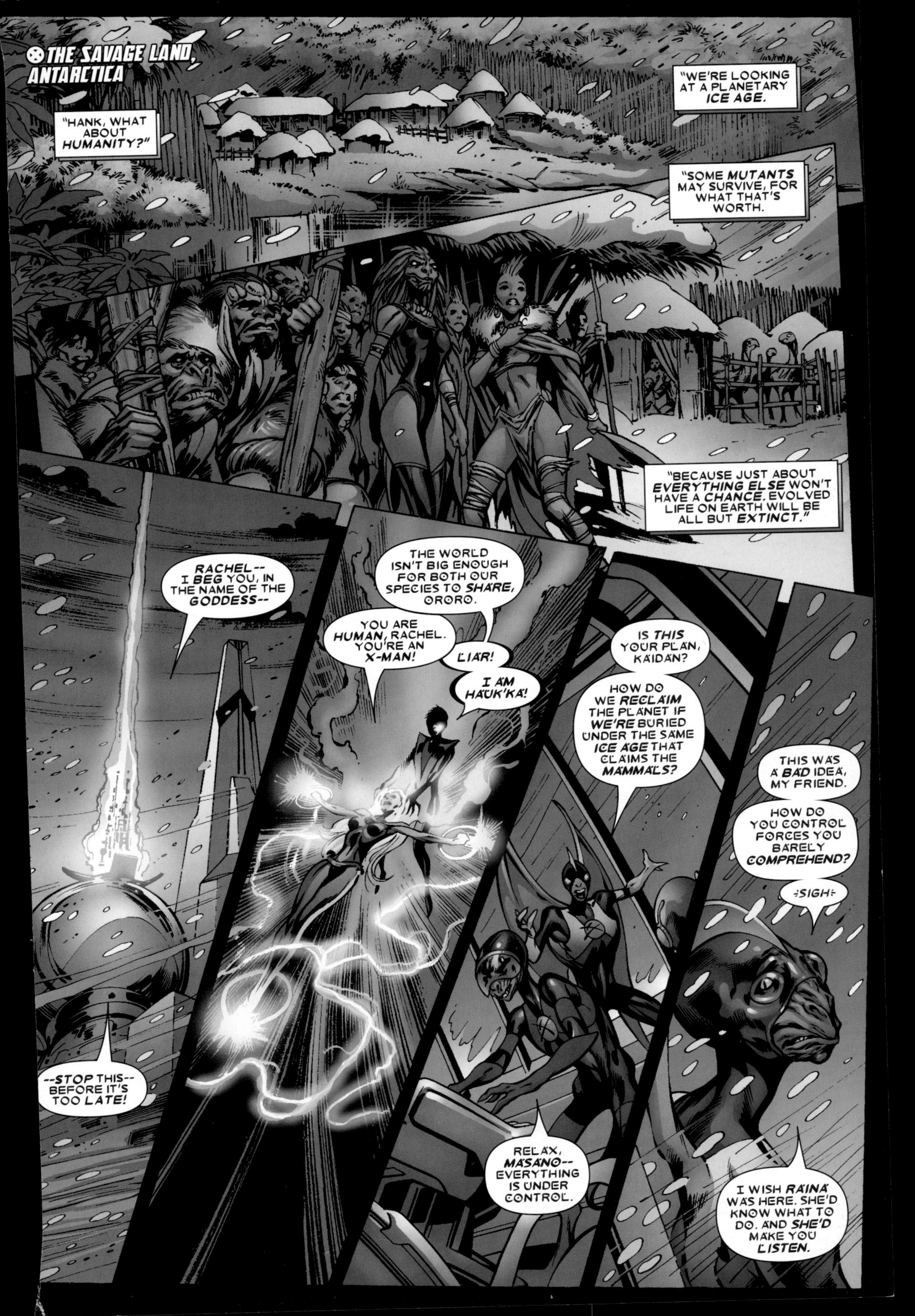

THE SAVAGE LAND, ANTARCTICA
"HANK, WHAT ABOUT HUMANITY?"
"WE'RE LOOKING AT A PLANETARY ICE AGE.
"SOME MUTANTS MAY SURVIVE, FOR WHAT THAT'S WORTH.
"BECAUSE JUST ABOUT EVERYTHING ELSE WON'T HAVE A CHANCE. EVOLVED LIFE ON EARTH WILL BE ALL BUT EXTINCT."
RACHEL-- I BEG YOU, IN THE NAME OF THE GODDESS--
--STOP THIS-- BEFORE IT'S TOO LATE!
THE WORLD ISN'T BIG ENOUGH FOR BOTH OUR SPECIES TO SHARE, ORORO.
YOU ARE HUMAN, RACHEL. YOU'RE AN X-MAN!
LIAR!
I AM HAUK'KA!
IS THIS YOUR PLAN, KAIDAN?
HOW DO WE RECLAIM THE PLANET IF WE'RE BURIED UNDER THE SAME ICE AGE THAT CLAIMS THE MAMMALS?
RELAX, MASANO-- EVERYTHING IS UNDER CONTROL.
THIS WAS A BAD IDEA, MY FRIEND.
HOW DO YOU CONTROL FORCES YOU BARELY COMPREHEND?
SIGH
I WISH RAINA WAS HERE. SHE'D KNOW WHAT TO DO. AND SHE'D MAKE YOU LISTEN.

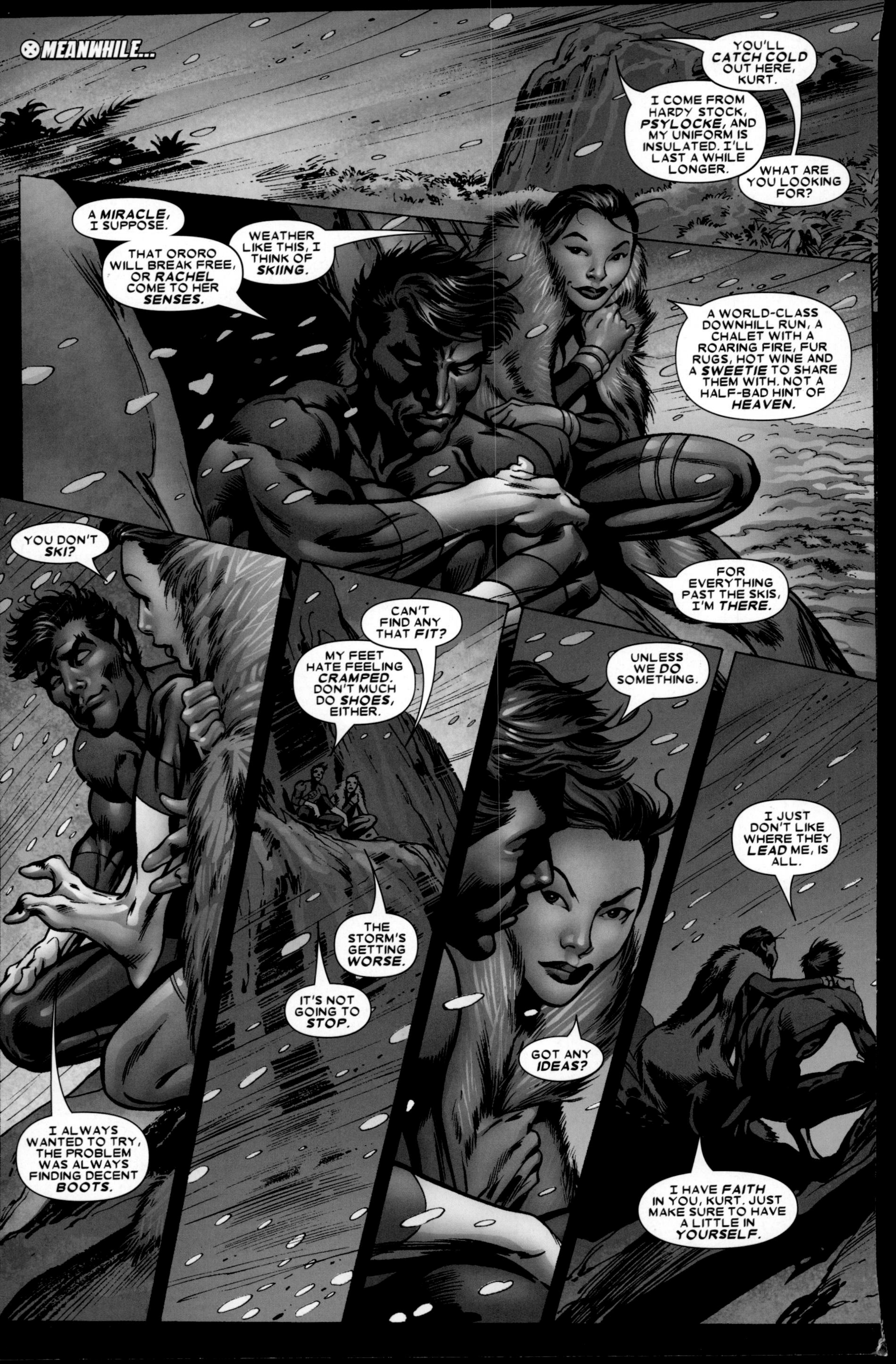
MEANWHILE...
YOU'LL CATCH COLD OUT HERE, KURT.
I COME FROM HARDY STOCK, PSYLOCKE, AND MY UNIFORM IS INSULATED. I'LL LAST A WHILE LONGER.
WHAT ARE YOU LOOKING FOR?
A MIRACLE, I SUPPOSE.
THAT ORORO WILL BREAK FREE, OR RACHEL COME TO HER SENSES.
WEATHER LIKE THIS, I THINK OF SKIING.
A WORLD-CLASS DOWNHILL RUN, A CHALET WITH A ROARING FIRE, FUR RUGS, HOT WINE AND A SWEETIE TO SHARE THEM WITH. NOT A HALF-BAD HINT OF HEAVEN.
FOR EVERYTHING PAST THE SKIS, I'M THERE.
YOU DON'T SKI?
I ALWAYS WANTED TO TRY, THE PROBLEM WAS ALWAYS FINDING DECENT BOOTS.
CAN'T FIND ANY THAT FIT?
MY FEET HATE FEELING CRAMPED. DON'T MUCH DO SHOES, EITHER.
THE STORM'S GETTING WORSE.
IT'S NOT GOING TO STOP.
UNLESS WE DO SOMETHING.
GOT ANY IDEAS?
I JUST DON'T LIKE WHERE THEY LEAD ME, IS ALL.
I HAVE FAITH IN YOU, KURT. JUST MAKE SURE TO HAVE A LITTLE IN YOURSELF.

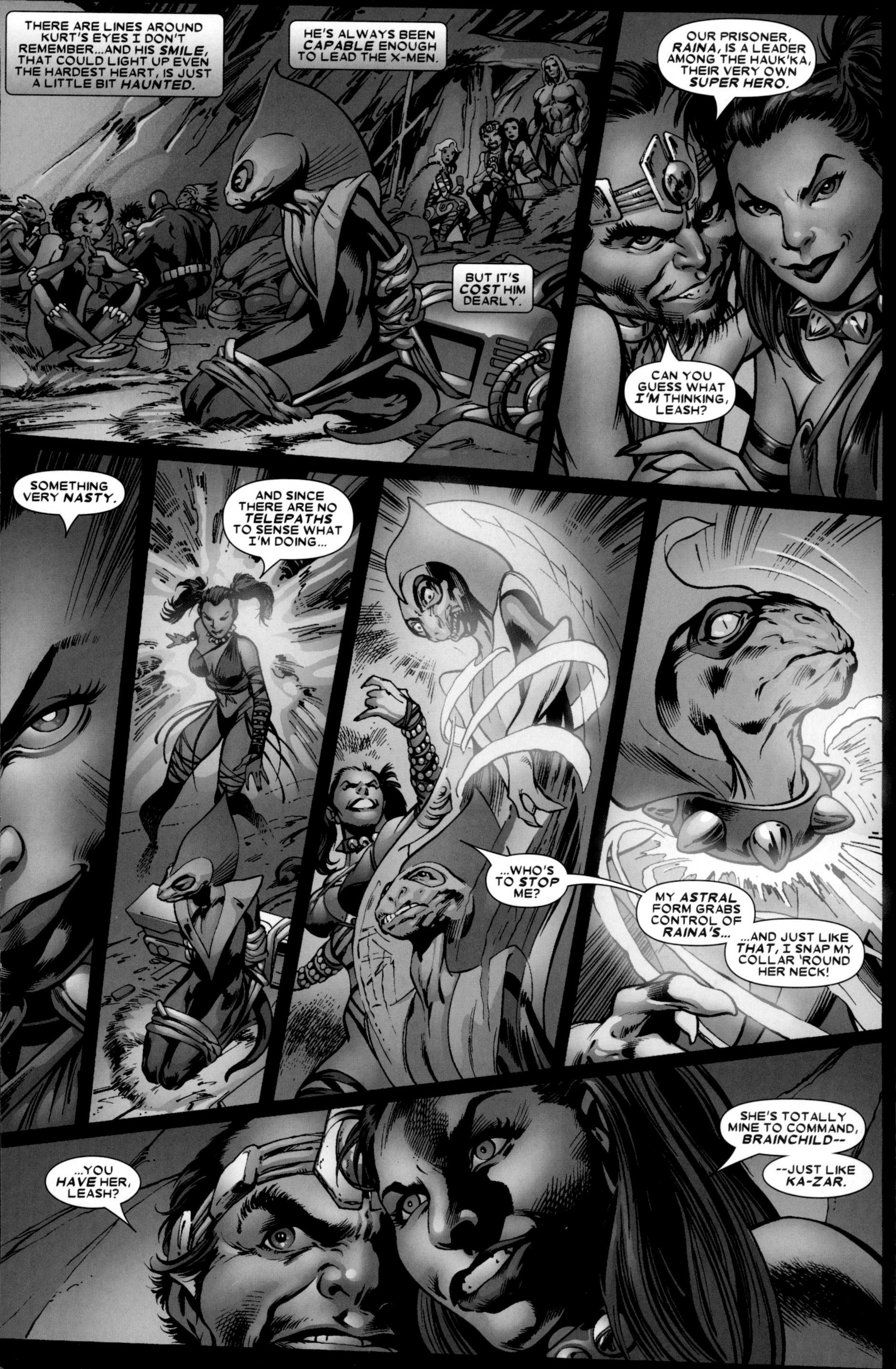

THERE ARE LINES AROUND KURT'S EYES I DON'T REMEMBER...AND HIS *SMILE*, THAT COULD LIGHT UP EVEN THE HARDEST HEART, IS JUST A LITTLE BIT *HAUNTED*.
HE'S ALWAYS BEEN *CAPABLE* ENOUGH TO LEAD THE X-MEN.
BUT IT'S *COST* HIM DEARLY.
OUR PRISONER, *RAINA*, IS A LEADER AMONG THE HAUK'KA, THEIR VERY OWN *SUPER HERO*.
CAN YOU GUESS WHAT *I'M* THINKING, LEASH?
SOMETHING VERY *NASTY*.
AND SINCE THERE ARE NO *TELEPATHS* TO SENSE WHAT I'M DOING...
...WHO'S TO *STOP* ME?
MY *ASTRAL* FORM GRABS CONTROL OF *RAINA'S*...
...AND JUST LIKE *THAT*, I SNAP MY COLLAR 'ROUND HER NECK!
SHE'S TOTALLY MINE TO COMMAND, *BRAINCHILD*--
--JUST LIKE *KA-ZAR*.
...YOU *HAVE* HER, LEASH?

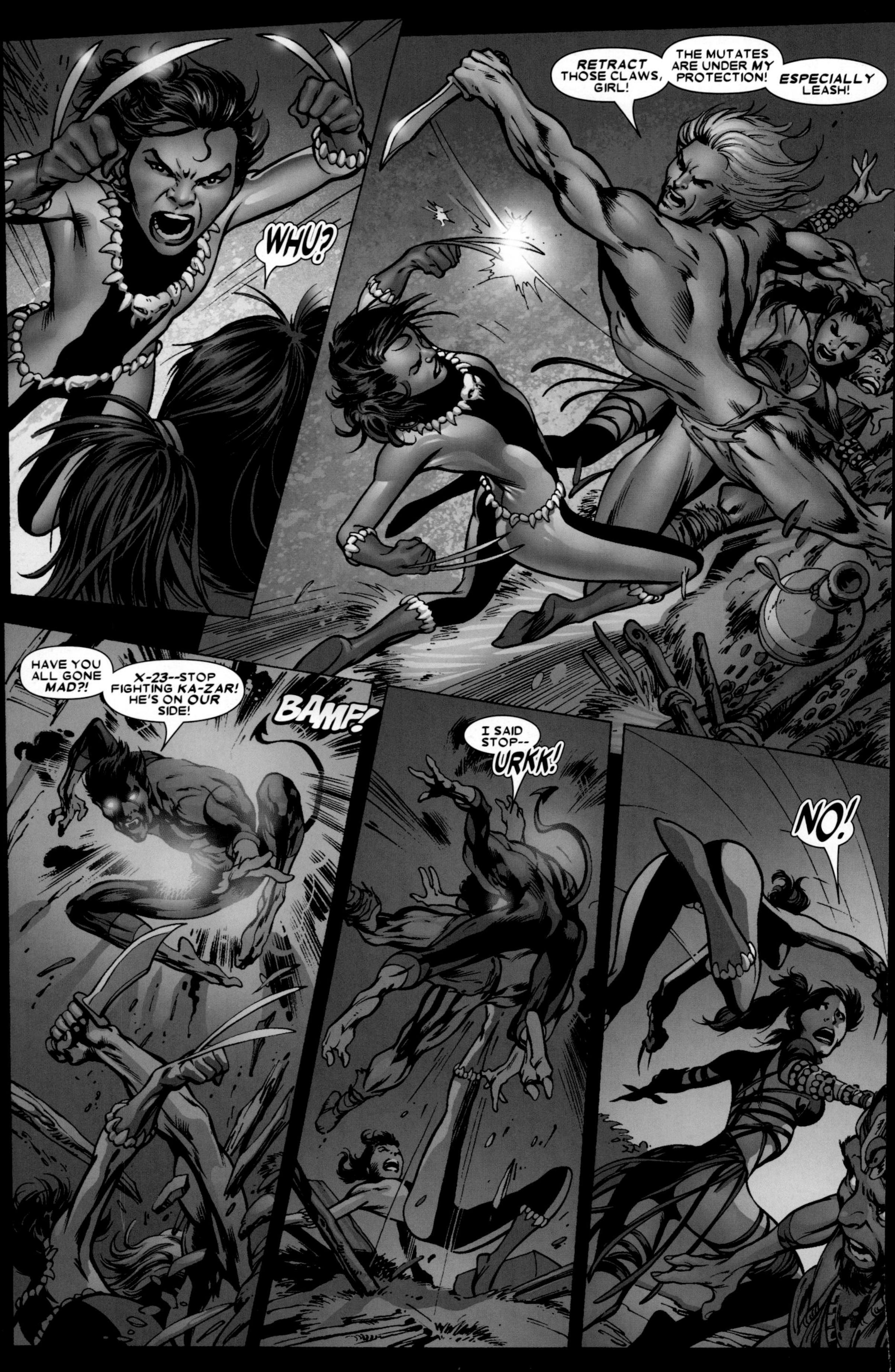

WHU?
RETRACT THOSE CLAWS, GIRL!
THE MUTATES ARE UNDER MY PROTECTION!
ESPECIALLY LEASH!
HAVE YOU ALL GONE MAD?!
X-23--STOP FIGHTING KA-ZAR! HE'S ON OUR SIDE!
BAMF!
I SAID STOP--
URKK!
NO!

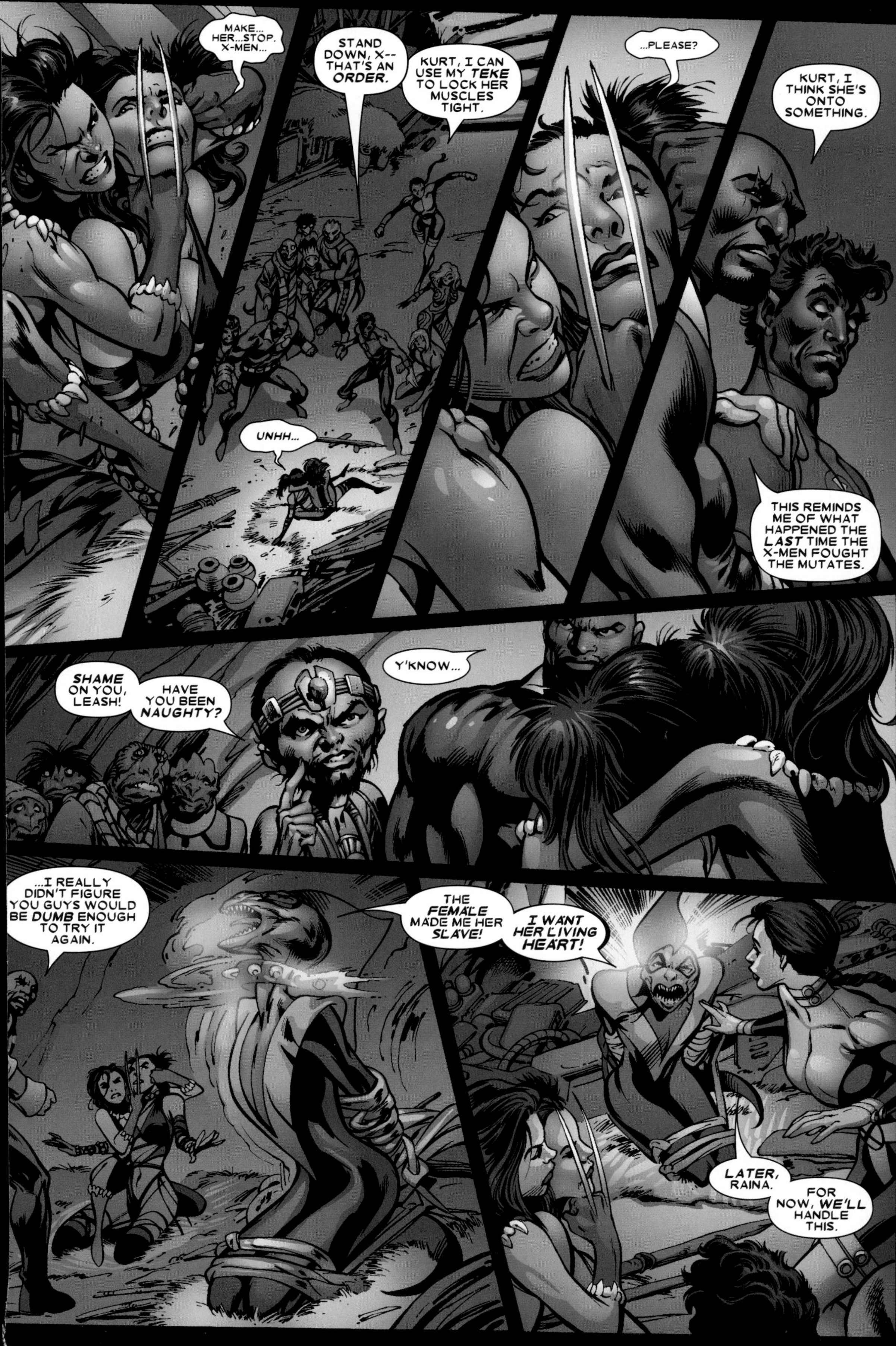
MAKE... HER...STOP. X-MEN...
STAND DOWN, X-- THAT'S AN *ORDER*.
KURT, I CAN USE MY *TEKE* TO LOCK HER MUSCLES TIGHT.
UNHH...
...PLEASE?
KURT, I THINK SHE'S ONTO SOMETHING.
THIS REMINDS ME OF WHAT HAPPENED THE *LAST* TIME THE X-MEN FOUGHT THE MUTATES.
SHAME ON YOU, LEASH!
HAVE YOU BEEN *NAUGHTY*?
Y'KNOW...
...I REALLY DIDN'T FIGURE YOU GUYS WOULD BE *DUMB* ENOUGH TO TRY IT AGAIN.
THE *FEMALE* MADE ME HER *SLAVE*!
I WANT HER LIVING HEART!
LATER, RAINA.
FOR NOW, *WE'LL* HANDLE THIS.

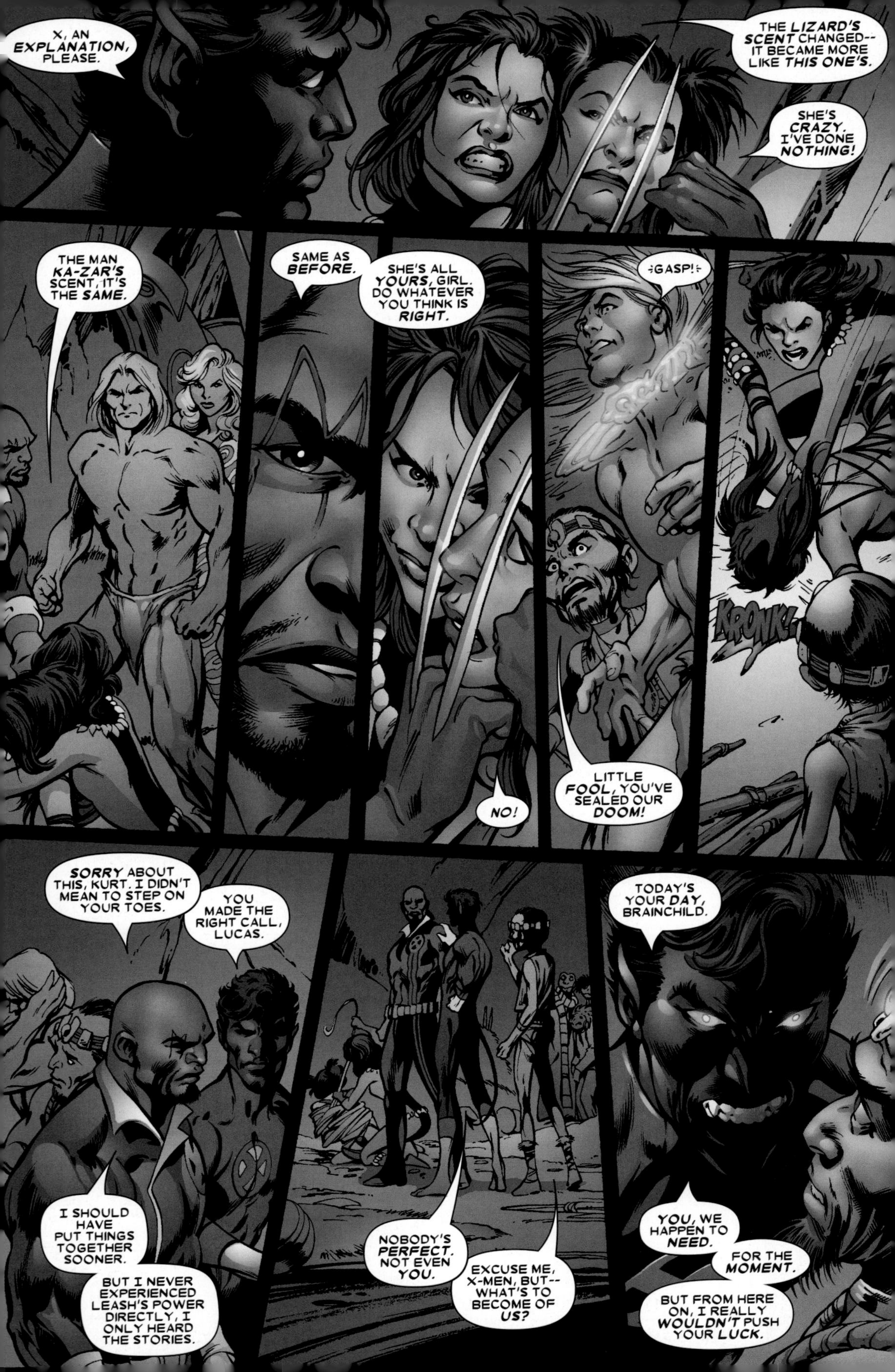
X, AN EXPLANATION, PLEASE.
THE LIZARD'S SCENT CHANGED-- IT BECAME MORE LIKE THIS ONE'S.
SHE'S CRAZY. I'VE DONE NOTHING!
THE MAN KA-ZAR'S SCENT, IT'S THE SAME.
SAME AS BEFORE.
SHE'S ALL YOURS, GIRL. DO WHATEVER YOU THINK IS RIGHT.
NO!
GASP!
LITTLE FOOL, YOU'VE SEALED OUR DOOM!
KRONK!
SORRY ABOUT THIS, KURT. I DIDN'T MEAN TO STEP ON YOUR TOES.
YOU MADE THE RIGHT CALL, LUCAS.
I SHOULD HAVE PUT THINGS TOGETHER SOONER.
BUT I NEVER EXPERIENCED LEASH'S POWER DIRECTLY, I ONLY HEARD THE STORIES.
NOBODY'S PERFECT. NOT EVEN YOU.
EXCUSE ME, X-MEN, BUT-- WHAT'S TO BECOME OF US?
TODAY'S YOUR DAY, BRAINCHILD.
YOU, WE HAPPEN TO NEED.
FOR THE MOMENT.
BUT FROM HERE ON, I REALLY WOULDN'T PUSH YOUR LUCK.

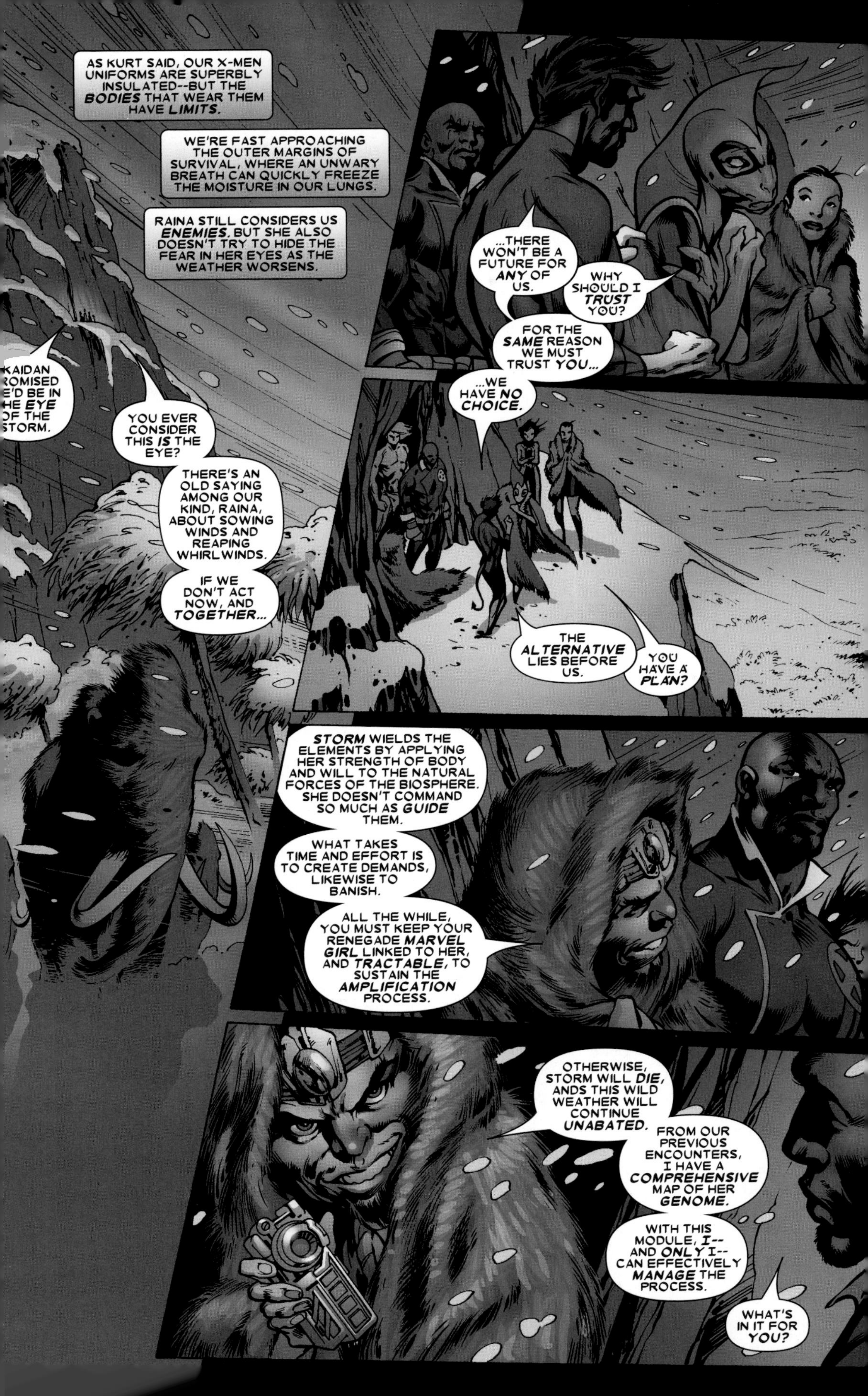

AS KURT SAID, OUR X-MEN UNIFORMS ARE SUPERBLY INSULATED--BUT THE BODIES THAT WEAR THEM HAVE LIMITS.
WE'RE FAST APPROACHING THE OUTER MARGINS OF SURVIVAL, WHERE AN UNWARY BREATH CAN QUICKLY FREEZE THE MOISTURE IN OUR LUNGS.
RAINA STILL CONSIDERS US ENEMIES. BUT SHE ALSO DOESN'T TRY TO HIDE THE FEAR IN HER EYES AS THE WEATHER WORSENS.
KAIDAN ROMISED E'D BE IN HE EYE OF THE STORM.
YOU EVER CONSIDER THIS IS THE EYE?
THERE'S AN OLD SAYING AMONG OUR KIND, RAINA, ABOUT SOWING WINDS AND REAPING WHIRLWINDS.
IF WE DON'T ACT NOW, AND TOGETHER...
...THERE WON'T BE A FUTURE FOR ANY OF US.
WHY SHOULD I TRUST YOU?
FOR THE SAME REASON WE MUST TRUST YOU...
...WE HAVE NO CHOICE.
THE ALTERNATIVE LIES BEFORE US.
YOU HAVE A PLAN?
STORM WIELDS THE ELEMENTS BY APPLYING HER STRENGTH OF BODY AND WILL TO THE NATURAL FORCES OF THE BIOSPHERE. SHE DOESN'T COMMAND SO MUCH AS GUIDE THEM.
WHAT TAKES TIME AND EFFORT IS TO CREATE DEMANDS, LIKEWISE TO BANISH.
ALL THE WHILE, YOU MUST KEEP YOUR RENEGADE MARVEL GIRL LINKED TO HER, AND TRACTABLE, TO SUSTAIN THE AMPLIFICATION PROCESS.
OTHERWISE, STORM WILL DIE, ANDS THIS WILD WEATHER WILL CONTINUE UNABATED.
FROM OUR PREVIOUS ENCOUNTERS, I HAVE A COMPREHENSIVE MAP OF HER GENOME.
WITH THIS MODULE, I--AND ONLY I--CAN EFFECTIVELY MANAGE THE PROCESS.
WHAT'S IN IT FOR YOU?

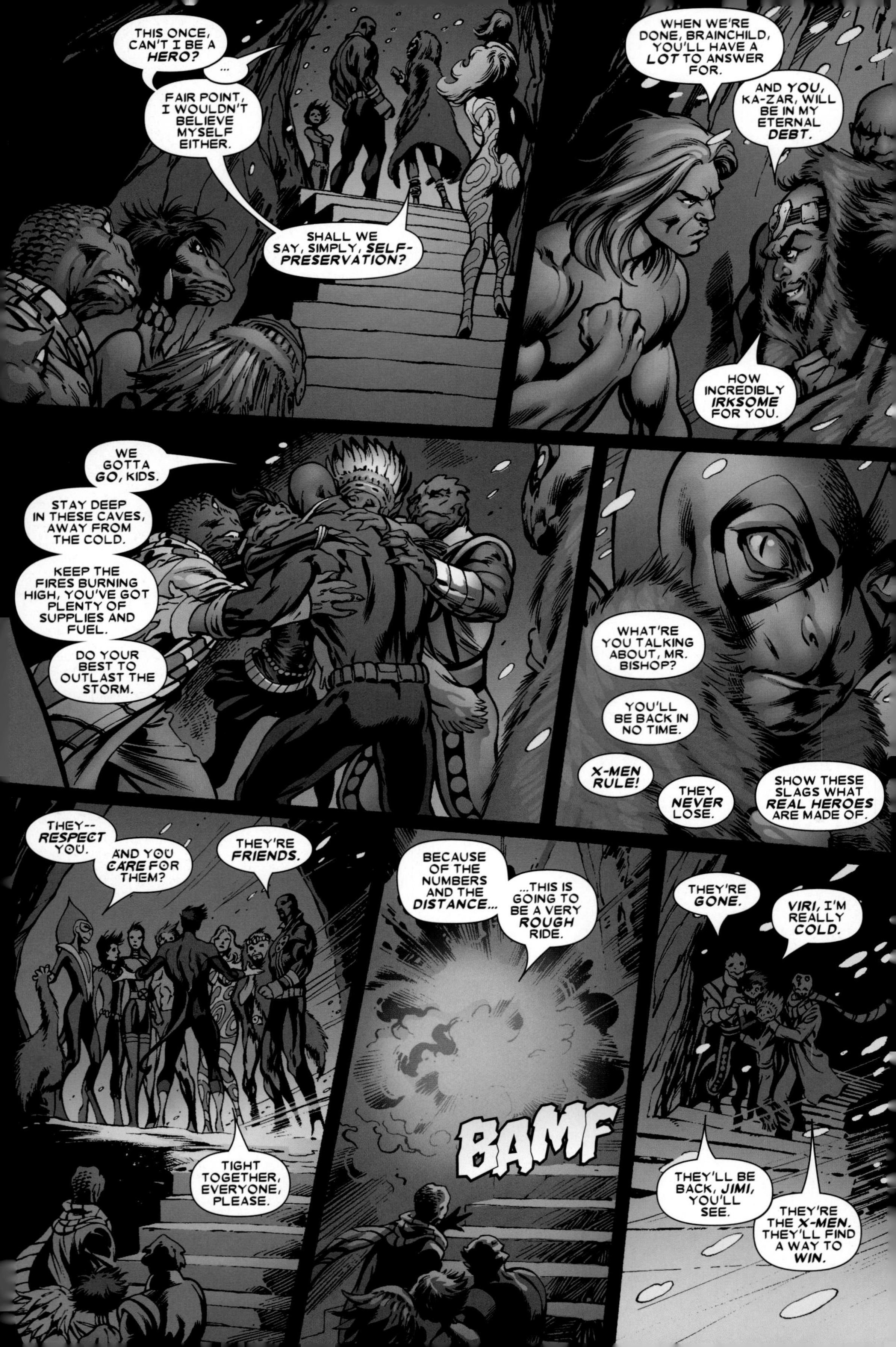
THIS ONCE, CAN'T I BE A HERO?
...
FAIR POINT, I WOULDN'T BELIEVE MYSELF EITHER.
SHALL WE SAY, SIMPLY, SELF-PRESERVATION?
WHEN WE'RE DONE, BRAINCHILD, YOU'LL HAVE A LOT TO ANSWER FOR.
AND YOU, KA-ZAR, WILL BE IN MY ETERNAL DEBT.
HOW INCREDIBLY IRKSOME FOR YOU.
WE GOTTA GO, KIDS.
STAY DEEP IN THESE CAVES, AWAY FROM THE COLD.
KEEP THE FIRES BURNING HIGH, YOU'VE GOT PLENTY OF SUPPLIES AND FUEL.
DO YOUR BEST TO OUTLAST THE STORM.
WHAT'RE YOU TALKING ABOUT, MR. BISHOP?
YOU'LL BE BACK IN NO TIME.
X-MEN RULE!
THEY NEVER LOSE.
SHOW THESE SLAGS WHAT REAL HEROES ARE MADE OF.
THEY-- RESPECT YOU.
AND YOU CARE FOR THEM?
THEY'RE FRIENDS.
TIGHT TOGETHER, EVERYONE, PLEASE.
BECAUSE OF THE NUMBERS AND THE DISTANCE...
...THIS IS GOING TO BE A VERY ROUGH RIDE.
BAMF
THEY'RE GONE.
VIRI, I'M REALLY COLD.
THEY'LL BE BACK, JIMI, YOU'LL SEE.
THEY'RE THE X-MEN. THEY'LL FIND A WAY TO WIN.

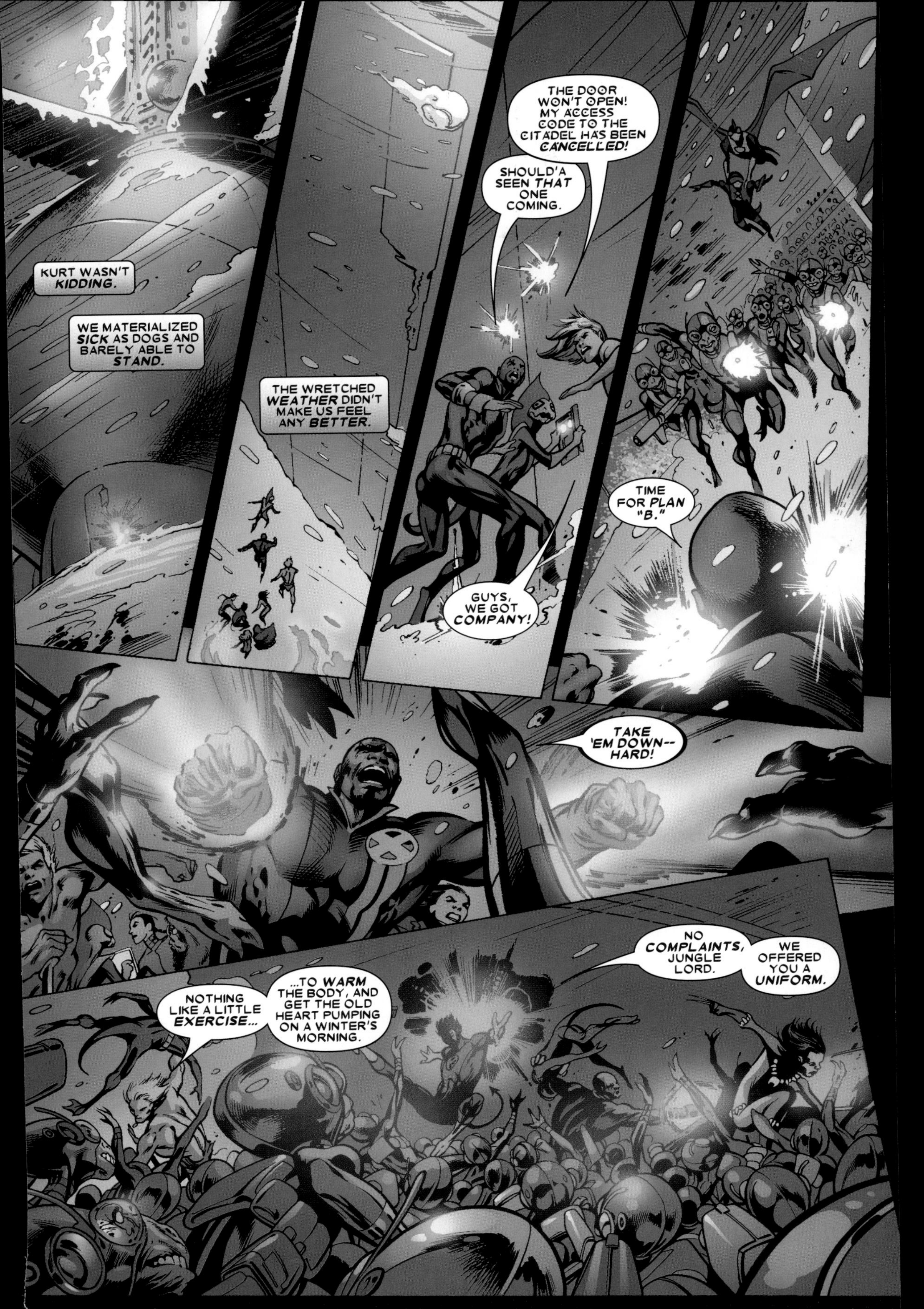
KURT WASN'T KIDDING.
WE MATERIALIZED SICK AS DOGS AND BARELY ABLE TO STAND.
THE WRETCHED WEATHER DIDN'T MAKE US FEEL ANY BETTER.
THE DOOR WON'T OPEN! MY ACCESS CODE TO THE CITADEL HAS BEEN CANCELLED!
SHOULD'A SEEN THAT ONE COMING.
GUYS, WE GOT COMPANY!
TIME FOR PLAN "B."
TAKE 'EM DOWN-- HARD!
NOTHING LIKE A LITTLE EXERCISE...
...TO WARM THE BODY, AND GET THE OLD HEART PUMPING ON A WINTER'S MORNING.
NO COMPLAINTS, JUNGLE LORD.
WE OFFERED YOU A UNIFORM.

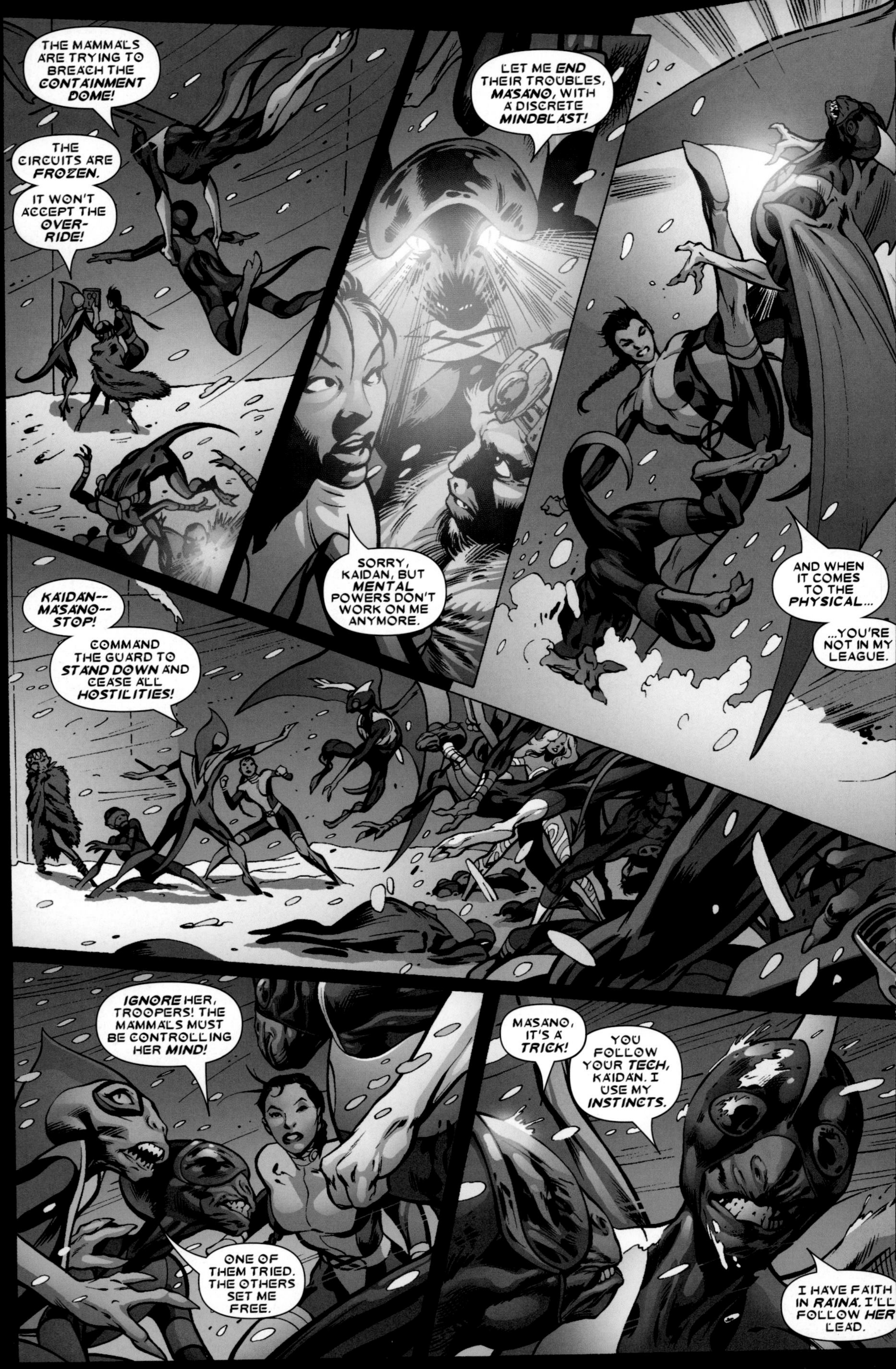
THE MAMMALS ARE TRYING TO BREACH THE CONTAINMENT DOME!
THE CIRCUITS ARE FROZEN.
IT WON'T ACCEPT THE OVER-RIDE!
LET ME END THEIR TROUBLES, MASANO, WITH A DISCRETE MINDBLAST!
SORRY, KAIDAN, BUT MENTAL POWERS DON'T WORK ON ME ANYMORE.
AND WHEN IT COMES TO THE PHYSICAL...
...YOU'RE NOT IN MY LEAGUE.
KAIDAN-- MASANO-- STOP!
COMMAND THE GUARD TO STAND DOWN AND CEASE ALL HOSTILITIES!
IGNORE HER, TROOPERS! THE MAMMALS MUST BE CONTROLLING HER MIND!
ONE OF THEM TRIED. THE OTHERS SET ME FREE.
MASANO, IT'S A TRICK!
YOU FOLLOW YOUR TECH, KAIDAN. I USE MY INSTINCTS.
I HAVE FAITH IN RAINA. I'LL FOLLOW HER LEAD.

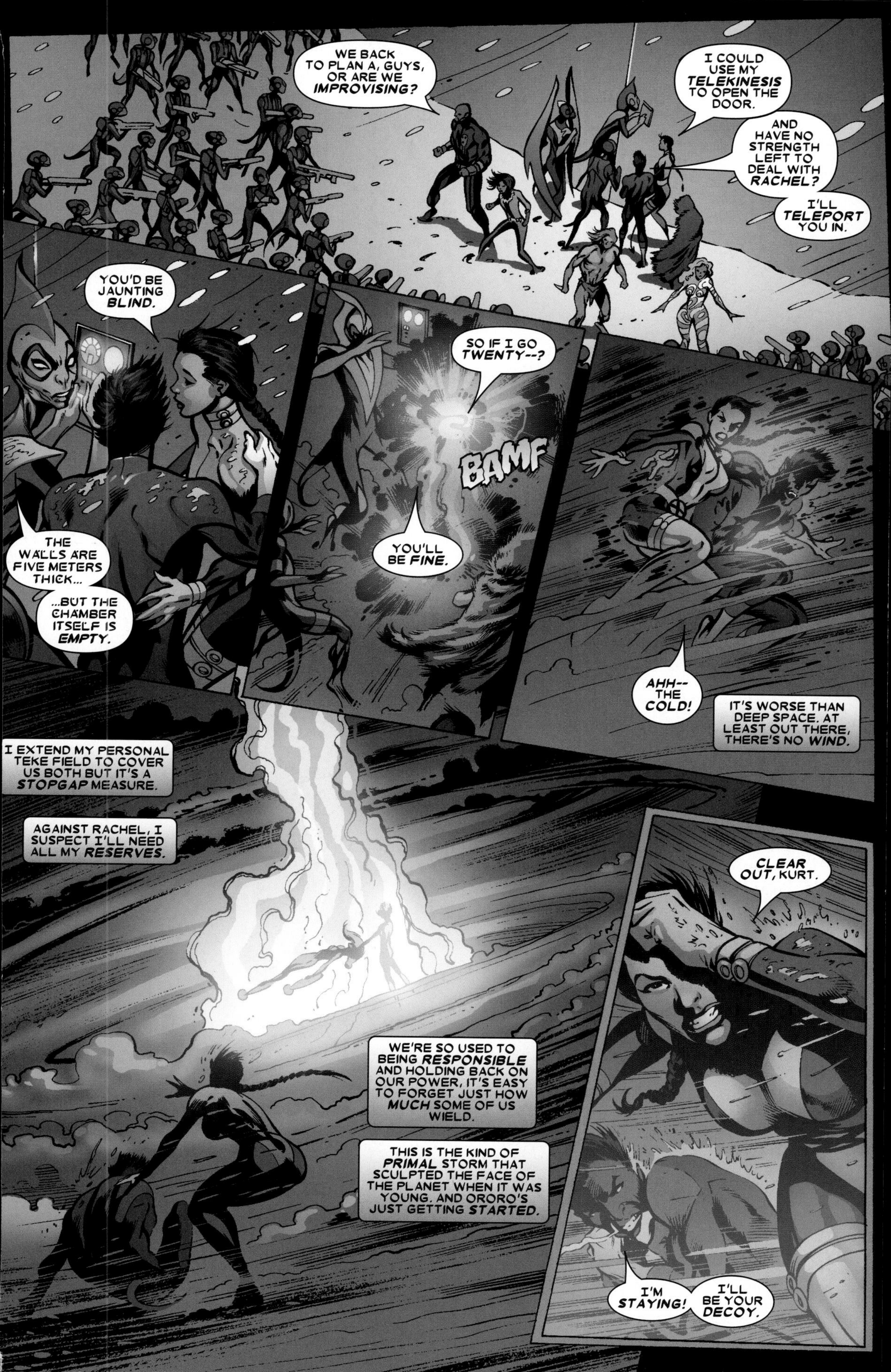
WE BACK TO PLAN A, GUYS, OR ARE WE IMPROVISING?
I COULD USE MY TELEKINESIS TO OPEN THE DOOR.
AND HAVE NO STRENGTH LEFT TO DEAL WITH RACHEL?
I'LL TELEPORT YOU IN.
YOU'D BE JAUNTING BLIND.
THE WALLS ARE FIVE METERS THICK...
...BUT THE CHAMBER ITSELF IS EMPTY.
SO IF I GO TWENTY--?
BAMF
YOU'LL BE FINE.
AHH--THE COLD!
IT'S WORSE THAN DEEP SPACE. AT LEAST OUT THERE, THERE'S NO WIND.
I EXTEND MY PERSONAL TEKE FIELD TO COVER US BOTH BUT IT'S A STOPGAP MEASURE.
AGAINST RACHEL, I SUSPECT I'LL NEED ALL MY RESERVES.
WE'RE SO USED TO BEING RESPONSIBLE AND HOLDING BACK ON OUR POWER, IT'S EASY TO FORGET JUST HOW MUCH SOME OF US WIELD.
THIS IS THE KIND OF PRIMAL STORM THAT SCULPTED THE FACE OF THE PLANET WHEN IT WAS YOUNG. AND ORORO'S JUST GETTING STARTED.
CLEAR OUT, KURT.
I'M STAYING!
I'LL BE YOUR DECOY.

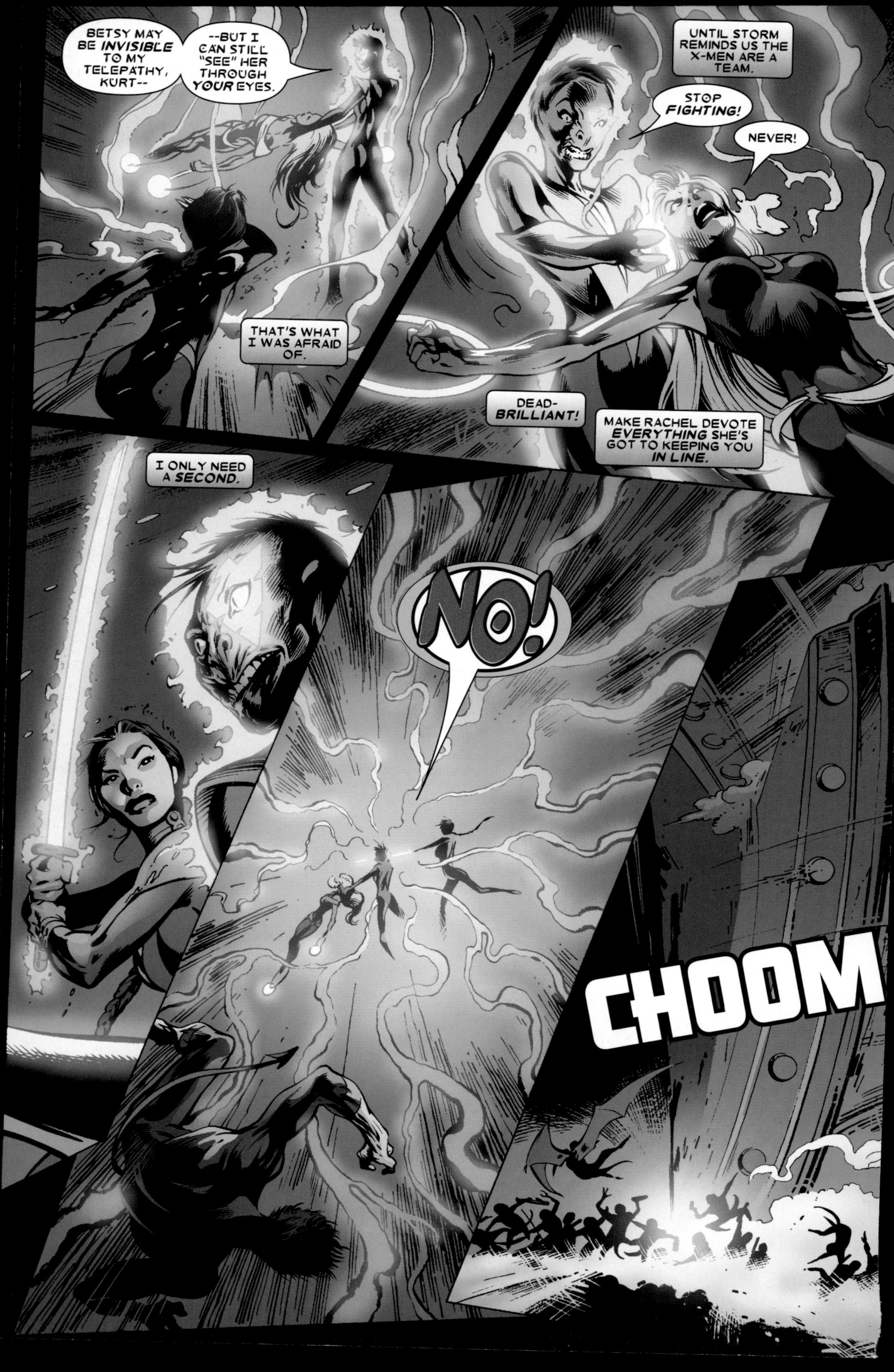
BETSY MAY BE INVISIBLE TO MY TELEPATHY, KURT--
--BUT I CAN STILL "SEE" HER THROUGH YOUR EYES.
THAT'S WHAT I WAS AFRAID OF.
UNTIL STORM REMINDS US THE X-MEN ARE A TEAM.
STOP FIGHTING!
NEVER!
DEAD-BRILLIANT!
MAKE RACHEL DEVOTE EVERYTHING SHE'S GOT TO KEEPING YOU IN LINE.
I ONLY NEED A SECOND.
NO!
CHOOM

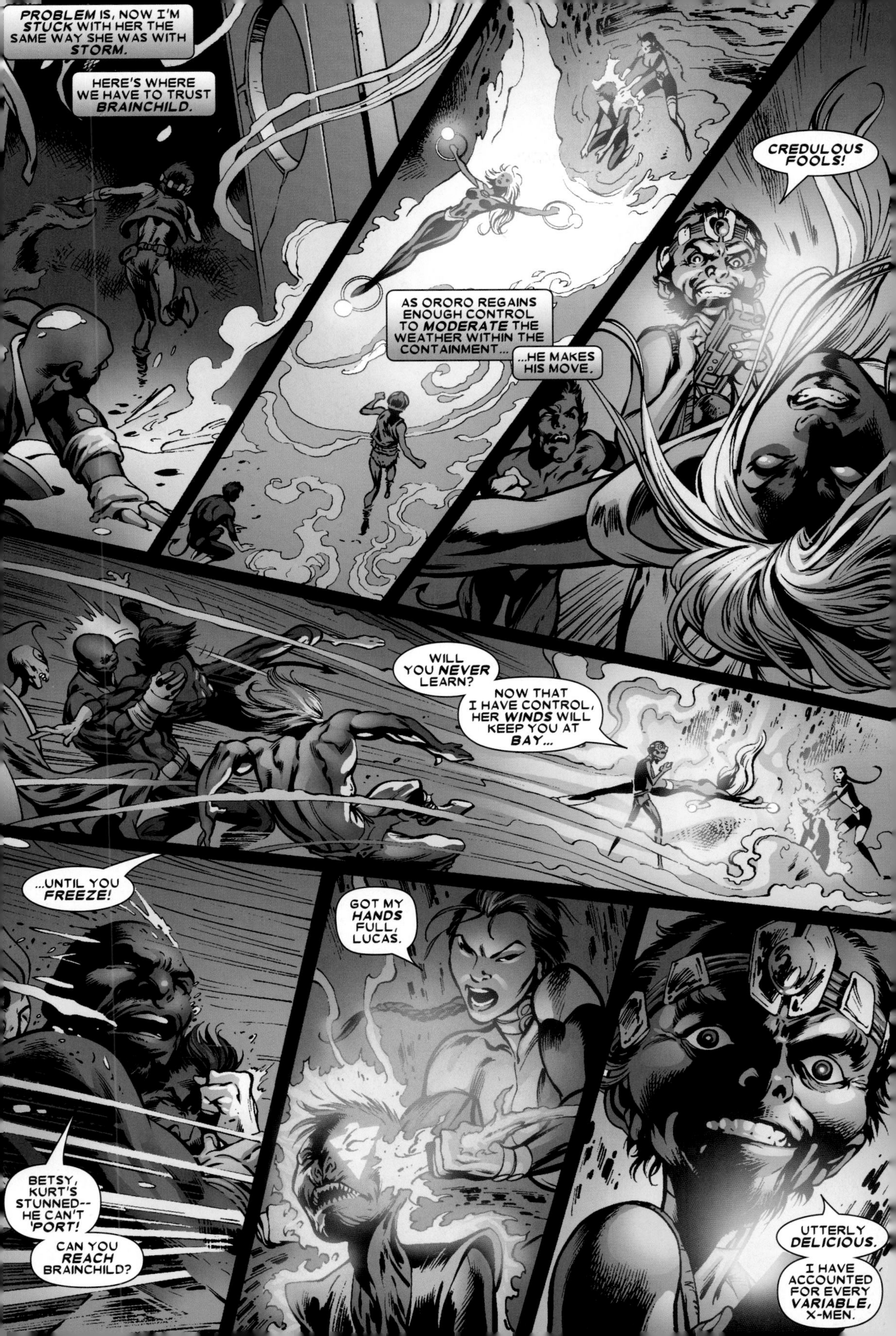
PROBLEM IS, NOW I'M STUCK WITH HER THE SAME WAY SHE WAS WITH STORM.
HERE'S WHERE WE HAVE TO TRUST BRAINCHILD.
AS ORORO REGAINS ENOUGH CONTROL TO MODERATE THE WEATHER WITHIN THE CONTAINMENT...
...HE MAKES HIS MOVE.
CREDULOUS FOOLS!
WILL YOU NEVER LEARN?
NOW THAT I HAVE CONTROL, HER WINDS WILL KEEP YOU AT BAY...
...UNTIL YOU FREEZE!
BETSY, KURT'S STUNNED-- HE CAN'T 'PORT!
CAN YOU REACH BRAINCHILD?
GOT MY HANDS FULL, LUCAS.
UTTERLY DELICIOUS.
I HAVE ACCOUNTED FOR EVERY VARIABLE, X-MEN.

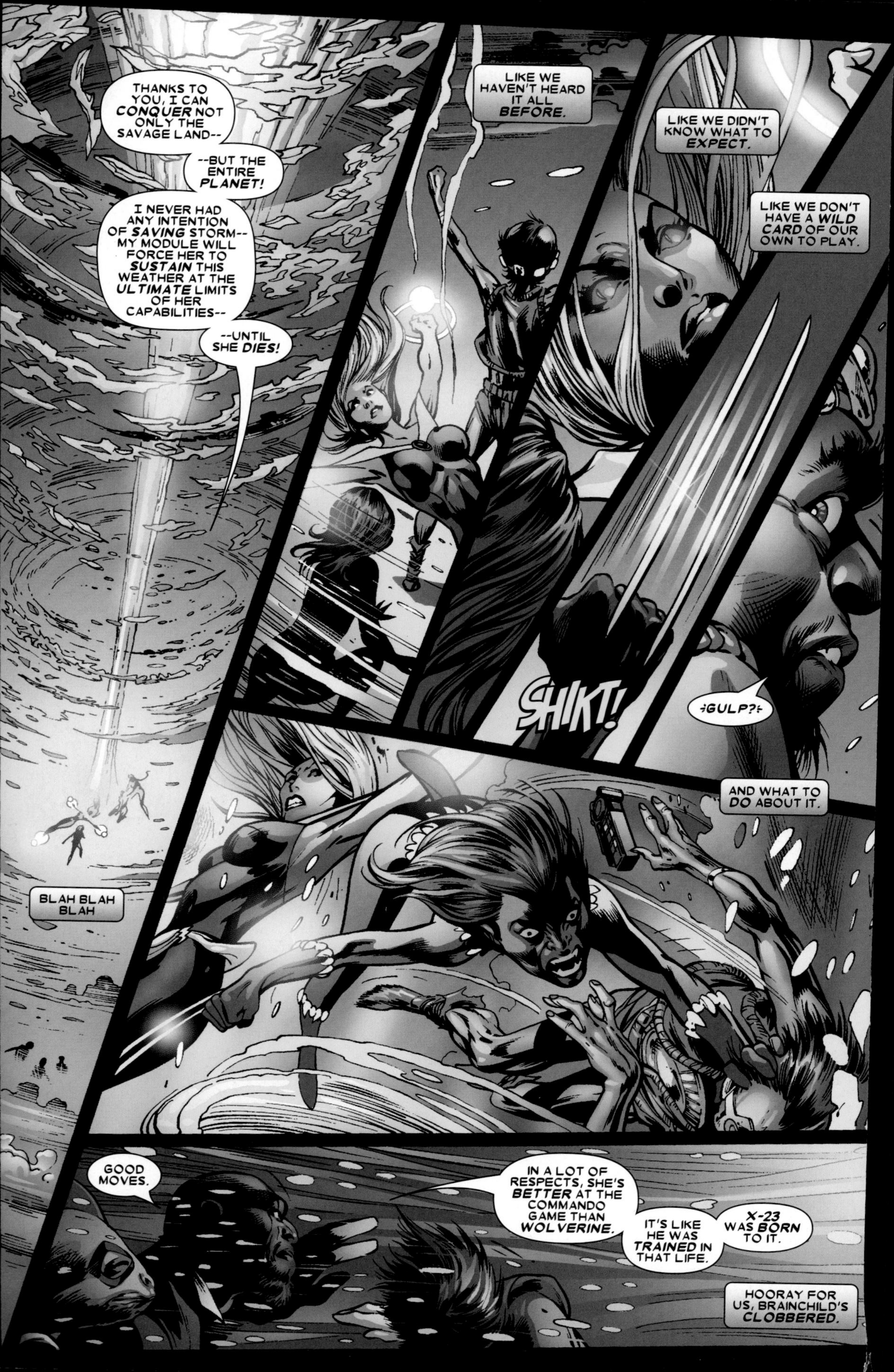
THANKS TO YOU, I CAN CONQUER NOT ONLY THE SAVAGE LAND--
--BUT THE ENTIRE PLANET!
I NEVER HAD ANY INTENTION OF SAVING STORM-- MY MODULE WILL FORCE HER TO SUSTAIN THIS WEATHER AT THE ULTIMATE LIMITS OF HER CAPABILITIES--
--UNTIL SHE DIES!
BLAH BLAH BLAH
LIKE WE HAVEN'T HEARD IT ALL BEFORE.
LIKE WE DIDN'T KNOW WHAT TO EXPECT.
LIKE WE DON'T HAVE A WILD CARD OF OUR OWN TO PLAY.
SHIKT!
GULP?
AND WHAT TO DO ABOUT IT.
GOOD MOVES.
IN A LOT OF RESPECTS, SHE'S BETTER AT THE COMMANDO GAME THAN WOLVERINE.
IT'S LIKE HE WAS TRAINED IN THAT LIFE.
X-23 WAS BORN TO IT.
HOORAY FOR US, BRAINCHILD'S CLOBBERED.

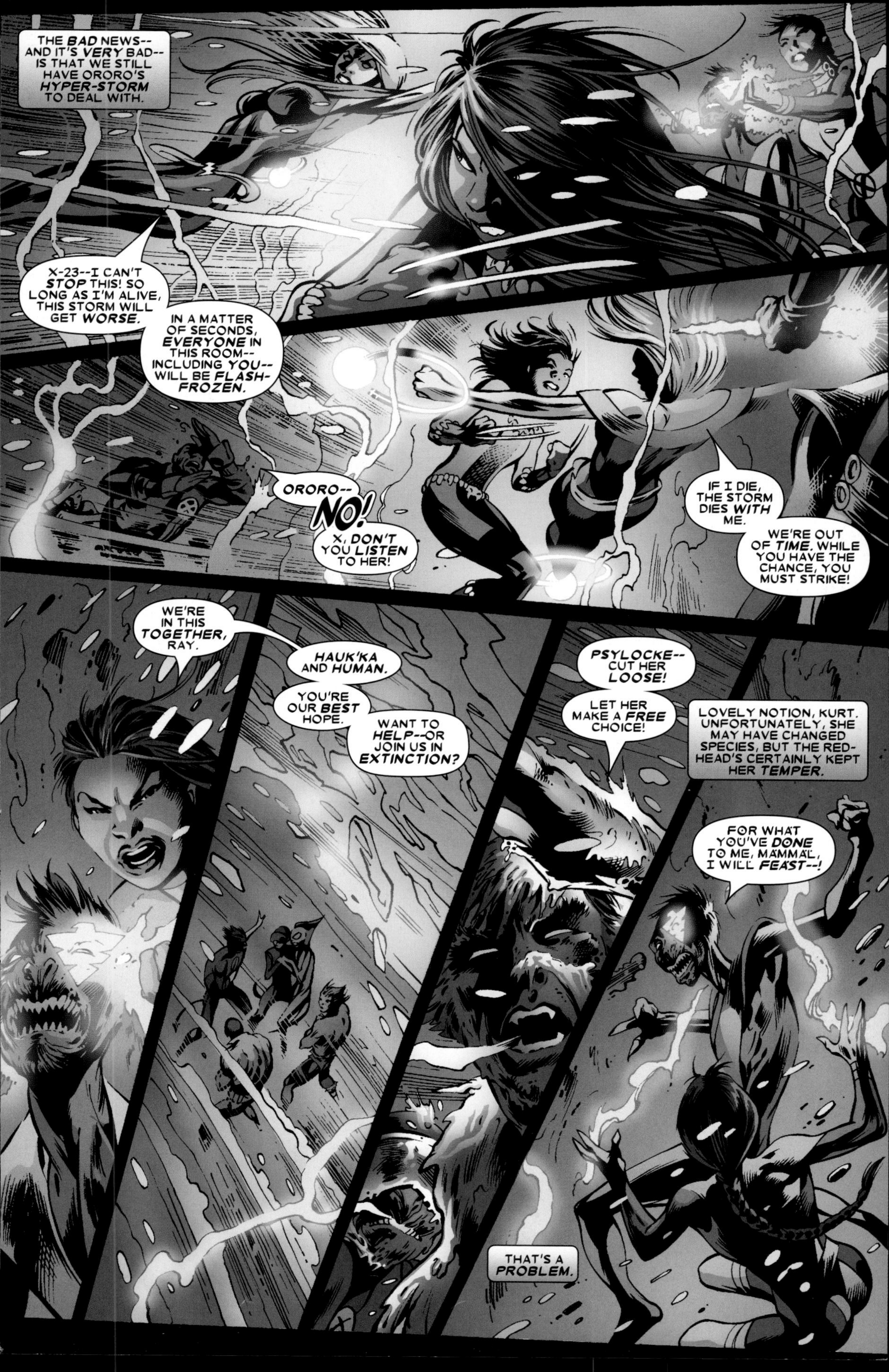
THE BAD NEWS-- AND IT'S VERY BAD-- IS THAT WE STILL HAVE ORORO'S HYPER-STORM TO DEAL WITH.
X-23--I CAN'T STOP THIS! SO LONG AS I'M ALIVE, THIS STORM WILL GET WORSE.
IN A MATTER OF SECONDS, EVERYONE IN THIS ROOM-- INCLUDING YOU-- WILL BE FLASH-FROZEN.
ORORO--
NO!
X, DON'T YOU LISTEN TO HER!
IF I DIE, THE STORM DIES WITH ME.
WE'RE OUT OF TIME. WHILE YOU HAVE THE CHANCE, YOU MUST STRIKE!
WE'RE IN THIS TOGETHER, RAY.
HAUK'KA AND HUMAN.
YOU'RE OUR BEST HOPE.
WANT TO HELP--OR JOIN US IN EXTINCTION?
PSYLOCKE-- CUT HER LOOSE!
LET HER MAKE A FREE CHOICE!
LOVELY NOTION, KURT. UNFORTUNATELY, SHE MAY HAVE CHANGED SPECIES, BUT THE RED-HEAD'S CERTAINLY KEPT HER TEMPER.
FOR WHAT YOU'VE DONE TO ME, MAMMAL, I WILL FEAST--!
THAT'S A PROBLEM.

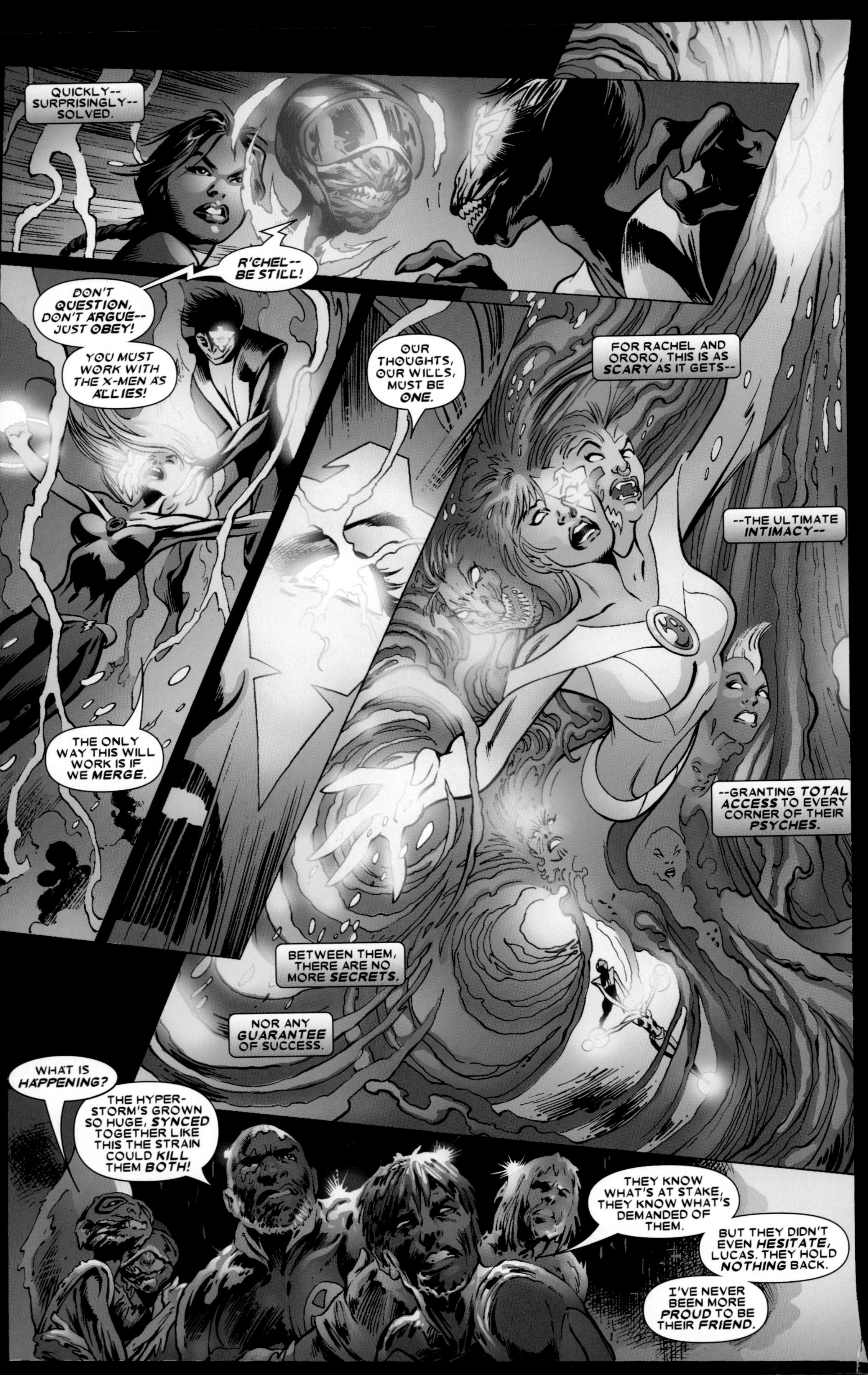
QUICKLY-- SURPRISINGLY-- SOLVED.
R'CHEL-- BE STILL!
DON'T QUESTION, DON'T ARGUE-- JUST OBEY!
YOU MUST WORK WITH THE X-MEN AS ALLIES!
THE ONLY WAY THIS WILL WORK IS IF WE MERGE.
OUR THOUGHTS, OUR WILLS, MUST BE ONE.
FOR RACHEL AND ORORO, THIS IS AS SCARY AS IT GETS--
--THE ULTIMATE INTIMACY--
--GRANTING TOTAL ACCESS TO EVERY CORNER OF THEIR PSYCHES.
BETWEEN THEM, THERE ARE NO MORE SECRETS.
NOR ANY GUARANTEE OF SUCCESS.
WHAT IS HAPPENING?
THE HYPER-STORM'S GROWN SO HUGE, SYNCED TOGETHER LIKE THIS THE STRAIN COULD KILL THEM BOTH!
THEY KNOW WHAT'S AT STAKE, THEY KNOW WHAT'S DEMANDED OF THEM.
BUT THEY DIDN'T EVEN HESITATE, LUCAS. THEY HOLD NOTHING BACK.
I'VE NEVER BEEN MORE PROUD TO BE THEIR FRIEND.

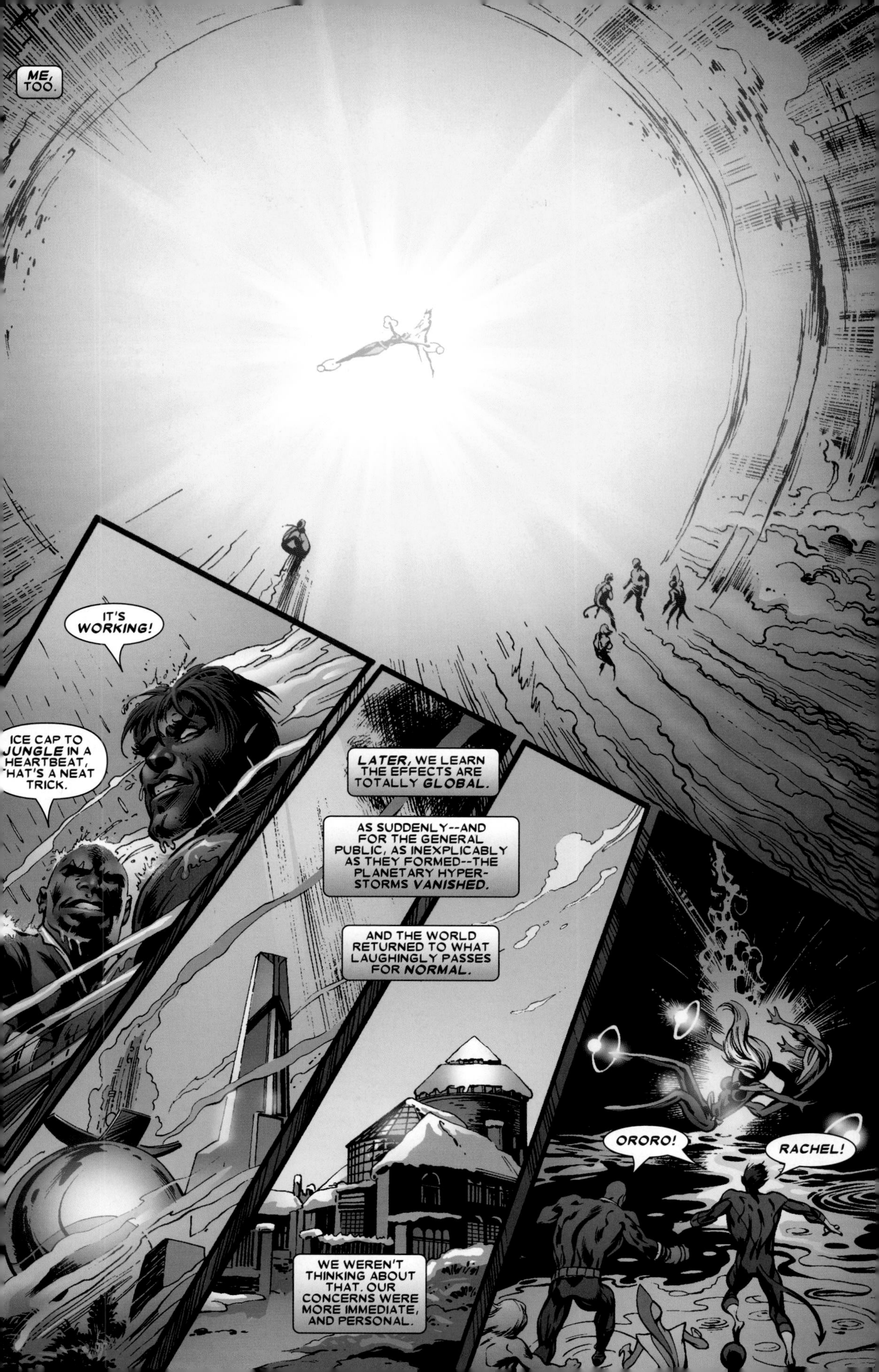
ME, TOO.
IT'S WORKING!
ICE CAP TO JUNGLE IN A HEARTBEAT, THAT'S A NEAT TRICK.
LATER, WE LEARN THE EFFECTS ARE TOTALLY GLOBAL.
AS SUDDENLY--AND FOR THE GENERAL PUBLIC, AS INEXPLICABLY AS THEY FORMED--THE PLANETARY HYPER-STORMS VANISHED.
AND THE WORLD RETURNED TO WHAT LAUGHINGLY PASSES FOR NORMAL.
WE WEREN'T THINKING ABOUT THAT. OUR CONCERNS WERE MORE IMMEDIATE, AND PERSONAL.
ORORO!
RACHEL!

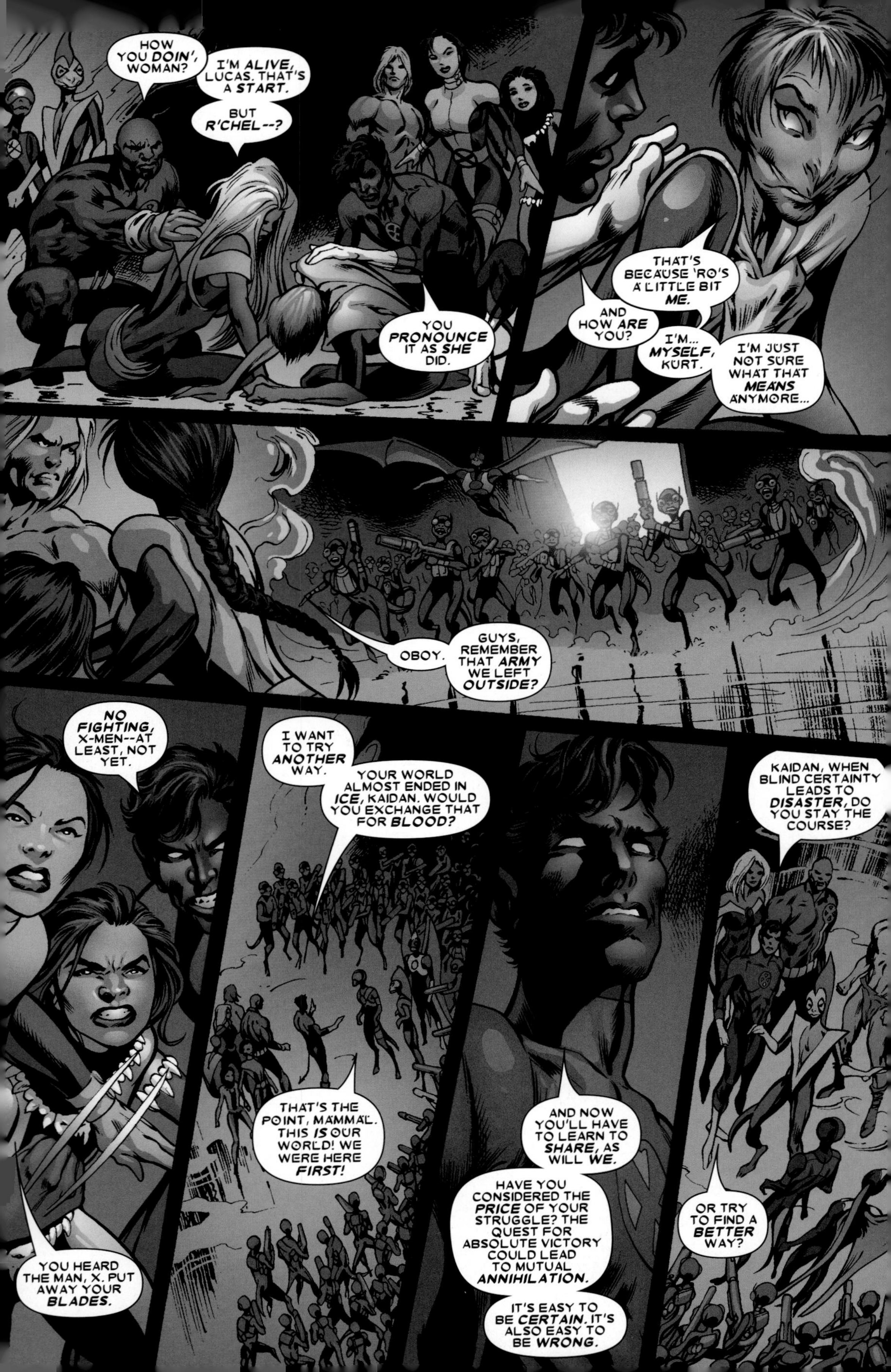
HOW YOU DOIN', WOMAN?
I'M ALIVE, LUCAS. THAT'S A START.
BUT R'CHEL--?
YOU PRONOUNCE IT AS SHE DID.
THAT'S BECAUSE 'RO'S A LITTLE BIT ME.
AND HOW ARE YOU?
I'M... MYSELF, KURT.
I'M JUST NOT SURE WHAT THAT MEANS ANYMORE...
OBOY.
GUYS, REMEMBER THAT ARMY WE LEFT OUTSIDE?
NO FIGHTING, X-MEN--AT LEAST, NOT YET.
YOU HEARD THE MAN, X. PUT AWAY YOUR BLADES.
I WANT TO TRY ANOTHER WAY.
YOUR WORLD ALMOST ENDED IN ICE, KAIDAN. WOULD YOU EXCHANGE THAT FOR BLOOD?
THAT'S THE POINT, MAMMAL. THIS IS OUR WORLD! WE WERE HERE FIRST!
AND NOW YOU'LL HAVE TO LEARN TO SHARE, AS WILL WE.
HAVE YOU CONSIDERED THE PRICE OF YOUR STRUGGLE? THE QUEST FOR ABSOLUTE VICTORY COULD LEAD TO MUTUAL ANNIHILATION.
IT'S EASY TO BE CERTAIN. IT'S ALSO EASY TO BE WRONG.
KAIDAN, WHEN BLIND CERTAINTY LEADS TO DISASTER, DO YOU STAY THE COURSE?
OR TRY TO FIND A BETTER WAY?

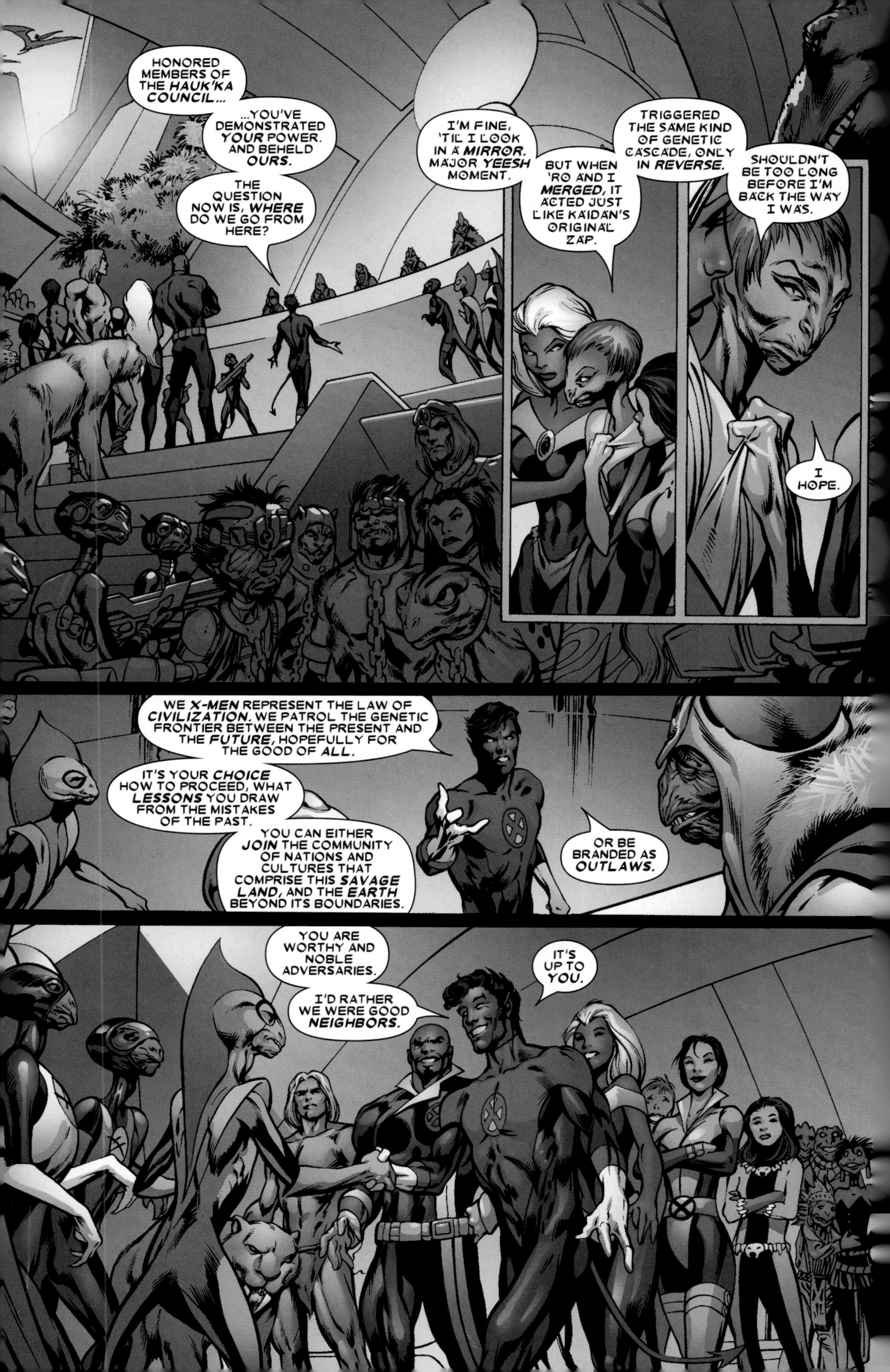

HONORED MEMBERS OF THE HAUK'KA COUNCIL...
...YOU'VE DEMONSTRATED YOUR POWER. AND BEHELD OURS.
THE QUESTION NOW IS, WHERE DO WE GO FROM HERE?
I'M FINE, 'TIL I LOOK IN A MIRROR. MAJOR YEESH MOMENT.
BUT WHEN 'RO AND I MERGED, IT ACTED JUST LIKE KAIDAN'S ORIGINAL ZAP.
TRIGGERED THE SAME KIND OF GENETIC CASCADE, ONLY IN REVERSE.
SHOULDN'T BE TOO LONG BEFORE I'M BACK THE WAY I WAS.
I HOPE.
WE X-MEN REPRESENT THE LAW OF CIVILIZATION. WE PATROL THE GENETIC FRONTIER BETWEEN THE PRESENT AND THE FUTURE, HOPEFULLY FOR THE GOOD OF ALL.
IT'S YOUR CHOICE HOW TO PROCEED, WHAT LESSONS YOU DRAW FROM THE MISTAKES OF THE PAST.
YOU CAN EITHER JOIN THE COMMUNITY OF NATIONS AND CULTURES THAT COMPRISE THIS SAVAGE LAND, AND THE EARTH BEYOND ITS BOUNDARIES.
OR BE BRANDED AS OUTLAWS.
YOU ARE WORTHY AND NOBLE ADVERSARIES.
I'D RATHER WE WERE GOOD NEIGHBORS.
IT'S UP TO YOU.

#460

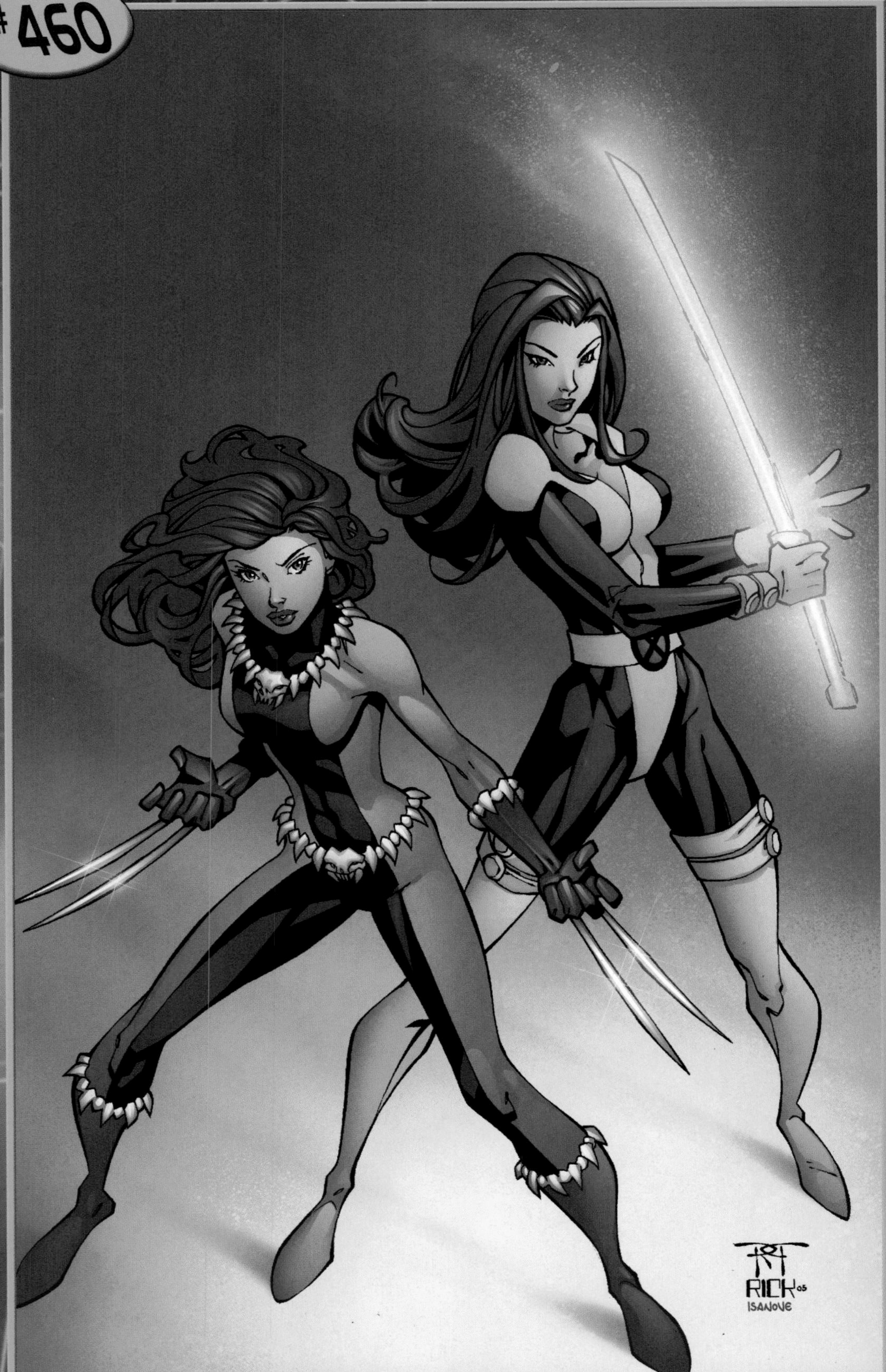
RICK 05
ISANOVE

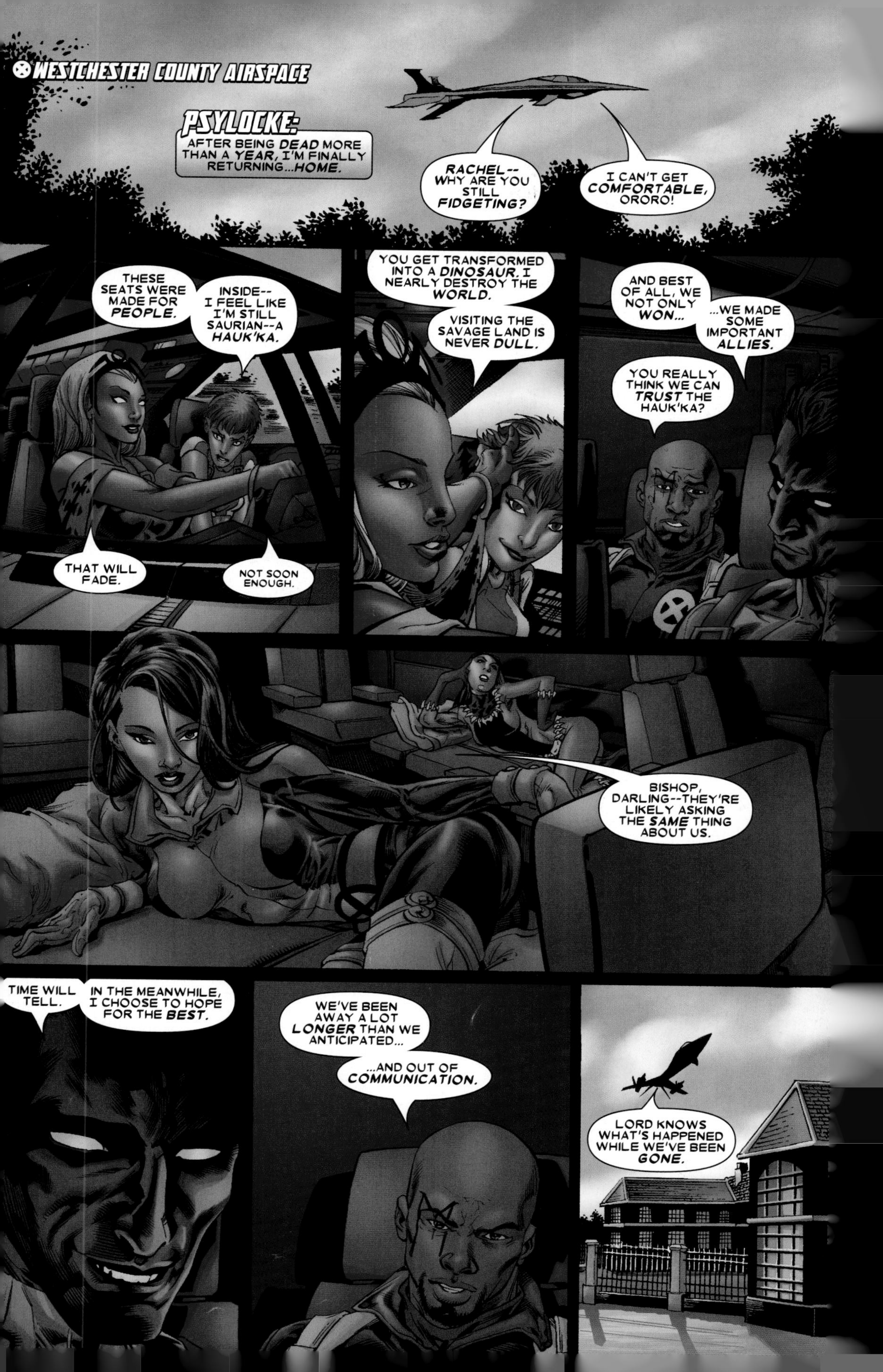
WESTCHESTER COUNTY AIRSPACE
PSYLOCKE:
AFTER BEING DEAD MORE THAN A YEAR, I'M FINALLY RETURNING...HOME.
RACHEL-- WHY ARE YOU STILL FIDGETING?
I CAN'T GET COMFORTABLE, ORORO!
THESE SEATS WERE MADE FOR PEOPLE.
INSIDE-- I FEEL LIKE I'M STILL SAURIAN--A HAUK'KA.
THAT WILL FADE.
NOT SOON ENOUGH.
YOU GET TRANSFORMED INTO A DINOSAUR. I NEARLY DESTROY THE WORLD.
VISITING THE SAVAGE LAND IS NEVER DULL.
AND BEST OF ALL, WE NOT ONLY WON...
...WE MADE SOME IMPORTANT ALLIES.
YOU REALLY THINK WE CAN TRUST THE HAUK'KA?
BISHOP, DARLING--THEY'RE LIKELY ASKING THE SAME THING ABOUT US.
TIME WILL TELL.
IN THE MEANWHILE, I CHOOSE TO HOPE FOR THE BEST.
WE'VE BEEN AWAY A LOT LONGER THAN WE ANTICIPATED...
...AND OUT OF COMMUNICATION.
LORD KNOWS WHAT'S HAPPENED WHILE WE'VE BEEN GONE.

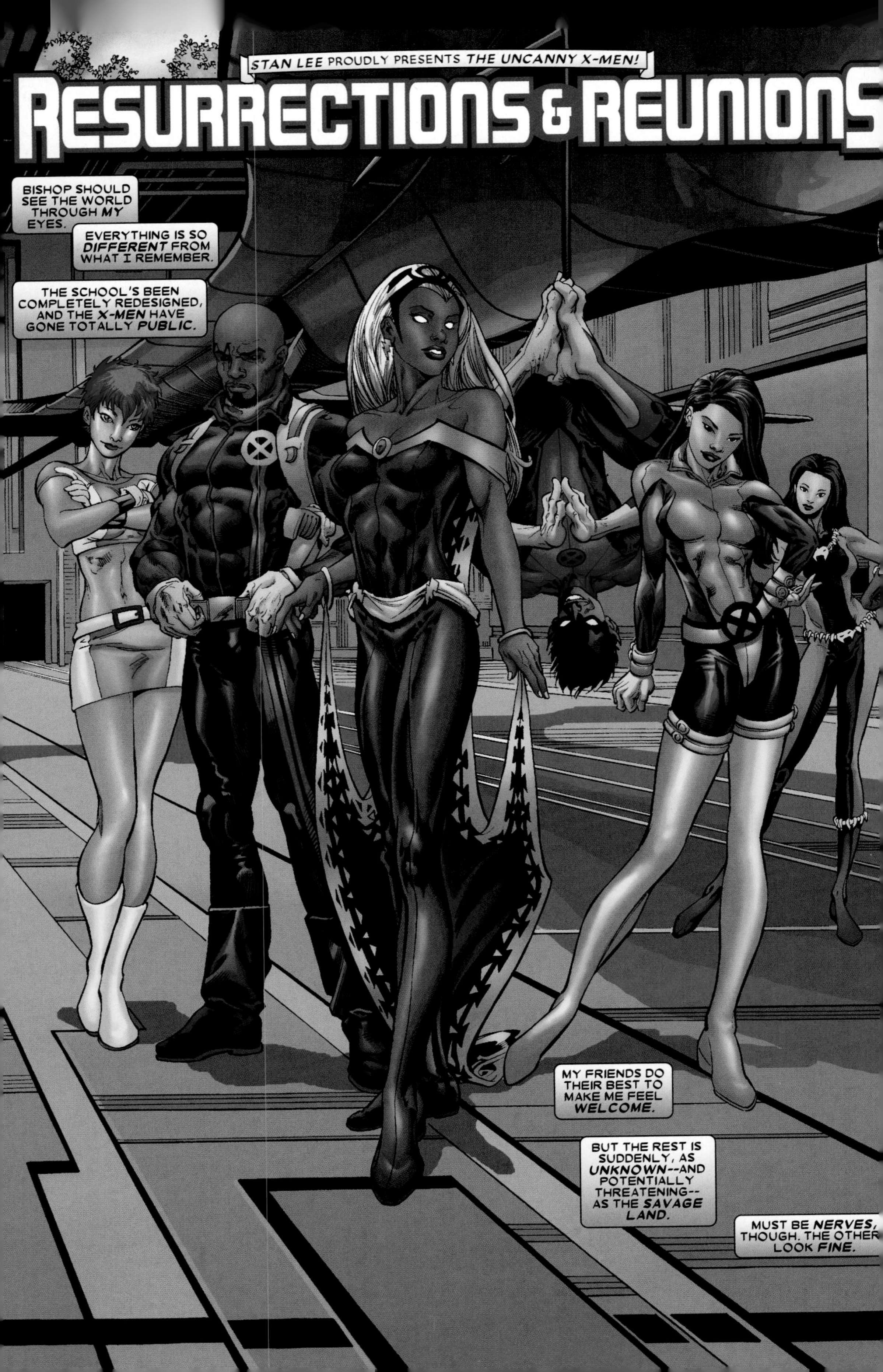
STAN LEE PROUDLY PRESENTS THE UNCANNY X-MEN!
RESURRECTIONS & REUNIONS
BISHOP SHOULD SEE THE WORLD THROUGH MY EYES.
EVERYTHING IS SO DIFFERENT FROM WHAT I REMEMBER.
THE SCHOOL'S BEEN COMPLETELY REDESIGNED, AND THE X-MEN HAVE GONE TOTALLY PUBLIC.
MY FRIENDS DO THEIR BEST TO MAKE ME FEEL WELCOME.
BUT THE REST IS SUDDENLY, AS UNKNOWN--AND POTENTIALLY THREATENING--AS THE SAVAGE LAND.
MUST BE NERVES, THOUGH. THE OTHER LOOK FINE.

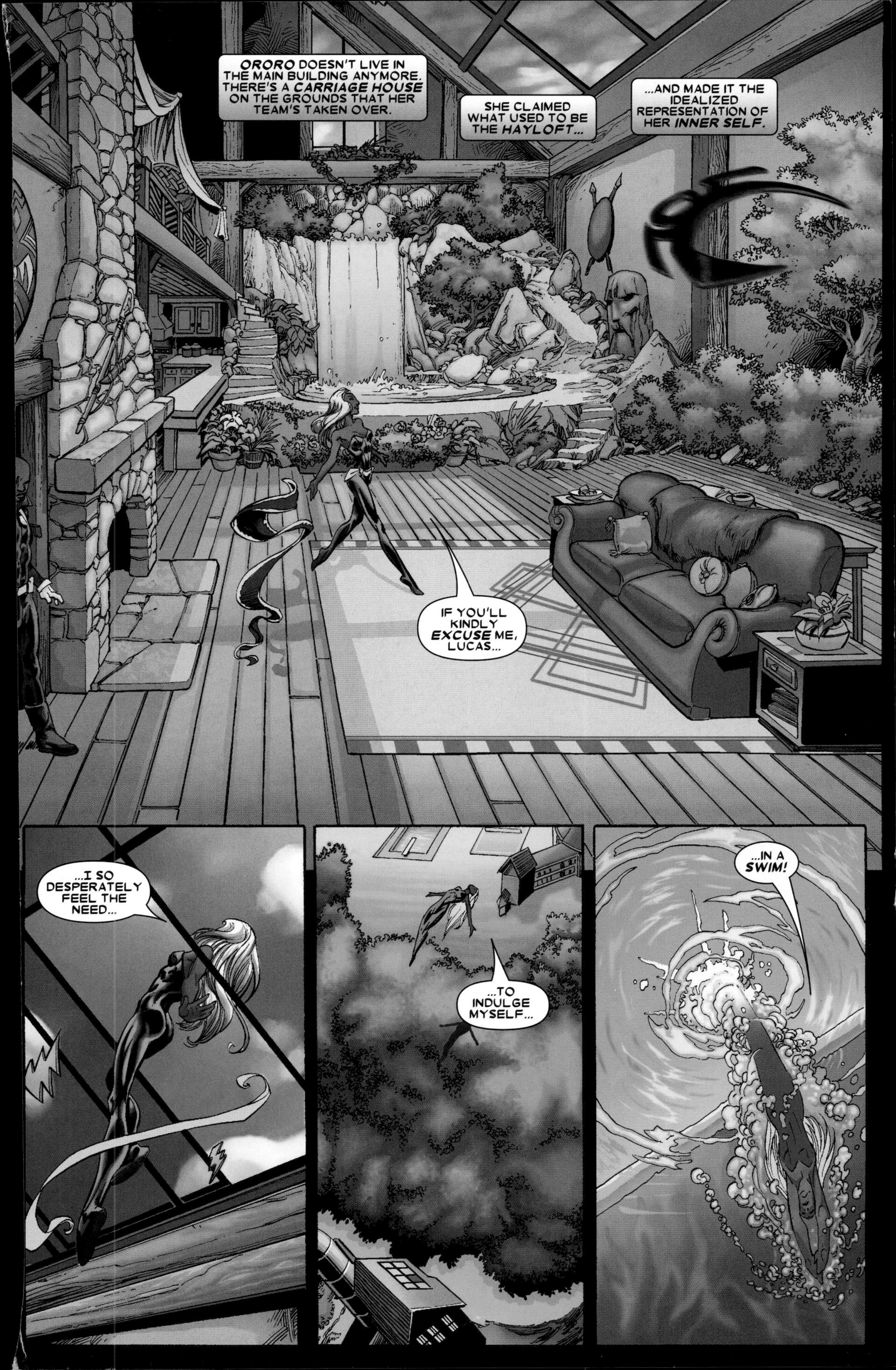
ORORO DOESN'T LIVE IN THE MAIN BUILDING ANYMORE. THERE'S A CARRIAGE HOUSE ON THE GROUNDS THAT HER TEAM'S TAKEN OVER.
SHE CLAIMED WHAT USED TO BE THE HAYLOFT...
...AND MADE IT THE IDEALIZED REPRESENTATION OF HER INNER SELF.
IF YOU'LL KINDLY EXCUSE ME, LUCAS...
...I SO DESPERATELY FEEL THE NEED...
...TO INDULGE MYSELF...
...IN A SWIM!

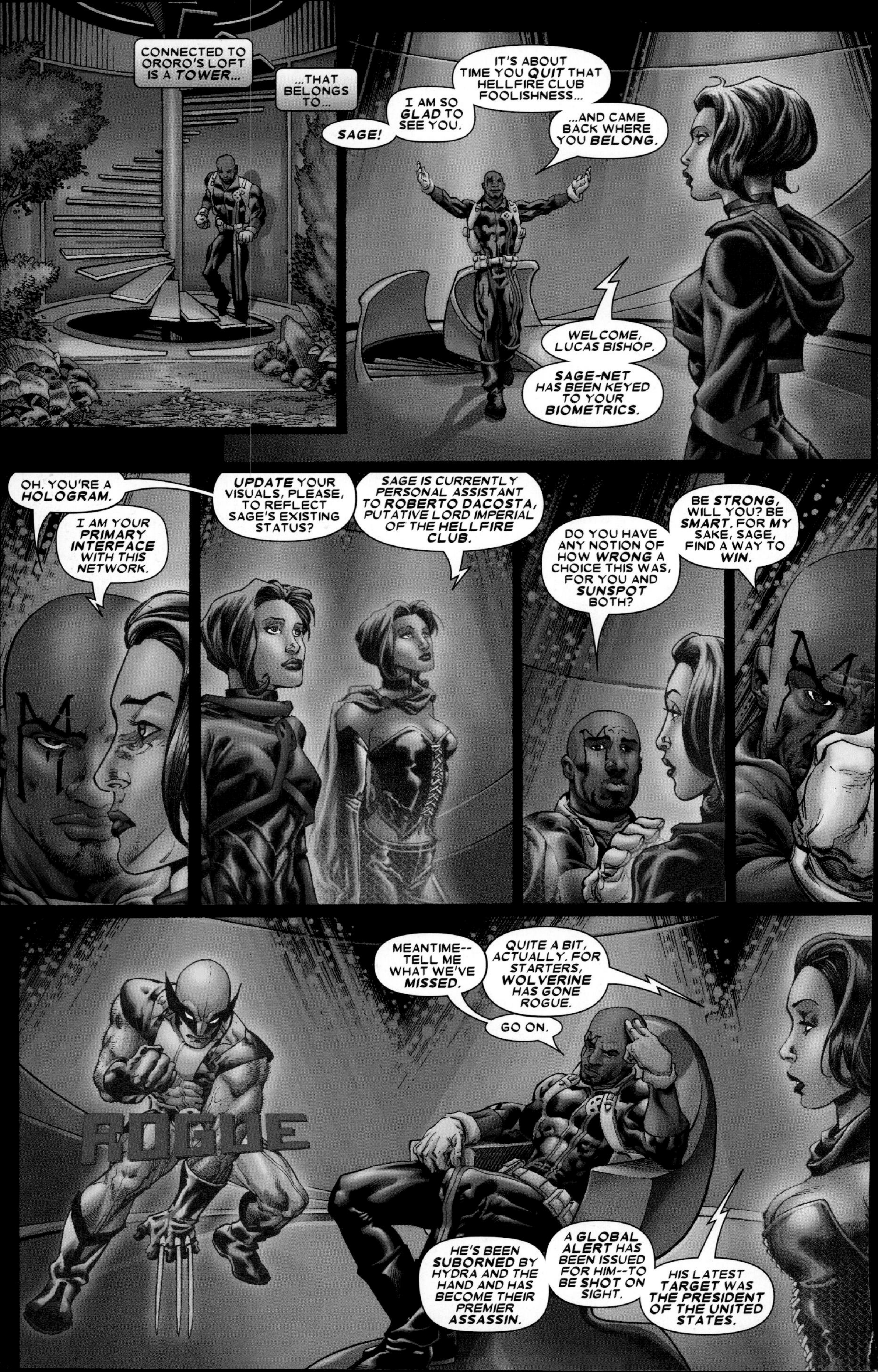
CONNECTED TO ORORO'S LOFT IS A TOWER...
...THAT BELONGS TO...
SAGE!
I AM SO GLAD TO SEE YOU.
IT'S ABOUT TIME YOU QUIT THAT HELLFIRE CLUB FOOLISHNESS...
...AND CAME BACK WHERE YOU BELONG.
WELCOME, LUCAS BISHOP.
SAGE-NET HAS BEEN KEYED TO YOUR BIOMETRICS.
OH. YOU'RE A HOLOGRAM.
I AM YOUR PRIMARY INTERFACE WITH THIS NETWORK.
UPDATE YOUR VISUALS, PLEASE, TO REFLECT SAGE'S EXISTING STATUS?
SAGE IS CURRENTLY PERSONAL ASSISTANT TO ROBERTO DACOSTA, PUTATIVE LORD IMPERIAL OF THE HELLFIRE CLUB.
DO YOU HAVE ANY NOTION OF HOW WRONG A CHOICE THIS WAS, FOR YOU AND SUNSPOT BOTH?
BE STRONG, WILL YOU? BE SMART. FOR MY SAKE, SAGE, FIND A WAY TO WIN.
MEANTIME-- TELL ME WHAT WE'VE MISSED.
QUITE A BIT, ACTUALLY. FOR STARTERS, WOLVERINE HAS GONE ROGUE.
GO ON.
ROGUE
HE'S BEEN SUBORNED BY HYDRA AND THE HAND AND HAS BECOME THEIR PREMIER ASSASSIN.
A GLOBAL ALERT HAS BEEN ISSUED FOR HIM--TO BE SHOT ON SIGHT.
HIS LATEST TARGET WAS THE PRESIDENT OF THE UNITED STATES.

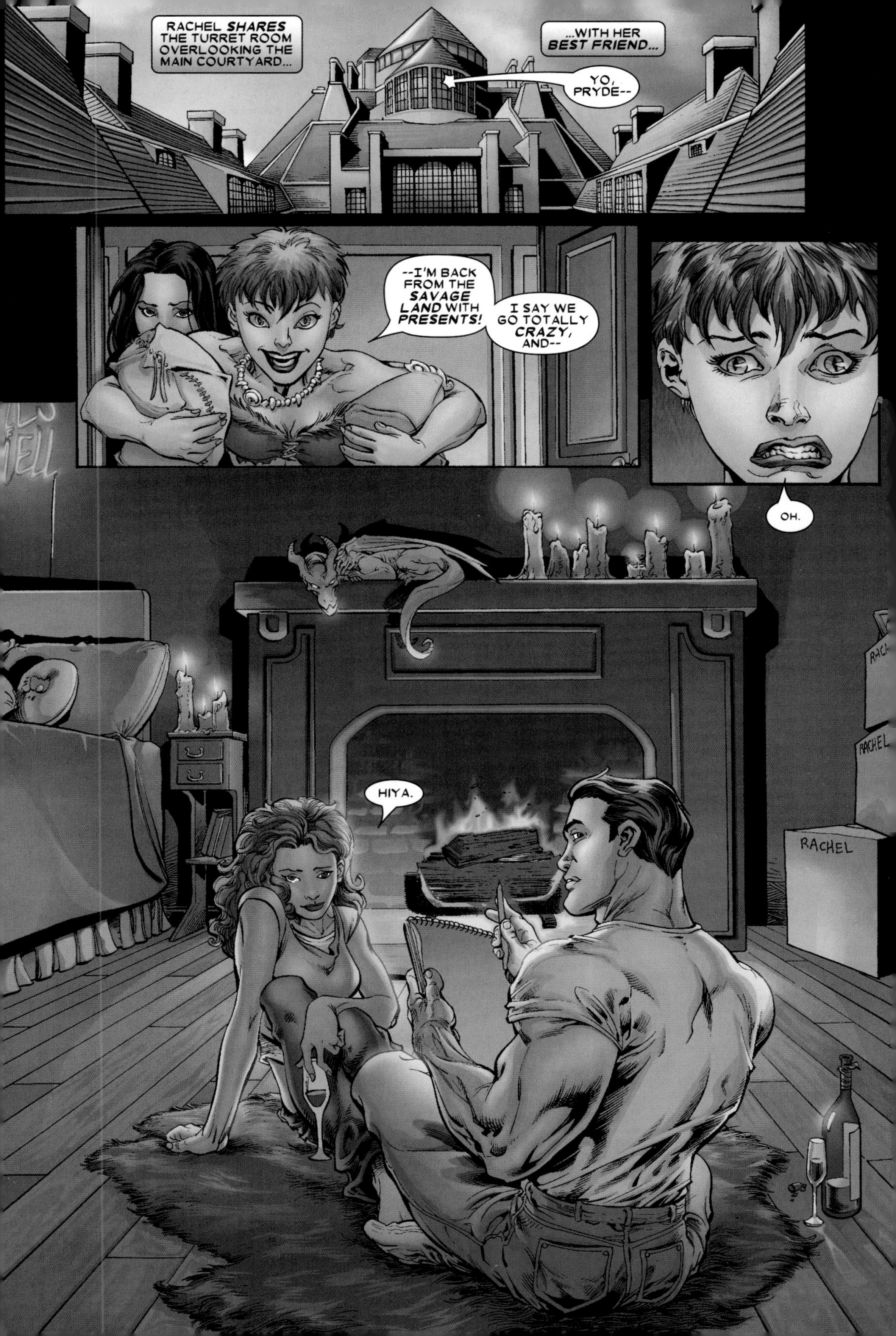
RACHEL SHARES THE TURRET ROOM OVERLOOKING THE MAIN COURTYARD...
...WITH HER BEST FRIEND...
YO, PRYDE--
--I'M BACK FROM THE SAVAGE LAND WITH PRESENTS!
I SAY WE GO TOTALLY CRAZY, AND--
OH.
HIYA.
RACHEL
RACHEL
RACHEL

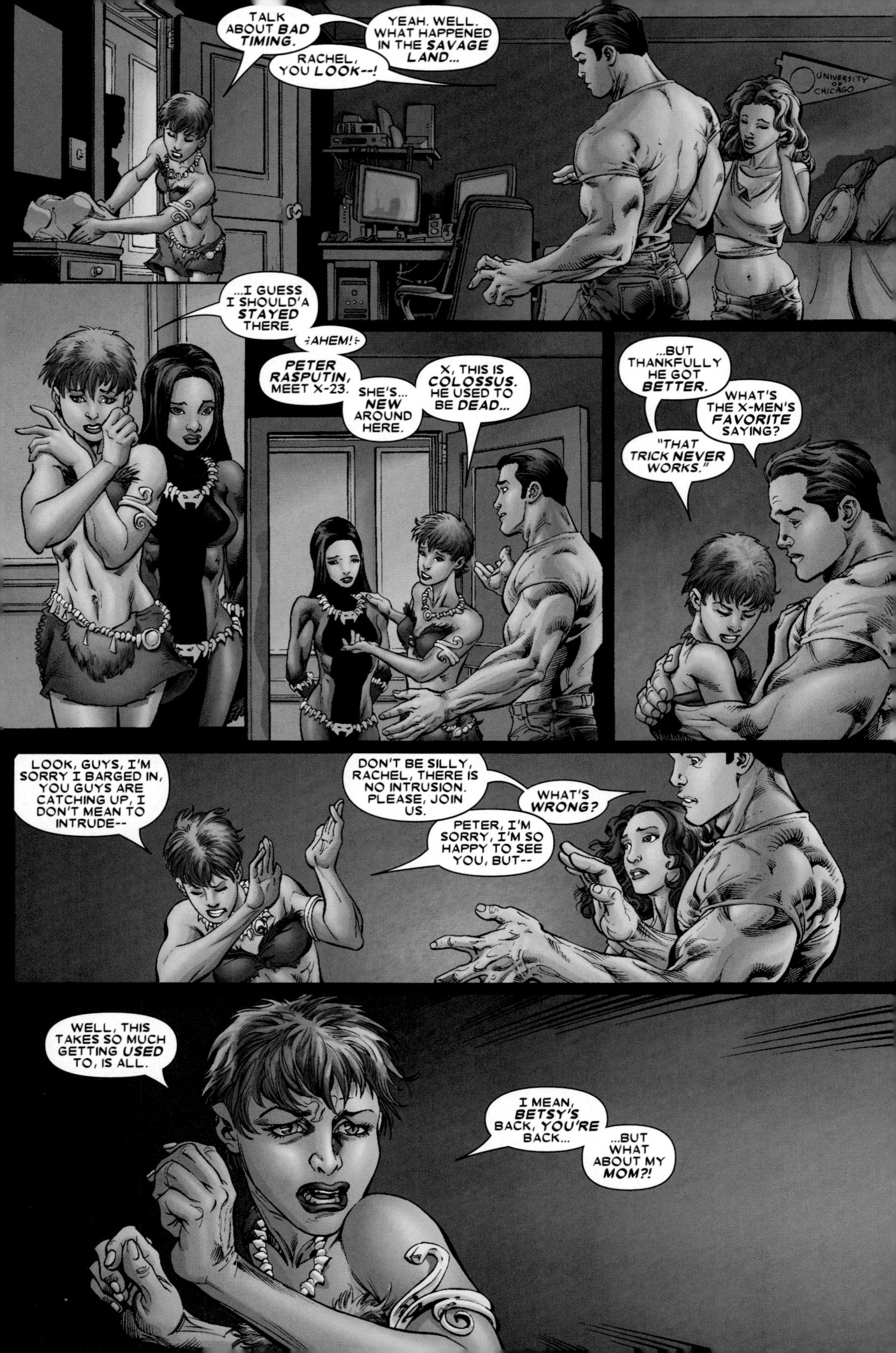

TALK ABOUT BAD TIMING.
RACHEL, YOU LOOK--!
YEAH. WELL. WHAT HAPPENED IN THE SAVAGE LAND...
UNIVERSITY OF CHICAGO
...I GUESS I SHOULD'A STAYED THERE.
AHEM!
PETER RASPUTIN, MEET X-23.
SHE'S... NEW AROUND HERE.
X, THIS IS COLOSSUS. HE USED TO BE DEAD...
...BUT THANKFULLY HE GOT BETTER.
WHAT'S THE X-MEN'S FAVORITE SAYING?
"THAT TRICK NEVER WORKS."
LOOK, GUYS, I'M SORRY I BARGED IN, YOU GUYS ARE CATCHING UP, I DON'T MEAN TO INTRUDE--
DON'T BE SILLY, RACHEL, THERE IS NO INTRUSION. PLEASE, JOIN US.
WHAT'S WRONG?
PETER, I'M SORRY, I'M SO HAPPY TO SEE YOU, BUT--
WELL, THIS TAKES SO MUCH GETTING USED TO, IS ALL.
I MEAN, BETSY'S BACK, YOU'RE BACK...
...BUT WHAT ABOUT MY MOM?!

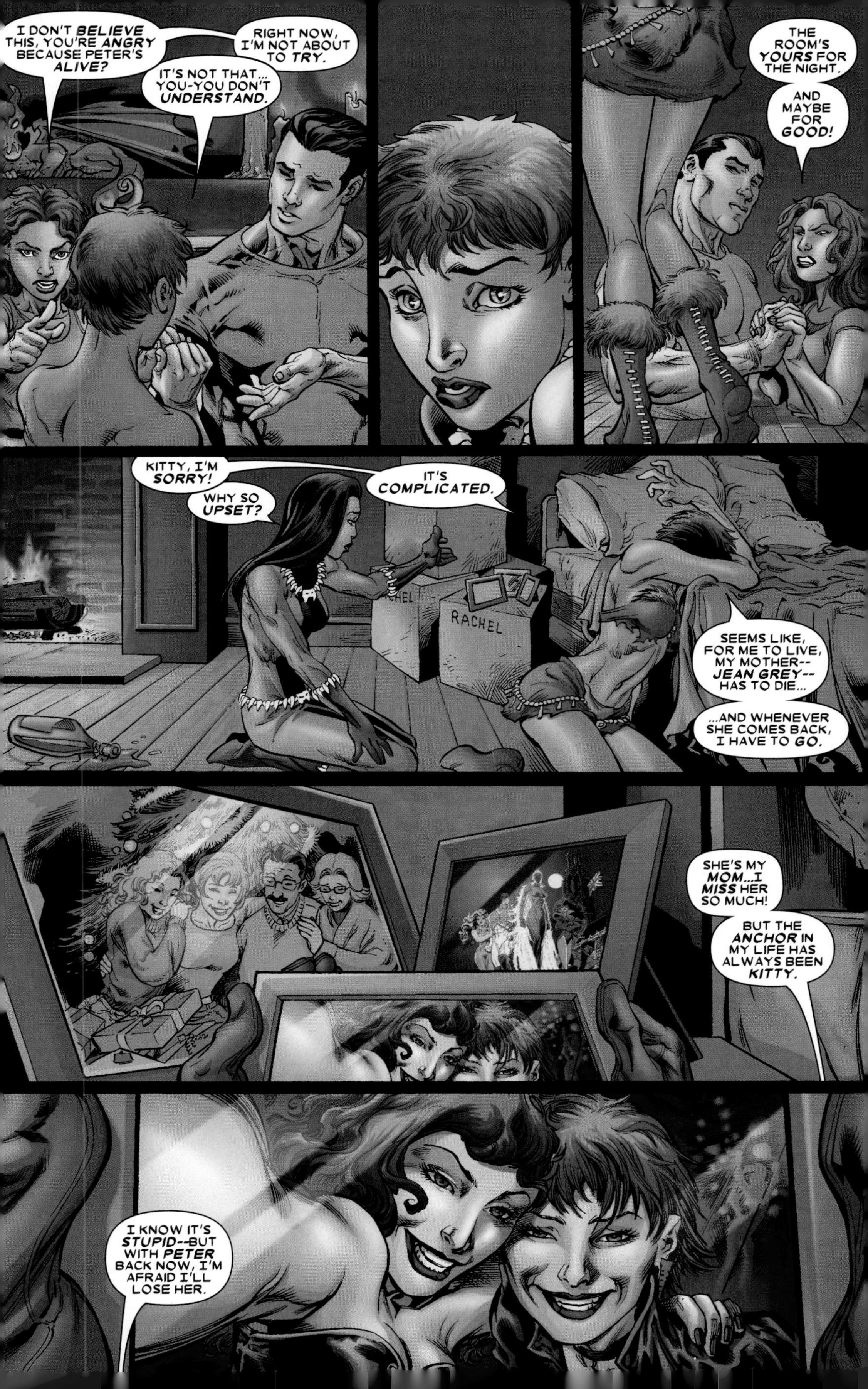

I DON'T BELIEVE THIS, YOU'RE ANGRY BECAUSE PETER'S ALIVE?
RIGHT NOW, I'M NOT ABOUT TO TRY.
IT'S NOT THAT... YOU-YOU DON'T UNDERSTAND.
THE ROOM'S YOURS FOR THE NIGHT.
AND MAYBE FOR GOOD!
KITTY, I'M SORRY!
IT'S COMPLICATED.
WHY SO UPSET?
RACHEL
RACHEL
SEEMS LIKE, FOR ME TO LIVE, MY MOTHER-- JEAN GREY-- HAS TO DIE...
...AND WHENEVER SHE COMES BACK, I HAVE TO GO.
SHE'S MY MOM...I MISS HER SO MUCH!
BUT THE ANCHOR IN MY LIFE HAS ALWAYS BEEN KITTY.
I KNOW IT'S STUPID--BUT WITH PETER BACK NOW, I'M AFRAID I'LL LOSE HER.

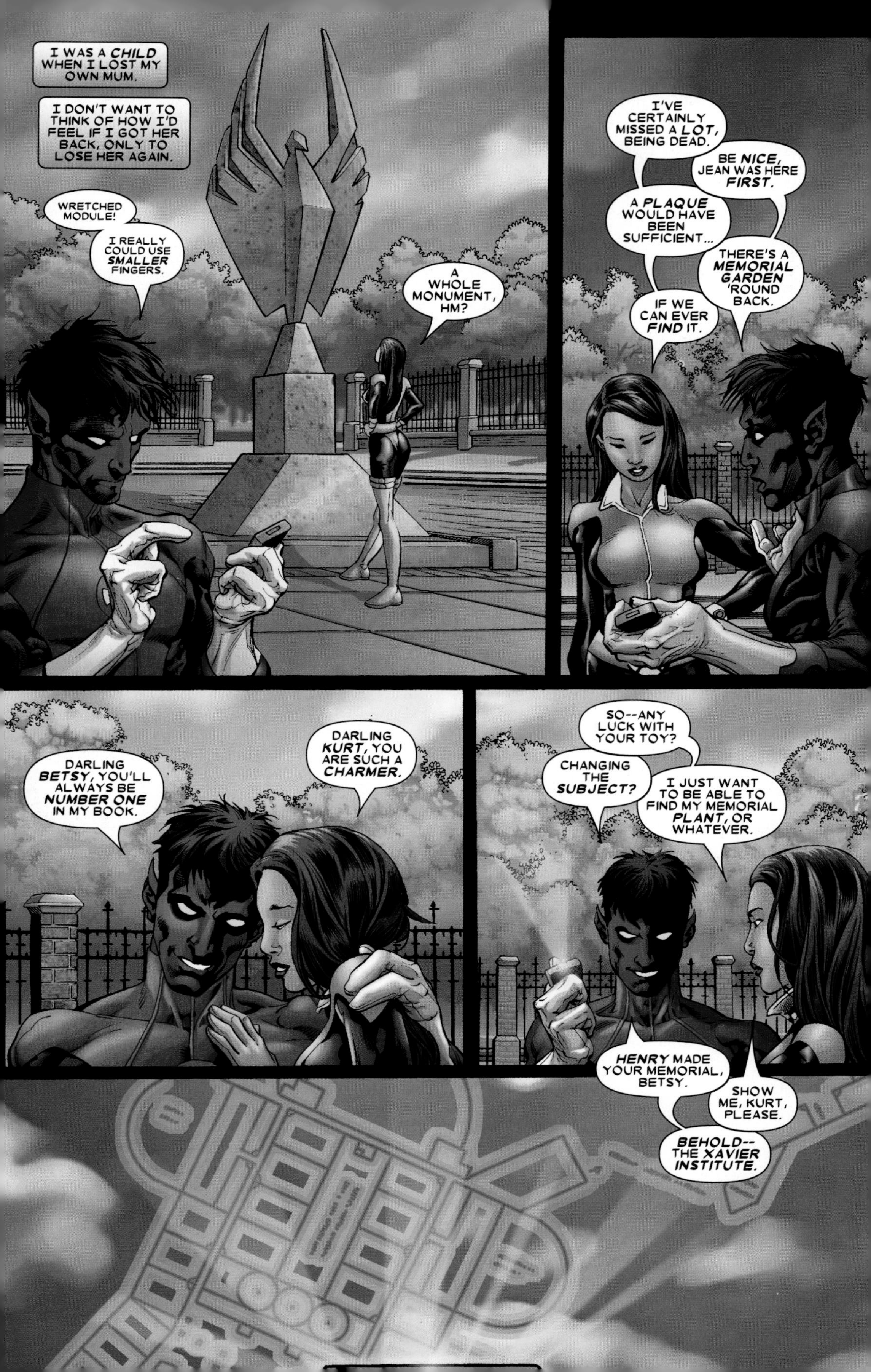
I WAS A CHILD WHEN I LOST MY OWN MUM.
I DON'T WANT TO THINK OF HOW I'D FEEL IF I GOT HER BACK, ONLY TO LOSE HER AGAIN.
WRETCHED MODULE!
I REALLY COULD USE SMALLER FINGERS.
A WHOLE MONUMENT, HM?
I'VE CERTAINLY MISSED A LOT, BEING DEAD.
BE NICE, JEAN WAS HERE FIRST.
A PLAQUE WOULD HAVE BEEN SUFFICIENT...
THERE'S A MEMORIAL GARDEN 'ROUND BACK.
IF WE CAN EVER FIND IT.
DARLING BETSY, YOU'LL ALWAYS BE NUMBER ONE IN MY BOOK.
DARLING KURT, YOU ARE SUCH A CHARMER.
SO--ANY LUCK WITH YOUR TOY?
CHANGING THE SUBJECT?
I JUST WANT TO BE ABLE TO FIND MY MEMORIAL PLANT, OR WHATEVER.
HENRY MADE YOUR MEMORIAL, BETSY.
SHOW ME, KURT, PLEASE.
BEHOLD-- THE XAVIER INSTITUTE.

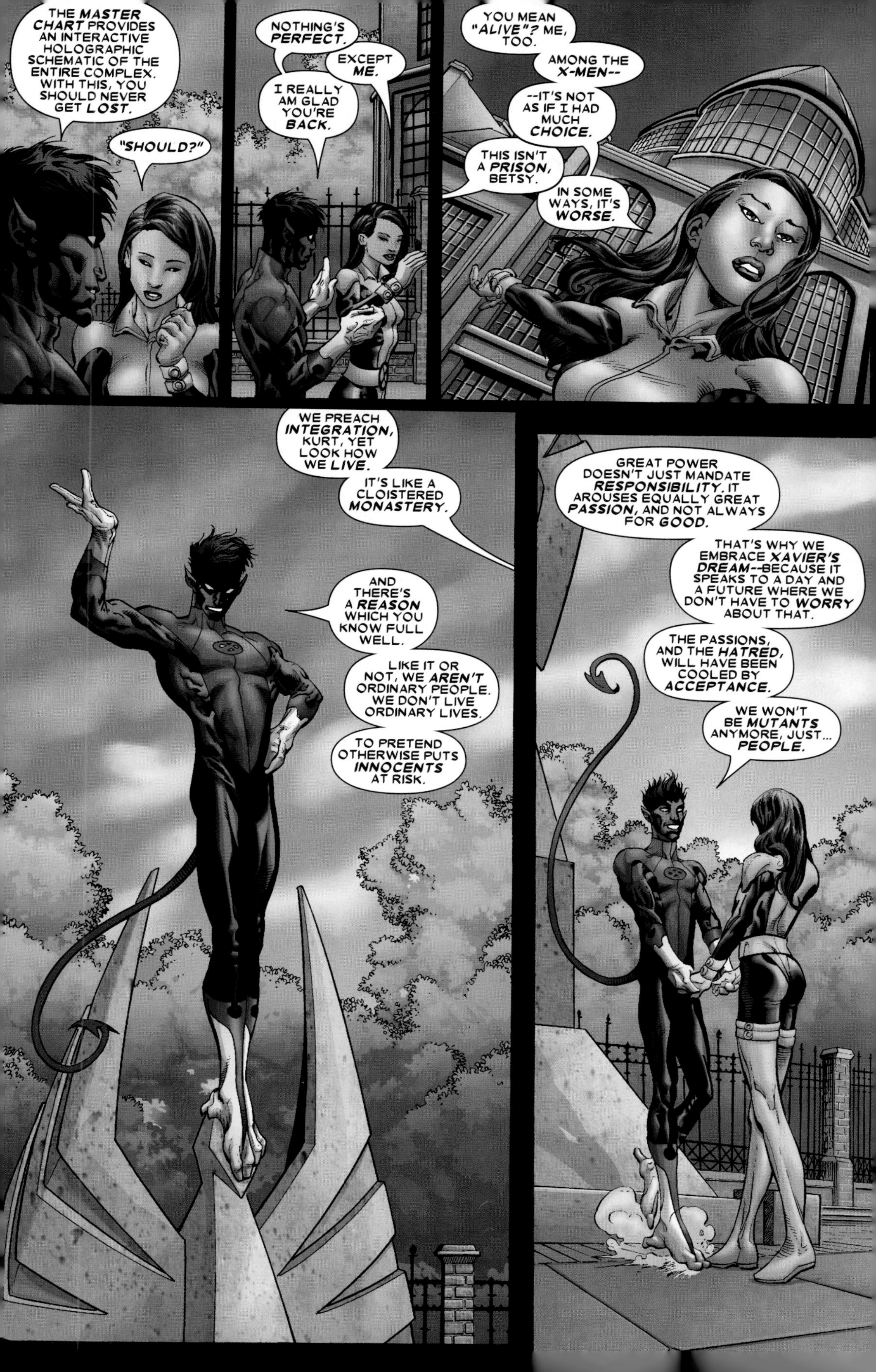
THE MASTER CHART PROVIDES AN INTERACTIVE HOLOGRAPHIC SCHEMATIC OF THE ENTIRE COMPLEX. WITH THIS, YOU SHOULD NEVER GET LOST.
"SHOULD?"
NOTHING'S PERFECT.
EXCEPT ME.
I REALLY AM GLAD YOU'RE BACK.
YOU MEAN "ALIVE"? ME, TOO.
AMONG THE X-MEN--
--IT'S NOT AS IF I HAD MUCH CHOICE.
THIS ISN'T A PRISON, BETSY.
IN SOME WAYS, IT'S WORSE.
WE PREACH INTEGRATION, KURT, YET LOOK HOW WE LIVE.
IT'S LIKE A CLOISTERED MONASTERY.
AND THERE'S A REASON WHICH YOU KNOW FULL WELL.
LIKE IT OR NOT, WE AREN'T ORDINARY PEOPLE. WE DON'T LIVE ORDINARY LIVES.
TO PRETEND OTHERWISE PUTS INNOCENTS AT RISK.
GREAT POWER DOESN'T JUST MANDATE RESPONSIBILITY. IT AROUSES EQUALLY GREAT PASSION, AND NOT ALWAYS FOR GOOD.
THAT'S WHY WE EMBRACE XAVIER'S DREAM--BECAUSE IT SPEAKS TO A DAY AND A FUTURE WHERE WE DON'T HAVE TO WORRY ABOUT THAT.
THE PASSIONS, AND THE HATRED, WILL HAVE BEEN COOLED BY ACCEPTANCE.
WE WON'T BE MUTANTS ANYMORE, JUST... PEOPLE.

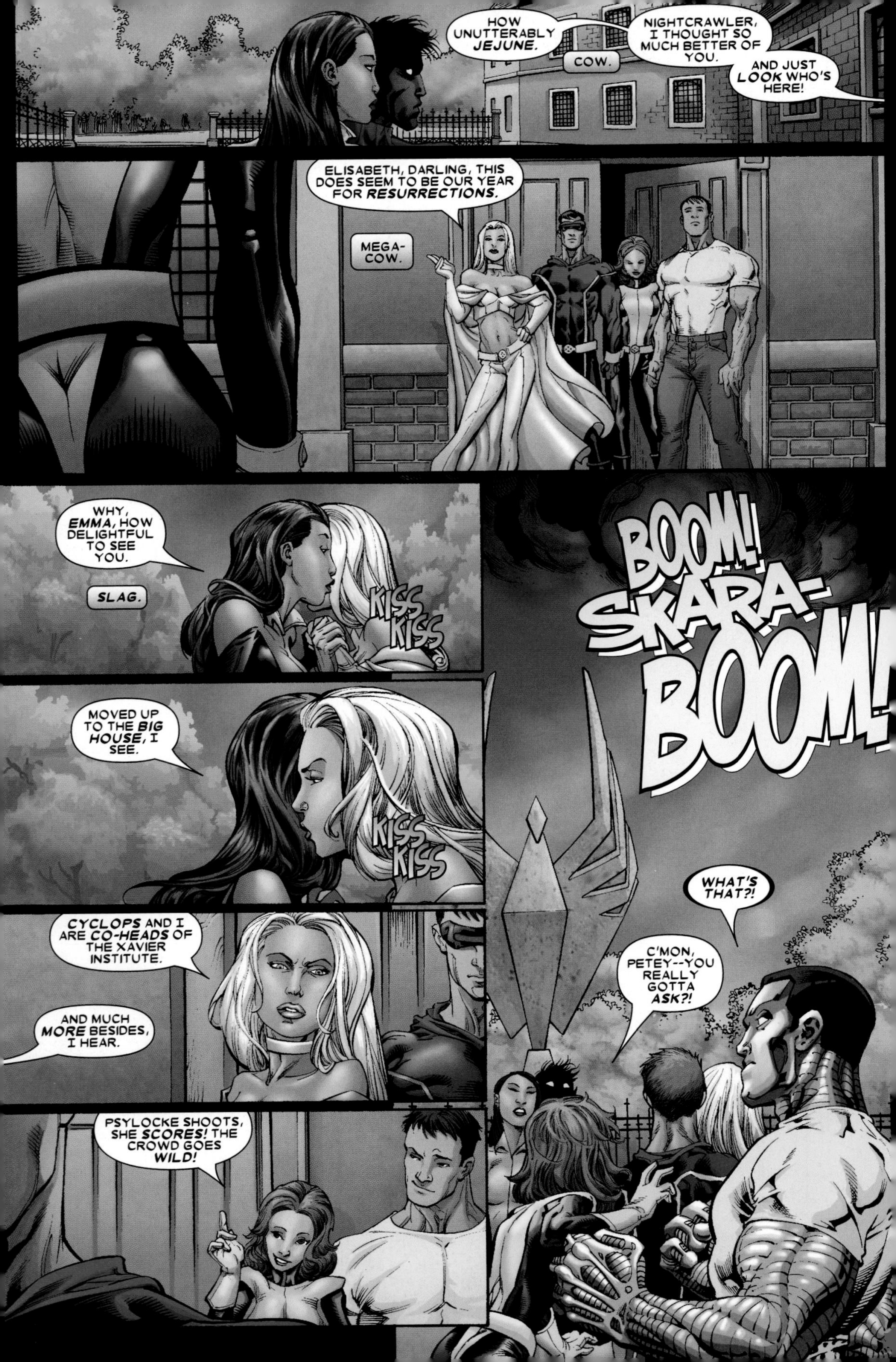
HOW UNUTTERABLY JEJUNE.
NIGHTCRAWLER, I THOUGHT SO MUCH BETTER OF YOU.
COW.
AND JUST LOOK WHO'S HERE!
ELISABETH, DARLING, THIS DOES SEEM TO BE OUR YEAR FOR RESURRECTIONS.
MEGA-COW.
WHY, EMMA, HOW DELIGHTFUL TO SEE YOU.
SLAG.
KISS KISS
MOVED UP TO THE BIG HOUSE, I SEE.
KISS KISS
CYCLOPS AND I ARE CO-HEADS OF THE XAVIER INSTITUTE.
AND MUCH MORE BESIDES, I HEAR.
PSYLOCKE SHOOTS, SHE SCORES! THE CROWD GOES WILD!
BOOM! SKARA-BOOM!
WHAT'S THAT?!
C'MON, PETEY--YOU REALLY GOTTA ASK?!

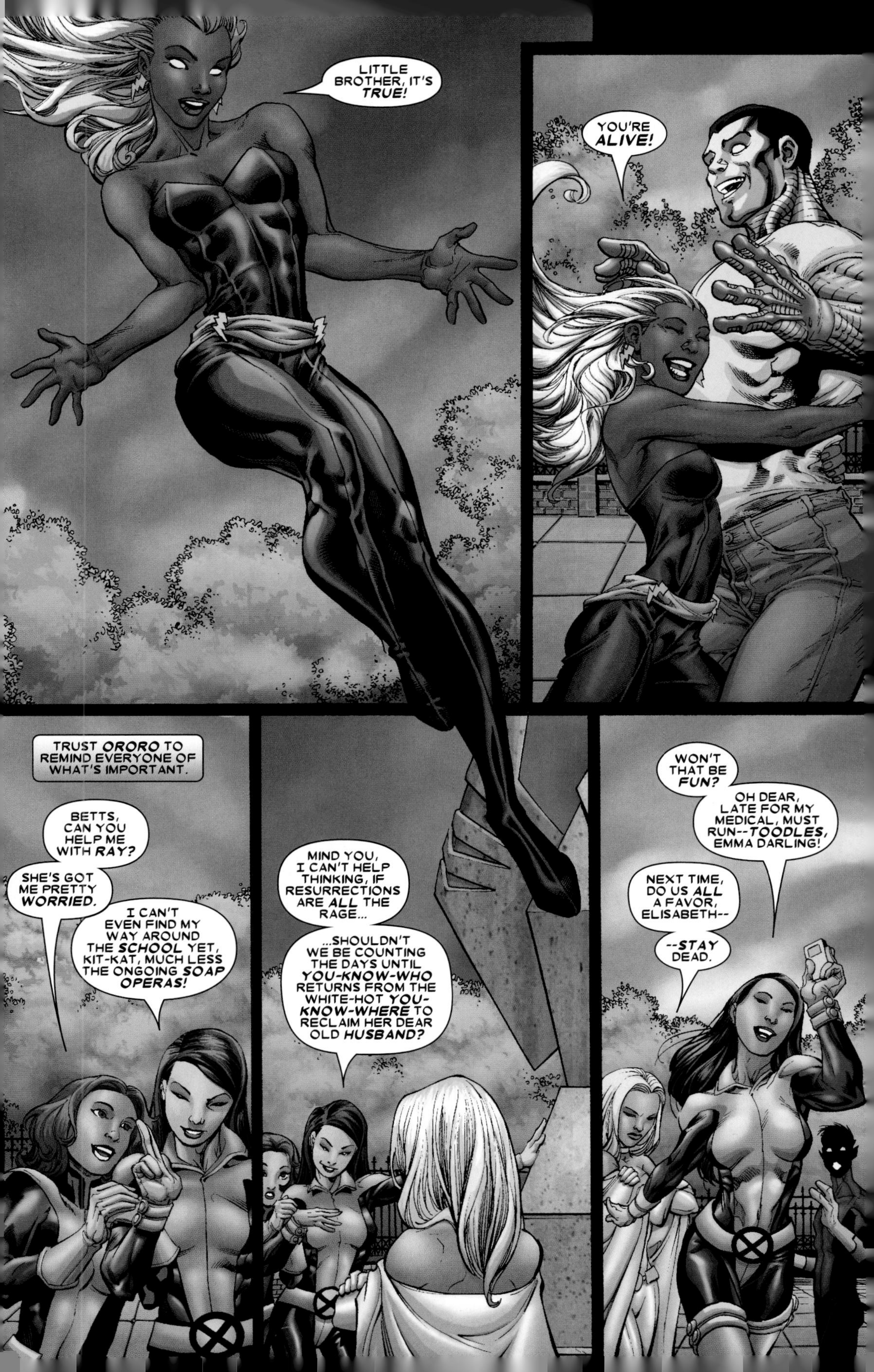

LITTLE BROTHER, IT'S TRUE!
YOU'RE ALIVE!
TRUST ORORO TO REMIND EVERYONE OF WHAT'S IMPORTANT.
BETTS, CAN YOU HELP ME WITH RAY?
SHE'S GOT ME PRETTY WORRIED.
I CAN'T EVEN FIND MY WAY AROUND THE SCHOOL YET, KIT-KAT, MUCH LESS THE ONGOING SOAP OPERAS!
MIND YOU, I CAN'T HELP THINKING, IF RESURRECTIONS ARE ALL THE RAGE...
...SHOULDN'T WE BE COUNTING THE DAYS UNTIL YOU-KNOW-WHO RETURNS FROM THE WHITE-HOT YOU-KNOW-WHERE TO RECLAIM HER DEAR OLD HUSBAND?
WON'T THAT BE FUN?
OH DEAR, LATE FOR MY MEDICAL, MUST RUN--TOODLES, EMMA DARLING!
NEXT TIME, DO US ALL A FAVOR, ELISABETH--
--STAY DEAD.

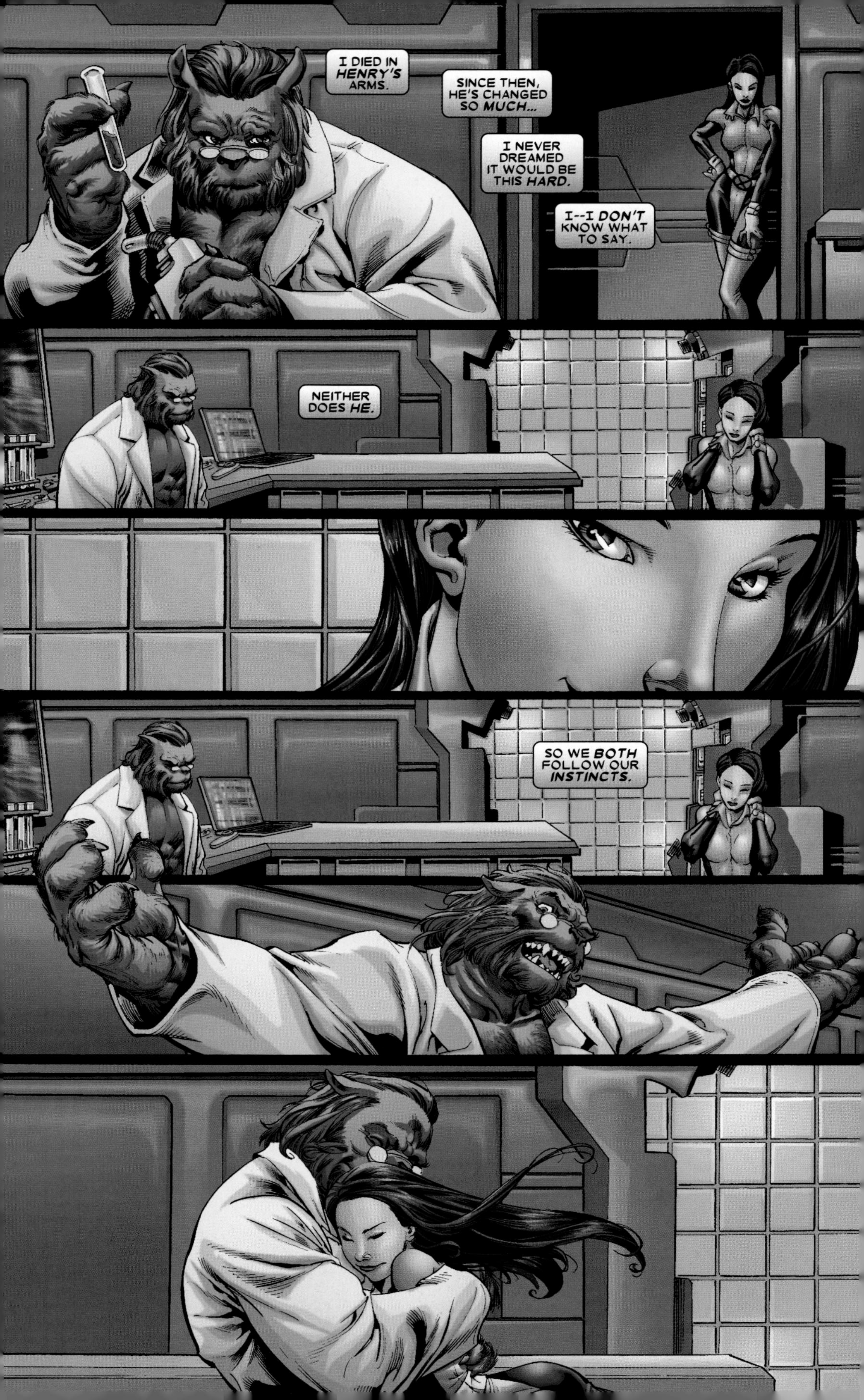
I DIED IN HENRY'S ARMS.
SINCE THEN, HE'S CHANGED SO MUCH...
I NEVER DREAMED IT WOULD BE THIS HARD.
I--I DON'T KNOW WHAT TO SAY.
NEITHER DOES HE.
SO WE BOTH FOLLOW OUR INSTINCTS.

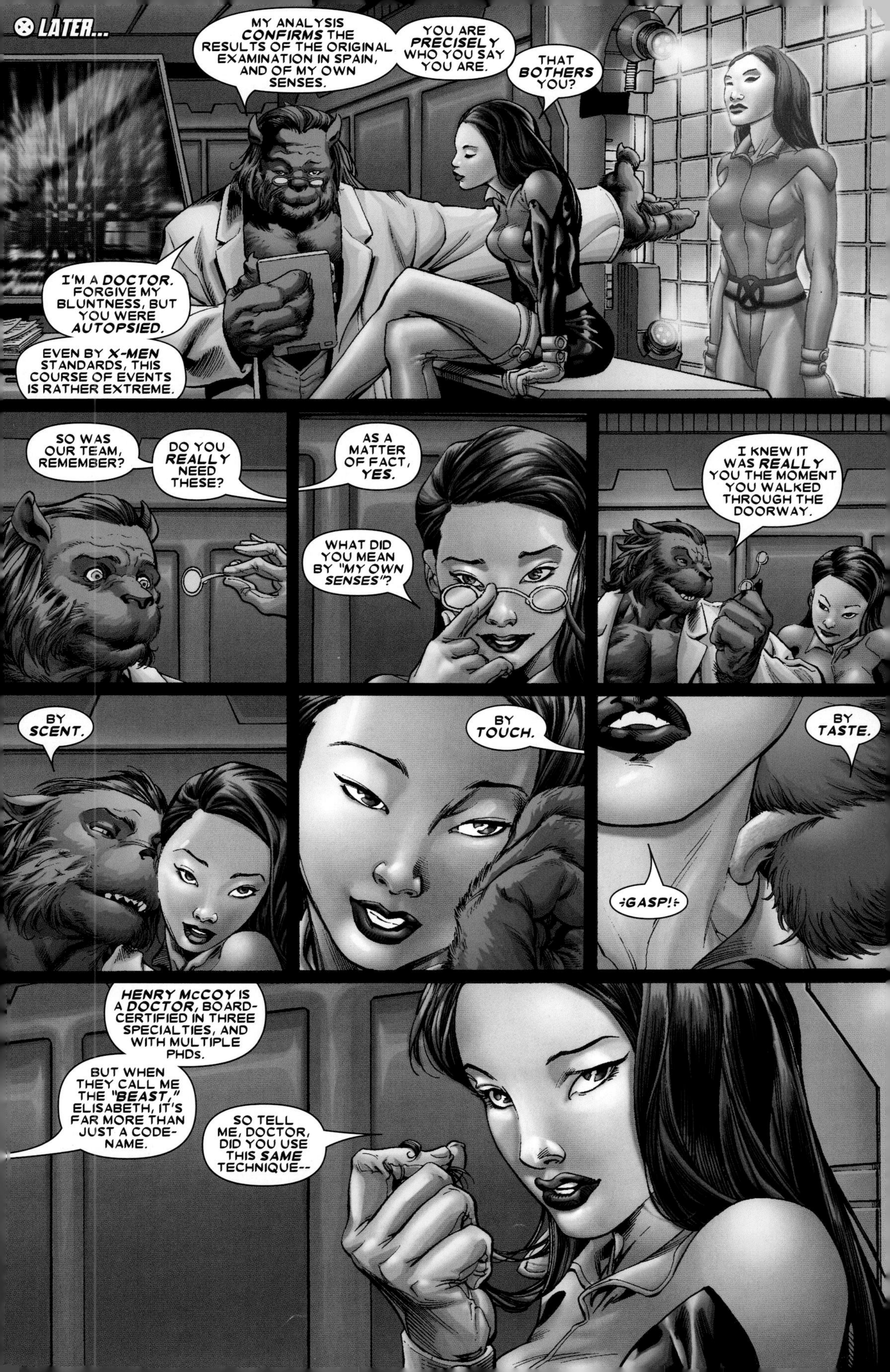
LATER...
MY ANALYSIS CONFIRMS THE RESULTS OF THE ORIGINAL EXAMINATION IN SPAIN, AND OF MY OWN SENSES.
YOU ARE PRECISELY WHO YOU SAY YOU ARE.
THAT BOTHERS YOU?
I'M A DOCTOR. FORGIVE MY BLUNTNESS, BUT YOU WERE AUTOPSIED.
EVEN BY X-MEN STANDARDS, THIS COURSE OF EVENTS IS RATHER EXTREME.
SO WAS OUR TEAM, REMEMBER?
DO YOU REALLY NEED THESE?
AS A MATTER OF FACT, YES.
WHAT DID YOU MEAN BY "MY OWN SENSES"?
I KNEW IT WAS REALLY YOU THE MOMENT YOU WALKED THROUGH THE DOORWAY.
BY SCENT.
BY TOUCH.
BY TASTE.
GASP!
HENRY McCOY IS A DOCTOR, BOARD-CERTIFIED IN THREE SPECIALTIES, AND WITH MULTIPLE PHDs.
BUT WHEN THEY CALL ME THE "BEAST," ELISABETH, IT'S FAR MORE THAN JUST A CODE-NAME.
SO TELL ME, DOCTOR, DID YOU USE THIS SAME TECHNIQUE--

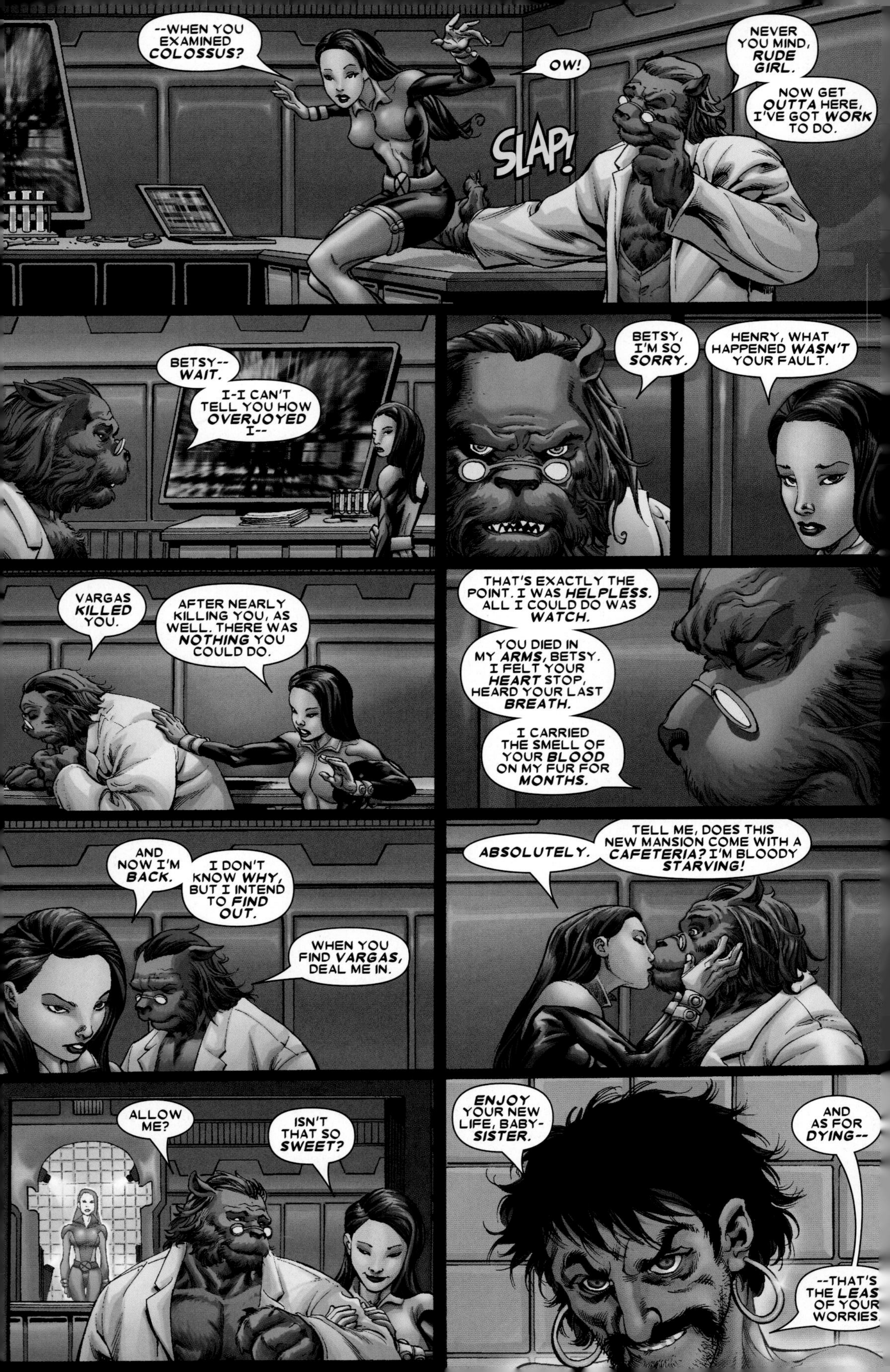

--WHEN YOU EXAMINED COLOSSUS?
OW!
SLAP!
NEVER YOU MIND, RUDE GIRL.
NOW GET OUTTA HERE, I'VE GOT WORK TO DO.
BETSY-- WAIT.
I-I CAN'T TELL YOU HOW OVERJOYED I--
BETSY, I'M SO SORRY.
HENRY, WHAT HAPPENED WASN'T YOUR FAULT.
VARGAS KILLED YOU.
AFTER NEARLY KILLING YOU, AS WELL. THERE WAS NOTHING YOU COULD DO.
THAT'S EXACTLY THE POINT. I WAS HELPLESS. ALL I COULD DO WAS WATCH.
YOU DIED IN MY ARMS, BETSY. I FELT YOUR HEART STOP, HEARD YOUR LAST BREATH.
I CARRIED THE SMELL OF YOUR BLOOD ON MY FUR FOR MONTHS.
AND NOW I'M BACK.
I DON'T KNOW WHY, BUT I INTEND TO FIND OUT.
WHEN YOU FIND VARGAS, DEAL ME IN.
ABSOLUTELY.
TELL ME, DOES THIS NEW MANSION COME WITH A CAFETERIA? I'M BLOODY STARVING!
ALLOW ME?
ISN'T THAT SO SWEET?
ENJOY YOUR NEW LIFE, BABY-SISTER.
AND AS FOR DYING--
--THAT'S THE LEAS OF YOUR WORRIES.

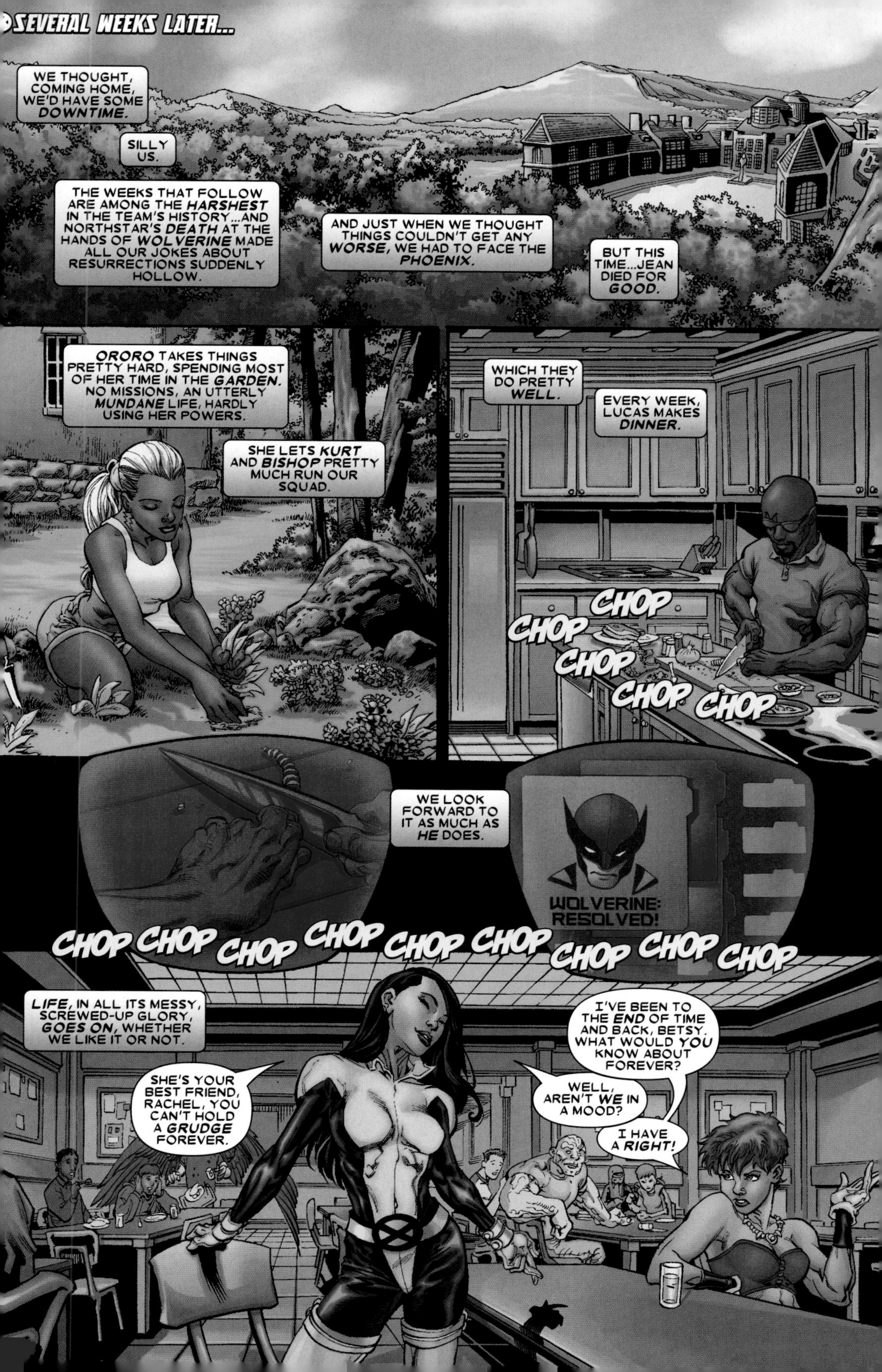
SEVERAL WEEKS LATER...
WE THOUGHT, COMING HOME, WE'D HAVE SOME DOWNTIME.
SILLY US.
THE WEEKS THAT FOLLOW ARE AMONG THE HARSHEST IN THE TEAM'S HISTORY...AND NORTHSTAR'S DEATH AT THE HANDS OF WOLVERINE MADE ALL OUR JOKES ABOUT RESURRECTIONS SUDDENLY HOLLOW.
AND JUST WHEN WE THOUGHT THINGS COULDN'T GET ANY WORSE, WE HAD TO FACE THE PHOENIX.
BUT THIS TIME...JEAN DIED FOR GOOD.
ORORO TAKES THINGS PRETTY HARD, SPENDING MOST OF HER TIME IN THE GARDEN. NO MISSIONS, AN UTTERLY MUNDANE LIFE, HARDLY USING HER POWERS.
SHE LETS KURT AND BISHOP PRETTY MUCH RUN OUR SQUAD.
WHICH THEY DO PRETTY WELL.
EVERY WEEK, LUCAS MAKES DINNER.
CHOP CHOP CHOP CHOP CHOP
WE LOOK FORWARD TO IT AS MUCH AS HE DOES.
WOLVERINE: RESOLVED!
CHOP CHOP CHOP CHOP CHOP CHOP CHOP CHOP CHOP
LIFE, IN ALL ITS MESSY, SCREWED-UP GLORY, GOES ON, WHETHER WE LIKE IT OR NOT.
SHE'S YOUR BEST FRIEND, RACHEL, YOU CAN'T HOLD A GRUDGE FOREVER.
I'VE BEEN TO THE END OF TIME AND BACK, BETSY. WHAT WOULD YOU KNOW ABOUT FOREVER?
WELL, AREN'T WE IN A MOOD?
I HAVE A RIGHT!

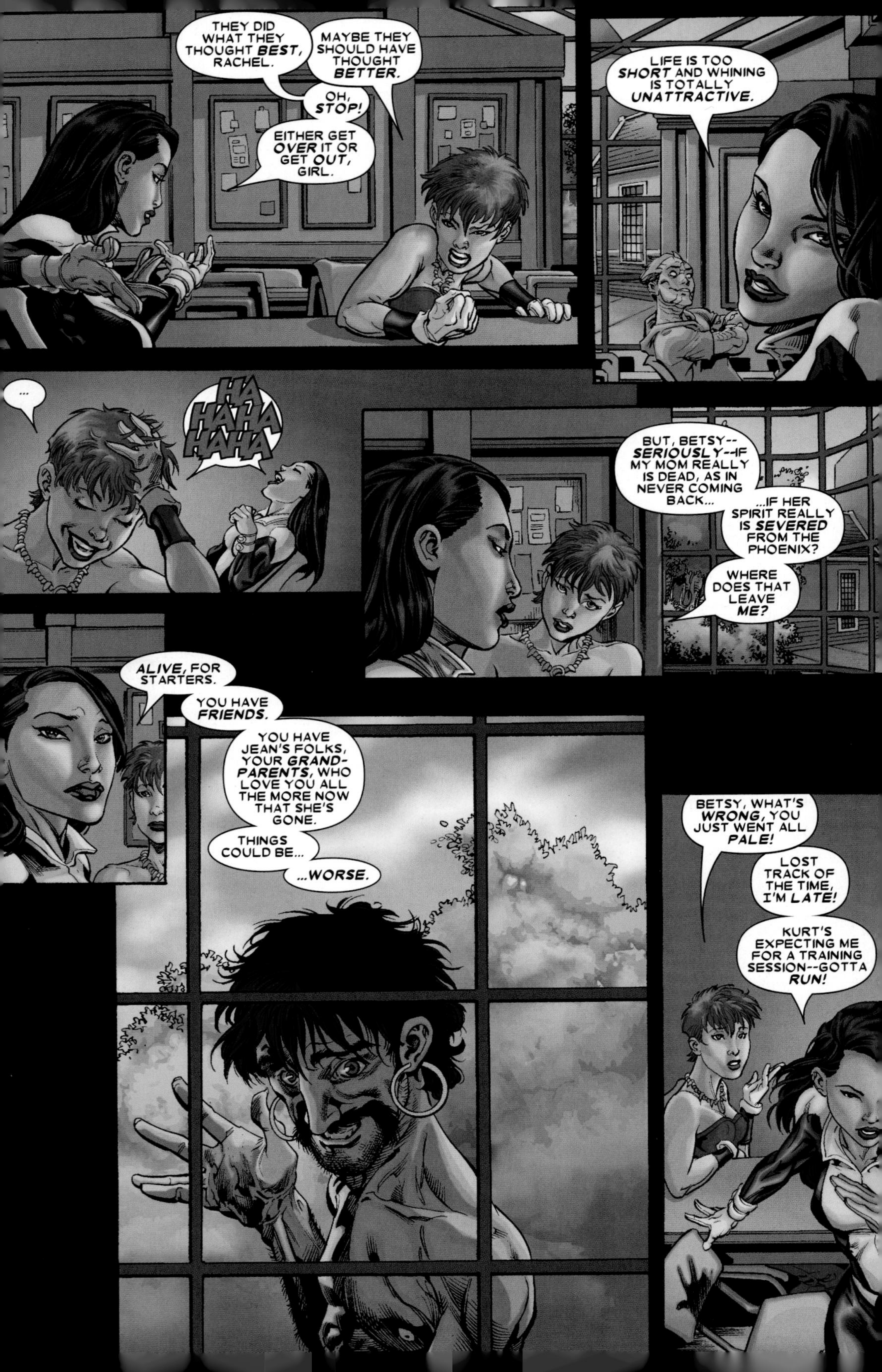
THEY DID WHAT THEY THOUGHT BEST, RACHEL.
MAYBE THEY SHOULD HAVE THOUGHT BETTER.
OH, STOP!
EITHER GET OVER IT OR GET OUT, GIRL.
LIFE IS TOO SHORT AND WHINING IS TOTALLY UNATTRACTIVE.
...
HA HAHAHA HAHA
BUT, BETSY-- SERIOUSLY--IF MY MOM REALLY IS DEAD, AS IN NEVER COMING BACK...
...IF HER SPIRIT REALLY IS SEVERED FROM THE PHOENIX?
WHERE DOES THAT LEAVE ME?
ALIVE, FOR STARTERS.
YOU HAVE FRIENDS.
YOU HAVE JEAN'S FOLKS, YOUR GRAND-PARENTS, WHO LOVE YOU ALL THE MORE NOW THAT SHE'S GONE.
THINGS COULD BE...
...WORSE.
BETSY, WHAT'S WRONG, YOU JUST WENT ALL PALE!
LOST TRACK OF THE TIME, I'M LATE!
KURT'S EXPECTING ME FOR A TRAINING SESSION--GOTTA RUN!

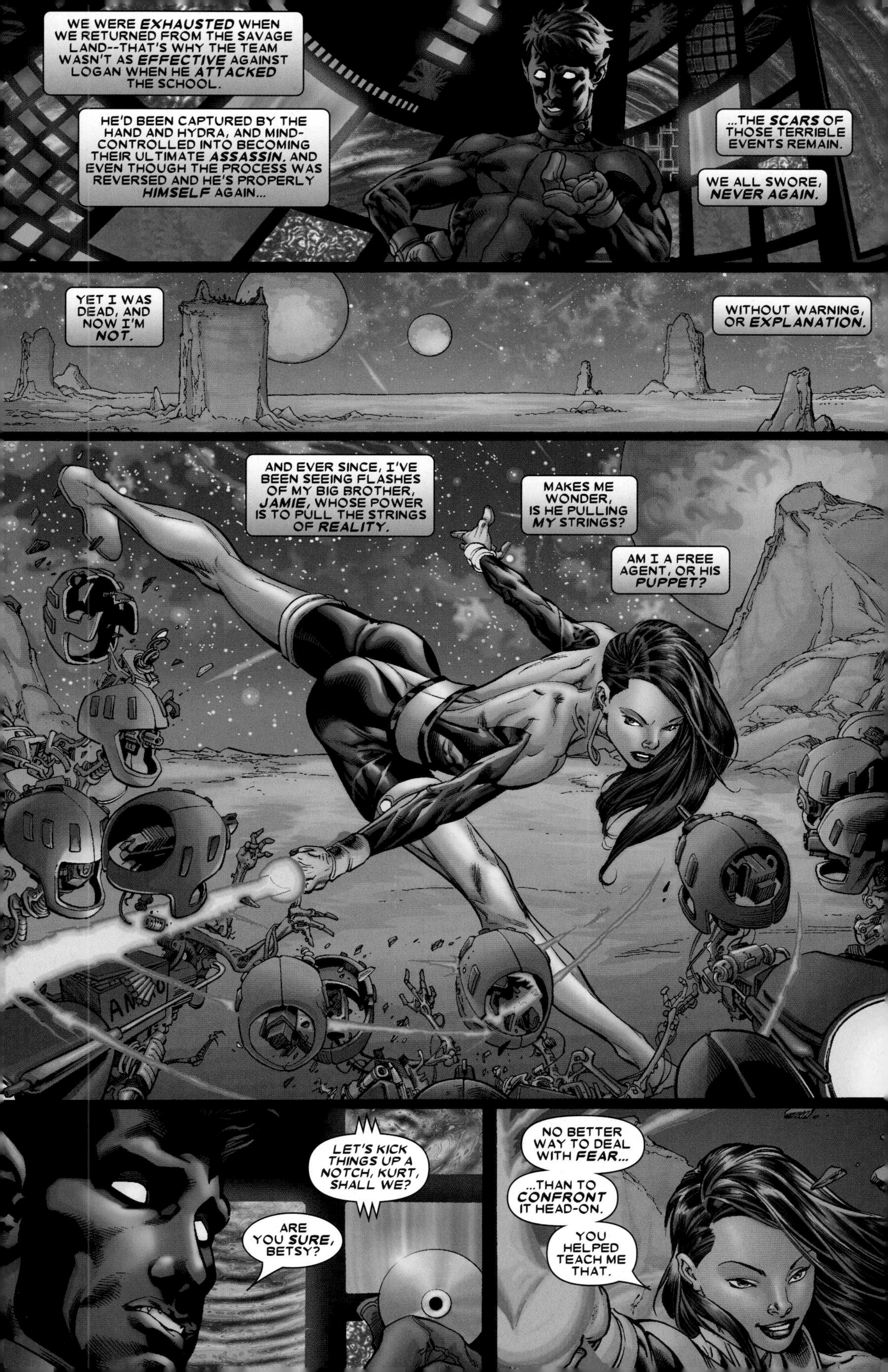
WE WERE EXHAUSTED WHEN WE RETURNED FROM THE SAVAGE LAND--THAT'S WHY THE TEAM WASN'T AS EFFECTIVE AGAINST LOGAN WHEN HE ATTACKED THE SCHOOL.
HE'D BEEN CAPTURED BY THE HAND AND HYDRA, AND MIND-CONTROLLED INTO BECOMING THEIR ULTIMATE ASSASSIN. AND EVEN THOUGH THE PROCESS WAS REVERSED AND HE'S PROPERLY HIMSELF AGAIN...
...THE SCARS OF THOSE TERRIBLE EVENTS REMAIN.
WE ALL SWORE, NEVER AGAIN.
YET I WAS DEAD, AND NOW I'M NOT.
WITHOUT WARNING, OR EXPLANATION.
AND EVER SINCE, I'VE BEEN SEEING FLASHES OF MY BIG BROTHER, JAMIE, WHOSE POWER IS TO PULL THE STRINGS OF REALITY.
MAKES ME WONDER, IS HE PULLING MY STRINGS?
AM I A FREE AGENT, OR HIS PUPPET?
LET'S KICK THINGS UP A NOTCH, KURT, SHALL WE?
ARE YOU SURE, BETSY?
NO BETTER WAY TO DEAL WITH FEAR...
...THAN TO CONFRONT IT HEAD-ON.
YOU HELPED TEACH ME THAT.

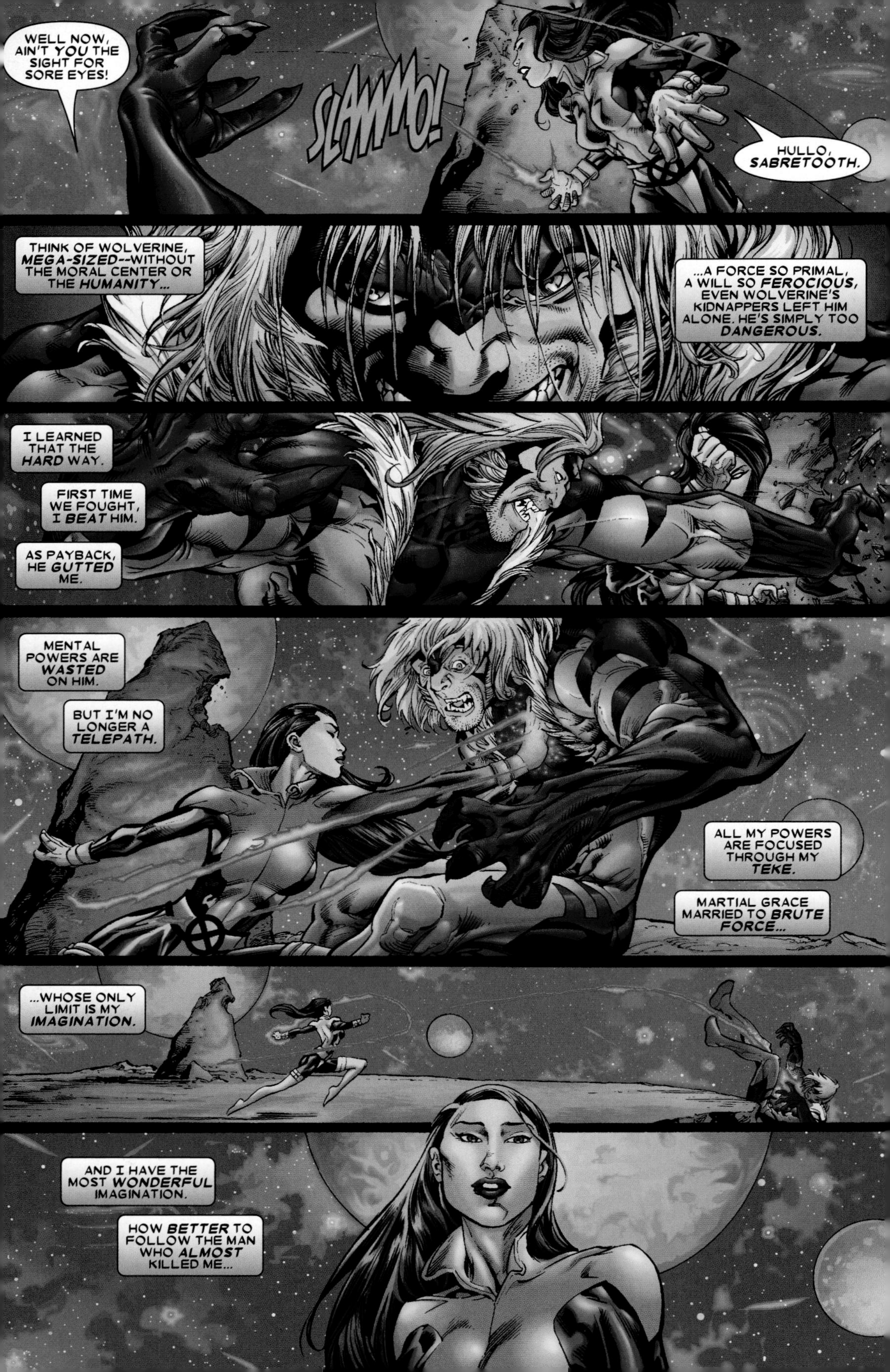
WELL NOW, AIN'T YOU THE SIGHT FOR SORE EYES!
SLAMMO!
HULLO, SABRETOOTH.
THINK OF WOLVERINE, MEGA-SIZED--WITHOUT THE MORAL CENTER OR THE HUMANITY...
...A FORCE SO PRIMAL, A WILL SO FEROCIOUS, EVEN WOLVERINE'S KIDNAPPERS LEFT HIM ALONE. HE'S SIMPLY TOO DANGEROUS.
I LEARNED THAT THE HARD WAY.
FIRST TIME WE FOUGHT, I BEAT HIM.
AS PAYBACK, HE GUTTED ME.
MENTAL POWERS ARE WASTED ON HIM.
BUT I'M NO LONGER A TELEPATH.
ALL MY POWERS ARE FOCUSED THROUGH MY TEKE.
MARTIAL GRACE MARRIED TO BRUTE FORCE...
...WHOSE ONLY LIMIT IS MY IMAGINATION.
AND I HAVE THE MOST WONDERFUL IMAGINATION.
HOW BETTER TO FOLLOW THE MAN WHO ALMOST KILLED ME...

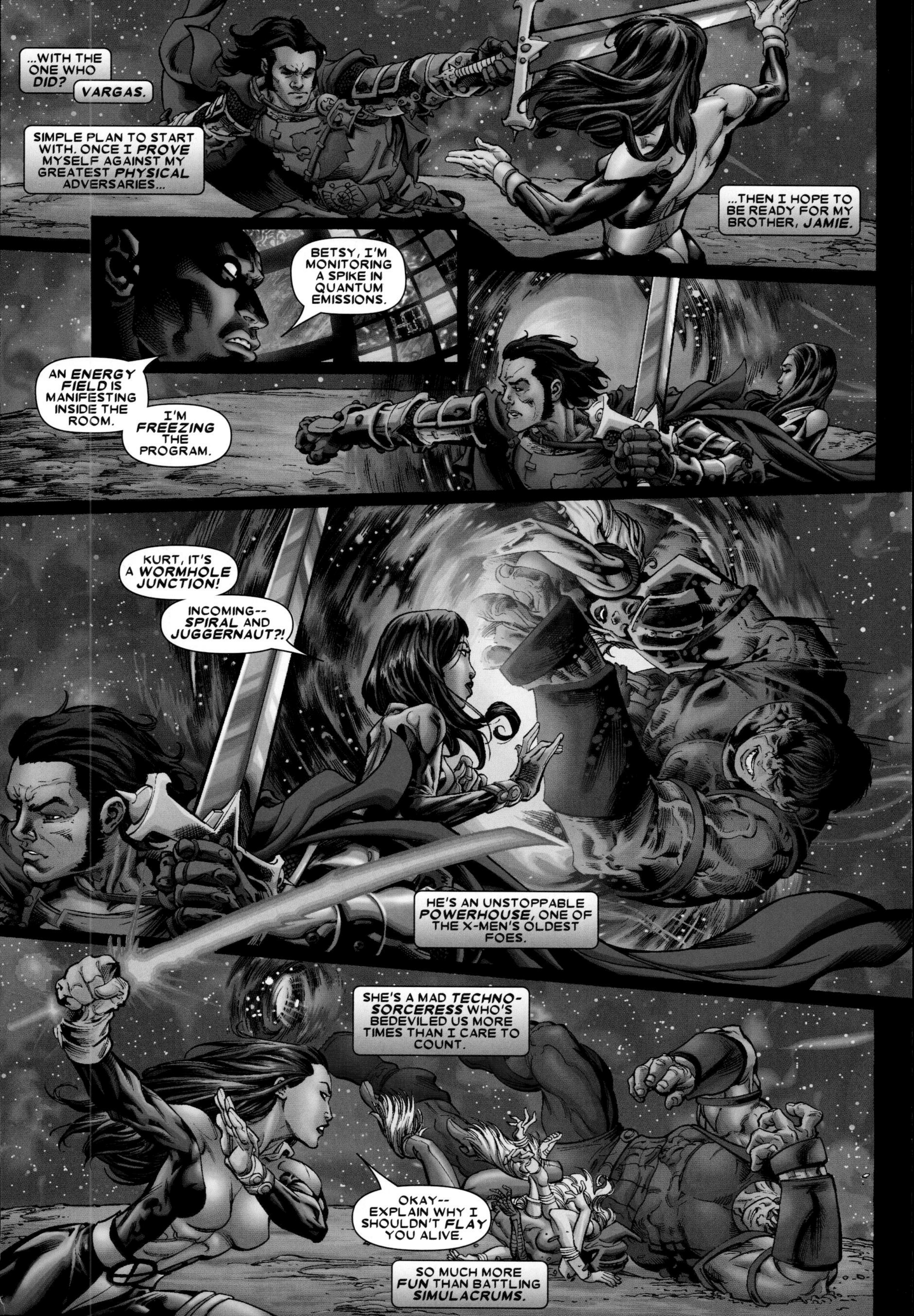
...WITH THE ONE WHO *DID*? *VARGAS.*
SIMPLE PLAN TO START WITH. ONCE I *PROVE* MYSELF AGAINST MY GREATEST *PHYSICAL* ADVERSARIES...
...THEN I HOPE TO BE READY FOR MY BROTHER, *JAMIE.*
BETSY, I'M MONITORING A SPIKE IN QUANTUM EMISSIONS.
AN *ENERGY FIELD* IS MANIFESTING INSIDE THE ROOM.
I'M *FREEZING* THE PROGRAM.
KURT, IT'S A *WORMHOLE JUNCTION!*
INCOMING-- *SPIRAL* AND *JUGGERNAUT?!*
HE'S AN UNSTOPPABLE *POWERHOUSE*, ONE OF THE X-MEN'S OLDEST FOES.
SHE'S A MAD *TECHNO-SORCERESS* WHO'S BEDEVILED US MORE TIMES THAN I CARE TO COUNT.
OKAY-- EXPLAIN WHY I SHOULDN'T *FLAY* YOU ALIVE.
SO MUCH MORE *FUN* THAN BATTLING *SIMULACRUMS.*

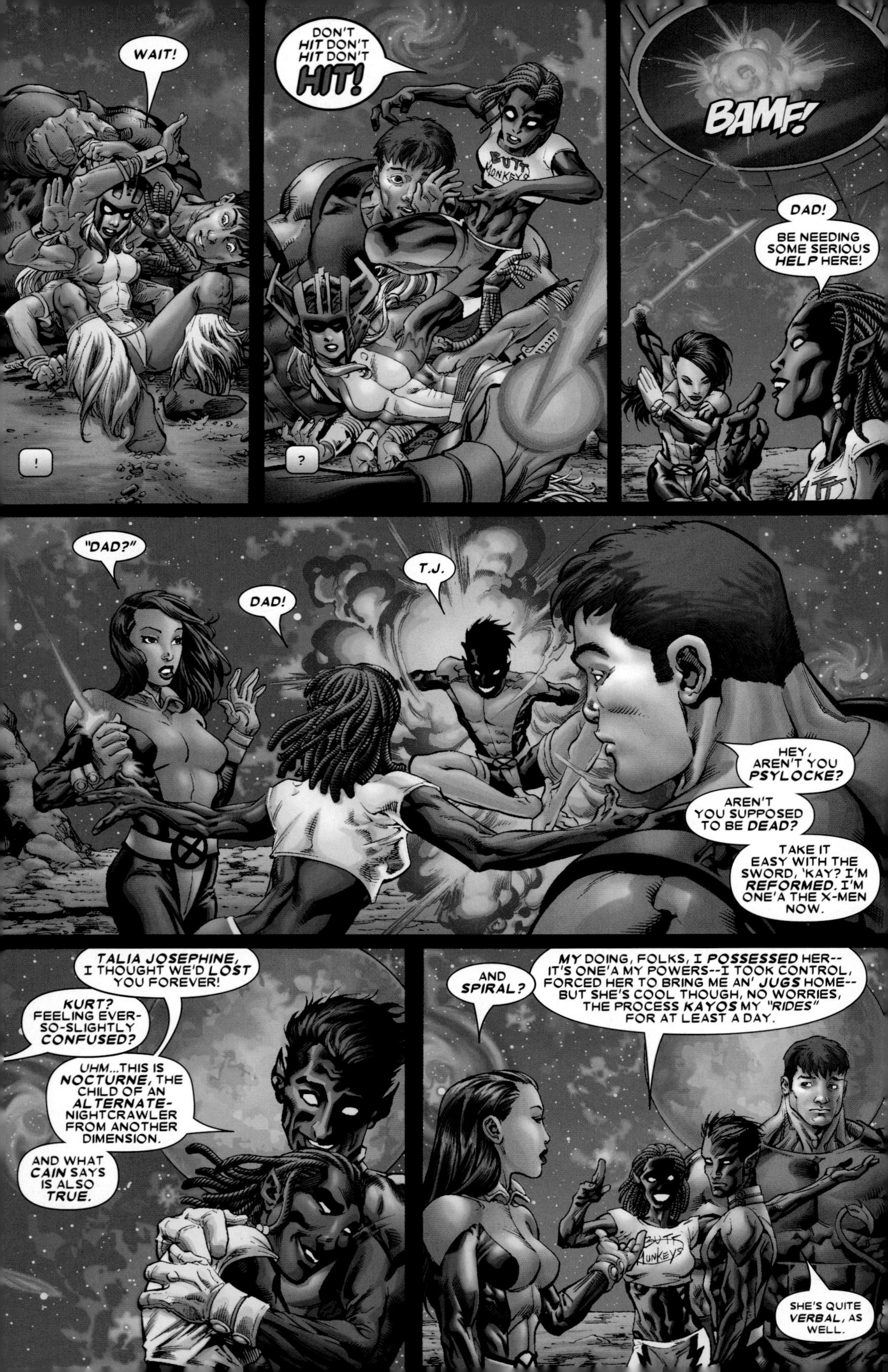

WAIT!
!
DON'T HIT DON'T HIT DON'T HIT!
?
BAMF!
DAD!
BE NEEDING SOME SERIOUS HELP HERE!
"DAD?"
DAD!
T.J.
HEY, AREN'T YOU PSYLOCKE?
AREN'T YOU SUPPOSED TO BE DEAD?
TAKE IT EASY WITH THE SWORD, 'KAY? I'M REFORMED. I'M ONE'A THE X-MEN NOW.
TALIA JOSEPHINE, I THOUGHT WE'D LOST YOU FOREVER!
KURT? FEELING EVER-SO-SLIGHTLY CONFUSED?
UHM...THIS IS NOCTURNE, THE CHILD OF AN ALTERNATE-NIGHTCRAWLER FROM ANOTHER DIMENSION.
AND WHAT CAIN SAYS IS ALSO TRUE.
AND SPIRAL?
MY DOING, FOLKS, I POSSESSED HER--IT'S ONE'A MY POWERS--I TOOK CONTROL, FORCED HER TO BRING ME AN' JUGS HOME--BUT SHE'S COOL THOUGH, NO WORRIES, THE PROCESS KAYOS MY "RIDES" FOR AT LEAST A DAY.
SHE'S QUITE VERBAL, AS WELL.

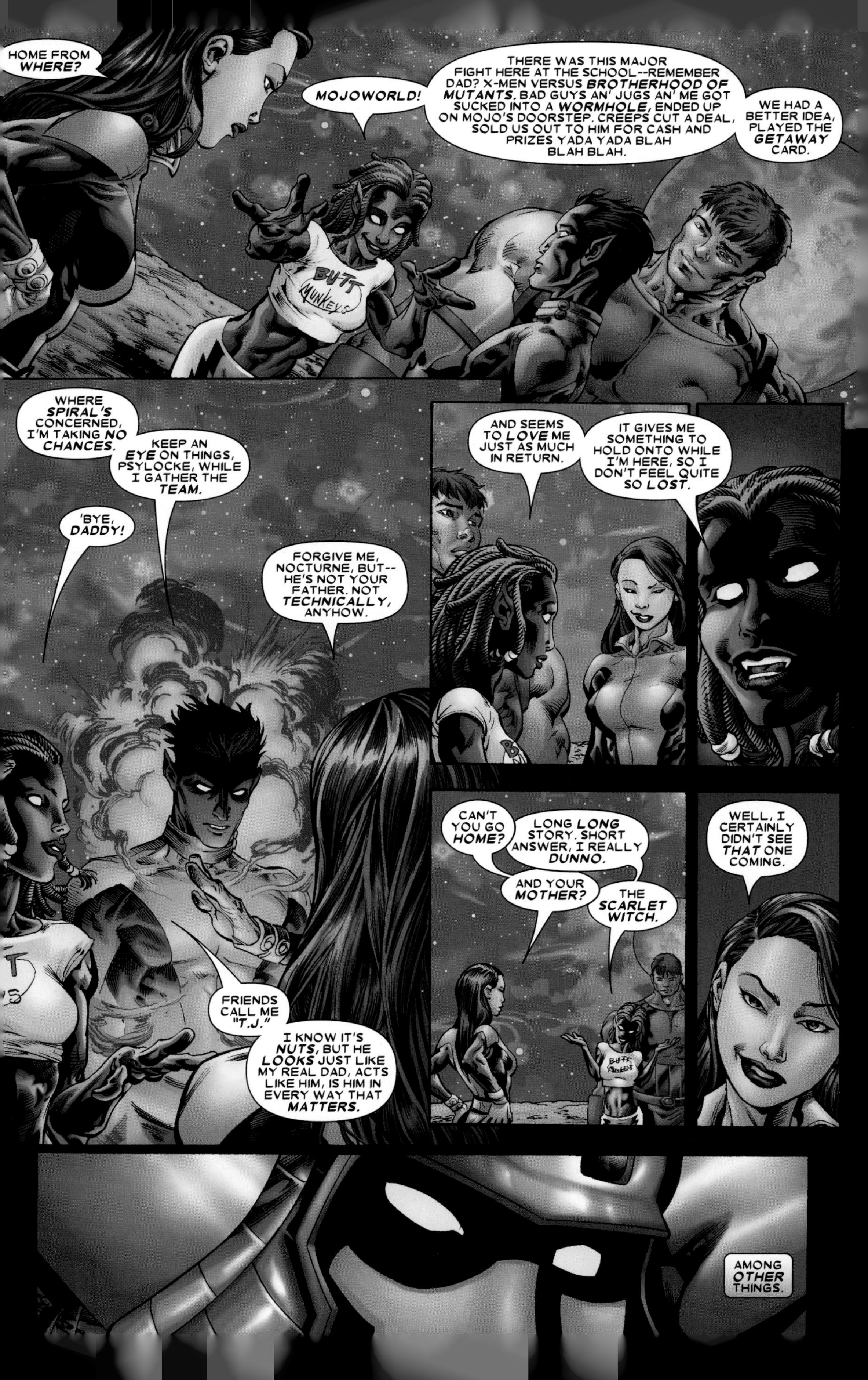
HOME FROM WHERE?
MOJOWORLD!
THERE WAS THIS MAJOR FIGHT HERE AT THE SCHOOL--REMEMBER DAD? X-MEN VERSUS BROTHERHOOD OF MUTANTS. BAD GUYS AN' JUGS AN' ME GOT SUCKED INTO A WORMHOLE, ENDED UP ON MOJO'S DOORSTEP. CREEPS CUT A DEAL, SOLD US OUT TO HIM FOR CASH AND PRIZES YADA YADA BLAH BLAH BLAH.
WE HAD A BETTER IDEA, PLAYED THE GETAWAY CARD.
WHERE SPIRAL'S CONCERNED, I'M TAKING NO CHANCES.
KEEP AN EYE ON THINGS, PSYLOCKE, WHILE I GATHER THE TEAM.
'BYE, DADDY!
FORGIVE ME, NOCTURNE, BUT-- HE'S NOT YOUR FATHER. NOT TECHNICALLY, ANYHOW.
FRIENDS CALL ME "T.J."
I KNOW IT'S NUTS, BUT HE LOOKS JUST LIKE MY REAL DAD, ACTS LIKE HIM, IS HIM IN EVERY WAY THAT MATTERS.
AND SEEMS TO LOVE ME JUST AS MUCH IN RETURN.
IT GIVES ME SOMETHING TO HOLD ONTO WHILE I'M HERE, SO I DON'T FEEL QUITE SO LOST.
CAN'T YOU GO HOME?
LONG LONG STORY. SHORT ANSWER, I REALLY DUNNO.
AND YOUR MOTHER?
THE SCARLET WITCH.
WELL, I CERTAINLY DIDN'T SEE THAT ONE COMING.
AMONG OTHER THINGS.

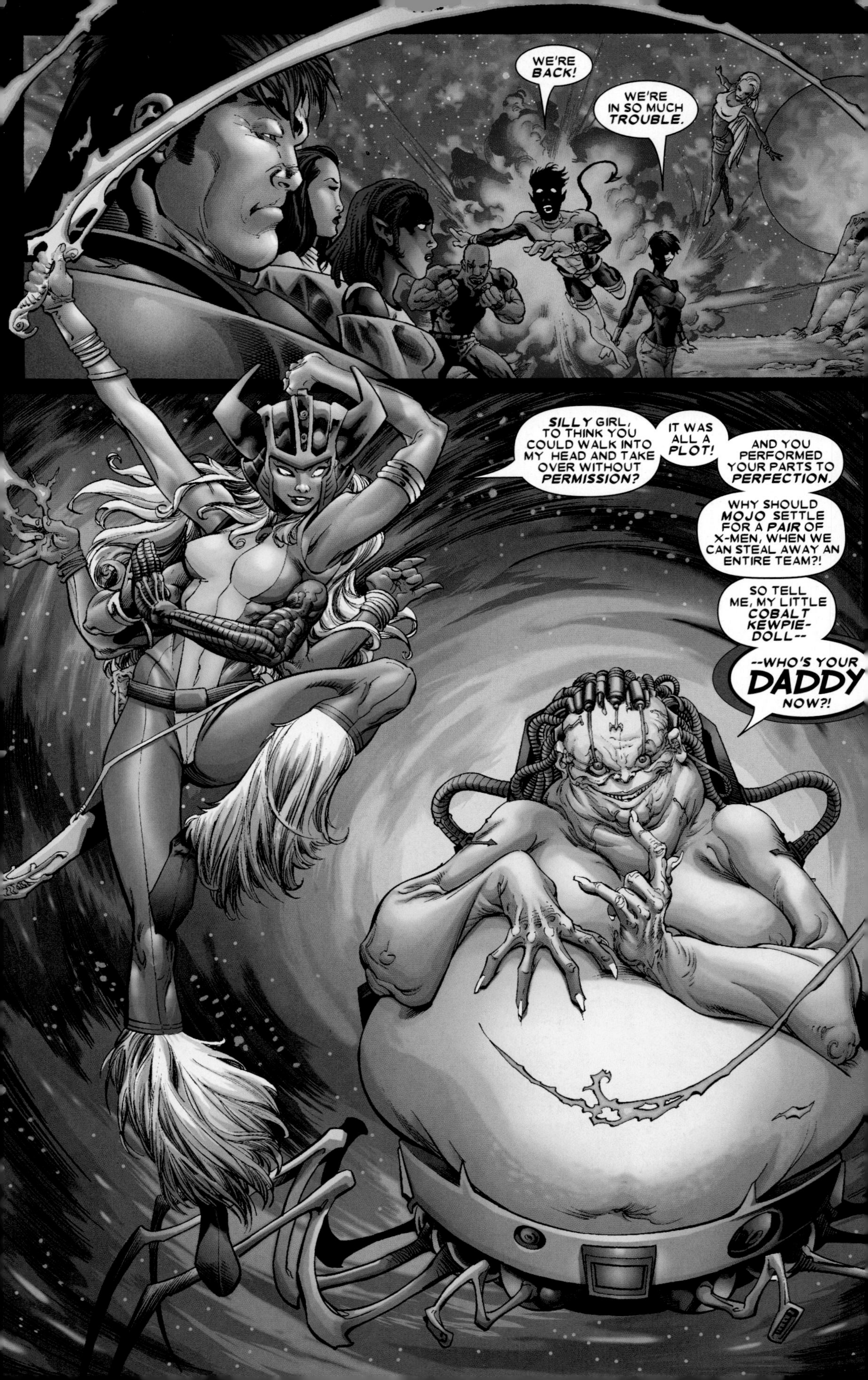
WE'RE BACK!
WE'RE IN SO MUCH TROUBLE.
SILLY GIRL, TO THINK YOU COULD WALK INTO MY HEAD AND TAKE OVER WITHOUT PERMISSION?
IT WAS ALL A PLOT!
AND YOU PERFORMED YOUR PARTS TO PERFECTION.
WHY SHOULD MOJO SETTLE FOR A PAIR OF X-MEN, WHEN WE CAN STEAL AWAY AN ENTIRE TEAM?!
SO TELL ME, MY LITTLE COBALT KEWPIE-DOLL--
--WHO'S YOUR DADDY NOW?!

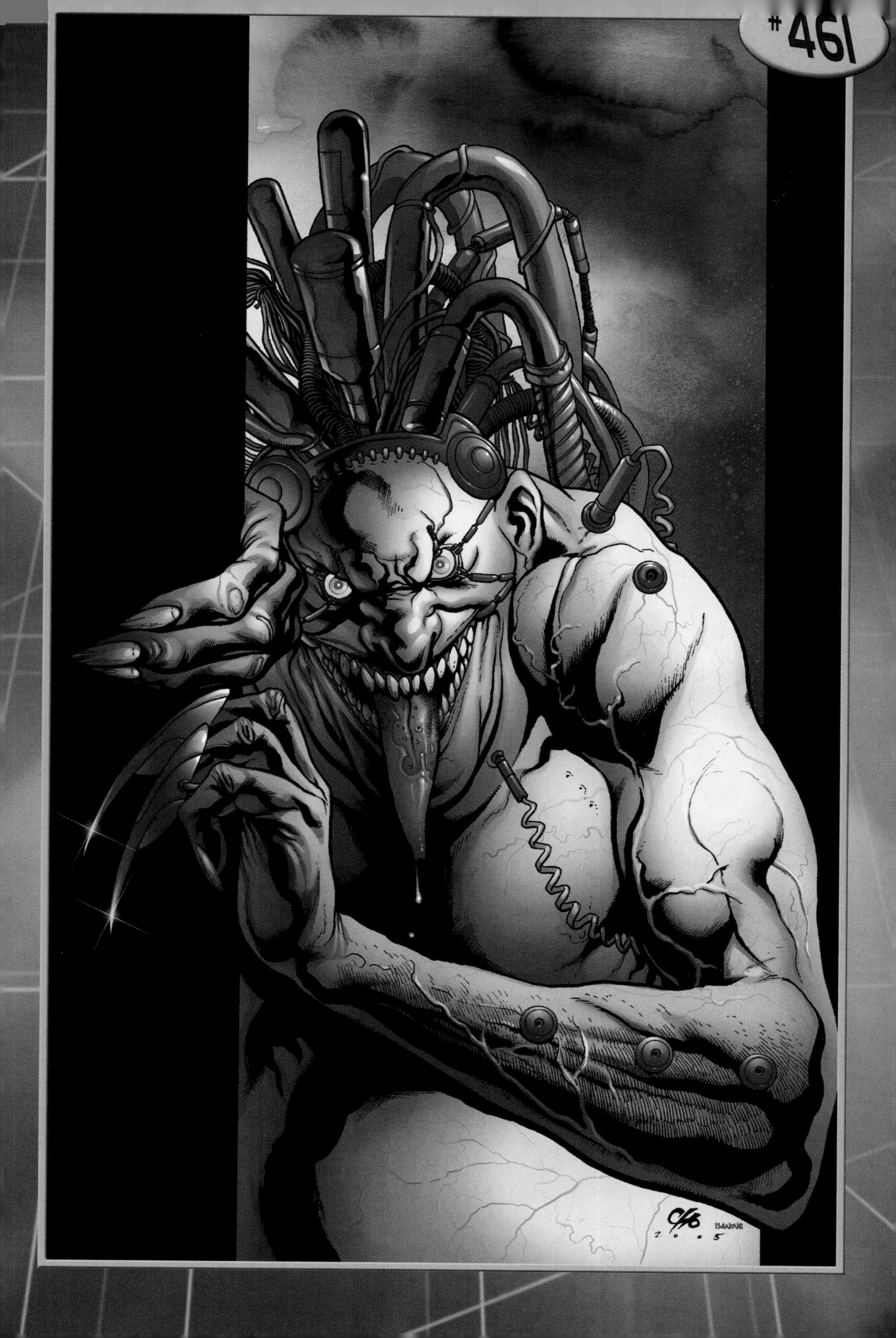
#461

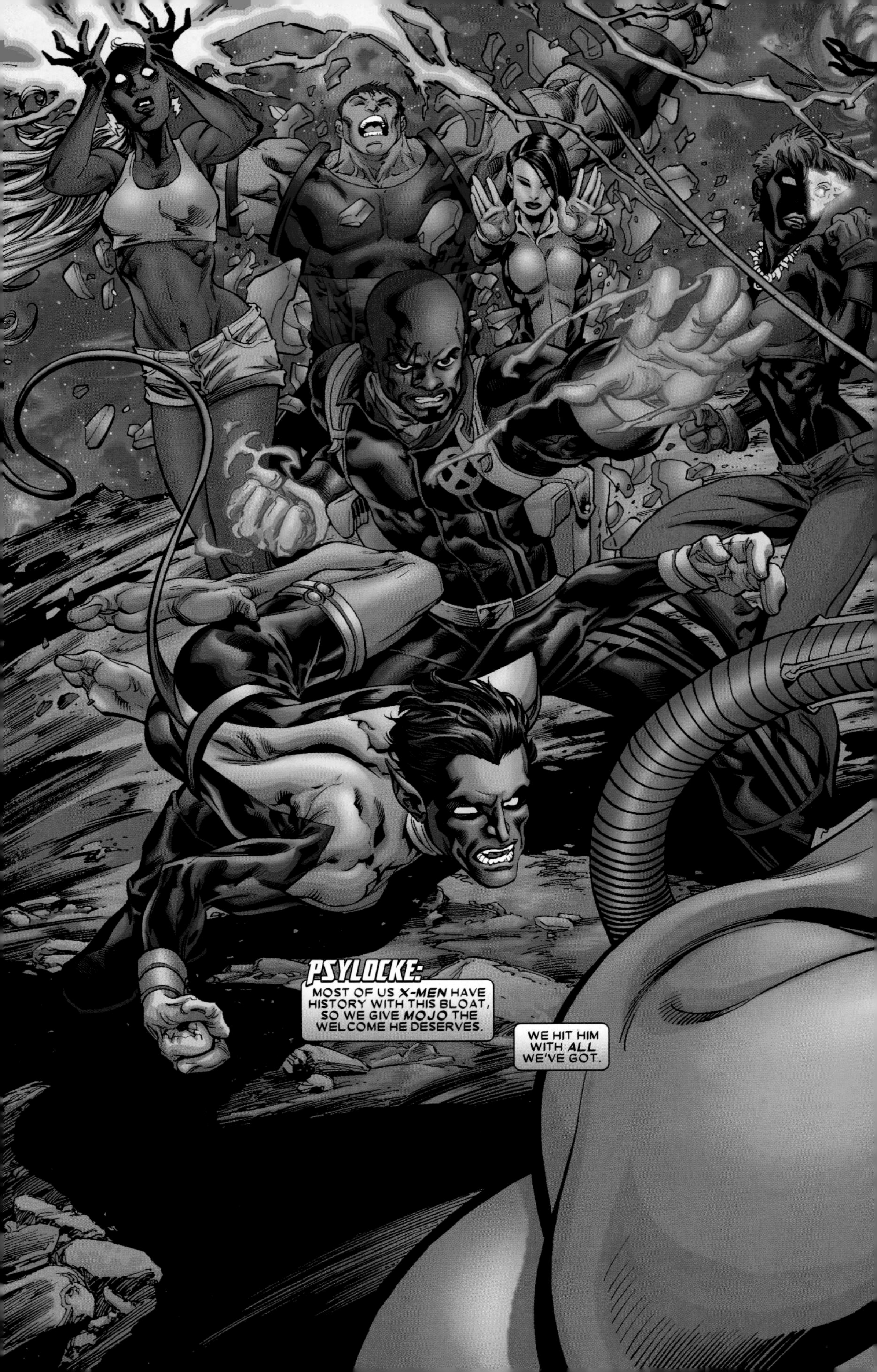
PSYLOCKE:
MOST OF US X-MEN HAVE HISTORY WITH THIS BLOAT, SO WE GIVE MOJO THE WELCOME HE DESERVES.
WE HIT HIM WITH ALL WE'VE GOT.

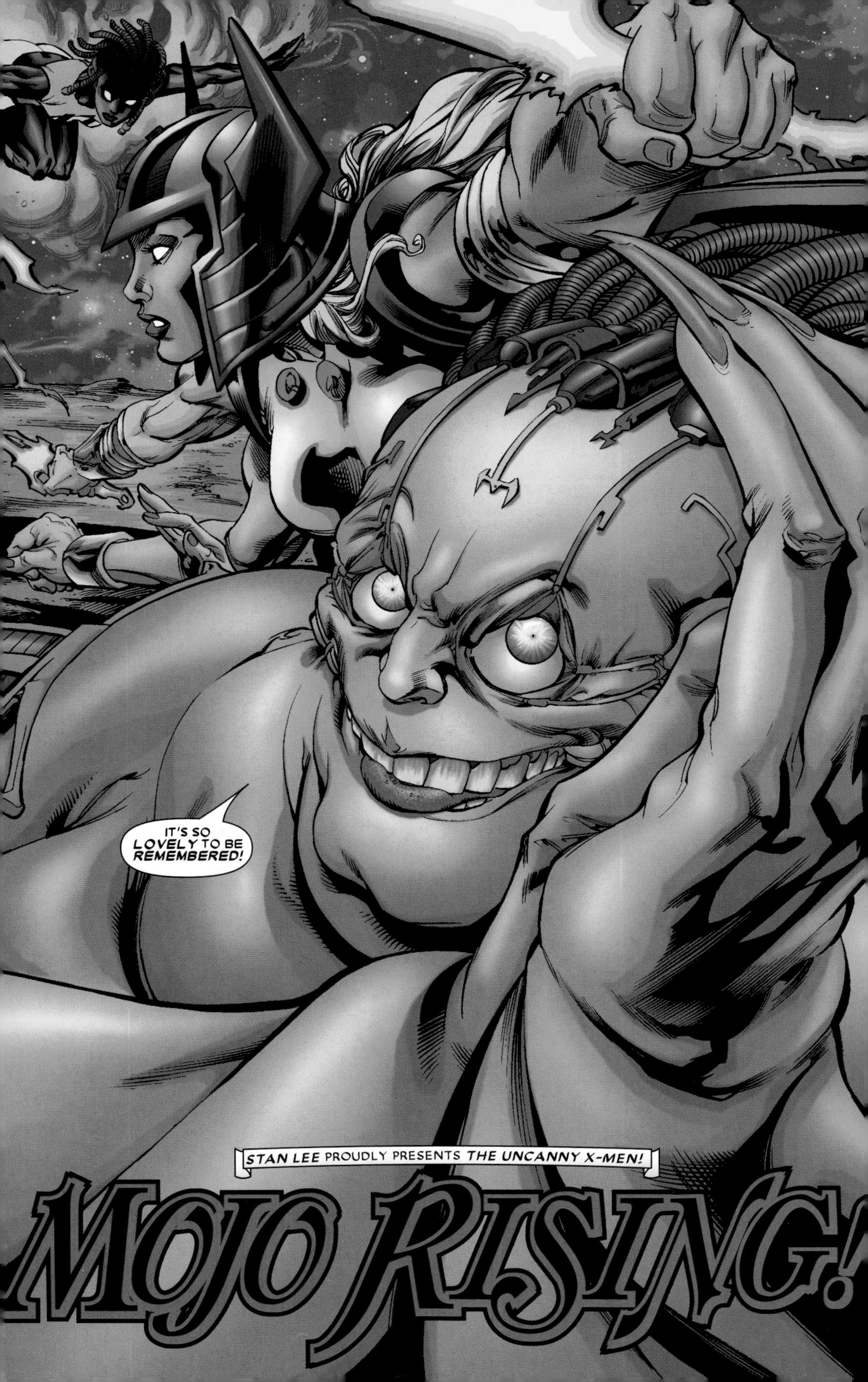
IT'S SO LOVELY TO BE REMEMBERED!
STAN LEE PROUDLY PRESENTS THE UNCANNY X-MEN!
MOJO RISING!

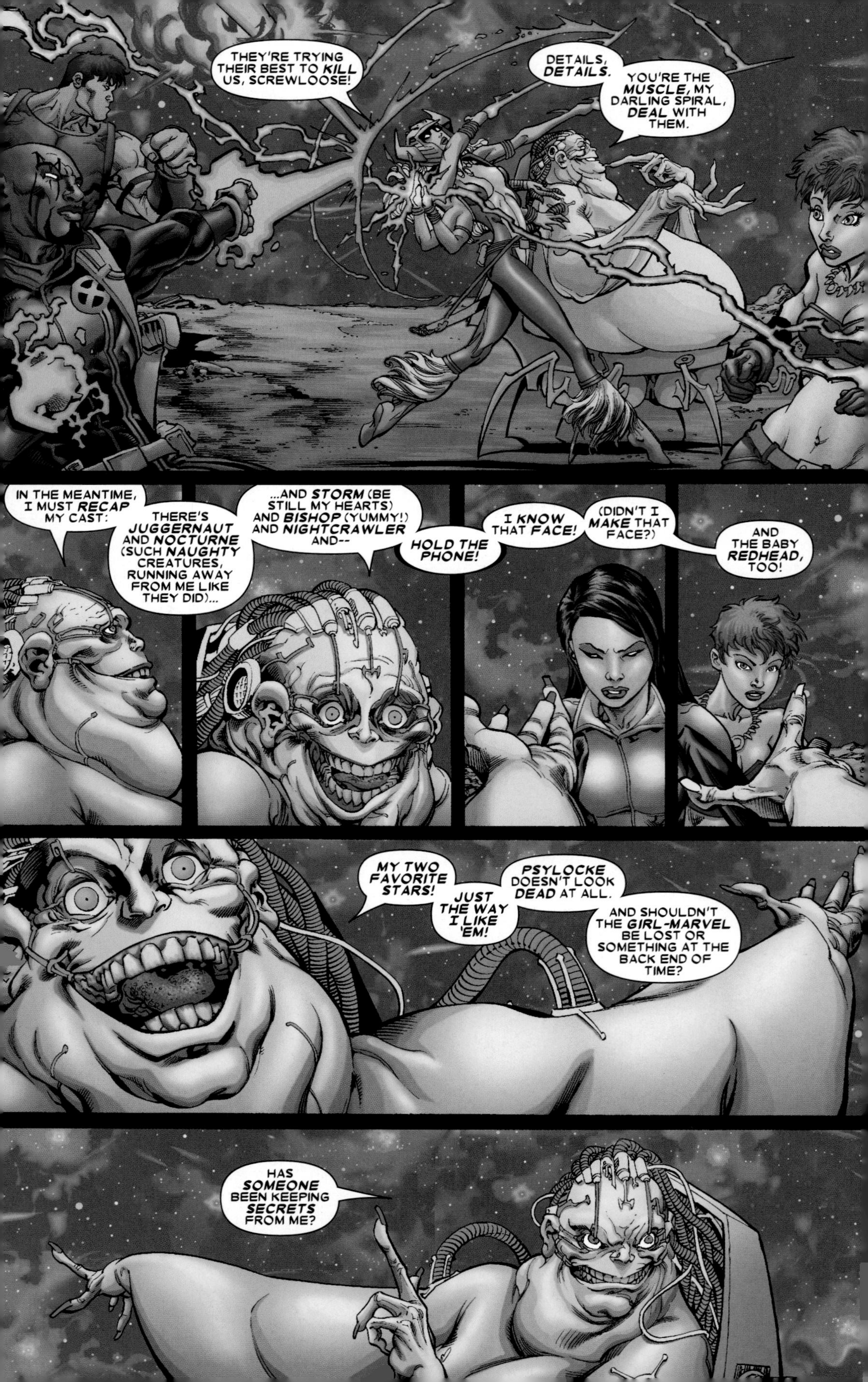
THEY'RE TRYING THEIR BEST TO KILL US, SCREWLOOSE!
DETAILS, DETAILS.
YOU'RE THE MUSCLE, MY DARLING SPIRAL, DEAL WITH THEM.
IN THE MEANTIME, I MUST RECAP MY CAST:
THERE'S JUGGERNAUT AND NOCTURNE (SUCH NAUGHTY CREATURES, RUNNING AWAY FROM ME LIKE THEY DID)...
...AND STORM (BE STILL MY HEARTS) AND BISHOP (YUMMY!) AND NIGHTCRAWLER AND--
HOLD THE PHONE!
I KNOW THAT FACE!
(DIDN'T I MAKE THAT FACE?)
AND THE BABY REDHEAD, TOO!
MY TWO FAVORITE STARS!
JUST THE WAY I LIKE 'EM!
PSYLOCKE DOESN'T LOOK DEAD AT ALL.
AND SHOULDN'T THE GIRL-MARVEL BE LOST OR SOMETHING AT THE BACK END OF TIME?
HAS SOMEONE BEEN KEEPING SECRETS FROM ME?

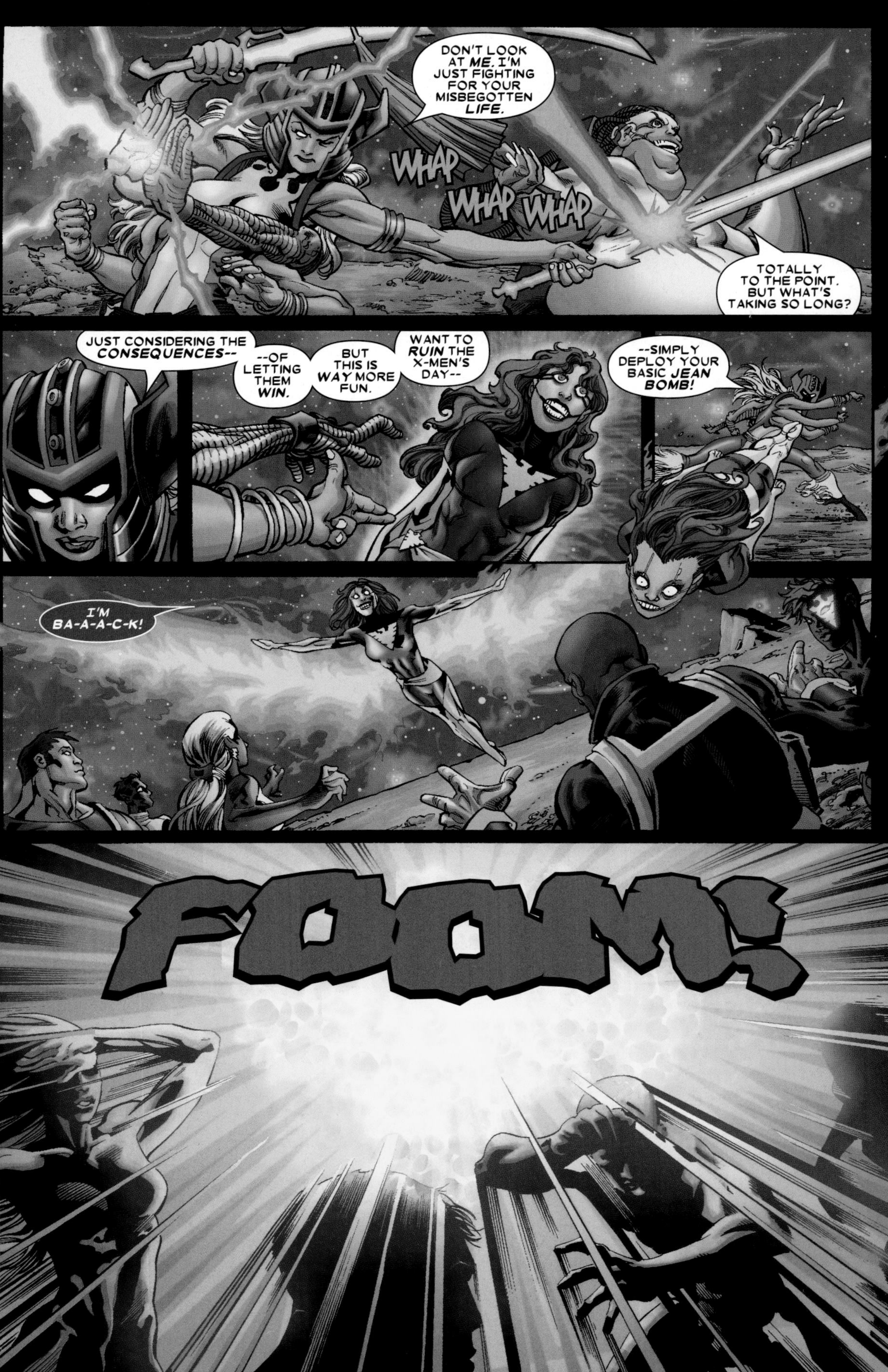
DON'T LOOK AT ME. I'M JUST FIGHTING FOR YOUR MISBEGOTTEN LIFE.
WHAP
WHAP WHAP
TOTALLY TO THE POINT. BUT WHAT'S TAKING SO LONG?
JUST CONSIDERING THE CONSEQUENCES--
--OF LETTING THEM WIN.
BUT THIS IS WAY MORE FUN.
WANT TO RUIN THE X-MEN'S DAY--
--SIMPLY DEPLOY YOUR BASIC JEAN BOMB!
I'M BA-A-A-C-K!
FOOM!

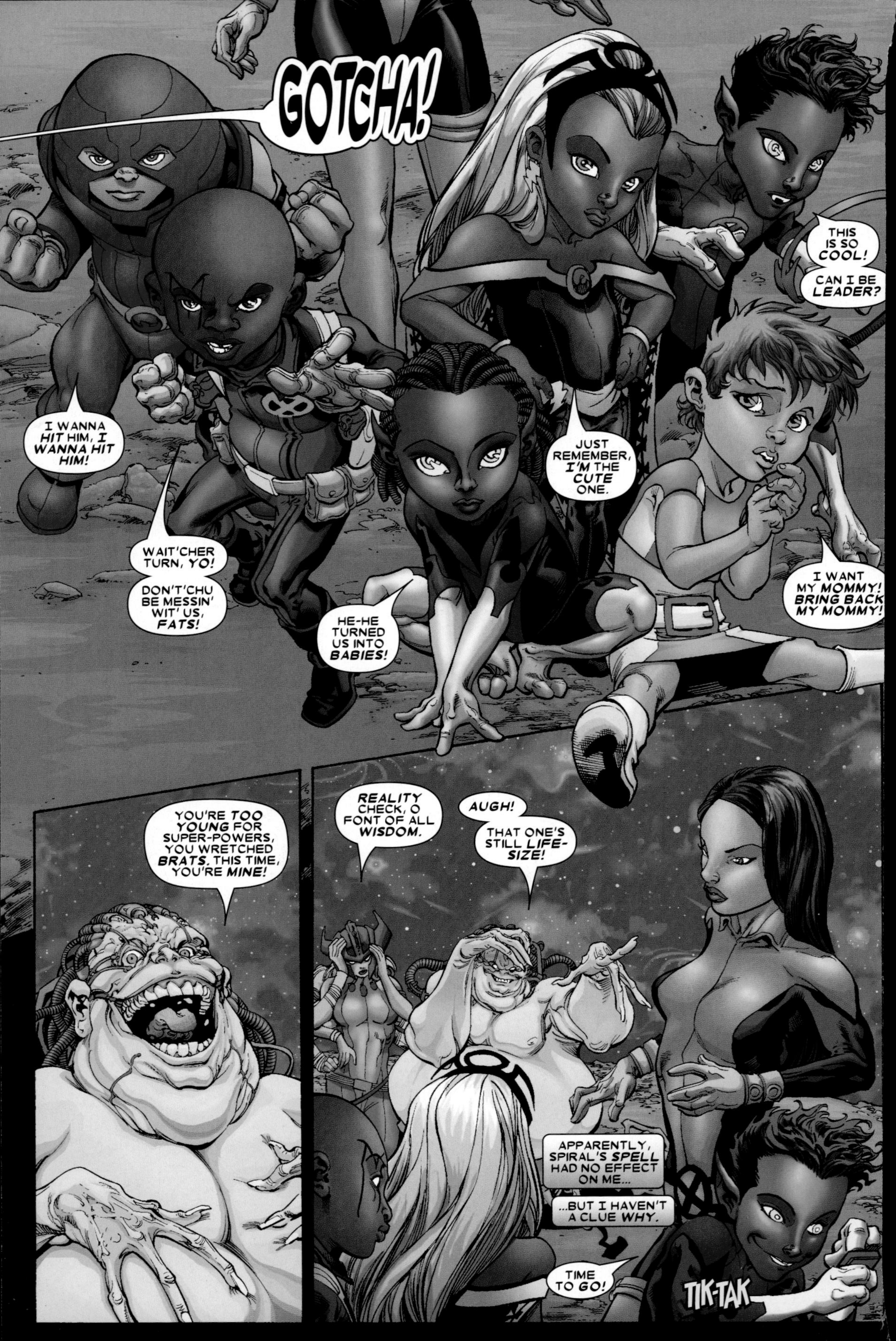
GOTCHA!
THIS IS SO COOL!
CAN I BE LEADER?
I WANNA HIT HIM, I WANNA HIT HIM!
JUST REMEMBER, I'M THE CUTE ONE.
WAIT'CHER TURN, YO!
DON'T'CHU BE MESSIN' WIT' US, FATS!
HE-HE TURNED US INTO BABIES!
I WANT MY MOMMY! BRING BACK MY MOMMY!
YOU'RE TOO YOUNG FOR SUPER-POWERS, YOU WRETCHED BRATS. THIS TIME, YOU'RE MINE!
REALITY CHECK, O FONT OF ALL WISDOM.
AUGH!
THAT ONE'S STILL LIFE-SIZE!
APPARENTLY, SPIRAL'S SPELL HAD NO EFFECT ON ME...
...BUT I HAVEN'T A CLUE WHY.
TIME TO GO!
TIK-TAK

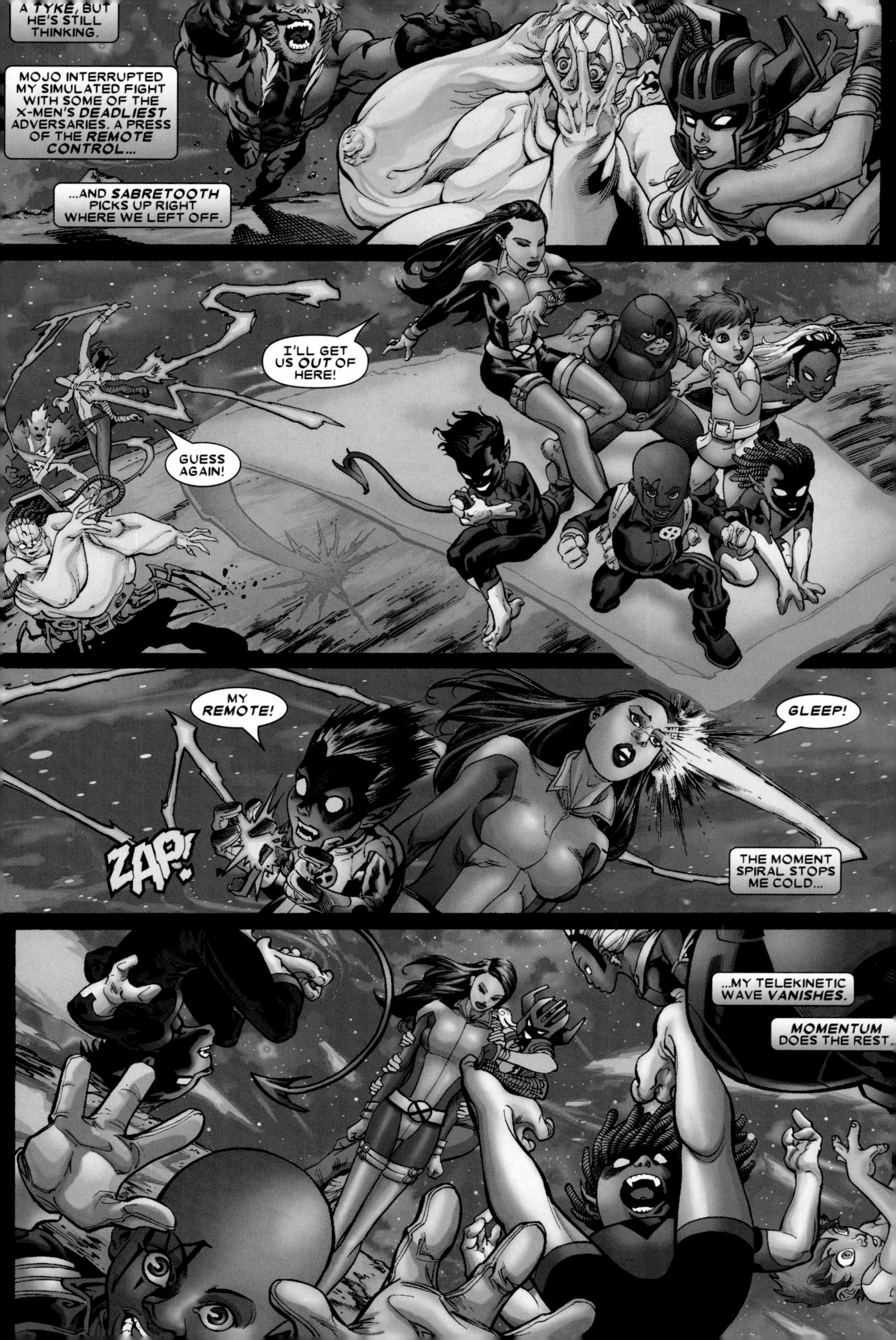

A TYKE, BUT HE'S STILL THINKING.
MOJO INTERRUPTED MY SIMULATED FIGHT WITH SOME OF THE X-MEN'S DEADLIEST ADVERSARIES. A PRESS OF THE REMOTE CONTROL...
...AND SABRETOOTH PICKS UP RIGHT WHERE WE LEFT OFF.
I'LL GET US OUT OF HERE!
GUESS AGAIN!
MY REMOTE!
GLEEP!
ZAP!
THE MOMENT SPIRAL STOPS ME COLD...
...MY TELEKINETIC WAVE VANISHES.
MOMENTUM DOES THE REST.

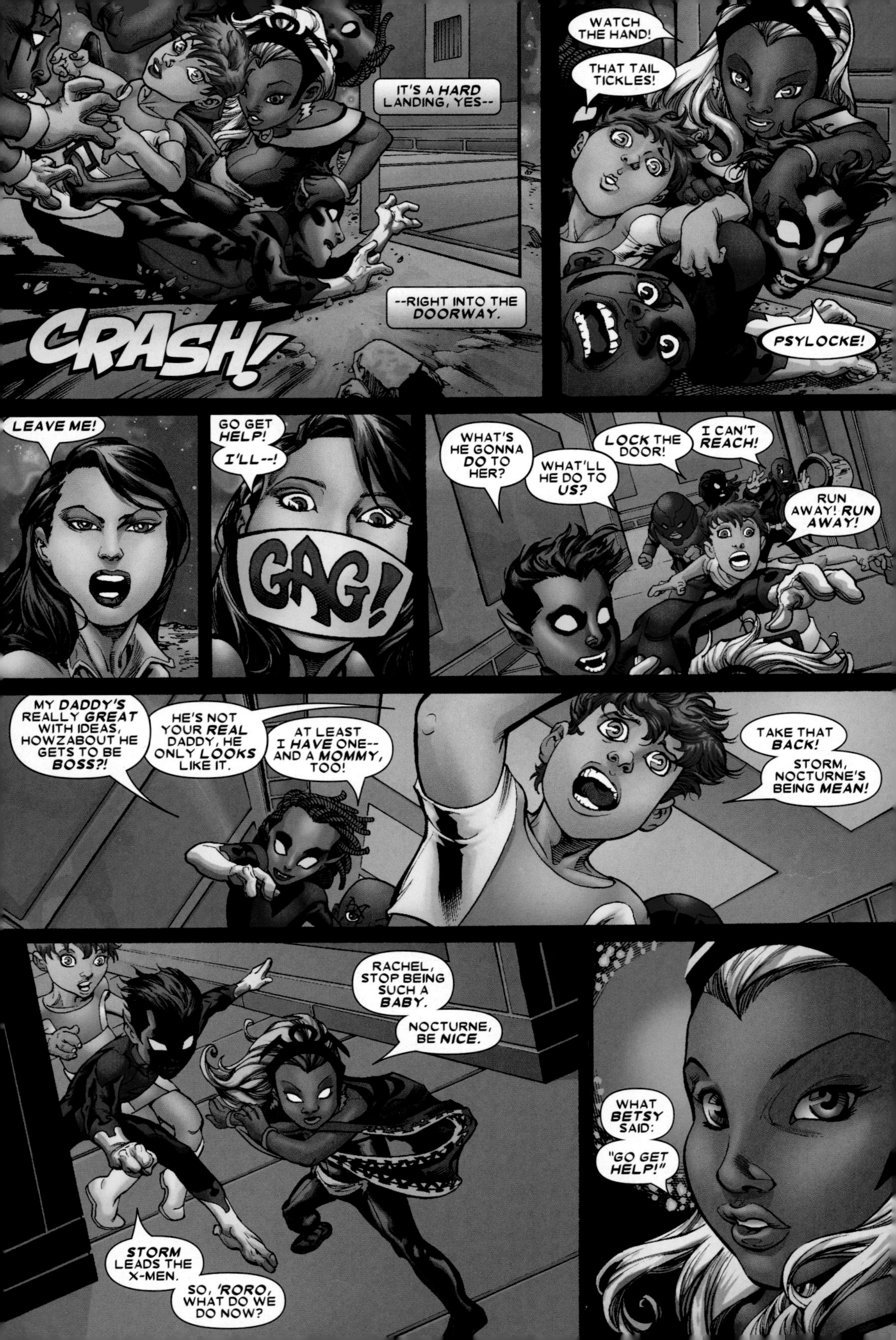
IT'S A HARD LANDING, YES--
--RIGHT INTO THE DOORWAY.
CRASH!
WATCH THE HAND!
THAT TAIL TICKLES!
PSYLOCKE!
LEAVE ME!
GO GET HELP!
I'LL--!
GAG!
WHAT'S HE GONNA DO TO HER?
WHAT'LL HE DO TO US?
LOCK THE DOOR!
I CAN'T REACH!
RUN AWAY! RUN AWAY!
MY DADDY'S REALLY GREAT WITH IDEAS, HOWZABOUT HE GETS TO BE BOSS?!
HE'S NOT YOUR REAL DADDY, HE ONLY LOOKS LIKE IT.
AT LEAST I HAVE ONE-- AND A MOMMY, TOO!
TAKE THAT BACK!
STORM, NOCTURNE'S BEING MEAN!
RACHEL, STOP BEING SUCH A BABY.
NOCTURNE, BE NICE.
STORM LEADS THE X-MEN.
SO, 'RORO, WHAT DO WE DO NOW?
WHAT BETSY SAID:
"GO GET HELP!"

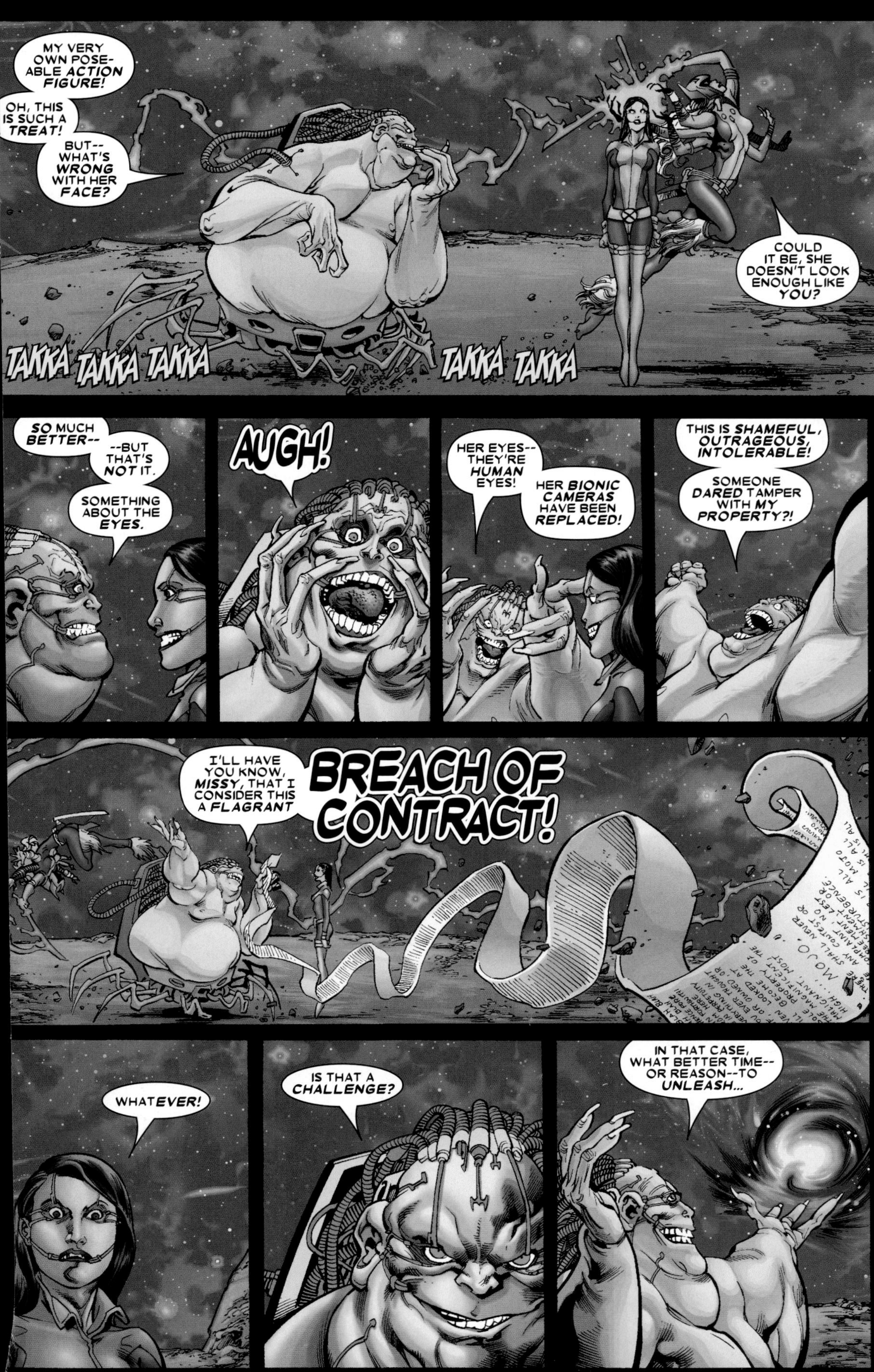

MY VERY OWN POSE-ABLE ACTION FIGURE!
OH, THIS IS SUCH A TREAT!
BUT--WHAT'S WRONG WITH HER FACE?
COULD IT BE, SHE DOESN'T LOOK ENOUGH LIKE YOU?
TAKKA TAKKA TAKKA
TAKKA TAKKA
SO MUCH BETTER--
--BUT THAT'S NOT IT.
SOMETHING ABOUT THE EYES.
AUGH!
HER EYES--THEY'RE HUMAN EYES!
HER BIONIC CAMERAS HAVE BEEN REPLACED!
THIS IS SHAMEFUL, OUTRAGEOUS, INTOLERABLE!
SOMEONE DARED TAMPER WITH MY PROPERTY?!
I'LL HAVE YOU KNOW, MISSY, THAT I CONSIDER THIS A FLAGRANT
BREACH OF CONTRACT!
WHATEVER!
IS THAT A CHALLENGE?
IN THAT CASE, WHAT BETTER TIME--OR REASON--TO UNLEASH...

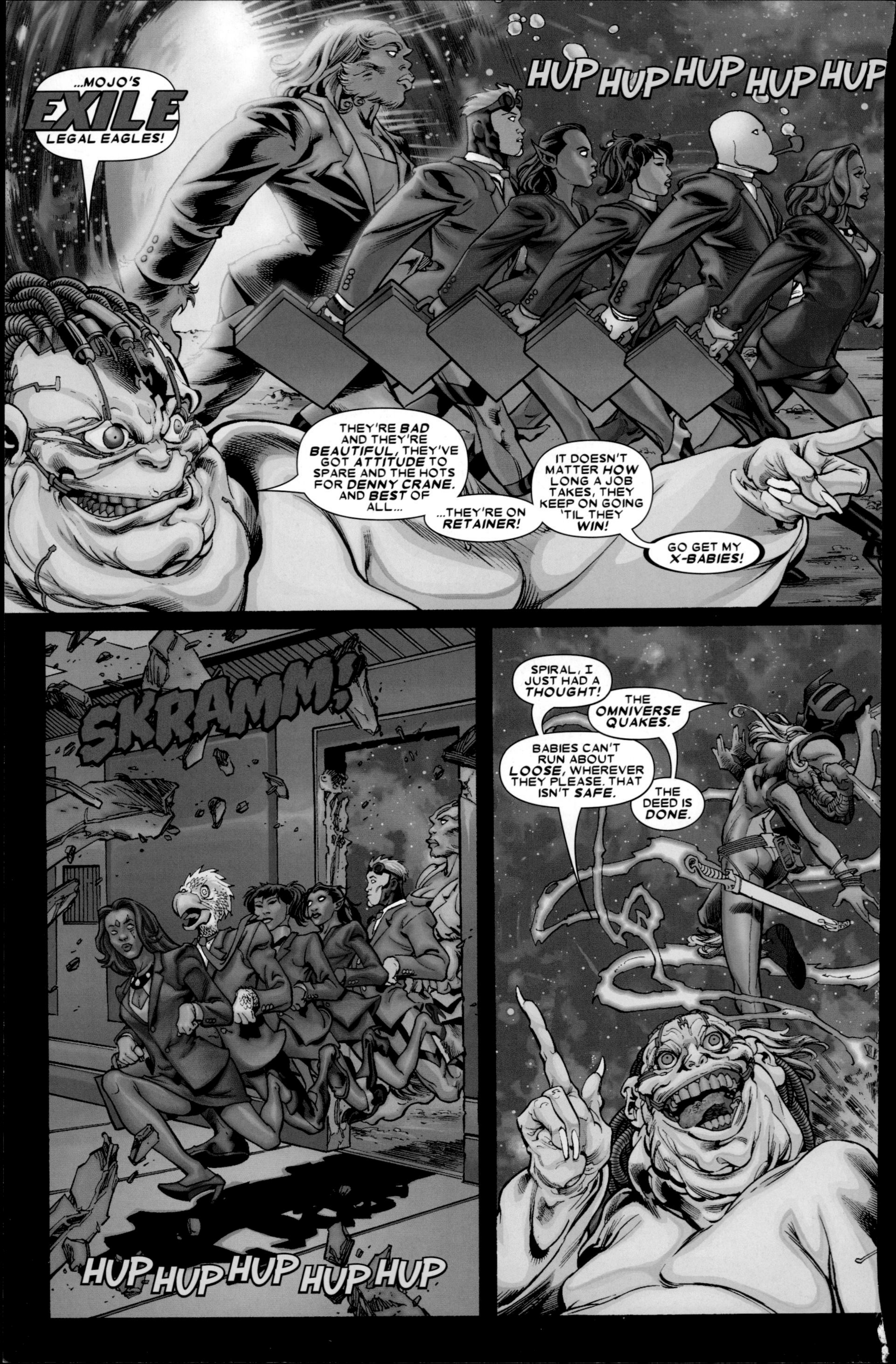
...MOJO'S EXILE LEGAL EAGLES!
HUP HUP HUP HUP HUP
THEY'RE BAD AND THEY'RE BEAUTIFUL, THEY'VE GOT ATTITUDE TO SPARE AND THE HOTS FOR DENNY CRANE. AND BEST OF ALL...
...THEY'RE ON RETAINER!
IT DOESN'T MATTER HOW LONG A JOB TAKES, THEY KEEP ON GOING 'TIL THEY WIN!
GO GET MY X-BABIES!
SKRAMM!
HUP HUP HUP HUP HUP
SPIRAL, I JUST HAD A THOUGHT!
THE OMNIVERSE QUAKES.
BABIES CAN'T RUN ABOUT LOOSE, WHEREVER THEY PLEASE. THAT ISN'T SAFE.
THE DEED IS DONE.

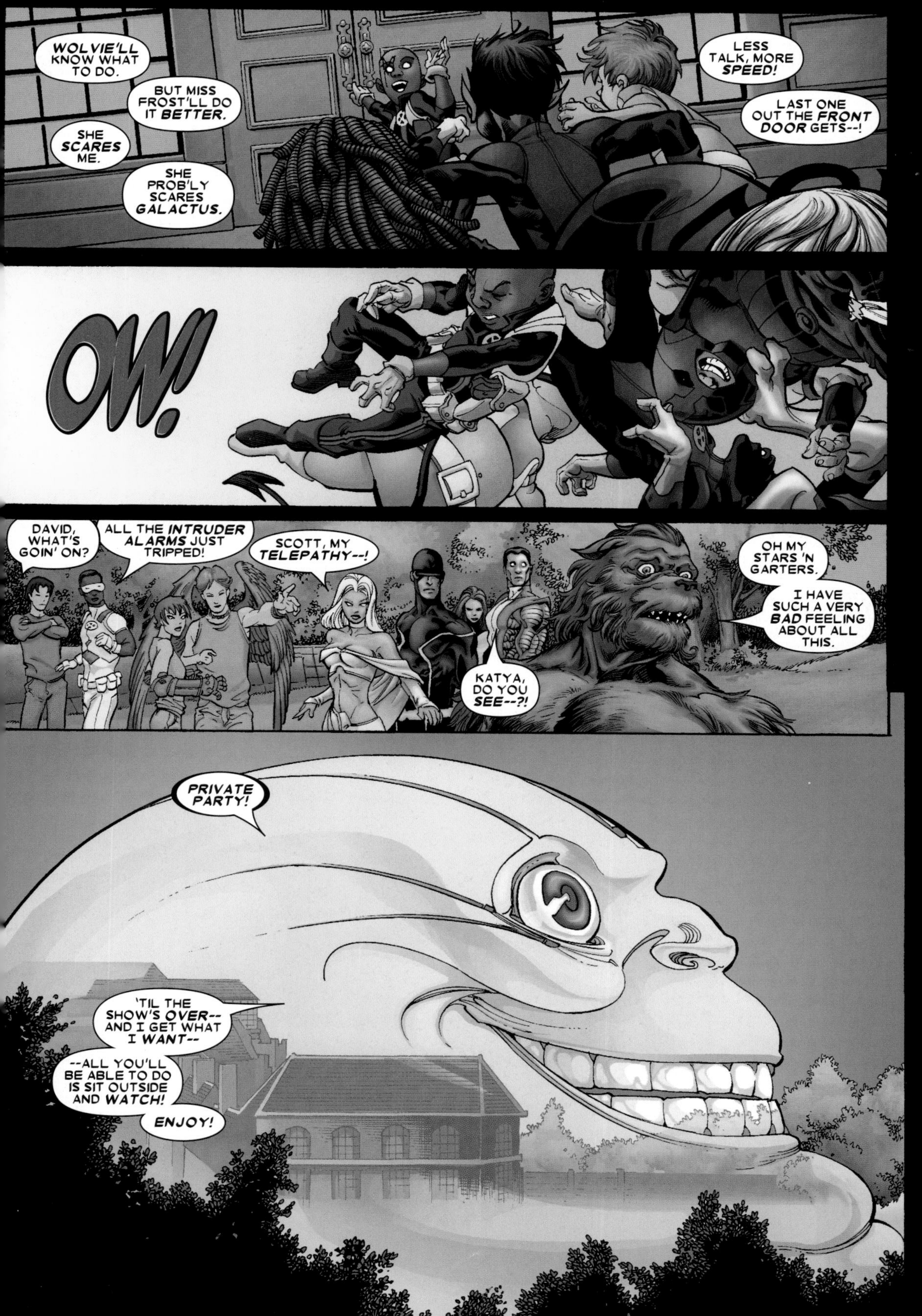
WOLVIE'LL KNOW WHAT TO DO.
BUT MISS FROST'LL DO IT BETTER.
SHE SCARES ME.
SHE PROB'LY SCARES GALACTUS.
LESS TALK, MORE SPEED!
LAST ONE OUT THE FRONT DOOR GETS--!
OW!
DAVID, WHAT'S GOIN' ON?
ALL THE INTRUDER ALARMS JUST TRIPPED!
SCOTT, MY TELEPATHY--!
KATYA, DO YOU SEE--?!
OH MY STARS 'N GARTERS.
I HAVE SUCH A VERY BAD FEELING ABOUT ALL THIS.
PRIVATE PARTY!
'TIL THE SHOW'S OVER-- AND I GET WHAT I WANT--
--ALL YOU'LL BE ABLE TO DO IS SIT OUTSIDE AND WATCH!
ENJOY!

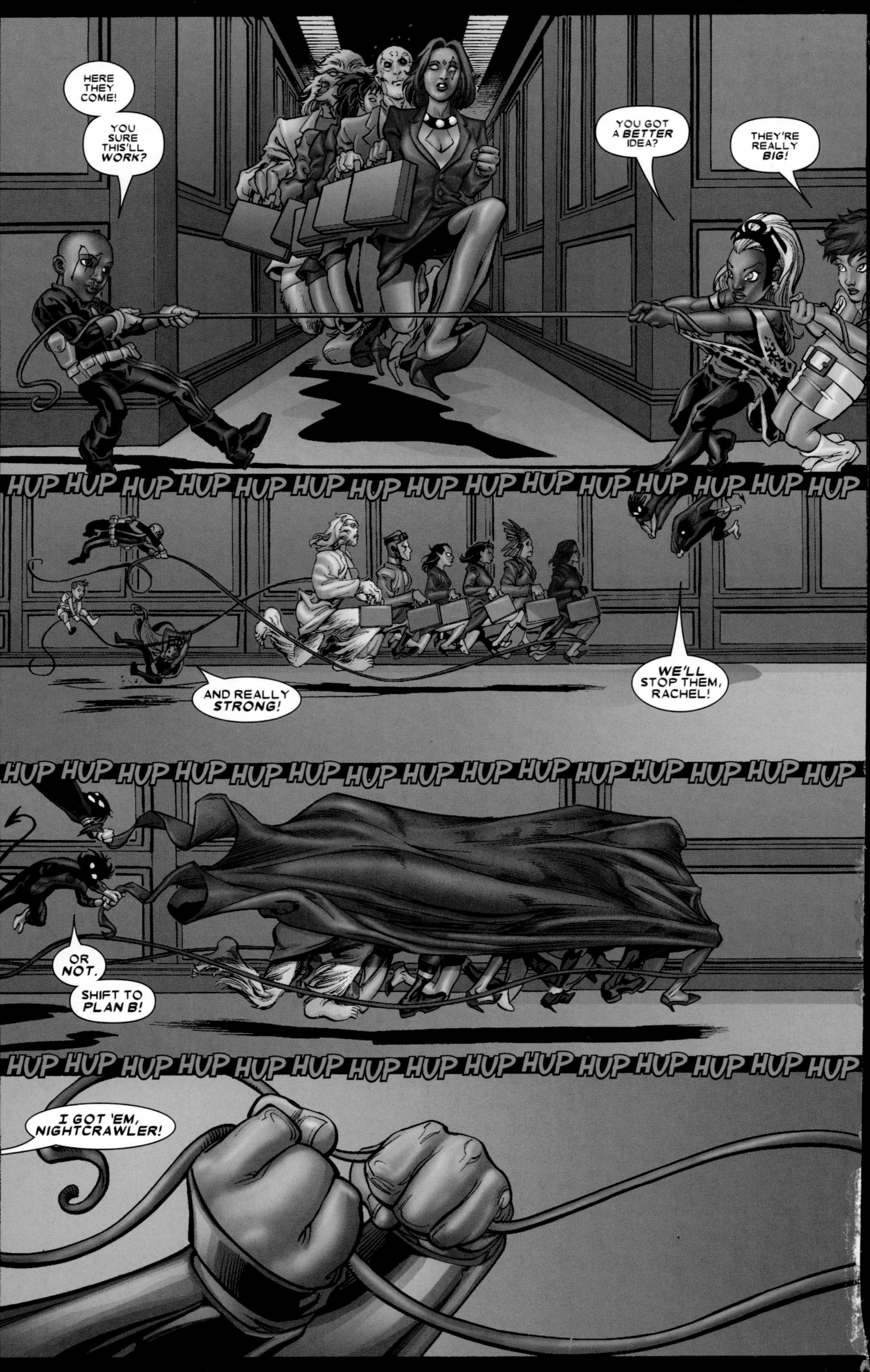
HERE THEY COME!
YOU SURE THIS'LL WORK?
YOU GOT A BETTER IDEA?
THEY'RE REALLY BIG!
HUP HUP HUP HUP HUP HUP HUP HUP HUP HUP HUP HUP HUP HUP HUP
AND REALLY STRONG!
WE'LL STOP THEM, RACHEL!
HUP HUP HUP HUP HUP HUP HUP HUP HUP HUP HUP HUP HUP HUP HUP
OR NOT.
SHIFT TO PLAN B!
HUP HUP HUP HUP HUP HUP HUP HUP HUP HUP HUP HUP HUP HUP HUP
I GOT 'EM, NIGHTCRAWLER!

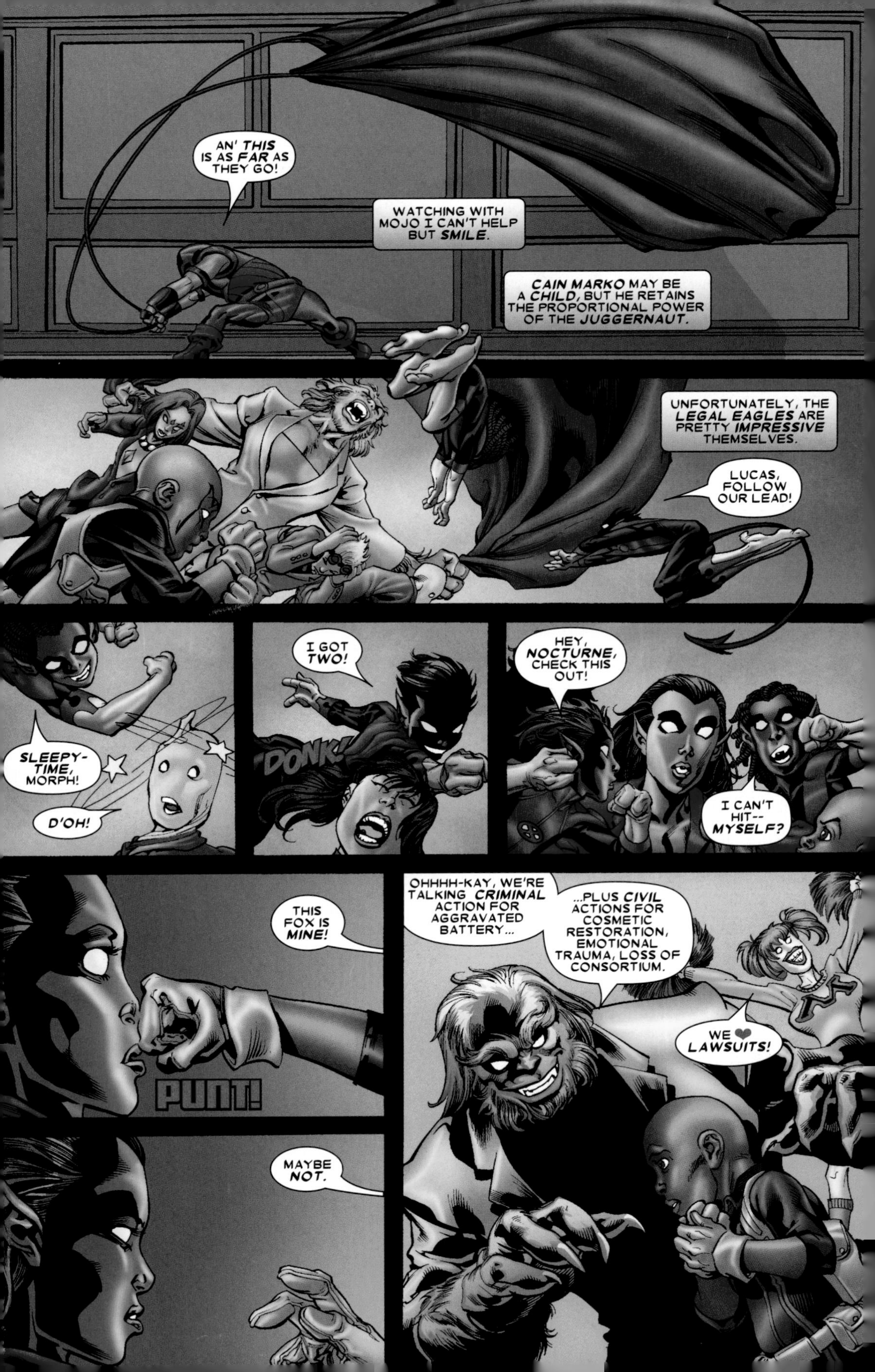
AN' THIS IS AS FAR AS THEY GO!
WATCHING WITH MOJO I CAN'T HELP BUT SMILE.
CAIN MARKO MAY BE A CHILD, BUT HE RETAINS THE PROPORTIONAL POWER OF THE JUGGERNAUT.
UNFORTUNATELY, THE LEGAL EAGLES ARE PRETTY IMPRESSIVE THEMSELVES.
LUCAS, FOLLOW OUR LEAD!
SLEEPY-TIME, MORPH!
D'OH!
I GOT TWO!
DONK!
HEY, NOCTURNE, CHECK THIS OUT!
I CAN'T HIT-- MYSELF?
THIS FOX IS MINE!
PUNT!
MAYBE NOT.
OHHHH-KAY, WE'RE TALKING CRIMINAL ACTION FOR AGGRAVATED BATTERY...
...PLUS CIVIL ACTIONS FOR COSMETIC RESTORATION, EMOTIONAL TRAUMA, LOSS OF CONSORTIUM.
WE ❤ LAWSUITS!

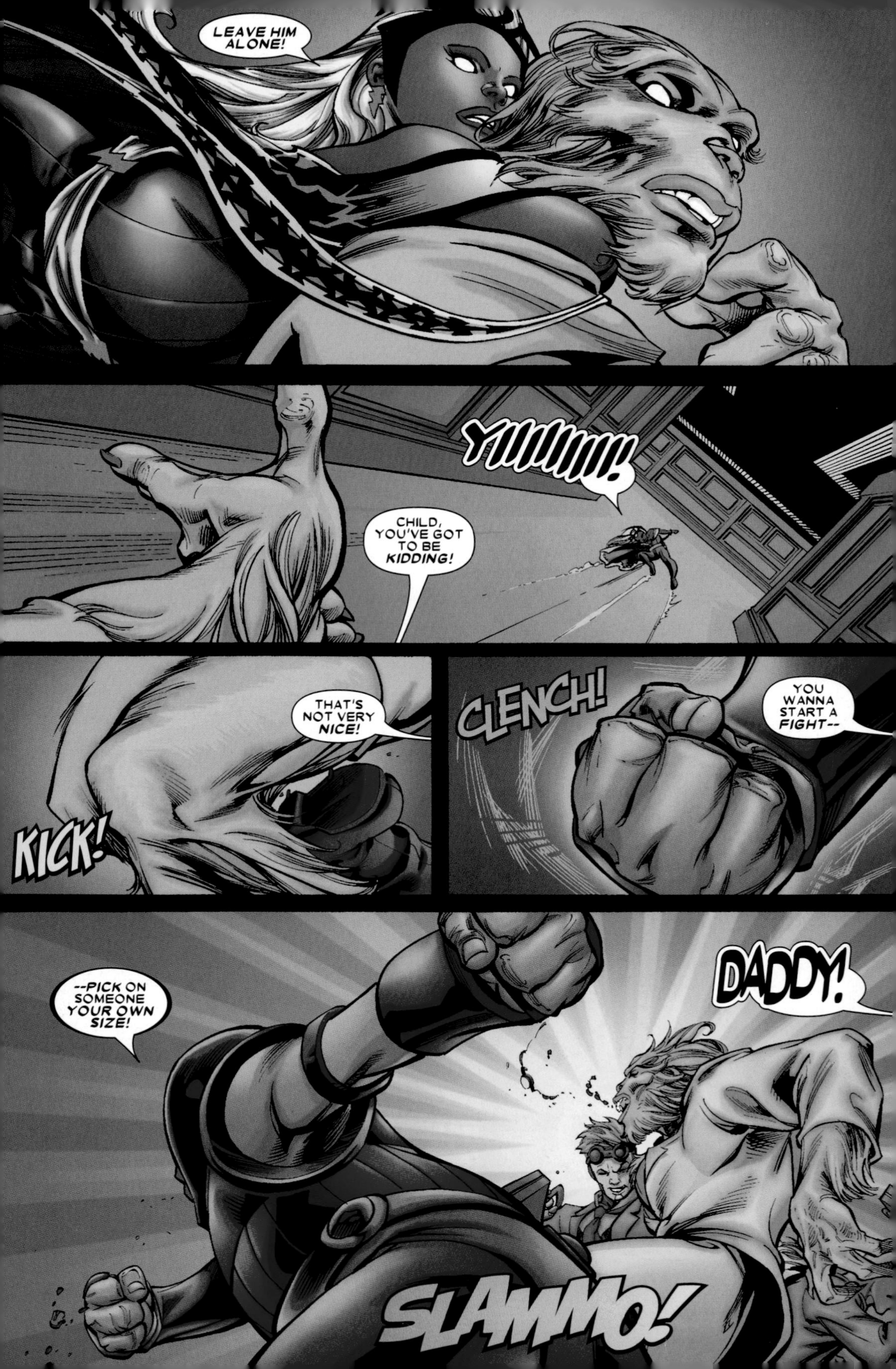
LEAVE HIM ALONE!
YIIIIIIIII!
CHILD, YOU'VE GOT TO BE KIDDING!
THAT'S NOT VERY NICE!
KICK!
CLENCH!
YOU WANNA START A FIGHT--
--PICK ON SOMEONE YOUR OWN SIZE!
DADDY!
SLAMMO!

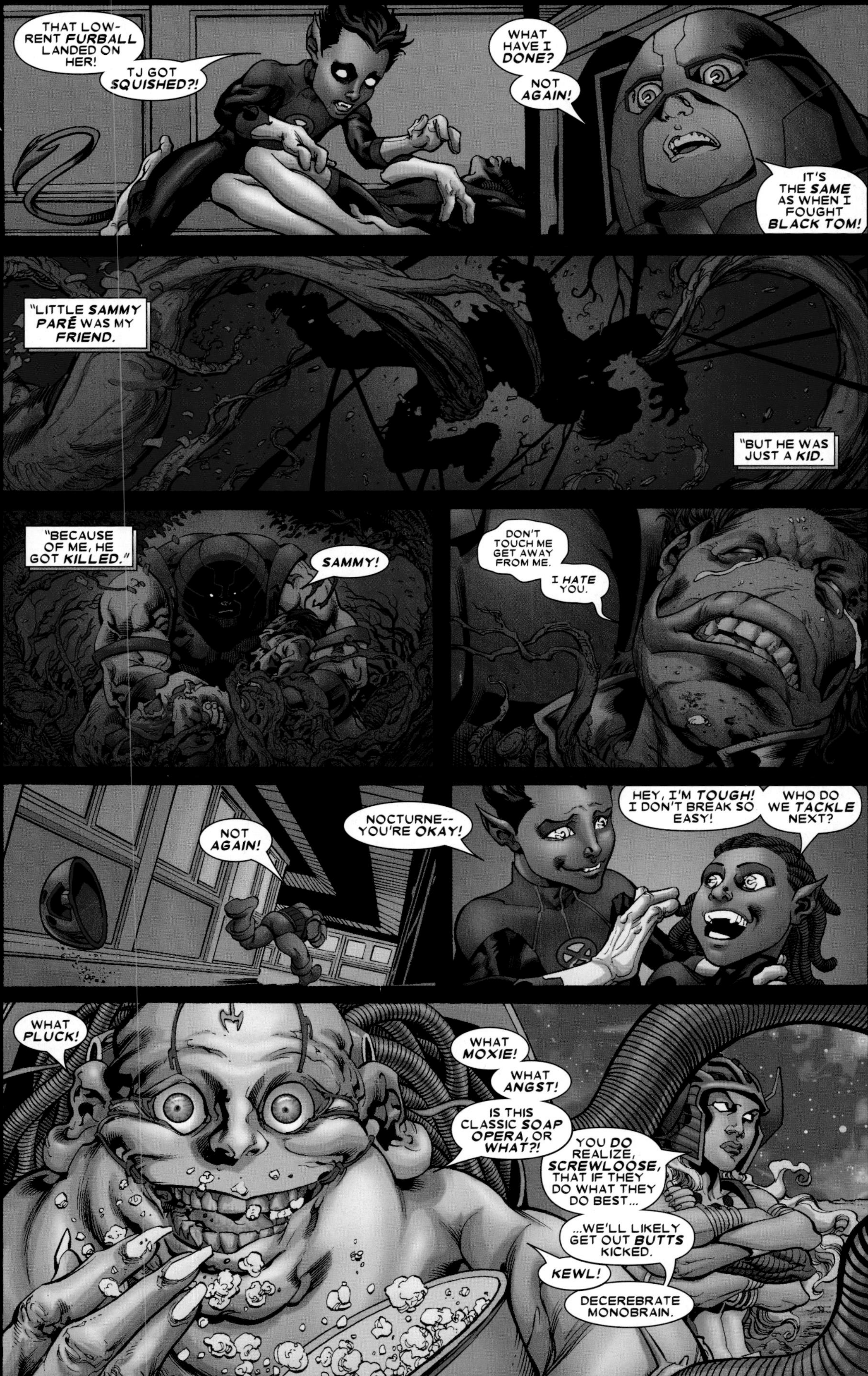
THAT LOW-RENT FURBALL LANDED ON HER!
TJ GOT SQUISHED?!
WHAT HAVE I DONE?
NOT AGAIN!
IT'S THE SAME AS WHEN I FOUGHT BLACK TOM!
"LITTLE SAMMY PARÉ WAS MY FRIEND.
"BUT HE WAS JUST A KID.
"BECAUSE OF ME, HE GOT KILLED."
SAMMY!
DON'T TOUCH ME GET AWAY FROM ME.
I HATE YOU.
NOT AGAIN!
NOCTURNE-- YOU'RE OKAY!
HEY, I'M TOUGH! I DON'T BREAK SO EASY!
WHO DO WE TACKLE NEXT?
WHAT PLUCK!
WHAT MOXIE!
WHAT ANGST!
IS THIS CLASSIC SOAP OPERA, OR WHAT?!
YOU DO REALIZE, SCREWLOOSE, THAT IF THEY DO WHAT THEY DO BEST...
...WE'LL LIKELY GET OUT BUTTS KICKED.
KEWL!
DECEREBRATE MONOBRAIN.

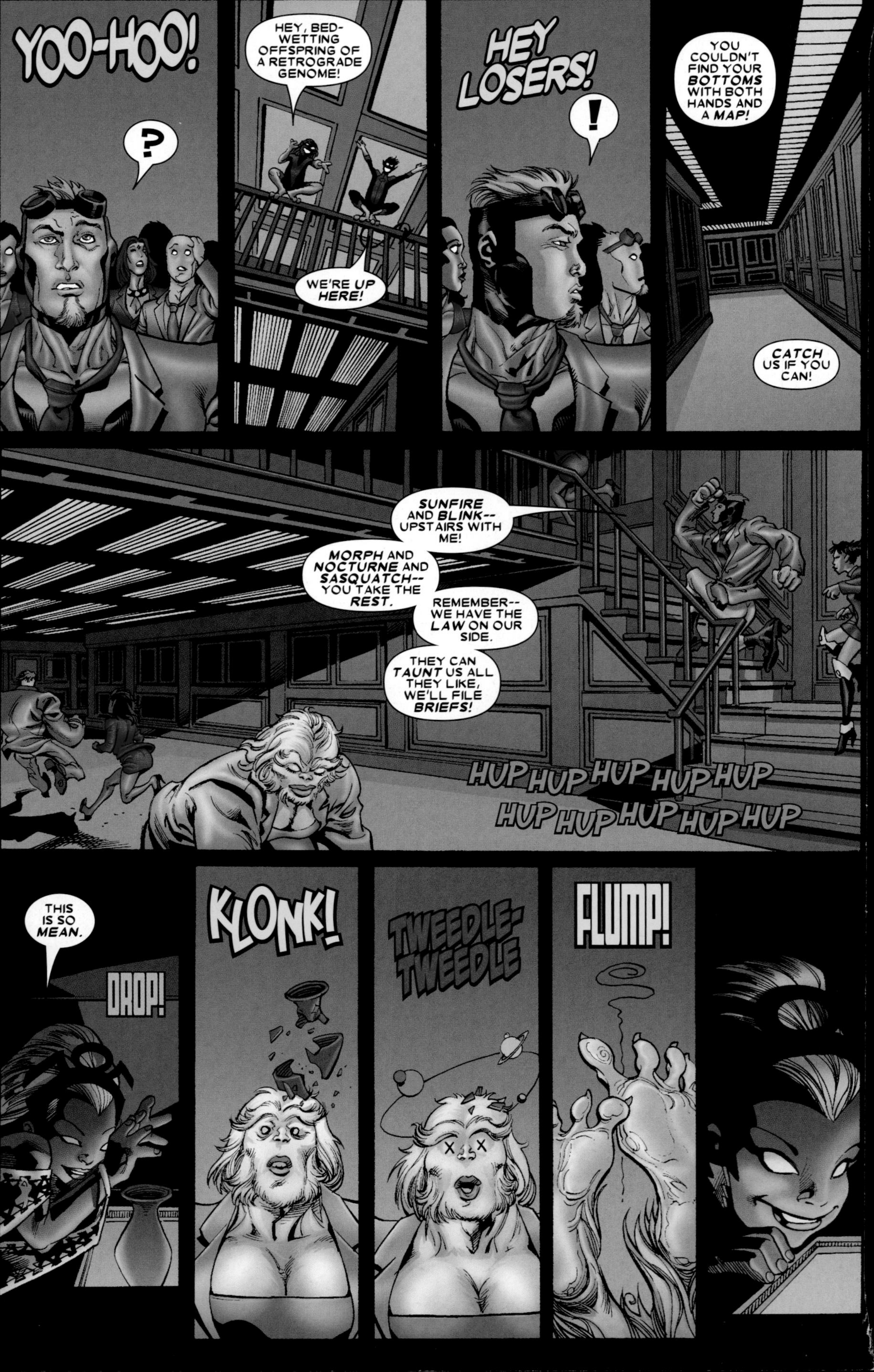
YOO-HOO!
?
HEY, BED-WETTING OFFSPRING OF A RETROGRADE GENOME!
WE'RE UP HERE!
HEY LOSERS!
!
YOU COULDN'T FIND YOUR BOTTOMS WITH BOTH HANDS AND A MAP!
CATCH US IF YOU CAN!
SUNFIRE AND BLINK-- UPSTAIRS WITH ME!
MORPH AND NOCTURNE AND SASQUATCH-- YOU TAKE THE REST.
REMEMBER-- WE HAVE THE LAW ON OUR SIDE.
THEY CAN TAUNT US ALL THEY LIKE, WE'LL FILE BRIEFS!
HUP HUP HUP HUP HUP
HUP HUP HUP HUP HUP
THIS IS SO MEAN.
DROP!
KLONK!
TWEEDLE-TWEEDLE
FLUMP!

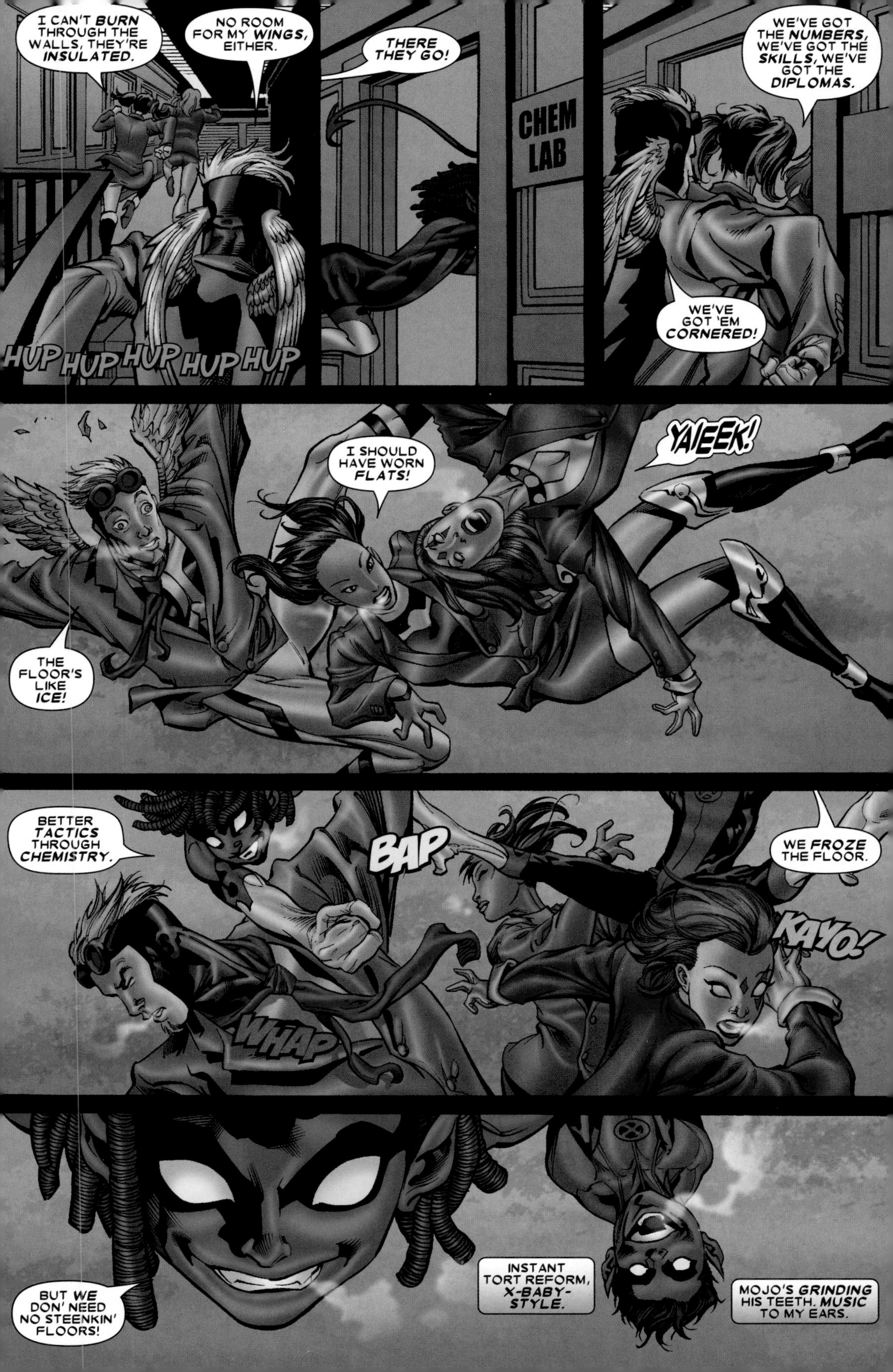
I CAN'T BURN THROUGH THE WALLS, THEY'RE INSULATED.
NO ROOM FOR MY WINGS, EITHER.
HUP HUP HUP HUP HUP
THERE THEY GO!
CHEM LAB
WE'VE GOT THE NUMBERS, WE'VE GOT THE SKILLS, WE'VE GOT THE DIPLOMAS.
WE'VE GOT 'EM CORNERED!
I SHOULD HAVE WORN FLATS!
YAIEEK!
THE FLOOR'S LIKE ICE!
BETTER TACTICS THROUGH CHEMISTRY.
BAP
WE FROZE THE FLOOR.
KAYO!
WHAP
BUT WE DON' NEED NO STEENKIN' FLOORS!
INSTANT TORT REFORM, X-BABY-STYLE.
MOJO'S GRINDING HIS TEETH. MUSIC TO MY EARS.

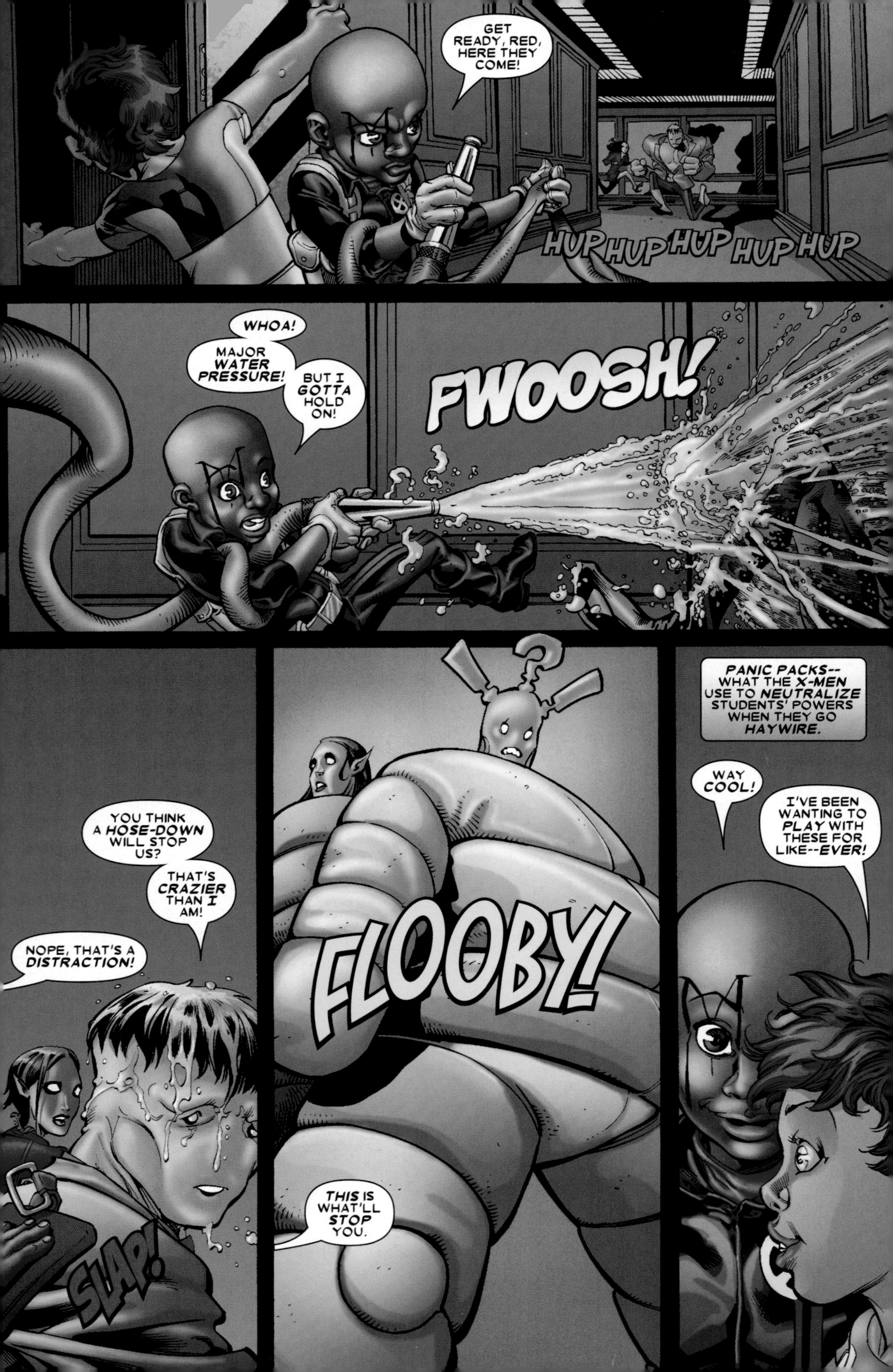
GET READY, RED, HERE THEY COME!
HUP HUP HUP HUP HUP
WHOA!
MAJOR WATER PRESSURE!
BUT I GOTTA HOLD ON!
FWOOSH!
YOU THINK A HOSE-DOWN WILL STOP US?
THAT'S CRAZIER THAN I AM!
NOPE, THAT'S A DISTRACTION!
SLAP!
FLOOBY!
THIS IS WHAT'LL STOP YOU.
PANIC PACKS--WHAT THE X-MEN USE TO NEUTRALIZE STUDENTS' POWERS WHEN THEY GO HAYWIRE.
WAY COOL!
I'VE BEEN WANTING TO PLAY WITH THESE FOR LIKE--EVER!

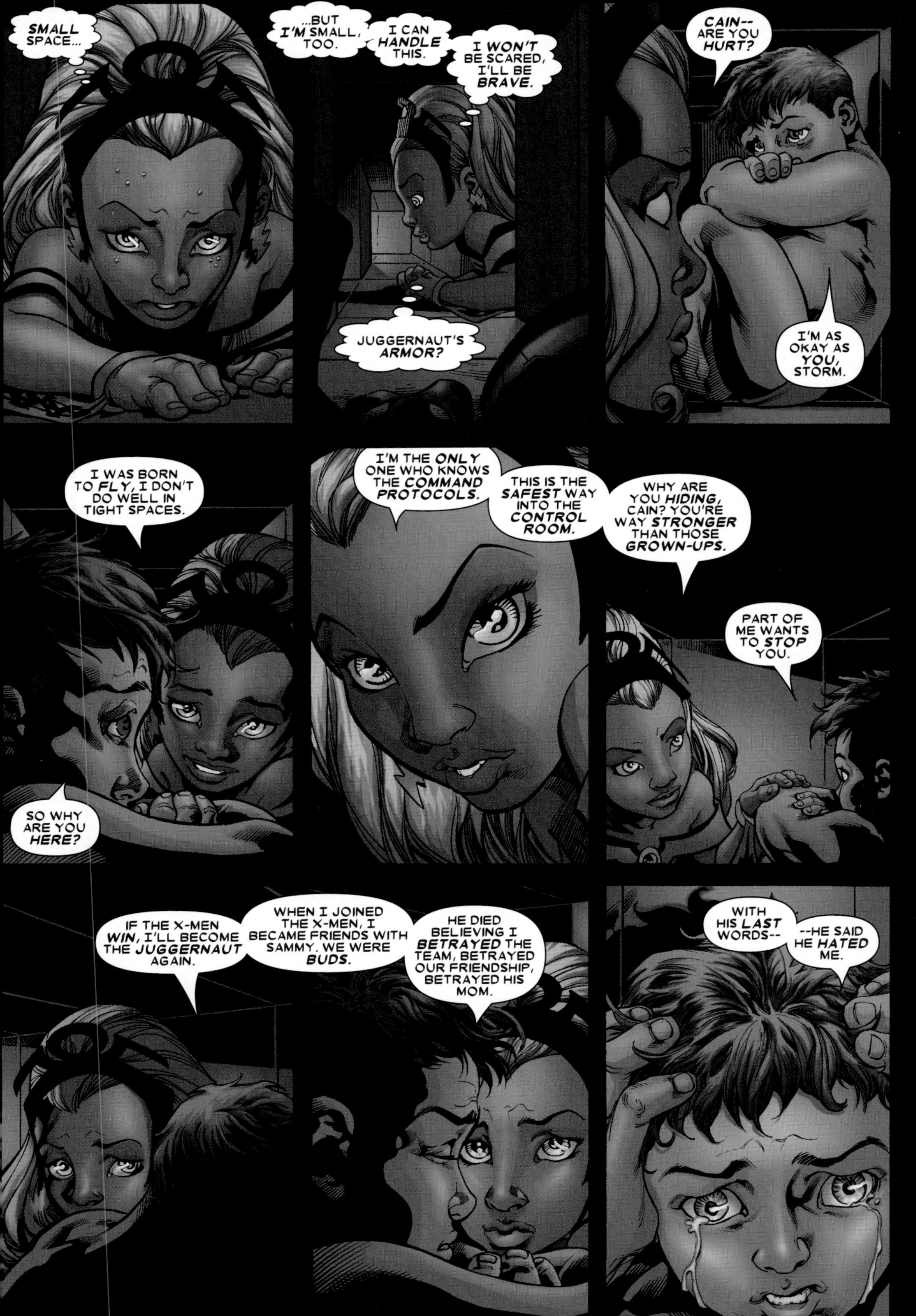
SMALL SPACE...
...BUT I'M SMALL, TOO.
I CAN HANDLE THIS.
I WON'T BE SCARED, I'LL BE BRAVE.
JUGGERNAUT'S ARMOR?
CAIN-- ARE YOU HURT?
I'M AS OKAY AS YOU, STORM.
I WAS BORN TO FLY, I DON'T DO WELL IN TIGHT SPACES.
SO WHY ARE YOU HERE?
I'M THE ONLY ONE WHO KNOWS THE COMMAND PROTOCOLS.
THIS IS THE SAFEST WAY INTO THE CONTROL ROOM.
WHY ARE YOU HIDING, CAIN? YOU'RE WAY STRONGER THAN THOSE GROWN-UPS.
PART OF ME WANTS TO STOP YOU.
IF THE X-MEN WIN, I'LL BECOME THE JUGGERNAUT AGAIN.
WHEN I JOINED THE X-MEN, I BECAME FRIENDS WITH SAMMY. WE WERE BUDS.
HE DIED BELIEVING I BETRAYED THE TEAM, BETRAYED OUR FRIENDSHIP, BETRAYED HIS MOM.
WITH HIS LAST WORDS--
--HE SAID HE HATED ME.

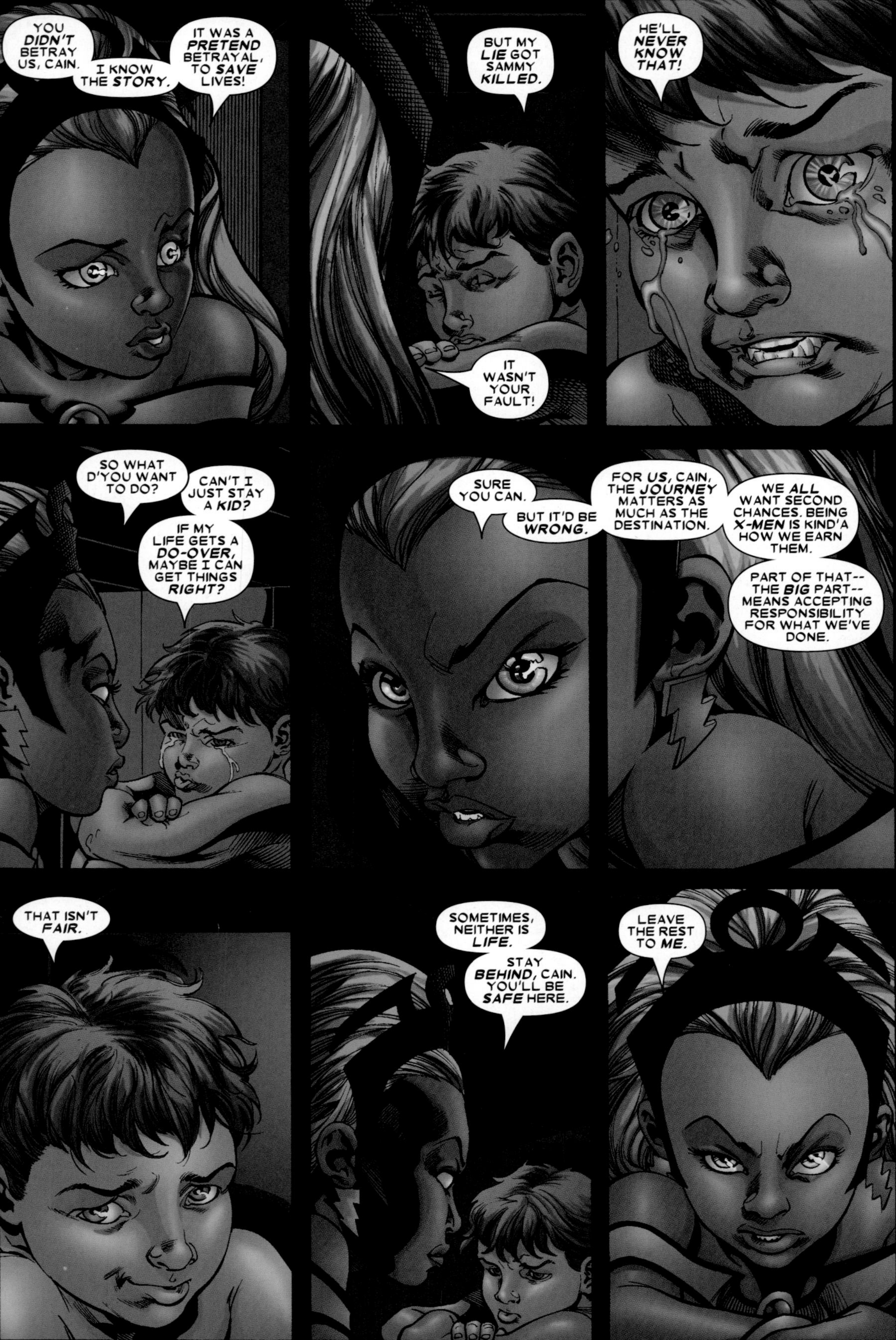
YOU DIDN'T BETRAY US, CAIN.
I KNOW THE STORY.
IT WAS A PRETEND BETRAYAL, TO SAVE LIVES!
BUT MY LIE GOT SAMMY KILLED.
IT WASN'T YOUR FAULT!
HE'LL NEVER KNOW THAT!
SO WHAT D'YOU WANT TO DO?
CAN'T I JUST STAY A KID?
IF MY LIFE GETS A DO-OVER, MAYBE I CAN GET THINGS RIGHT?
SURE YOU CAN.
BUT IT'D BE WRONG.
FOR US, CAIN, THE JOURNEY MATTERS AS MUCH AS THE DESTINATION.
WE ALL WANT SECOND CHANCES. BEING X-MEN IS KIND'A HOW WE EARN THEM.
PART OF THAT-- THE BIG PART-- MEANS ACCEPTING RESPONSIBILITY FOR WHAT WE'VE DONE.
THAT ISN'T FAIR.
SOMETIMES, NEITHER IS LIFE.
STAY BEHIND, CAIN. YOU'LL BE SAFE HERE.
LEAVE THE REST TO ME.

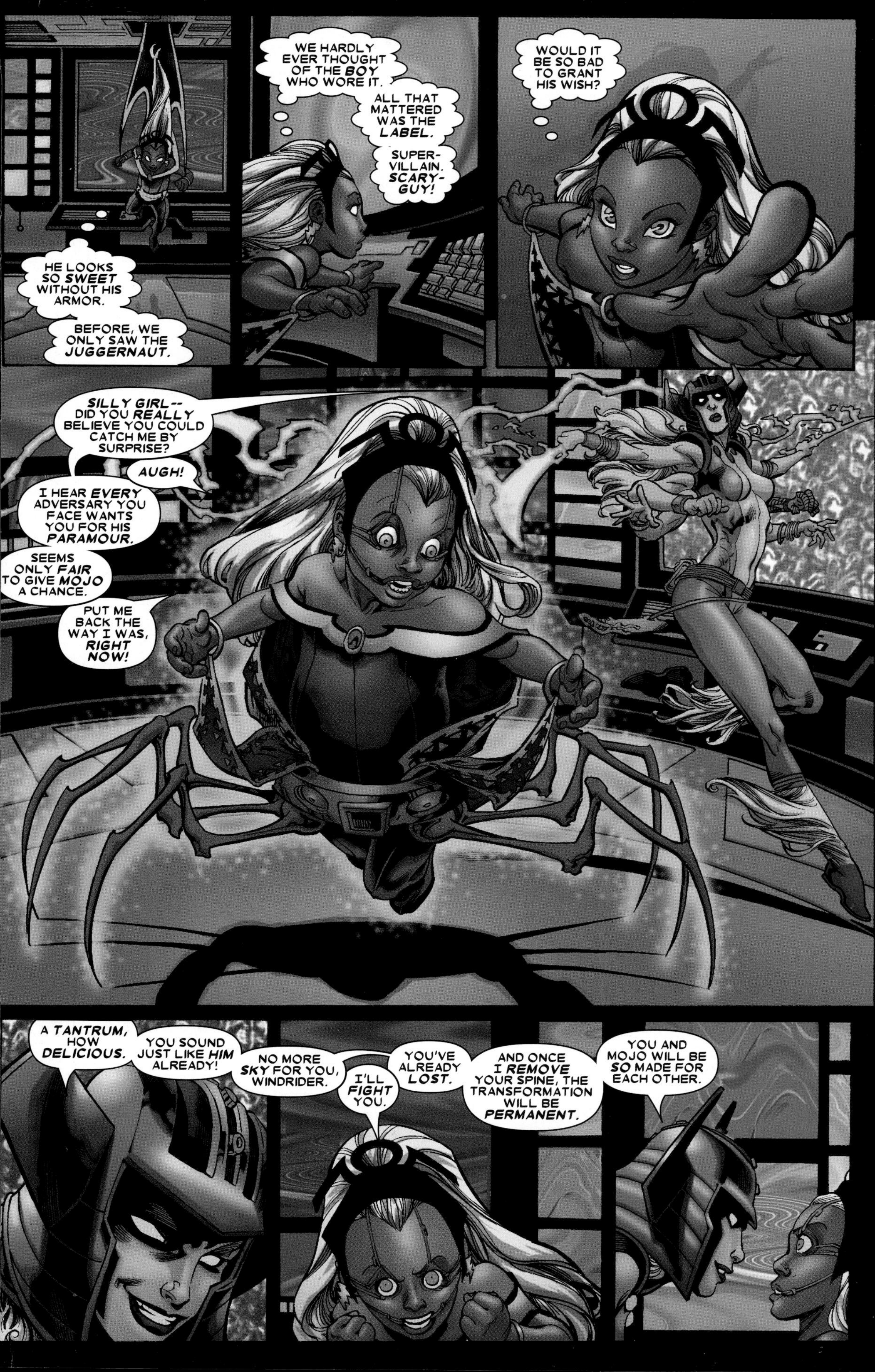
HE LOOKS SO SWEET WITHOUT HIS ARMOR.
BEFORE, WE ONLY SAW THE JUGGERNAUT.
WE HARDLY EVER THOUGHT OF THE BOY WHO WORE IT.
ALL THAT MATTERED WAS THE LABEL.
SUPER-VILLAIN. SCARY-GUY!
WOULD IT BE SO BAD TO GRANT HIS WISH?
SILLY GIRL-- DID YOU REALLY BELIEVE YOU COULD CATCH ME BY SURPRISE?
AUGH!
I HEAR EVERY ADVERSARY YOU FACE WANTS YOU FOR HIS PARAMOUR.
SEEMS ONLY FAIR TO GIVE MOJO A CHANCE.
PUT ME BACK THE WAY I WAS, RIGHT NOW!
A TANTRUM, HOW DELICIOUS.
YOU SOUND JUST LIKE HIM ALREADY!
NO MORE SKY FOR YOU, WINDRIDER.
I'LL FIGHT YOU.
YOU'VE ALREADY LOST.
AND ONCE I REMOVE YOUR SPINE, THE TRANSFORMATION WILL BE PERMANENT.
YOU AND MOJO WILL BE SO MADE FOR EACH OTHER.

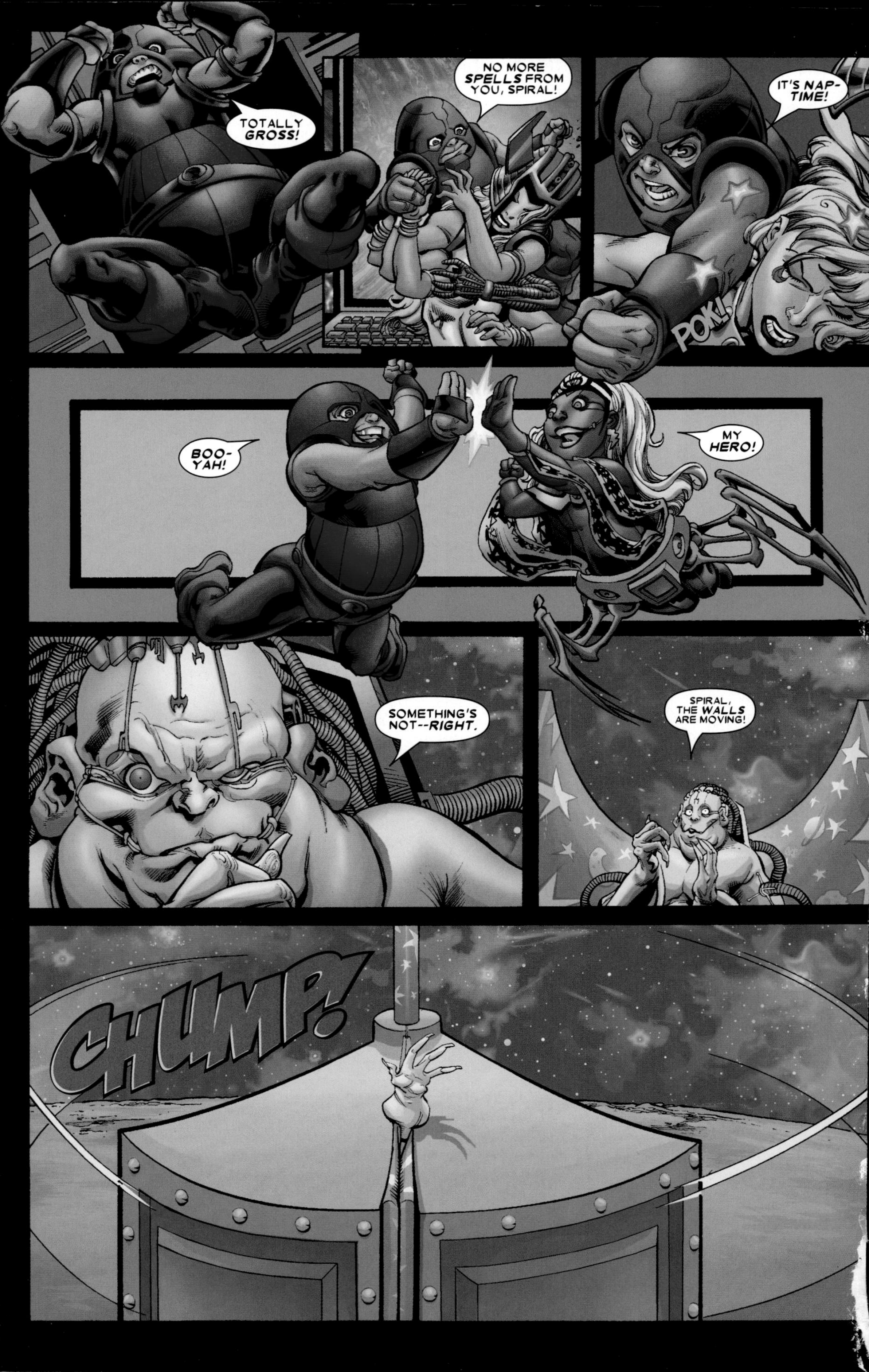
TOTALLY GROSS!
NO MORE SPELLS FROM YOU, SPIRAL!
IT'S NAP-TIME!
POK!
BOO-YAH!
MY HERO!
SOMETHING'S NOT--RIGHT.
SPIRAL, THE WALLS ARE MOVING!
CHUMP!

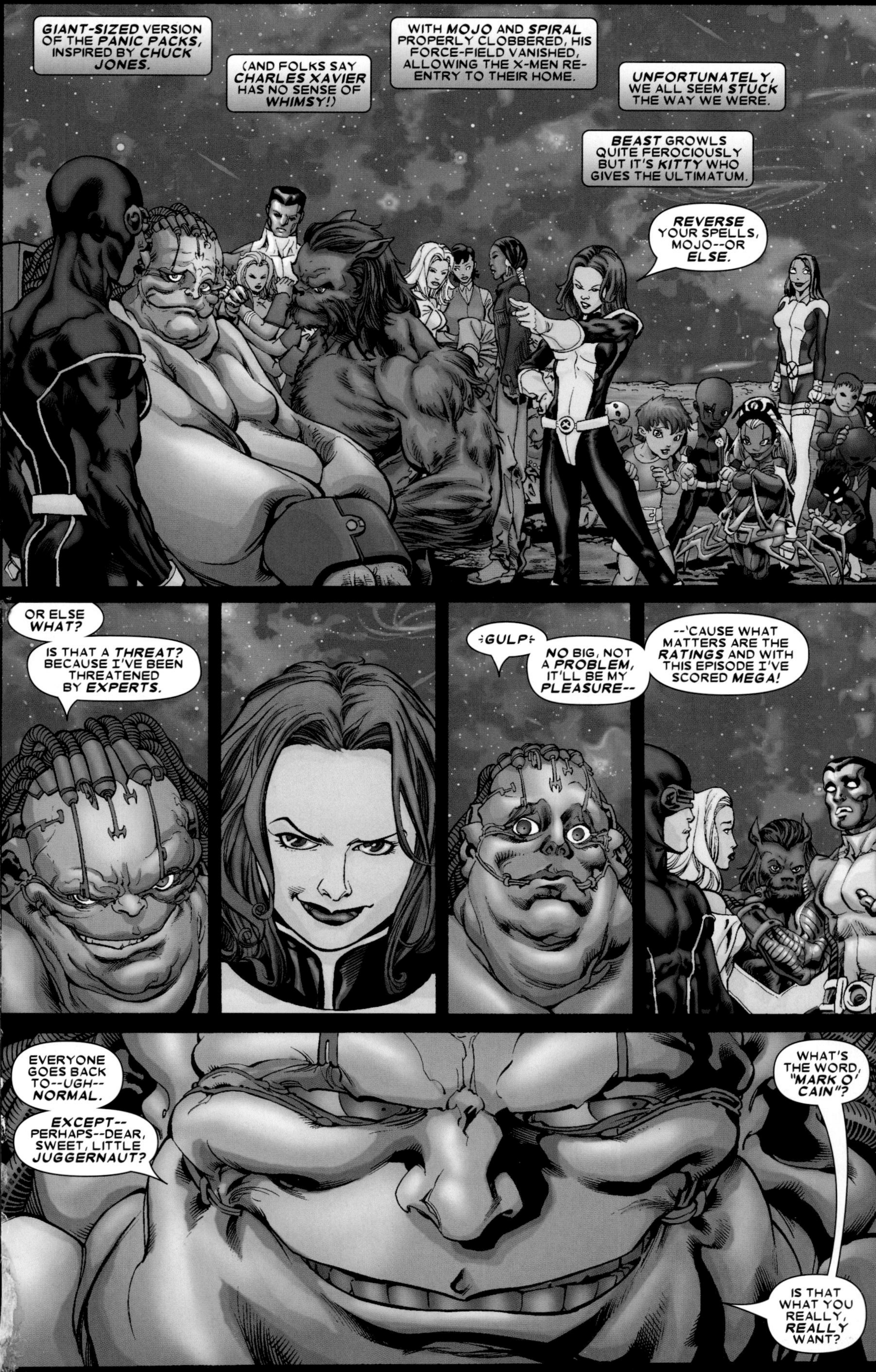
GIANT-SIZED VERSION OF THE PANIC PACKS, INSPIRED BY CHUCK JONES.
(AND FOLKS SAY CHARLES XAVIER HAS NO SENSE OF WHIMSY!)
WITH MOJO AND SPIRAL PROPERLY CLOBBERED, HIS FORCE-FIELD VANISHED, ALLOWING THE X-MEN RE-ENTRY TO THEIR HOME.
UNFORTUNATELY, WE ALL SEEM STUCK THE WAY WE WERE.
BEAST GROWLS QUITE FEROCIOUSLY BUT IT'S KITTY WHO GIVES THE ULTIMATUM.
REVERSE YOUR SPELLS, MOJO--OR ELSE.
OR ELSE WHAT?
IS THAT A THREAT? BECAUSE I'VE BEEN THREATENED BY EXPERTS.
GULP
NO BIG, NOT A PROBLEM, IT'LL BE MY PLEASURE--
--'CAUSE WHAT MATTERS ARE THE RATINGS AND WITH THIS EPISODE I'VE SCORED MEGA!
EVERYONE GOES BACK TO--UGH--NORMAL.
EXCEPT--PERHAPS--DEAR, SWEET, LITTLE JUGGERNAUT?
WHAT'S THE WORD, "MARK O' CAIN"?
IS THAT WHAT YOU REALLY, REALLY WANT?

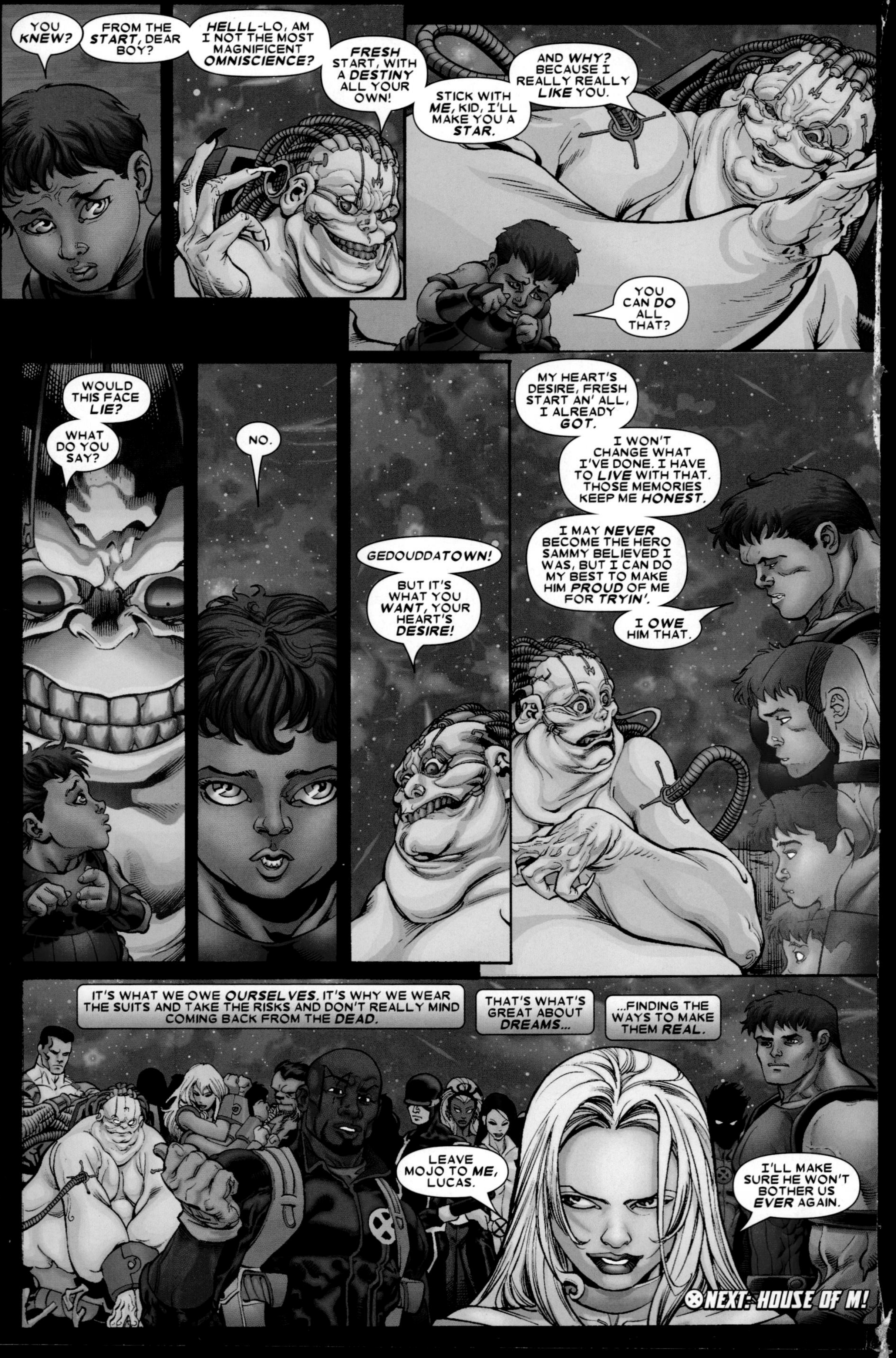
YOU KNEW?
FROM THE START, DEAR BOY?
HELLL-LO, AM I NOT THE MOST MAGNIFICENT OMNISCIENCE?
FRESH START, WITH A DESTINY ALL YOUR OWN!
STICK WITH ME, KID, I'LL MAKE YOU A STAR.
AND WHY? BECAUSE I REALLY REALLY LIKE YOU.
YOU CAN DO ALL THAT?
WOULD THIS FACE LIE?
WHAT DO YOU SAY?
NO.
GEDOUDDATOWN!
BUT IT'S WHAT YOU WANT, YOUR HEART'S DESIRE!
MY HEART'S DESIRE, FRESH START AN' ALL, I ALREADY GOT.
I WON'T CHANGE WHAT I'VE DONE. I HAVE TO LIVE WITH THAT. THOSE MEMORIES KEEP ME HONEST.
I MAY NEVER BECOME THE HERO SAMMY BELIEVED I WAS, BUT I CAN DO MY BEST TO MAKE HIM PROUD OF ME FOR TRYIN'.
I OWE HIM THAT.
IT'S WHAT WE OWE OURSELVES. IT'S WHY WE WEAR THE SUITS AND TAKE THE RISKS AND DON'T REALLY MIND COMING BACK FROM THE DEAD.
THAT'S WHAT'S GREAT ABOUT DREAMS...
...FINDING THE WAYS TO MAKE THEM REAL.
LEAVE MOJO TO ME, LUCAS.
I'LL MAKE SURE HE WON'T BOTHER US EVER AGAIN.
NEXT: HOUSE OF M!

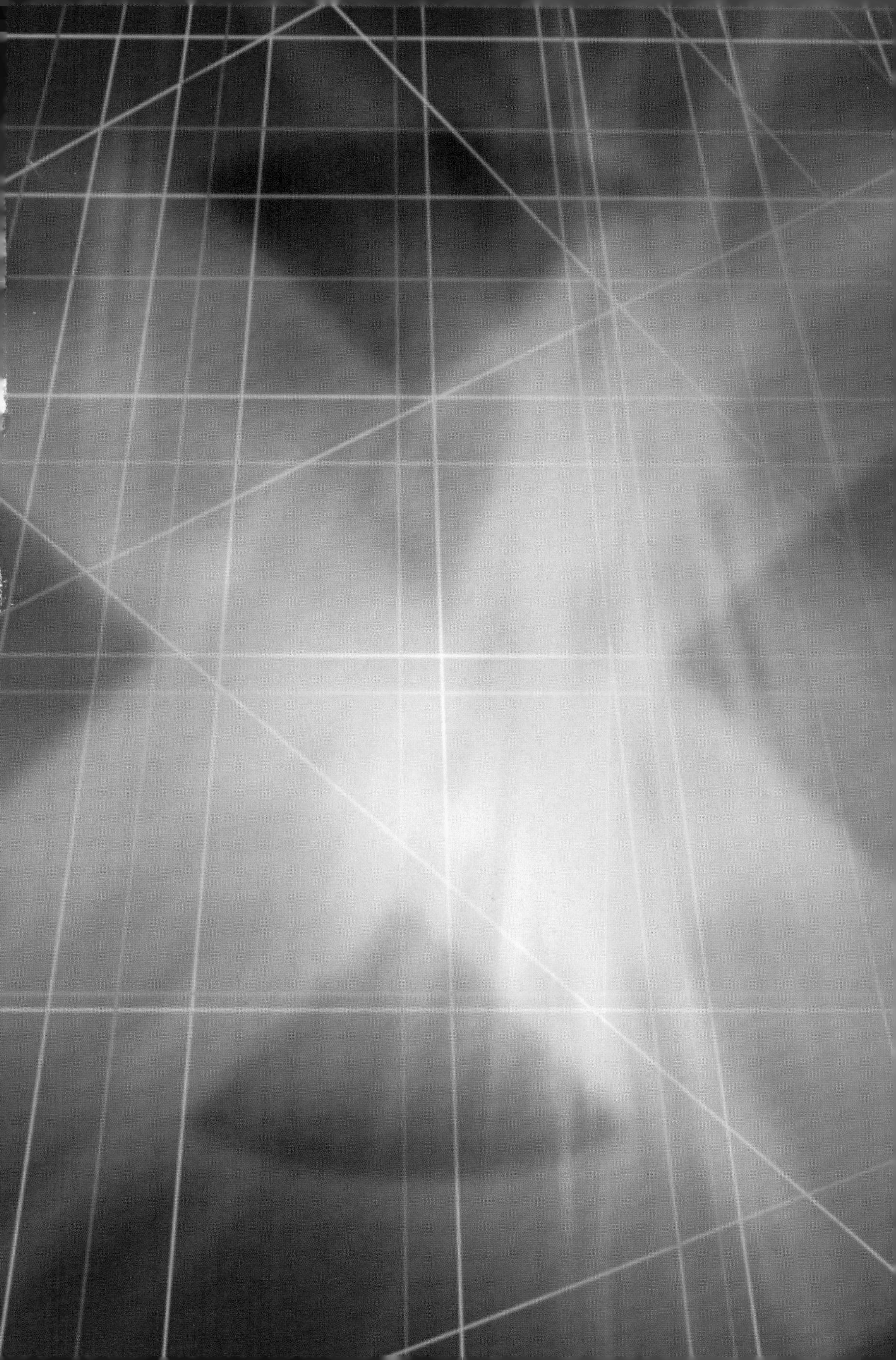

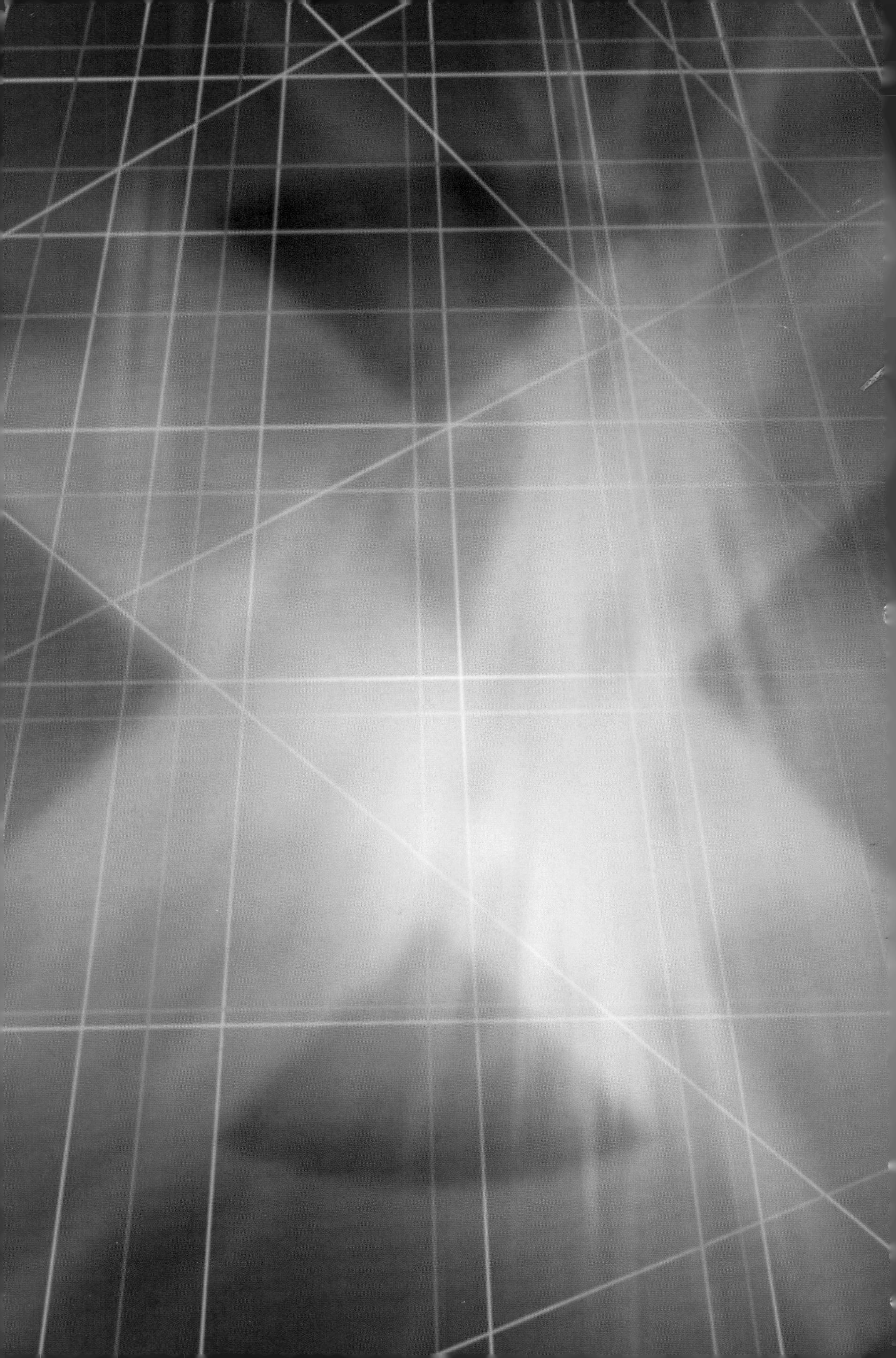